THE CAMPAIGN OF 1776
AROUND NEW YORK
AND BROOKLYN

A Da Capo Press Reprint Series

THE ERA OF THE AMERICAN REVOLUTION

GENERAL EDITOR: LEONARD W. LEVY

Claremont Graduate School

THE CAMPAIGN OF 1776 AROUND NEW YORK AND BROOKLYN

By Henry P. Johnston

DA CAPO PRESS • NEW YORK • 1971

A Da Capo Press Reprint Edition

This Da Capo Press edition of
The Campaign of 1776 Around New York and Brooklyn
is an unabridged republication of the first
edition published in Brooklyn, New York, in 1878
as Volume III of the *Memoirs of the Long Island
Historical Society.*

Library of Congress Catalog Card Number 74-157827
SBN 306-70169-3

Published by Da Capo Press, Inc.
A Subsidiary of Plenum Publishing Corporation
227 West 17th Street, New York, N. Y. 10011

Manufactured in the United States of America

THE

CAMPAIGN OF 1776

AROUND

NEW YORK AND BROOKLYN.

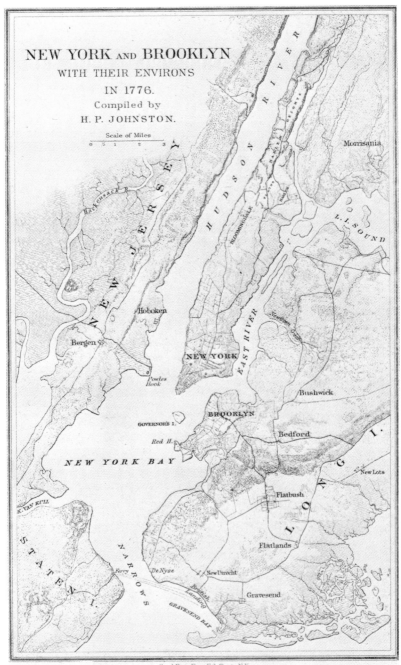

NEW YORK AND BROOKLYN
WITH THEIR ENVIRONS
IN 1776.
Compiled by
H. P. JOHNSTON.

Scale of Miles
0   ½   1   2   3

Morrisania

L. I. SOUND

HUDSON RIVER

NEW JERSEY

Hackensack R.

Hoboken

Bergen

Powles Hook

NEW YORK

EAST RIVER

Newtown Creek

Bushwick

GOVERNORS I.

BROOKLYN

Bedford

Red H.

NEW YORK BAY

LONG I.

New Lots

Flatbush

K. VAN KULL

STATEN I.

NARROWS

Flatlands

Ferry

De Nyse

New Utrecht

Brooklyn Landing

Gravesend

GRAVESEND BAY

Steel Engr. F von Egloffstein N.Y.

THE

CAMPAIGN OF 1776

AROUND

NEW YORK AND BROOKLYN.

INCLUDING A NEW AND CIRCUMSTANTIAL ACCOUNT OF

THE BATTLE OF LONG ISLAND AND THE LOSS OF NEW YORK,

WITH A

REVIEW OF EVENTS TO THE CLOSE OF THE YEAR.

CONTAINING MAPS, PORTRAITS, AND ORIGINAL DOCUMENTS.

BY

HENRY P. JOHNSTON.

————•♦•————

BROOKLYN, N. Y:

PUBLISHED BY THE LONG ISLAND HISTORICAL SOCIETY.

1878.

S. W. GREEN,
PRINTER AND ELECTROTYPER,
16 and 18 Jacob Street,
New York.

PREFACE.

THE site now occupied by the two cities of New York and Brooklyn, and over which they continue to spread, is pre-eminently " Revolutionary soil." Very few of our historic places are more closely associated with the actual scenes of that struggle. As at Boston in 1775, so here in 1776, we had the war at our doors and all about us. In what is now the heart of Brooklyn Revolutionary soldiers lay encamped for months, and in the heat of a trying summer surrounded themselves with lines of works. What have since been converted into spots of rare beauty—Greenwood Cemetery and Prospect Park—became, with the ground in their vicinity, a battle-field. New York, which was then taking its place as the most flourishing city on the continent, was transformed by the emergency into a fortified military base. Troops quartered in Broad Street and along the North and East rivers, and on the line of Grand Street permanent camps were established. Forts, redoubts, batteries, and intrenchments encircled the town. The streets were barricaded, the roads blocked, and efforts made to obstruct the navigation of both rivers. Where we have stores and warehouses, Washington fixed alarm and picket posts; and at points where costly residences stand, men fought, died, and were buried. In 1776 the cause had become general; soldiers gathered here from ten of the original thirteen States, and the contest assumed serious proportions It was here around New York and Brooklyn that the War of the Revolution began in earnest.

The record of what occurred in this vicinity at that interesting period has much of it been preserved in our standard histories by Gordon, Marshall, Irving, Hildreth, Lossing, Bancroft, Carrington, and others. In the present volume it is given as a single connected account, with many additional particulars which have but recently come to light. This new material, gathered largely from the descendants of officers and soldiers who participated in that campaign, is published with other documents in Part II. of this work, and is presented as its principal feature. What importance should be attached to it must be left to the judgment of the reader.

The writer himself has made use of these documents in filling gaps and correcting errors. Such documents, for example, as the orders issued by Generals Greene and Sullivan on Long Island, with the original letters of Generals Parsons, Scott, and other officers, go far towards clearing up the hitherto doubtful points in regard to operations on the Brooklyn side. There is not a little, also, that throws light on the retreat to

New York; while material of value has been un-earthed respecting events which terminated in the capture of the city by the British. Considerable space has been devoted to the preparations made by both sides for the campaign, but as the nature of those preparations illustrates the very great importance attached to the struggle that was to come, it may not appear disproportionate. The narrative also is continued so as to include the closing incidents of the year, without which it would hardly be complete, although they take us beyond the limits of New York.

But for the cheerful and in many cases painstaking co-operation of those who are in possession of the documents referred to, or who have otherwise rendered assistance, the preparation of the work could not have been possible. The writer finds himself especially under obligations to Miss Harriet E. Henshaw, of Leicester, Mass.; Miss Mary Little and Benjamin Hale, Esq., Newburyport; Charles J. Little, Esq., Cambridge; Mr. Francis S. Drake, Roxbury; Rev. Dr. I. N. Tarbox and John J. Soren, Boston; Prof. George Washington Greene, East Greenwich, R. I.; Hon. J. M. Addeman, Secretary of State of Rhode Island, and Rev. Dr. Stone, Providence; Hon. Dwight Morris, Secretary of State of Connecticut; Dr. P. W. Ellsworth and Captain John C. Kinney, Hartford; Miss Mary L. Huntington, Norwich; Benjamin Douglas, Esq., Middletown; Mr. Henry M. Selden, Haddam Neck; Hon. G. H. Hollister, Bridgeport; Hon. Teunis G. Bergen,

Mr. Henry E. Pierrepont, J. Carson Brevoort, Esq., Rev. Dr. H. M. Scudder, and Mr. Gerrit H. Van Wagenen, Brooklyn; Mr. Henry Onderdonk, Jr., Jamaica, L. I.; Frederick H. Wolcott, Esq., Astoria, L. I.; Hon. John Jay, Charles I. Bushnell, Esq., Miss Troup, Mrs. Kernochan, Prof. and Mrs. O. P. Hubbard, Gen. Alex. S. Webb, Rev. A. A. Reinke, New York City; Mr. William Kelby, New York Historical Society; Prof. Asa Bird Gardner, West Point; Hon. W. S. Stryker, Adjutant-General, Trenton, N. J.; Richard Randolph Parry, Esq., Hon. Lewis A. Scott, and Mr. J. Jordan, Philadelphia; Hon. John B. Linn, Harrisburg; Mrs. S. B. Rogers and Mr. D. M. Stauffler, Lancaster; Dr. Dalrymple, Maryland Historical Society, Baltimore; Hon. Cæsar A. Rodney, J. R. Walter, and W. S. Boyd, Wilmington, Del.; Oswald Tilghman, Esq., Easton, Md.; Hon. Edward McPherson, Rev. Dr. John Chester, and Lieutenant-Colonel T. Lincoln Casey, Washington; President Andrews and Mr. Holden, Librarian, Marietta College; and Mr. Henry E. Parsons and Edward Welles, Ashtabula, Ohio.

The cordial and constant encouragement extended by the Rev. Dr. Richard S. Storrs, President of the Long Island Historical Society, and the interest taken in the work by Hon. Henry C. Murphy, Benjamin D. Silliman, Esq., and the Librarian, Mr. George Hannah, are gratefully acknowledged.

New York City, June, 1878.

CONTENTS.

PART I.

PART II

LIST OF MAPS.

———

PORTRAITS.

PART I.

————•◆•————

THE CAMPAIGN.

CHAPTER I.

"OUR affairs are hastening fast to a crisis; and the approaching campaign will, in all probability, determine forever the fate of America."

So wrote John Hancock, President of Congress, June 4th, 1776, to the governors and conventions of the Eastern and Middle colonies, as, in the name of that body, he reminded them of the gravity of the struggle on which they had entered, and urged the necessity of increasing their exertions for the common defence. That this was no undue alarm, published for effect, but a well-grounded and urgent warning to the country, is confirmed by the situation at the time and the whole train of events that followed. The campaign of 1776 did indeed prove to be a crisis, a turning-point, in the fortunes of the Revolution. It is not investing it with an exaggerated importance, to claim that it was the decisive period of the war; that, whatever anxieties and fears were subsequently experienced, this was the year in which the greatest dangers were encountered and passed. "Should the united colonies be able to keep their ground this campaign," continued Hancock, "I am under no apprehensions on account of any future one." "We expect a very bloody summer in New York and Canada," wrote Washington to his brother John Augustine, in May; and repeatedly, through the days of preparation, he represented to his troops what vital interests were at stake and how much was to depend upon their discipline and courage in the field.

But let the significance of the campaign be measured by the record itself, to which the following pages are devoted. It will be found to have been the year in which Great Britain made her most strenuous efforts to suppress the colonial revolt, and in which both sides mustered the largest forces raised during the war; the year in which the issues of the contest were clearly defined and America first fought for independence; a year, for the most part, of defeats and losses for the colonists, and when their faith and resolution were put to the severest test; but a year, also, which ended with a broad ray of hope, and whose hard experiences opened the road to final success. It was the year from which we date our national existence. A period so interesting and, in a certain sense, momentous is deserving of illustration with every fact and detail that can be gathered.

What was the occasion or necessity for this campaign; what the plans and preparations made for it both by the mother country and the colonies?

The opening incidents of the Revolution, to which these questions refer us, are a familiar chapter in its history. On the morning of the 19th of April, 1775, an expedition of British regulars, moving out from Boston, came upon a company of provincials hastily forming on Lexington Common, twelve miles distant. The attitude of these countrymen represented the last step to which they had been driven by the aggressive acts of the home Parliament. Up to this moment the controversy over colonial rights and privileges had been confined, from the days of the Stamp Act, to argument, protest, petition, and legislative proceedings; but these failing to convince or conciliate either party, it only remained for Great Britain to exercise her authority in the case with force.

The expedition in question had been organized for the purpose of seizing the military stores belonging to the Massachusetts Colony, then collected at Concord, and which the king's authorities regarded as too dangerous material to be in the hands of the people at that stage of the crisis. The provincials, on the other hand, watched them jealously. King and Parliament might question their rights, block up their port, ruin their trade, proscribe their leaders, and they could bear all without offering open resistance. But the attempt to deprive them of the means of self-defence at a time when the current of affairs clearly indicated that, sooner or later, they would be compelled to defend themselves, was an act to which they would not submit, as already they had shown on more than one occasion. To no other right did the colonist cling more tenaciously at this juncture than to his right to his powder. The men at Lexington, therefore, drew up on their village grounds, not defiantly, but in obedience to the most natural impulse. Their position was a logical one. To have remained quietly in their homes would have been a stultification of their whole record from the beginning of the troubles; stand they must, some time and somewhere. Under the circumstances, a collision between the king's troops and the provincials that morning was inevitable. The commander of the former, charged with orders to disperse all "rebels," made the sharp demand upon the Lexington company instantly to lay down their arms. A moment's confusion and delay—then scattering shots—then a full volley from the regulars—and ten men fell dead and wounded upon the green. Here was a shock, the ultimate consequences of which few of the participants in the scene could have forecast ; but it was the alarm-gun of the Revolution.

Events followed rapidly. The march of the British to Concord, the destruction of the stores, the skirmish at the bridge, and, later in the day, the famous road-fight kept up by the farmers down to Charlestown, ending in the signal demoralization and defeat of the expedition, combined with the Lexington episode to make the 19th of April an historic date. The rapid spread of the news, the excitement in New England, the uprising of the militia and their hurried march to Boston to resist any further excursions of the regulars, were the immediate consequence of this collision.

Nor was the alarm confined to the Eastern colonies, then chiefly affected. A courier delivered the news in New York three days later, on Sunday noon, and the liberty party at once seized the public military stores, and prevented vessels loaded with supplies for the British in Boston from leaving port. Soon came fuller accounts of the expedition and its rout. Expresses carried them southward, and their course can be followed for nearly a thousand miles along the coast. On the 23d and 24th they passed through Connecticut, where at Wallingford the dispatches quaintly describe the turning out of the militiamen : " The country beyond here are all gone." They reached New York at two o'clock on the 25th, and Isaac Low countersigns. Relays taking them up in New Jersey, report at Princeton on the 26th, at " 3.30 A.M." They are at Philadelphia at noon, and "forwarded at the same time." We find them at New Castle, Delaware, at nine in the evening; at Baltimore at ten on the following night; at Alexandria, Virginia, at sunset on the 29th; at Williamsburg, May 2d; and at Edenton, North Carolina, on the 4th, with directions to the next Committee of Safety: "Disperse the material passages [of the accounts] through all your parts." Down through the deep pine regions, stopping at Bath and Newbern, ride the horsemen, reaching Wilmington at 4 P.M. on the 8th. "Forward it by night and day," say the committee. At Brunswick at nine the indorsement is entered: "Pray don't neglect a moment in forwarding." At Georgetown, South Carolina, where the dispatches arrive at 6.30 P.M. on the 10th, the committee address a note to their Charleston brethren: "We send you by express a letter and newspapers with momentous intelligence this instant arrived." The news reaching Savannah, a party of citizens immediately took possession of the government powder.

The wave of excitement which follows the signal of a coming struggle was thus borne by its own force throughout the length of the colonies. And from the coast the intelligence spread inland as far as settlers had found their way. In distant Westmoreland County, Pennsylvania, men heard it, and began to organize and drill. At Charlotte, North Carolina, they sounded the first note for independence. From many points brave and sympathetic words were sent to the people of Massachusetts Bay, and in all quarters people discussed the probable effect of the startling turn matters had taken in that colony. The likelihood of a general rupture with the mother country now came to be seriously entertained.

Meanwhile the situation to the eastward assumed more and more a military aspect. On the 10th of May occurred

the surprise and capture, by Ethan Allen and his party, of
the important post of Ticonderoga, where during the summer the provincials organized a force to march upon and, if
possible, secure the Canadas. The Continental Congress
at Philadelphia, after resolving that the issue had been
forced upon them by Great Britain, voted to prepare for
self-defence. They adopted the New England troops,
gathered around Boston, as a Continental force, and appointed Washington to the chief command. Then on the
17th of June Bunker Hill was fought, that first regular
action of the war, with its far-reaching moral effect; and
following it came the siege of Boston, or the hemming in of
the British by the Americans, until the former were finally
compelled to evacuate the city.

It is here in these culminating events of the spring and
summer of 1775 that we find the occasion for the preparations made by Great Britain for the campaign of 1776.
Little appreciating the genius of the colonists, underrating
their resources and capacity for resistance, mistaking also
their motives, King George and his party imagined that on
the first display of England's power all disturbance and
attempts at rebellion across the sea would instantly cease.
But the sudden transition from peace to war, and the complete mastery of the situation which the colonists appeared
to hold, convinced the home government that "the American business" was no trifling trouble, to be readily settled
by a few British regiments. As the season advanced, they
began to realize the fact that General Gage, and then Howe
succeeding him, with their force of ten thousand choice
troops, were helplessly pent up in Boston; that Montreal
and Quebec were threatened; that colonists in the undisturbed sections were arming; and that Congress was sup-

planting the authority of Parliament. A more rigorous treatment of the revolt had become necessary; and as the time had passed to effect any thing on a grand scale during the present year, measures were proposed to crush all opposition in the next campaign. Follow, briefly, the course of the British Government at this crisis.

Parliament convened on the 26th day of October. The king's speech, with which it opened, was necessarily devoted to the American question, and it declared his policy clearly and boldly. His rebellious subjects must be brought to terms. "They have raised troops," he said, "and are collecting a naval force; they have seized the public revenue, and assumed to themselves legislative, executive, and judicial powers, which they already exercise, in the most arbitrary manner, over the persons and properties of their fellow subjects: and although many of these unhappy people may still retain their loyalty, and may be too wise not to see the fatal consequence of this usurpation and wish to resist it, yet the torrent of violence has been strong enough to compel their acquiescence, till a sufficient force shall appear to support them. The authors and promoters of this desperate conspiracy have, in the conduct of it, derived great advantage from the difference of our intentions and theirs. They meant only to amuse by vague expressions of attachment to the parent state, and the strongest protestations of loyalty to me, whilst they were preparing for a general revolt. On our part, though it was declared in your last session that a rebellion existed within the province of the Massachusetts' Bay, yet even that province we wished rather to reclaim than to subdue. . . . . The rebellious war now levied is become more general, and is manifestly carried on for the purpose of establishing an independent empire. I need not dwell upon the fatal effects of the success of such a plan. . . . . It is now become the part of wisdom, and (in its effects) of clemency, to put a speedy end to these disorders, by the most decisive exertions. For this purpose, I have increased my naval establishment, and greatly augmented my land forces, but in such a manner as may be the least burthensome to my kingdoms. I have also the satisfaction to inform you, that I have received the most friendly offers of foreign assistance, and if I shall make any treaties in consequence thereof, they shall be laid before you."

A stranger in Parliament, knowing nothing of the merits of the controversy, would have assumed from the tone of this speech that the home government had been grossly wronged by the American colonists, or at least a powerful faction among them, and that their suppression was a matter of national honor as well as necessity. But the speech was inexcusably unjust to the colonists. The charge of design and double-dealing could not be laid against them, for the ground of their grievances had been the same from the outset, and their conduct consistent with single motives; and if independence had been mentioned at all as yet, it was only as an ulterior resort, and not as an aim or ambition. The king and the Ministry, on the other hand, were wedded to strict notions of authority in the central government, and measured a citizen's fidelity by the readiness with which he submitted to its policy and legislation. Protests and discussion about "charters" and "liberties" were distasteful to them, and whoever disputed Parliament in any case was denounced as strong-headed and factious. The king's speech, therefore, was no more than what was expected from him. It reflected the sentiments of the ruling party.

As usual, motions were made in both houses that an humble address in reply be presented to his Majesty, professing loyalty to his person, and supporting his views and measures. The mover in the Commons was Thomas Ackland, who, in the course of his speech at the time, strongly urged the policy of coercion, and emphasized his approval of it by declaring that it would have been better for his country that America had never been known than that "a great consolidated western empire" should exist independent of Britain. Lyttleton, who seconded the motion, was equally uncompromising. He objected to making the Americans any further conciliatory offers, and insisted that they ought to be conquered first before mercy was shown them.

The issue thus fairly stated by and for the government immediately roused the old opposition, that "ardent and powerful opposition," as Gibbon, who sat in the Commons, describes it ; and again the House echoed to attack and invective. Burke, Fox, Conway, Barré, Dunning, and others, who on former occasions had cheered America with their stout defence of her rights, were present at this session to resist any further attempt to impair them. Of the leading spirits, Chatham, now disabled from public service, alone was absent.

Lord John Cavendish led the way on this side, by moving a substitute for Ackland's address which breathed a more moderate spirit, and in effect suggested to his Majesty that the House review the whole of the late proceedings in the colonies, and apply, in its own way, the most effectual means of restoring order and confidence there. Of course this meant concession to America, and it became the signal for the opening of an impassioned debate. Wilkes, Lord Mayor of London, poured out a torrent of remonstrances against the conduct of the Ministry, who had precipitated the nation into "an unjust, ruinous, felonious, and murderous war." Sir Adam Fergusson, speaking less vehemently and with more show of sense, defended the government. Whatever causes may have brought on the troubles, the present concern with him was how to treat them as they then existed. There was but one choice, in his estimation—either to support the authority of Great Britain with vigor, or abandon America altogether. And who, he asked, would be bold enough to advise abandonment? The employment of force, therefore, was the only alternative; and, said the speaker, prudence and humanity required that the army sent out should be such a one as would carry its point and override opposition in every quarter—not merely beat the colonists, but "deprive them of all idea of resistance." Gov. Johnstone, rising in reply, reviewed the old questions at length, and in the course of his speech took occasion to eulogize the bravery of the provincials at Bunker Hill. It was this engagement, more than any incident of the war thus far, that had shown the determination of the "rebels" to fight for their rights; and their friends in Parliament presented it as a foretaste of what was to come, if England persisted in extreme measures. Johnstone besought the House not to wreak its vengeance upon such men as fought that day; for their courage was deserving, rather, of admiration, and their conduct of forgiveness. Honorable Temple Lutrell followed with an attack upon the "evil counsellors who had so long poisoned the ear of the Sovereign." Conway, who on this occasion spoke with his old fire, and held the close attention of the House, called for more information as to the condition of affairs in the colonies, and at the same time rejected the idea of reducing them to submission by force. Barré entered minutely into the particulars and results of the campaign since the 19th of April, as being little to England's credit, and urged the Ministry to embrace the present opportunity for an accommodation with America, or that whole country would be lost to them forever. Burke, in the same vein, represented the impolicy of carrying on the war, and advised the government to meet the colonists with a friendly countenance, and no longer allow Great Britain to appear like "a porcupine, armed all over with acts of Parliament oppressive to trade and America." Fox spoke of Lord North as "a blundering pilot," who had brought the nation into its present dilemma. Neither Lord Chatham nor the King of Prussia, not even Alexander the Great, he declared, ever gained more in one campaign than the noble lord had lost—he had lost an entire continent. While not justifying all the proceedings of the colonists, he called upon the Administration to place America where she stood in 1763, and to repeal every act passed since that time which affected either her freedom or her commerce. Wedderburne and Dunning, the ablest lawyers in the House, took opposite sides. The former, as Solicitor-General, threw the weight of his opinion in favor of rigorous measures, and hoped that an army of not less than sixty thousand men would be sent to enforce Parliamentary authority. Dunning, his predecessor in office, questioned the legality of the king's preparations for war without the previous consent of the Commons. Then, later in the debate, rose Lord North, the principal figure in the Ministry, and whom the Opposition held mainly responsible for the colonial troubles, and defended both himself and the king's address. Speaking forcibly and to the point, he informed the House that, in a word, the measures intended by the government were to send a powerful sea and land armament against the colonists, and at the same time to proffer terms of mercy upon a proper submission. "This," said the Minister, "will show we are in earnest, that we are prepared to punish, but are nevertheless ready to forgive; and this is, in my opinion, the most likely means of producing an honorable reconciliation."

But all the eloquence, reasoning and appeal of the Opposition failed to have any more influence now than in the earlier stages of the controversy, and it again found itself in a hopeless minority. Upon a division of the House, the king was supported by a vote of 278 to 110. The address presented to him closed with the words: "We hope and trust that we shall, by the blessing of God, put such strength and force into your Majesty's hands, as may soon defeat and suppress this rebellion, and enable your Majesty to accomplish your gracious wish of re-establishing order, tranquillity, and happiness through all parts of your United Empire." In the House of Lords, where Camden, Shelburne, Rockingham, and their compeers stood between America and the Ministry, the address was adopted by a vote of 69 to 33.[1]

This powerful endorsement of the king's policy by Parliament, however, cannot be taken as representing the sense

---

[1] Outside of Parliament, all shades of opinion found expression through the papers, pamphlets, and private correspondence. Hume, the historian, wrote, October 27th, 1775 : "I am an American in my principles, and wish we could let them alone, to govern or misgovern themselves as they think proper. The affair is of no consequence, or of little consequence to us." But he wanted those "insolent rascals in London and Middlesex" punished for inciting opposition at home. This would be more to the point than "mauling the poor infatuated Americans in the other hemisphere." William Strahan, the eminent printer, replied to Hume: "I differ from you *toto cælo* with regard to America. I am entirely for coercive methods with those obstinate madmen." Dr. Robertson, author of *The History of America*, wrote : "If our leaders do not exert the power of the British Empire in its full force, the struggle will be long, dubious, and disgraceful. We are past the hour of lenitives and half exertions." Early in 1776, Dr. Richard Price, the Dissenting preacher, issued his famous pamphlet on the *Nature of Civil Liberty, the Principles of Government, and the Justice and Policy of the War*, which had a great run. Taking sides with the colonists, he said : "It is madness to resolve to butcher them. Freemen are not to be governed by force, or dragooned into compliance. If capable of bearing to be so treated, it is a disgrace to be connected with them."

of the nation at large. It may be questioned whether even a bare majority of the English people were ready to go to the lengths proposed in his Majesty's address. The Ministry, it is true, pointed to the numerous ratifying "addresses" that flowed in, pledging the support of towns and cities for the prosecution of the war. Some were sent from unexpected quarters. To the surprise of both sides and the particular satisfaction of the king, both Manchester and Sheffield, places supposed to be American in sentiment, came forward with resolutions of confidence and approval; and in ministerial circles it was made to appear that substantially all England was for coercion. But this claim was unfounded. As the king predicted, the loyal addresses provoked opposition addresses. Edinburgh and Glasgow, despite the efforts of their members, refused to address. Lynn was said to have addressed, but its members denied the assertion, and claimed that the war was unpopular in that town. The paper from Great Yarmouth was very thinly signed, while Bristol, Glasgow, Liverpool, Manchester, Birmingham, Wolverhampton, Dudley, and other places sent in counter-petitions against the war. The justices of Middlesex unanimously voted that it was expedient to reduce the colonies to a proper sense of their duty ; but at a meeting of the freeholders of the same county, held at Mile-end, to instruct their members in Parliament, little unanimity prevailed, "much clamor arose," a protest was entered against the proposed resolutions, and only one of the sheriffs consented to sign them all. London, as the country well knew, sympathized largely with America, but in a manner which nullified her influence elsewhere. Her populace was noisy and threatening ; Wilkes, her Lord Mayor, was hated at court ; her solid men kept to business. "Are the London merchants," wrote the king to Lord

North,[1] " so thoroughly absorbed in their private interests not to feel what they owe to the constitution which has enriched them, that they do not either show their willingness to support, either by an address, or, what I should like better, a subscription, to furnish many comforts to the army in America?" An address from this quarter, signed by " respectable names," he thought might have a good effect, and one was presented on October 11th, with 941 signatures; but it was entirely neutralized by the presentation, three days before, of another address more numerously signed by "gentlemen, merchants, and traders of London," in which the measures of government were condemned. When the point was made in the Commons that the war was a popular measure in England, Lutrell promptly replied that he had made many a journey through the interior of the country during the summer season, and had conversed with "a multitude of persons widely different in station and description," only to find that the masses were in sympathy with the colonists. The division of sentiment was probably correctly represented by Lord Camden early in the year, in his observation that the landed interest was almost wholly anti-American, while the merchants, tradesmen, and the common people were generally opposed to a war.[2]

Having voted to push the war in earnest, Parliament proceeded to supply the sinews. On November 3d, Lord Barrington brought in the army estimates for 1776. Fifty-five thousand men, he reported, was the force necessary and intended to be raised for the purposes of the nation, the ordinary expense of maintaining which would be something over

---

[1] "Correspondence with Lord North." Donne.

[2] Upon this point Dr. Price said : "Let it be granted, *though probably far from true*, that the *majority* of the kingdom favor the present measures. No good argument could be drawn from thence against receding."

£1,300,000. Of these troops, twenty thousand would be retained to garrison Great Britain, ten thousand for the West Indies, Gibraltar, Minorca and the coast of Africa, while the actual force destined for America was to be increased to thirty-four battalions, each of 811 men, including two regiments of light horse, amounting, in the aggregate, to upwards of twenty-five thousand men. Barrington, at the same time, frankly acknowledged to the House that these figures showed well only on paper, as none of the regiments for America were complete, and, what was a still more unwelcome admission, that great difficulty was experienced in enlisting new recruits. Nothing, he said, had been left untried to secure them. The bounty had been raised and the standard lowered, and yet men were not forthcoming. Anticipating this dearth, he had warned the king of it as early as July, when the latter first determined to increase the army. " I wish, sir, most cordially," wrote this faithful secretary, " that the force intended for North America may be raised in time to be sent thither next spring; but I not only fear, but am confident, the proposed augmentation cannot possibly be raised, and ought not to be depended on."

Barrington was compelled to give an explanation of this state of things, for the point had been made in and out of Parliament that few recruits could be had in England, because the particular service was odious to the people in general. For the government to admit this would have been clearly fatal; and Barrington argued, per contra, that the scarcity of soldiers was to be traced to other and concurrent causes. The great influx of real and nominal wealth of recent years, the consequent luxury of the times, the very flourishing state of commerce and the manufactures, and the increased employment thus furnished to the lower classes, all contributed to keep men out of the army. Above all, it was represented that the true and natural cause was an actual lack of men, which was due chiefly to the late increase of the militia, who could not be called upon to serve except in extreme cases, and who were not available for the regular force. Barrington, a veteran in official service, true to the king, and justifying the war—though not at all clear as to the right of taxing the colonies—no doubt expressed his honest convictions in making this explanatory speech to the House. There was much, also, that was true in his words; but, whatever the absolute cause, the fact did not then, and cannot now escape notice, that in preparing to uphold the authority of Parliament, and preserve the integrity of her empire in America, Great Britain, in 1775, found it impossible to induce a sufficient number of her own subjects to take up arms in her behalf.

It remained, accordingly, to seek foreign aid. Europe must furnish England with troops, or the war must stop. The custom of employing mercenaries was ancient, and universally exercised on the Continent. Great Britain herself had frequently taken foreign battalions into her pay, but these were to fight a foreign enemy. It would be a thing new in her history to engage them to suppress fellow-Englishmen. But the king regarded war as war, and rebellion a heinous offence; and the character of the troops serving for him in this case became a secondary matter. A more serious question was where to get them. No assistance could be expected from France. Holland declined to lend troops to conquer men who were standing out for their rights on their own soil. In Prussia, Frederick the Great expressed the opinion that it was at least problematical whether America could be conquered, it being difficult to govern men by force at such a distance. "If you intend conciliation," he said in conversation to a party of Englishmen, "some of your measures are too rough; and if subjection, too gentle. In short, I do not understand these matters; I have no colonies. I hope you will extricate yourselves advantageously, but I own the affair seems rather perplexing." [1]

Of all the European powers, Russia and the German principalities alone presented a possible field of encouragement.[2] To the former, King George looked first; for England's friendly attitude had been of the greatest advantage to Russia in her campaigns against Turkey. The king, therefore, at an early date, gave directions that Gunning, the British Minister at Moscow, should approach the Empress Catherine on the subject of lending aid; and, on the proper occasion, Gunning held an interview with Panin, the Russian Prime Minister. Catherine promptly returned what appeared to be a very favorable reply. To use Gunning's own words communicating Russia's answer: "The empress had ordered him (Panin) to give the strongest assurances, and to express them in the strongest terms, of her entire readiness on this and all other occasions to give his Majesty every assistance he could desire, in whatever mode or manner he might think proper. She embraced with satisfaction this occasion of testifying her gratitude to the king and nation for the important services she had received in the late war—favors she the more valued and should not forget

---

[1] "A View of Society and Manners in France, Switzerland, and Germany." By John Moore, M.D. Lond., 1786. Vol. V., Letter 75.

[2] Respecting sentiment in Europe on American affairs, the English traveller Moore wrote as follows from Vienna in 1775 : "Our disputes with the colonies have been a prevailing topic of conversation wherever we have been since we left England. The warmth with which this subject is handled increases every day. At present the inhabitants of the Continent seem as impatient as those of Great Britain for news from the other side of the Atlantic; but with this difference, that here they are all of one mind— all praying for success to the Americans, and rejoicing in every piece of bad fortune which happens to our army."—*Moore's View*, etc. Letter 96.

as they were spontaneously bestowed. . . . We were as fully entitled to every succor from her as if the strongest treaties subsisted."[1]

Greatly elated by this unequivocal tender of aid, King George wrote to the empress in his own hand, thanking her for the proffer; and Gunning at the same time was instructed to ask for twenty thousand Russians, and enter into a treaty formally engaging their services. If he could not secure twenty thousand, he was to get all he could. But Gunning's negotiations were to fail completely. To his surprise and chagrin, when he opened the subject of hiring Russian troops, the empress and Panin answered with dignity that it was impossible to accommodate him; that Russia's relations with Sweden, Poland, and Turkey were unsettled, and that it was beneath her station to interfere in a domestic rebellion which no foreign Power had recognized. This sudden change in Catherine's attitude, which without doubt was the result of court intrigue,[2] filled the English king with mortification and disappointment, and compelled him to seek assistance where he finally obtained it—in the petty states of the " Hessian" princes.

[1] " History of England from the Accession of George III. to 1783." By J. Adolphus. Vol. II., p. 326.

[2] Two views have been expressed in regard to this. The English historian Adolphus charges Frederick of Prussia and secret French agents with having changed Catherine's mind, and he gives apparently good authority for the statement. The secret seems to have been known in English circles very soon after Catherine's refusal. On November 10th Shelburne said in the House of Lords: " There are Powers in Europe who will not suffer such a body of Russians to be transported to America. I speak from information. The Ministers know what I mean. Some power has already interfered to stop the success of the Russian negotiation." Mr. Bancroft, on the other hand, concludes (Vol. V., Chap. L., Rev. Ed.) that " no foreign influence whatever, not even that of the King of Prussia, had any share in determining the empress;" and Vergennes is quoted as saying that he could not reconcile Catherine's " elevation of soul with the dishonorable idea of trafficking in the blood of her subjects." But since

Success in this direction compensated in part for the Russian failure. What the British agent, Colonel Faucett, was able to accomplish, what bargains were struck to obtain troops, how much levy money was to be paid per man, and how much more if he never returned, is all a notorious record. From the Landgrave of Hesse-Cassel, Faucett hired twelve thousand infantry; from the Duke of Brunswick, three thousand nine hundred and a small body of cavalry; and from the reigning Count of Hanau, a corps six hundred and sixty strong. These constituted the " foreign troops" which England sent to America with her own soldiers for the campaign of 1776.

The plans for the campaign were laid out on a scale corresponding with the preparations. When Sir William Howe was sent out to reinforce General Gage at Boston, in the spring of 1775, it was assumed by the Ministry that operations would be confined to that quarter, and that if Massachusetts were once subdued there would be nothing to fear elsewhere. But the continued siege of Boston changed the military status. Howe was completely locked in, and could effect nothing. The necessity of transferring the seat of war to a larger field became apparent after Bunker Hill, and military plans were broached and discussed in the Cabinet, in the army, and in Parliament. Lord Barrington, who well knew that men enough could not be had from England to conquer the colonies, advocated operations by sea. An effective blockade of the en-

Catherine, four years later, in 1779, proposed to offer to give England effective assistance in America in order to be assured of her aid in return against the Turks, it may be questioned how far " elevation of soul" prompted the decision in 1775. (See Eaton's " Turkish Empire," p. 409.) In view of England's relations with most of the Continental Powers at that time, Shelburne and Adolphus have probably given the correct explanation of the matter.

tire American coast, depriving the colonists of their trade, might, in his view, bring them to terms. Mr. Innes, in the House, proposed securing a strong foothold in the south, below the Delaware, and shutting up the northern ports with the fleet. But the basis of the plan adopted appears to have been that suggested by Burgoyne at Boston in the summer of 1775, and by Howe in January, 1776. "If the continent," wrote the former to Lord Rochfort, Secretary of State for the Colonies, "is to be subdued by arms, his Majesty's councils will find, I am persuaded, the proper expedients; but I speak confidently as a soldier, because I speak the sentiments of those who know America best, that you can have no prospect of bringing the war to a speedy conclusion with any force that Great Britain and Ireland can supply. A large army of foreign troops such as might be hired, to begin their operations up the Hudson River; another army, composed partly of old disciplined troops and partly of Canadians, to act from Canada; a large levy of Indians, and a supply of arms for the blacks to awe the southern provinces, conjointly with detachments of regulars; and a numerous fleet to sweep the whole coast, might possibly do the business in one campaign."[1] To Lord Dartmouth, Howe represented that with an army of twenty thousand men, twelve thousand of whom should hold New York, six thousand land on Rhode Island, and two thousand protect Halifax, with a separate force at Quebec, offensive operations could be pushed so as to put "a very different aspect" on the situation by the close of another year.

The plan as finally arranged was a modification of these two views. It was decided that Howe should occupy

---

[1] *Fonblanque's Life of Burgoyne*, p. 152.

New York City with the main body of the army, and secure that important base; while Carleton, with Burgoyne as second in command, should move down from Canada to Ticonderoga and Albany. By concert of action on the part of these forces, New England could be effectually cut off from co-operation with the lower colonies, and the unity of their movements broken up. It was proposed at the same time to send an expedition under Lord Cornwallis and Admiral Parker, to obtain a footing in Virginia or either of the Carolinas, and encourage the loyal element in the South to organize, and counteract the revolt in that quarter. By carrying out this grand strategy, King George and his advisers confidently expected to end all resistance in America at one blow.

Thus Great Britain, instead of attempting to recover her authority over the colonists by a candid recognition of privileges which they claimed as Englishmen, resolved in 1775 to enforce it. The government went to war, with the nation's wealth and influence at its back, but with only half its popular sympathies and moral support. Parliament refused to listen to the appeals of its ablest members to try the virtues of concession and conciliation. A heavy war budget was voted, the Continent of Europe was ransacked for troops which could not be enlisted in England, and every effort made to insure the complete submission of the colonies in 1776.

How America prepared to meet the coming storm is properly the subject of the succeeding chapter of this work. But we find her in no position in 1775 to assume the character of a public enemy towards the mother country. She still claimed to be a petitioner to the king for the redress of grievances. If she had taken up arms, it was simply in self-

3

defence, and these she was ready to lay down the moment her rights were acknowledged. A revolution, involving separation from England, was not thought of by the mass of the American people at this time. The most they hoped for was, that by offering a stout resistance to an enforcement of the ministerial policy they could eventually compel a change in that policy, and enjoy all that they demanded under the British constitution. Towards the close of the year, however, when the intelligence came that the king had ignored the last petition from Congress, and had proposed extreme war measures, the colonists felt that serious work was before them. Independence now began to be more generally discussed; Washington's troops were re-enlisted for service through the following year, and Congress took further steps for the common defence.

Future military operations were necessarily dependent on the plans to be developed by the British. But as the siege of Boston progressed, it became obvious that that point at least could not be made a base for the ensuing campaign. No other was more likely to be selected by the enemy than New York; and to New York the war finally came.

The topography of this new region, the transfer to it of the two armies, and the preparations made for its defence by the Americans, next claim attention.

CHAPTER II.

NEW YORK CITY, in 1776, lay at the end of Manhattan Island, in shape somewhat like an arrow-head, with its point turned towards the sea and its barbs extended at uneven lengths along the East and Hudson rivers. It occupied no more space than is now included within the five lower and smallest of its twenty-four wards. Excepting a limited district laid out on the east side, in part as far as Grand street, the entire town stood below the line of the present Chambers street, and covered an area less than one mile square. Then, as now, Broadway was its principal thoroughfare. Shaded with rows of trees, and lined mainly with residences, churches, and public-houses, it stretched something more than a mile to the grounds of the old City Hospital, near Duane street. Its starting-point was the Battery at the end of the island, but not the Battery of to-day; for, under the system of "harbor encroachments," the latter has more than trebled in size, and is changed both in its shape and its uses. The city defences at that time occupied the site. Here at the foot of Broadway old Fort George had been erected upon the base of the older Fort Amsterdam, to guard the entrance to the rivers, and with its outworks was the only protection against an attack by sea. It was a square bastioned affair, with walls of stone, each face eighty feet in length, and within it stood magazines, barracks, and, until destroyed by fire, the mansion of the colonial governors. For additional security, about the time of the French war, an extensive stone battery, with merlons of cedar joists, had been built just below the fort along the water's edge, enclosing the point from river to river, and pierced for ninety-one pieces of cannon.[1]

At this period, the city represented a growth of one hundred and sixty years. Give it a population of twenty-five thousand souls[2]—more rather than less—and line its streets with four thousand buildings, and we have its census statistics approximately. The linear characteristics of the old town are still sharply preserved. Upon the west side, the principal streets running to the North River—Chambers, Warren, Murray, Barclay, Vesey, Dey, and Cortlandt—retain their names and location; but the water-line was then marked by Greenwich street. The present crowded section

[1] The site of Fort George is now covered in part by the buildings at the west corner of the Bowling Green block, where the steamship companies have their offices. South and west of this point the Battery is almost entirely made-land. (Compare Ratzer's map of 1767 with the maps recently compiled by the New York Dock Department.) As to other old defences of the city, Wm. Smith, the historian, writing about 1766, says: "During the late war a line of palisadoes was run from Hudson's to the East River, at the other end of the city [near the line of Chambers street], with block-houses at small distances. The greater part of these still remain as a monument of our folly, which cost the province about £8000."

[2] The last census before the Revolution was taken in 1771, when the population of the city and county of New York was returned at 21,863. (Doc. Hist. of N. Y., Vol. I.) At the time of the war alarm, in 1775, this total must have risen to full 25,000. Philadelphia's population was somewhat larger; Boston's, less.

to the west of it, including Washington and West streets and the docks, is built on new ground, made within the century. Behind Trinity Church, and as far down as the Battery, the shore rose to a very considerable bluff. Necessarily, much the greater part of the city then lay east of Broadway. The irregular streets to be found on this side are relics of both the Dutch and English foundation; of their buildings, however, as they stood in 1776, scarcely one remains at the present time. New streets have been built on the East River as well as on the North, materially changing the water boundary of this part of the island. Front and South streets had no existence at that date. On the line of Wall street, the city has nearly doubled in width since the Revolution.

Before its contraction, and in view of its convenience and protection from storms, the East River was the harbor proper of New York. Most of the docks were on that side, and just above Catherine street lay the ship-yards, where at times, in colonial days, an eight-hundred-ton West Indiaman might be seen upon the stocks.

What is now the City Hall Park was called in 1776 "the Fields," or "The Common." The site of the City Hall was occupied by the House of Correction; the present Hall of Records was the town jail, and the structure then on a line with them at the corner of Broadway was the "Bridewell." The City Hall of that day stood in Wall street, on the site of the present Custom-House, and King's, now Columbia, College in the square bounded by Murray, Barclay, Church, and West Broadway. Queen, now Pearl, was the principal business street; fashion was to be found in the vicinity of the Battery, and Broad and Dock streets; the Vauxhall Gardens were at the foot of Reade; and to pass out of town, one would have to turn off Broadway into Chatham street, which extended through Park Row, and keep on to the Bowery.

John Adams has left us a brief description of New York, as he saw it when passing through to the first Congress at Philadelphia in 1774, in company with Cushing, Paine, and Samuel Adams. His diary runs:

" *Saturday, Aug. 20.*—Lodged at Cock's, at Kingsbridge, a pretty place. . . . Breakfasted at Day's [127th street], and arrived in the city of New York at ten o'clock, at Hull's, a tavern, the sign the Bunch of Grapes. We rode by several very elegant country-seats before we came to the city. . . . After dinner, Mr. McDougall and Mr. Platt came, and walked with us to every part of the city. First we went to the fort, where we saw the ruins of that magnificent building, the Governor's house [burned Dec. 29, 1773]. From the Parade, before the fort, you have a fine prospect of Hudson River, and of the East River, or the Sound, and of the harbor; of Long Island, beyond the Sound River, and of New Jersey beyond Hudson's River. The walk round this fort is very pleasant, though the fortifications are not strong. Between the fort and the city is a beautiful ellipsis of land [Bowling Green], railed in with solid iron, in the centre of which is a statue of his majesty on horseback, very large, of solid lead gilded with gold, standing on a pedestal of marble, very high. We then walked up the Broad Way, a fine street, very wide, and in a right line from one end to the other of the city. In this route we saw the old Church and the new Church [Trinity]. The new is a very magnificent building—cost twenty thousand pounds, York currency. The prison is a large and a handsome stone building; there are two sets of barracks. We saw the New York College, which is also a large stone building. A new hospital is building, of stone. We then walked down to a ship-yard. Then we walked round through another street, which is the principal street of business. Saw the several markets.

After this we went to the coffee-house, which was full of gentlemen ; read the newspapers, etc. . . . The streets of this town are vastly more regular and elegant than those in Boston, and the houses are more grand, as well as neat. They are almost all painted, brick buildings and all."

Other glimpses we get from English sources. The traveler Smyth, while visiting this city during the British occupation, has this to say :[1] " Nothing can be more delightful than the situation of New York, commanding a variety of the most charming prospects that can be conceived. It is built chiefly upon the East River, which is the best and safest harbour, and is only something more than half a mile wide. The North River is better than two miles over to Powles Hook, which is a strong work opposite to New York, but is exposed to the driving of the ice in winter, whereby ships are prevented from lying therein during that season of the year. The land on the North River side is high and bold, but on the East River it gradually descends in a beautiful declivity to the water's edge. . . . Amongst the multitude of elegant seats upon this island, there are three or four uncommonly beautiful, viz., Governor Elliot's, Judge Jones's, Squire Morris's, and Mr. Bateman's. And opposite, upon the Continent, just above Hell-gates, there is a villa named Morrisania, which is inferior to no place in the world for the beauties, grandeur, and extent of perspective, and the elegance of its situation." Eddis, who had been compelled to leave Maryland on account of his loyal sentiments, was hardly less impressed with the city's appearance when he stopped here on his way to England in 1777. " The capital of this province," he wrote, August 16th, " is situated on the southern extremity of the island ; on one side

---

[1] " A Tour in the United States," etc.   By J. F. D. Smyth.   London, 1784.

runs the North, and on the other the East River, on the latter of which, on account of the harbour, the city is principally built.   In several streets, trees are regularly planted, which afford a grateful shelter during the intense heat of the summer.   The buildings are generally of brick, and many are erected in a style of elegance. . . .   Previous to the commencement of this unhappy war, New York was a flourishing, populous, and beautiful town. . . .   Notwithstanding the late devastation [fire of 1776], there are still many elegant edifices remaining, which would reflect credit on any metropolis in Europe." [1]

Beyond the limits of the city, Manhattan Island retained much of its primitive appearance.   Roads, farms, country-seats, interspersed it, but not thickly ; and as yet the salient features were hills, marshes, patches of rocky land, streams, and woods.   Just upon the outskirts, midway between the rivers, at about the corner of Grand and Centre Streets, the ground rose to a commanding elevation on the farm of William Bayard, which overlooked the city and the island above a distance of more than three miles.   Further east, a little north of the intersection of Grand and Division Streets, stood another hill, somewhat lower, where Judge Jones lived, from which opened an extensive view of the East River and harbor.   On the west side, on this line, the surface sank from Bayard's mount into a spreading marsh as far as the Hudson, and over which now run portions of Canal and Grand and their cross streets.   Where we have the Tombs and surrounding blocks, stood the " Fresh Water" lake or " Collect," several fathoms deep, with high sloping banks on the north and west, and on whose surface were made the earliest experiments in steam navigation in 1796.

[1] " Letters from America, 1769–1777."   By Wm. Eddis.   London.

One nearly central highway, known as the King's Bridge or Post Road, ran the entire length of the island. Where it left the city at Chatham Square, it was properly the Bowerie or Bowery Lane. Continuing along the present street by this name, it fell off into the line of Fourth Avenue as far as Fourteenth Street, crossed Union Square diagonally to Broadway, and kept the course of the latter to Madison Square at Twenty-third Street. Crossing this square, also diagonally, the road stretched along between Fourth and Second Avenues to Fifty-third Street, passed east of Second Avenue, and then turning westerly entered Central Park at Ninety-second Street. Leaving the Park at a hollow in the hills known as "McGowan's Pass," just above the house of Andrew McGowan, on the line of One Hundred and Seventh Street, west of Fifth Avenue, it followed Harlem Lane to the end of the island. Here, on the other side of King's Bridge, then "a small wooden bridge,"[1] the highway diverged easterly to New England and northerly to Albany.

This portion of the island above the city was known as its "Out-ward," and had been divided at an early date into three divisions, under the names of the Bowery, Harlem, and Bloomingdale divisions. Each contained points of settlement. The Bowery section included that part of the city laid out near Fresh Water Pond and around Chatham Square below Grand Street, and the stretch of country above beyond the line of Twenty-third Street. In this division were to be found some of the notable residences and country-seats of that day. James De Lancey's large estate extended from the Bowery to the East River,

[1] "King's Bridge, which joins the northern extremity of this island to the continent, is only a small wooden bridge, and the country around is mountainous, rocky, broken, and disagreeable, but very strong."—*Smyth's Tour*, *etc.*, vol. ii., p. 376.

and from Division nearly to the line of Houston Street. The Rutgers' Mansion stood attractively on the slopes of the river bank about the line of Montgomery Street, and above De Lancey's, on the Bowery, were the De Peysters, Dyckmans, and Stuyvesants.

The Harlem division of the Out-ward, with which are associated some of the most interesting events of 1776, included what is now known as Harlem, with the island above it as far as King's Bridge. Dutch farmers had settled here a hundred years before the Revolution. As early as 1658, the Director-General and Council of New Netherland gave notice that "for the further promotion of Agriculture, for the security of this Island, and the cattle pasturing thereon, as well as for the greater recreation and amusement of this city of Amsterdam in New Netherland, they have resolved to form a New Village or Settlement at the end of the Island, and about the lands of Jochem Pietersen, deceased, and those which adjoin thereto." The first settlers were to receive lots to cultivate, be furnished with a guard of soldiers, and allowed a ferry across the Harlem River, for "the better and greater promotion of neighborly correspondence with the English of the North."[1] In 1776, the division was interspersed with houses and fields, especially in the stretch of plains or flat land just above One Hundred and Tenth Street, and from the East River to the line of Ninth Avenue. The church and centre of the village were on the east side, in the vicinity of One Hundred and Twenty-fifth Street, and the old road by which they were reached from the city branched off from the main highway at McGowan's Pass.

[1] *Laws and Ordinances of New Netherlands.*

Bloomingdale was a scattered settlement, containing nearly all the houses to be found along the Bloomingdale Road, but the name appears to have identified principally the upper section beyond Fiftieth Street. Here lived the Apthorpes at Ninety-second Street ; the Strikers, Joneses, and Hogelands above ; and, lower down, the Somerindykes and Harsens. As fixed by law, at that time, this road started from the King's Bridge Road, at the house of John Horn, now the corner of Twenty-third Street and Fifth Avenue, and followed the line of the present Broadway and the recent Bloomingdale Road to the farm of Adrian Hogeland, at One Hundred and Eighth Street.[1] Nearly on a line with Hogeland, but considerably east of him, lived Benjamin Vandewater ; and these two were the most northerly residents in the division.

Still another suburb of the city was the village of Greenwich, overlooking the Hudson on the west side, in the vicinity of Fourteenth Street, to which the Greenwich Road, now Greenwich Street, led along the river bank in nearly a straight line. The road above continued further east about as far as Forty-fifth Street, and there connected, by a lane running southwesterly, with the Bloomingdale Road at Forty-third Street. Among the country-seats in this village were those of the Jeaunceys, Bayards, and Clarkes ; and above, at Thirty-third Street and Ninth Avenue, stood the ample and conspicuous residence of John Morin Scott, one of the leading lawyers of the city, and a powerful supporter of the American cause.

[1] The caption to the act in the case passed 1751, and remaining unchanged in 1773, reads : "*An Act for mending and keeping in Repair the publick Road or Highway, from the House of John Horne, in the Bowry Division of the Outward of the City of New York, through the Bloomendale Division in the said ward, to the house of Adrian Hoogelandt.*"

Across the East River, the "Sister City" of Brooklyn in 1776 was as yet invisible from New York. A clump of low buildings at the old ferry, and an occasional manor-seat, were the only signs of life apparent on that side. Columbia Heights, whose modern blocks and row of wharves and bonded stores suggest commercial activity alone, caught the eye a century ago as "a noble bluff," crowned with fields and woods, and meeting the water at its base with a shining beach. The parish or village proper was the merest cluster of houses, nestled in the vicinity of the old Dutch church, which stood in the middle of the road a little below Bridge Street. The road was the King's highway, and it ran from Fulton Ferry — where we have had a ferry for two hundred and forty years at least—along the line of Fulton Street, and on through Jamaica to the eastern end of Long Island. Besides the settlements that had grown up at these two points— the church and the ferry, which were nearly a mile and a half apart—a village centre was to be found at Bedford, further up the highway, another in the vicinity of the Wallabout, and still another, called Gowanus, along the branch road skirting the bay. These all stood within the present municipal limits of Brooklyn.

As it had been for more than a century before, the population on the Long Island side was largely Dutch at the time of the Revolution. The first-comers, in 1636 and after, introduced themselves to the soil and the red man as the Van Schows, the Cornelissens, the Manjes, and the like—good Walloon patronimics—and the Dutch heritage is still preserved in the names of old families, and even more permanently in the name of the place itself; for the word Brooklyn is but the English corruption of Breukelen, the ancient Holland village [1] of which our modern city appears to have been the namesake. Smyth, the English traveler, makes the general statement towards the close of the Revolution, that two thirds of the inhabitants of Long Island, especially those on the west end, were of Dutch extraction, who continued "to make use of their customs and language in preference to English," which, however, they also understood. "The people of King's County [Brooklyn]," he says, "are almost entirely Dutch. In Queen's County, four fifths of the people are so likewise, but the other fifth, and all Suffolk County, are English as they call themselves, being from English ances-

[1] The Hon. Henry C. Murphy, who visited this place in 1859, says of it: "The town lies in the midst of a marshy district, and hence its name; for Breukelen—pronounced Brurkeler—means marsh land." "There are some curious points of coincidence," continues Mr. Murphy, "both as regards the name and situation of the Dutch Breukelen and our Brooklyn. The name with us was originally applied exclusively to the hamlet which grew up along the main road now embraced within Fulton Avenue, and between Smith Street and Jackson Street; and we must, therefore, not confound it with the settlements at the Waalebought, Gowanus, and the Ferry, now Fulton Ferry, which were entirely distinct, and were not embraced within the general name of Brooklyn, until after the organization of the township of that name by the British Colonial Government. Those of our citizens who remember the lands on Fulton Avenue near Nevins Street and De Kalb Avenue before the changes which were produced by the filling-in of those streets, will recollect that their original character was marshy and springy, being in fact the bed of the valley which received the drain of the hills extending on either side of it from the Waalebought to Gowanus Bay. This would lead to the conclusion that the name was given on account of the locality; but though we have very imperfect accounts as to who were the first settlers of Brooklyn proper, still, reasoning from analogy in the cases of New Utrecht and New Amersfoort, we cannot probably err in supposing that Brooklyn owes its name to the circumstance that its first settlers wished to preserve in it a memento of their homes in Fatherland. After the English conquest, there was a continual struggle between the Dutch and English orthography. . . . Thus it is spelled Breucklyn, Breuckland, Brucklyn, Broucklyn, Brookland, Brookline, and several other ways. At the end of the last century it settled down into the present Brooklyn. In this form it still retains sufficiently its original signification of the *marsh* or *brook land*."—*Stiles' History of Brooklyn*, vol. i., App. 4.

tors, and using no other language." Major Baurmeister, one of the officers of the Hessian division which participated in the battle of Long Island, leaves us something more than statistics in the case. He appears to have noted every thing with lively appreciation. To a friend in Germany, for instance, we find him writing as follows: " The happiness of the inhabitants, whose ancestors were all Dutch, must have been great; genuine kindness and real abundance is everywhere; any thing worthless or going to ruin is nowhere to be perceived. The inhabited regions resemble the Westphalian peasant districts; upon separate farms the finest houses are built, which are planned and completed in the most elegant fashion. The furniture in them is in the best taste, nothing like which is to be seen with us, and besides so clean and neat, that altogether it surpasses every description. The female sex is universally beautiful and delicately reared, and is finely dressed in the latest European fashion, particularly in India laces, white cotton and silk gauzes; not one of these women but would consider driving a double team the easiest of work. They drive and ride out alone, having only a negro riding behind to accompany them. Near every dwelling-house negroes (their slaves) are settled, who cultivate the most fertile land, pasture the cattle, and do all the menial work." [1] That the English element, however, had crept in to a considerable extent around Brooklyn at this time, is a matter of record.

The topography of this section of Long Island was peculiar, presenting strong contrasts of high and low land. Originally, and indeed within the memory of citizens still

---

[1] Part II., Document 33. On the other hand, some later English descriptions are not as pleasant; but the wretchedness the writers saw during the war was what the war had caused.

living, that part of Brooklyn lying south and west of the line of Nevins Street was practically a peninsula, with the Wallabout Bay or present Navy Yard on one side of the neck, and on the other, a mile across, the extensive Gowanus creek and marsh, over which now run Second, Third, and Fourth Avenues. The creek set in from the bay where the Gowanus Canal is retained, and rendered the marsh impassable at high-water as far as the line of Baltic Street. Blocks of buildings now stand on the site of mills that were once worked by the ebb and flow of the tides. The lower part of what is known as South Brooklyn was largely swamp land in 1776. Here the peninsula terminated in a nearly isolated triangular piece of ground jutting out into the harbor, called Red Hook, which figured prominently in the military operations. From this projection to the furthest point on the Wallabout was a distance of three miles, and the scenery along the bank presented a varied and attractive appearance to the resident of New York. The "heights" rose conspicuously in all the beauty of their natural outline ; lower down the shore might be seen a quaint Dutch mill or two ; on the bluffs opposite the Battery, the mansions of Philip and Robert Livingston were prominent ; and not far from where the archway crosses Montague Street stood the Remsen and, nearer the ferry, the Colden and Middagh residences. From every point of view the perspective was rural and inviting.[1]

---

[1] In describing some of the characteristic features of Long Island, Smyth, the traveler already quoted, mentions what seemed to him " two very extraordinary places." " The first," he says, " is a very dangerous and dreadful strait or passage, called *Hell-Gates,* between the East River and the Sound ; where the two tides meeting cause a horrible whirlpool, the vortex of which is called the Pot, and drawing in and swallowing up every thing that approaches near it, dashes them to pieces upon the rocks at the bottom. . . . Before the late war, a top-sail vessel was seldom ever known to pass

Vastly changed to-day is all this region, which was now to be disturbed by the din and havoc of war. Its picturesqueness long since disappeared. Upon Manhattan Island, the city's push "uptown"-ward has been like the cut of a drawing knife, a remorseless process of levelling and "filling-in." Forty times in population and twenty in area has it expanded beyond the growth of 1776. Brooklyn is a new creation. Would its phlegmatic denizen of colonial times recognize the site of his farms or his mills? Even the good Whig ferryman, Waldron, might be at a loss to make out his bearings, for the green banks of the East River have vanished, and its points become confused. The extent of its contraction he could learn from the builders of the bridge, who have set the New York pier eight hundred feet out from the high-water mark of 1776, and the Brooklyn pier two hundred or more, narrowing the stream at that point to a strait of but sixteen hundred feet in width.

The first active steps looking to the occupation of New York were taken by the Americans early in January of this year. Reports had reached Washington's head-

through Hell-Gates ; but since the commencement of it, fleets of transports, with frigates for their convoy, have frequently ventured and accomplished it ; the Niger, indeed, a very fine frigate of thirty-two guns, generally struck on some hidden rock, every time she attempted this passage. But what is still more extraordinary, that daring veteran, Sir James Wallace, to the astonishment of every person who ever saw or heard of it, carried his Majesty's ship, the Experiment, of fifty guns, safe through Hell-Gates, from the east end of the Sound to New York ; when the French fleet under D'Estaing lay off Sandy Hook, and blocked up the harbor and city of New York, some ships of the line being also sent by D'Estaing round the east end of Long Island to cruise in the Sound for the same purpose, so that the Experiment must inevitably have fallen into their hands, had it not been for this bold and successful attempt of her gallant commander." The other spot was Hempstead Plains, which presented the " singular phenomenon," for America, of having no trees.

quarters that the British were fitting out an expedition by sea, whose destination was kept a profound secret. In Boston, rumors were afloat that it was bound for Halifax or Rhode Island. In reality it was the expedition with which Sir Henry Clinton was to sail to North Carolina, and there meet Cornwallis, from England, to carry out the southern diversion. Ignorant of the British plans, and suspecting that Clinton might suddenly appear at New York, Washington on the 4th of January called the attention of Congress to the movement, and suggested that it would be " consistent with prudence" to have some New Jersey troops thrown into the city to prevent the " almost irremediable" evil which would follow its occupation by the enemy. Two days later, General Charles Lee, holding rank in the American army next to Washington, pressed a plan of his own, to the effect that he be sent himself by the commander-in-chief to secure New York, and that the troops for the purpose (there being none to spare from the force around Boston) be hastily raised in Connecticut. This was approved at head-quarters, and on the 8th inst. Lee received instructions as follows:

" Having undoubted intelligence of the fitting out of a fleet at Boston, and of the embarkation of troops from thence, which, from the season of the year and other circumstances, must be destined for a southern expedition; and having such information as I can rely on, that the inhabitants, or a great part of them, on Long Island in the colony of New York, are not only inimical to the rights and liberties of America, but by their conduct and public professions have discovered a disposition to aid and assist in the reduction of that colony to ministerial tyranny; and as it is a matter of the utmost importance to prevent the enemy from taking possession of the City of New York and the North River, as they will thereby command the country, and the communication with Canada—it is of too much consequence to hazard such a post at so alarming a crisis. . . .

" You will therefore, with such volunteers as are willing to join you,

4

and can be expeditiously raised, repair to the City of New York, and calling upon the commanding officer of the forces of New Jersey for such assistance as he can afford, and you shall require, you are to put that city into the best posture of defence which the season and circumstances will admit, disarming all such persons upon Long Island and elsewhere (and if necessary otherwise securing them), whose conduct and declarations have rendered them justly suspected of designs unfriendly to the views of Congress. . . . . I am persuaded I need not recommend dispatch in the prosecution of this business. The importance of it alone is a sufficient incitement." [1]

Washington wrote at the same time to Governor Trumbull, of Connecticut, Colonel Lord Stirling, of New Jersey, and the New York Committee of Safety, urging them to give Gen. Lee all the assistance in their power.

Lee, who had been an officer in the British army, serving at one time under Burgoyne in Portugal, had already established a reputation for himself in Washington's camp as a military authority, and enjoyed the full confidence of the commander-in-chief, despite certain eccentricities of manner and an over-confidence in his own judgment and experience. The defects and weaknesses of his character, which eventually brought him into disgrace as a soldier, were not as yet displayed or understood. At the present time he was eager to be of essential service to the colonies, and he entered into the New York project with spirit. In Connecticut the governor promptly seconded his efforts, by calling out two regiments of volunteers to serve for six weeks under the general, and appointed Colonels David

[1] Washington had some misgivings as to his authority to assume military control of New York, and he sought the advice of John Adams, who was then at Watertown. The latter replied without hesitation that under his commission as commander-in-chief he had full authority. To President Hancock, Washington wrote : " I hope the Congress will approve of my conduct in sending General Lee upon this expedition. I am sure I mean it well, as experience teaches us that it is much easier to prevent an enemy from posting themselves, than it is to dislodge them after they have got possession."

Waterbury, of Stamford, and Andrew Ward, of Guilford, to their command. By the 20th, Lee found himself ready to proceed; but while on his way, near Stamford, he received a communication from the Committee of Safety at New York, representing that the rumors of his coming had created great alarm in the city, and earnestly requesting him to halt his troops on the Connecticut border, until his object were better known to the committee. Here was something of a dilemma, and it may be asked how it should have arisen. Why, indeed, was it necessary to organize a force outside of New York to secure it? Was not this the time for the city to prepare for her defence, and welcome assistance from whatever quarter offered? The answer is to be found in the exceptional political temperament of New York at this time. Her population contained a large and powerful loyalist element, which hoped, with the assistance of the three or four British men-of-war then in the harbor, to be able to give the place, at the proper moment, into the hands of the king's troops. Only a short time before, Governor Tryon had informed Howe that it only needed the presence of a small force to secure it, and develop a strong loyal support among the inhabitants of both the city and colony. The patriotic party had abated none of its zeal, but it recognized the danger of precipitating matters, and accordingly pursued what appeared to colonists elsewhere to be a temporizing and timid policy, but which proved the wisest course in the end. The city was at the mercy of the men-of-war. Any attempt to seize it could be answered with a bombardment. The situation required prudent management; above all, it required delay on the part of the Americans until they were ready for a decisive step. That the Committee of Safety was thoroughly true to the country, no one can doubt a moment after reading their daily proceedings. In their letter to Lee they say: " This committee and the Congress whose place we fill in their recess, are, we flatter ourselves, as unanimously zealous in the cause of America as any representative body on the continent : so truly zealous, that both the one and the other will cheerfully devote this city to sacrifice for advancing that great and important cause." But knowing the state of affairs in their midst better than others, they urged caution instead of haste in bringing the war to New York. In this case, they informed Lee that no works had been erected in the city, that they had but little powder, that they were sending out ships for more without molestation from the men-of-war, their object being kept secret, and that a general alarm then in the dead of winter, driving women and children into the country, would work great distress. " For these reasons," continue the committee, " we conceive that a just regard to the public cause, and our duty to take a prudent care of this city, dictate the impropriety of provoking hostilities at present, and the necessity of saving appearances with the ships of war till at least the month of March. Though we have been unfortunate in our disappointments with respect to some of our adventures, yet be assured, sir, we have not been idle. Our intrenching tools are almost completed to a sufficient number ; we are forming a magazine of provisions for five thousand men for a month in a place of safety, and at a convenient distance from this city ; we have provided ourselves with six good brass field-pieces ; have directed carriages to be made for our other artillery, and are raising a company of artillery for the defence of the colony on the Continental establishment. These things, when accomplished, with other smaller matters, and with the arrival of some gunpowder, the prospect of which is not unpromising, will enable us to face our enemies with some countenance." Lee, with due consideration, replied to the committee that he should comply with their request about the troops, and do nothing that could endanger the city.

It was not until the 4th of February that the general entered New York. On the same day Clinton arrived in the harbor from Boston, with his southern expedition, but only to make a brief stay. The coming of these officers threw the city into great excitement. Many of the inhabitants expected an immediate collision, and began to leave the place. One Garish Harsin, writing from New York to William Radclift at Rhyn Beck, sums up in a single sentence the effect of the harbor news :[1] " It is impossible to describe the confusion the place was in on account of the regulars being come." And when rumors magnified Clinton's two or three transports into a British fleet of nineteen sail, Harsin informs his friend that the people were taking themselves out of town "as if it were the Last Day." Pastor Shewkirk, of the Moravian Church, in his interesting diary[2] of passing events, tells us that " the inhabitants began now to move away in a surprising manner," and that " the whole aspect of things grew frightful, and increased so from day to day." To add to the discomfort and suffering of the people, the weather was very cold, and the rivers full of ice.

The Committee of Safety, in their anxiety as to the effect of Lee's occupation of the city, had already written to the

---

[1] " New York in the Revolution." Published by the New York Mercantile Library Association.
[2] Part II., Document 37.

Continental Congress on the subject, and that body at once sent up a committee, consisting of Messrs. Harrison, Lynch, and Allen, to advise with Lee and the New York Committee. The latter accepted the situation, consented to the entry of the troops into town, and at a conference with Lee and the Congress Committee on the 6th, agreed to the immediate prosecution of defensive measures.

Upon his arrival, the general sent his engineer, Captain William Smith, " an excellent, intelligent, active officer," to survey and report upon the salient points of the position, especially around Hell Gate and on Long Island. Lee and Stirling also went over the ground several times. As a result of these inspections, the general became convinced that to attempt a complete defence of the city would be impracticable, because the ample sea-room afforded by the harbor and rivers gave the enemy every advantage, enabling them, with their powerful fleet, to threaten an attack in front and flank. Lee saw this at once, and reported his views to Washington, February 19th. " What to do with the city," he wrote, " I own, puzzles me. It is so encircled with deep navigable waters, that whoever commands the sea must command the town ;" and to the New York Committee ne said that it would be impossible to make the place absolutely secure. In view of this, he proposed to construct a system of defences that should have an alternative object, namely, that in case they should prove inadequate for the city's protection, they should at least be sufficient to prevent the enemy from securing a permanent foothold in it.

Under this plan, the line of the East River required the principal attention, as here it seemed possible to offer the best resistance to British attempts upon the city.

First, to cut off the enemy's communication between the Sound and the river, it was proposed to blockade the passage at Hell Gate by a fort on Horn's Hook, at the foot of East Eighty-eighth Street, as well as by works opposite, on the present Hallet's Point. A further object of these forts was to secure safe transit between Long Island and New York. In the next place, batteries were planned for both sides of the river at its entrance into the harbor, where the city was chiefly exposed. On the New York side, a battery was located at the foot of Catherine Street at the intersection of Cherry, and where the river was narrowest. This was called Waterbury's Battery. To cover its fire a stronger work was ordered to be built on Rutgers' "first hill," just above, which was named Badlam's Redoubt, after Captain Badlam, then acting as Lee's chief artillery officer. Lower down a battery was sunk in a cellar on Ten Eyck's wharf, Coenties Slip, a short distance below Wall Street, and called Coenties Battery. These three, with part of the Grand Battery and Fort George, included all the works planned by Lee to guard the East River from the New York side.

In connection with these, works were laid out on the bank opposite on Long Island, the importance of which was apparent. Not only was the site well adapted for guns to sweep the channel and prevent the enemy's ships from remaining in the river long enough to do the city serious damage, but it also commanded the city, so as to make it untenable by the British should they succeed in occupying it. This bluff, "Columbia Heights," was in fact the key to the entire situation. Lee considered its possession and security of "greater importance" than New York; and to hold it he proposed establishing there an intrenched camp[1] for three or four thousand men, fortified by "a chain of redoubts mutually supporting each other." Of these redoubts, one was located on the edge of the bluff opposite the Coenties Battery, and stood on the line of Columbia Street, at about the foot of the present Clark Street. This came to be known as Fort Stirling. In its rear, near the corner of Henry and Pierrepont streets, it was proposed to erect a large citadel; but this, although begun, was never completed.[2] Lee's scheme of defence did not include the fortifying of either Red Hook or Governor's Island.

The East River thus provided for, attention was paid to the city and the North River side. Lee examined Fort George and the Grand Battery, but gave it as his opinion that neither of them could be held under the concentrated fire of large ships. He advised, accordingly, that the northern face of the fort be torn down, and a traverse built across Broadway above it at the Bowling Green, from which the interior of the work could be raked, should the enemy attempt to land and hold it. As the North River was "so extremely wide and deep," the general regarded the obstruction of its passage to the ships as out of the question. Batteries, however, could be erected at various points along the west side where it rose to a ridge, and the power of the ships to injure the town very considerably diminished. All the streets leading up from the water were ordered to be barricaded to prevent the

[1] Lee wrote to Washington, February 19th: "I wait for some more force to prepare a post or retrenched encampment on Long Island, opposite to the city, for 3000 men. This is, I think, a capital object; for, should the enemy take possession of New York, when Long Island is in our hands, they will find it almost impossible to subsist."

[2] The location and strength of Fort Stirling, the citadel, and the other works on Long Island, are noted more in detail further along in this chapter.

enemy from coming up on the flanks; forts were to be erected on Jones', Bayard's, and Lispenard's hills, north of the town, covering the approach by land from that direction; the roads obstructed to artillery; and redoubts, redans, and flêches thrown up at defensible points throughout the entire island, as far as King's Bridge.[1] "I must observe," said Lee to the Committee of Safety, "that New York, from its circumstances, can with difficulty be made a regular tenable fortification; but it may be made a most advantageous field of battle—so advantageous, indeed, that, if our people behave with common spirit, and the commanders are men of discretion, it must cost the enemy many thousands of men to get possession of it."

To construct these extensive works Lee could muster, two weeks after his arrival, but seventeen hundred men. Waterbury's Connecticut regiment was first on the ground; the First New Jersey Continentals, as yet incomplete, under Colonel the Earl of Stirling, soon followed; and from Westchester County, New York, came two hundred minutemen under Colonel Samuel Drake. Dutchess County sent down Colonels Swartwout and Van Ness with about three hundred more; and on the 24th Colonel Ward arrived with his Connecticut regiment, six hundred strong, which had rendezvoused at Fairfield. Stirling's regiment was quartered principally in the lower barracks at the Battery; Waterbury's at the upper, on the site of the new Court

[1] "*Feb.* 23ᵈ, 1776.— . . . General Lee is taking every necessary step to fortify and defend this city. The men-of-war are gone out of our harbor; the Phœnix is at the Hook; the Asia lays near Beedlow's Island; so that we are now in a state of perfect peace and security, was it not for our apprehensions of future danger. To see the vast number of houses shut up, one would think the city almost evacuated. Women and children are scarcely to be seen in the streets. Troops are daily coming in; they break open and quarter themselves in any houses they find shut up. Necessity knows no law."—*Letter from F. Rhinelander.* "*Life of Peter Van Schaack.*"

House; Ward's was sent to Long Island; and Drake's minute-men were posted at Horn's Hook, opposite Hell Gate, where they began work on the first battery marked out for the defence of New York City during the Revolution.

But Lee's stay at this point was to be brief. The Continental Congress appointed him to the command of the newly created Department of the South, and on the 7th of March he left New York in charge of Lord Stirling, who, a month before, had been promoted by Congress to the rank of brigadier-general. This officer's energy was conspicuous. His predecessor had already found him "a great acquisition," and he pushed on the defences of the city as rapidly as his resources would permit. The force under his immediate command, according to the returns of the 13th, amounted to a total of two thousand four hundred and twenty-two officers and men,[1] besides the city independent companies under Colonels John Lasher and William Heyer, and local militia,[2] who swelled the number to about four thousand. On the 14th, Washington wrote to Stirling that the enemy appeared to be on the point of evacuating Boston, and that it was more than probable they would sail southward. " I am of opinion," he wrote, " that New York is their place of destination. It is an object worthy of their attention, and it is the place that we must use every endeavor to keep from them. For, should they get that town, and the command of the North River, they can stop the intercourse

[1] Privates present fit for duty: Stirling's regiment, 407 ; Waterbury's, 457 ; Ward's, 489 ; Drake's, 104 ; Swartwout's, 186 ; Van Ness', 110 ; Captain Ledyard's company, N. Y., 64.

[2] In the chapter on " The Two Armies," some further account is given of the troops furnished during the campaign by New York and the Brooklyn villages.

COLONEL FIRST NEW YORK CITY BATTALION
1775–1776.

Steel Engr F von Egloffstein N.Y.

between the Northern and Southern colonies, upon which depends the safety of America. My feelings upon this subject are so strong, that I would not wish to give the enemy a chance of succeeding at your place. . . . The plan of defence formed by General Lee is, from what little I know of the place, a very judicious one. I hope, nay, I dare say, it is carrying into execution with spirit and industry. You may judge of the enemy's keeping so long possession of the town of Boston against an army superior in numbers, and animated with the noble spirit of liberty; I say, you may judge by that how much easier it is to keep an enemy from forming a lodgment in a place, than it will be to dispossess them when they get themselves fortified." Stirling immediately sent urgent appeals for troops in every direction. He ordered over the Third New Jersey Continental Regiment under Colonel Dayton, and wrote for three hundred picked men from each of the six nearest counties of that State. Ward's and Waterbury's regiments, which were impatient to return home to attend to their spring farming, were many of them induced to remain two weeks beyond their term of enlistment until Governor Trumbull could supply their places with troops under Colonels Silliman and Talcott. Congress also ordered forward five or six Pennsylvania regiments. Meanwhile the New York Committee of Safety co-operated zealously with the military authorities.[1] At Stirling's request they voted to call out all the male

----

[1] The committee humored Governor Tryon, however, with a few civilities as late as April 4th, when they provided his fleet with "the following articles, viz.: 1300 lbs. beef for the 'Asia'; 1000 lbs. beef for the 'Phœnix,' with 18*s.* worth vegetables; 2 qrs. beef, 1 doz. dishes, 2 doz. plates, 1 doz. spoons, 2 mugs, 2 barrels ale, for the packet; 6 barrels of beer, 2 quarters of beef for the governor's ship, 'Duchess of Gordon.'"—*Journal of the Provincial Congress.*

inhabitants of the city, black and white, capable of doing "fatigue duty," to work on the fortifications—the blacks to work every day, the whites every other day;[1] and the same orders were conveyed to the committee of King's County, where the inhabitants were directed to report to Colonel Ward, with spades, hoes and pickaxes. To troops needing quarters the committee turned over the empty houses in the city, or those that were "least liable to be injured;" coarse sheets were ordered for the straw beds in the barracks; the upper story of the "Bridewell" was converted into a laboratory or armory for repairing guns and making cartridges; and all necessary details provided for as far as possible. In case of an alarm, the troops were to parade immediately at the Battery, in the Common, and in front of Trinity Church. To annoy expected British men-of-war, the committee despatched Major William Malcolm, of the Second city battalion, to dismantle the Sandy Hook Light, which the major effected in a thorough manner, breaking what glasses he could not move, and carrying off the oil. On Long Island, a guard of King's County troopers was posted at the Narrows, and another at Rockaway, to report the approach of ships; and in the city, cannon were mounted in the batteries as fast as they were completed. On the 20th, Stirling could report that everybody turned to "with great spirit and industry," and that the work went on "amazingly well."

[1] Stirling's orders, March 13th, 1776 : "It is intended to employ one half of the inhabitants every other day, changing, at the works for the defence of this city; and the whole of the slaves every day, until this place is put in a proper posture of defence. The Town Major is immediately to disperse these orders."—*Force*, 4th series, vol. v., p. 219.

The citizens were divided off into reliefs or "beats." In the "N. Y. Hist. Manuscripts," vol. i., p. 267, may be found the "Amount of officers and Privates of yᵉ 22d Beat at work 17 March"—59 men under Captain Benj. Egbert. Negroes belonging to the 22d Beat—"Pomp, Cæsar, Peter, Sam, Jo, Cubitt, Simms, John, Cato," etc., 11 in all.

On the same date Brigadier-General Thompson, of Pennsylvania, reported at New York, and held the command until the arrival, a few days later, of Brigadier-General Heath, of Massachusetts, who in turn was relieved, April 4th, by Major-General Putnam.

Affairs at Boston now reached a crisis. The siege, which the provincial troops had so successfully maintained for ten months, terminated to their own unbounded credit and the secret mortification of the enemy. On the 17th of March the city was evacuated by the British, and immediately occupied by the Americans—an event that had been foreseen and provided for at a council of war held on the 13th, at General Ward's headquarters in Roxbury. The commander-in-chief there stated that every indication pointed to an early departure of the enemy from Boston, with the probability that they were destined for New York, and he questioned whether it was not advisable to send a part of the army to that point without delay. The council coincided in this opinion, and on the following day the rifle regiment under Lieutenant-Colonel Hand, and the three companies of Virginia riflemen, under Captain Stephenson, were put on the march southward. These were followed on the 18th by five regiments under Brigadier-General Heath, who had been ordered to march by way of Providence, Norwich, New London, and the Sound. As the enemy's transports lingered around Boston for several days, no more troops were sent southward until the 29th, when six regiments were ordered on, under Brigadier-General Sullivan. On the same date Major-General Putnam received orders to proceed to New York, assume command, and continue the work of fortifying the city upon the plan adopted by General Lee.

On the 1st of April, Brigadier-General Greene's brigade moved in the same direction, and was followed in a day or two by General Spencer's. Five regiments remained at Boston, under Major-General Ward.

Waiting until all the troops were on the march, Washington, on April 4th, himself set out from Cambridge for New York. Crowned with his first honors as the deliverer of Boston, he was greeted on his route with respectful admiration and enthusiasm. He had come to New England comparatively unknown—"a Mr. Washington, of Virginia;" he left it secure in the affections and pride of its people. Expecting him at Providence the next day, the 5th, General Greene, who had been delayed at that place, ordered two regiments of his brigade—Hitchcock's Rhode Island and Little's Massachusetts—to appear in their best form and escort the general into the city. The minuteness of Greene's directions on the occasion furnishes us with the material for a picture of the personal appearance of the early Continental soldier when on parade. As preserved among the papers of the Massachusetts colonel, the order runs as follows:

"*Providence April* 4, 1776.—Col⁰. Hitchcock's and Col⁰. Little's regiments are to turn out to-morrow morning to escort his Excellency into town, to parade at 8 o'clock, both officers & men dressed in uniform, & none to turn out except those dressed in uniform, & those of the non-commissioned officers & soldiers that turn out to be washed, both face & hands, clean, their beards shaved, their hair combed & powdered, & their arms cleaned. The General hopes that both officers & soldiers will exert themselves for the honour of the regiment & brigade to which they belong. He wishes to pay the honours to the Commander in Chief in as decent & respectable a manner as possible." [1]

Governor Cooke, of Rhode Island, was not less attentive,

[1] MS. Order Book of Colonel Moses Little.

and in addition to calling out " the several companies of cadets, of grenadiers, and light infantry" in Providence to meet the commander-in-chief, he had a house prepared for his reception and the accommodation of his suite, which, besides his officers, included Lady Washington and Mr. and Mrs. Custis.[1] Passing on to New London, where he hurried the embarkation of the troops, Washington kept on along the shore road, reached New Haven on the 11th, and on the 13th arrived at the city of New York. Putnam had come ten days earlier. Owing to insufficient transportation and slow sailing on the Sound, it was April 24th before the last of the soldiers reported on the ground.

The new military base in this vicinity was thus fairly established, and the commander-in-chief, after personally inspecting the position, urged on the work of defence. As the regiments on their arrival had been quartered at haphazard in the city, he first arranged the army into five brigades, with the view of putting them into suitable and permanent camps. To the command of these he assigned Heath, Spencer, Sullivan, Greene, and Stirling, in the order of their rank. The twenty-five battalions which made up the force at this date numbered together not quite ten thousand men.

But hardly were the orders for this new arrangement issued before events required its modification. Our affairs proving to be in a bad way in the direction of Canada, it became necessary to despatch General Sullivan with six regiments to the northward, and on the 29th of April the troops in New York were formed anew into four brigades, and assigned to their respective camps. Heath's first brigade was posted on the Hudson, just without the city

[1] R. I. Hist. Coll. Vol. VI.

above the Canal Street marsh and about Richmond Hill;
Spencer's second, on the East River, around the Rutgers'
farm and Jones' Hill; and Stirling's fourth, in the centre,
near Bayard's Hill and the Bowery Road; while Greene's
third brigade was assigned to "the ground marked out
upon Long Island." But one work now lay before these
soldiers, namely, to put New York and its vicinity in a
complete state of defence in the shortest possible time.
Howe and his Boston army, it was now known, had gone
to Halifax instead of sailing for New York; but he could
still reach, and, with reinforcements from England, attack
the city before the Americans were ready to receive him.
The situation, accordingly, admitted of no delays, and
digging was made the order of the day. No one could
have anticipated, however, that preparations were to be
continued full four months longer before active campaign-
ing opened.

This interval of fortifying is not without its interest;
and we may cross, first, with Greene to Long Island, to
note what further was done towards securing that "capital" point in the general system of defence.

From the orders of April 24th and 25th it would appear
that it was Washington's original intention to give the
Brooklyn command, not to Greene, but to Sullivan. The
latter was assigned to the Third Brigade before going to
Canada, and on the 25th the encampment of this brigade
was ordered to be marked out "upon Long Island." The
fact that Sullivan was senior to Greene in rank, and was
entitled, as between the two, to the honor and responsibility of the separate command, was doubtless the ground
of his assignment in this case. But a greater responsibility
was reserved for Sullivan in Canada, and Greene was sent

to Long Island. Owing to bad weather, it was the 3d or
4th of May before the latter crossed with troops. He
took with him his old brigade, consisting of Colonel Edward Hand's Pennsylvania Riflemen, his two favorite
Rhode Island regiments under Colonels James Mitchell
Varnum and Daniel Hitchcock, and Colonel Moses Little's
regiment from Massachusetts. These ranked as the First,
Ninth, Eleventh, and Twelfth of the Continental Establishment, and were as well armed and under as good discipline as any troops in Washington's army. Hand's
regiment, numbering four hundred and seventy officers
and men, was already on Long Island, having come from
Boston in advance of the brigades, and was engaged in
scouting and patrol duty at the Narrows and along the
coast. Varnum's, Hitchcock's, and Little's, having an
average strength of three hundred and eighty each, were
the only troops around Brooklyn.[1] The Long Island
militia were not as yet in the field, and the small company
of Brooklyn troopers under Captain Waldron and Lieutenant Boerum, which had patrolled the coast during the
early spring, do not appear on duty again until late in the
season.

It now remained for these regiments to go on fortifying
the water-front of this site to keep the ships out of the

[1] Ward's, we have seen, was the first regiment stationed on Long Island.
It was there from February 24th until about the end of March. The *N. Y.
Packet* of February 29th, 1776, says : "Saturday last Col. Ward's regiment
arrived here from Connecticut, and embarked in boats and landed on
Nassau [Long] Island." Lee gave orders that a Pennsylvania battalion,
supposed to be on its way to New York, should encamp from the Wallabout to Gowanus, but no Pennsylvania troops are included in Stirling's
return, and certainly none were on Long Island until Hand's riflemen came
from Boston. It is probable that Colonel Chas. Webb's Connecticut Continentals relieved Ward, as Captain Hale writes that it had been there three
weeks, sometime before May 20th. Greene's brigade were the next troops
to cross over.

river, and, in addition, to secure themselves against an attack by land. What Lee's plan was in reference to Columbia Heights has already been seen. Here he proposed to establish a camp with Fort Stirling and the Citadel among its defences, the former of which had been nearly completed and the latter begun by Ward's regiment and the inhabitants. In consequence, however, of a move made by General Putnam soon after his arrival, it had evidently become necessary to enlarge this plan. Governor's Island, just off the edge of which were moored the British men-of-war, had not been occupied by either Lee or Stirling; but it lay within cannon-shot of the Battery and Columbia Heights, and an enemy once lodged there could work us mischief. General Putnam noticed its position, and he had not been here three days before he wrote, April 7th, to the President of Congress: "After getting the works [in New York] in such forwardness as will be prudent to leave, I propose immediately to take possession of Governor's Island, which I think a very important post. Should the enemy arrive here, and get post there, it will not be possible to save the city, nor could we dislodge them without great loss."[1] On the very next night he carried out his proposal, as appears from the following account of the manœuvre preserved among the papers of Colonel G. Selleck Silliman, of Fairfield, Connecticut, who had recently come down to relieve the troops under Ward and Waterbury:

"*Tuesday Morning, 9th April.*—Last Evening Draughts were made from a Number of Regiments here, mine among the Rest, to the Amount of 1,000 Men. With these and a proper Number of Officers Gen[l] Putnam at

---

[1] *Force,* Fourth Series, vol. v., p. 811.

Candle lighting embarked on Board of a Number of Vessels with a large Number of intrenching Tools and went directly on the Island a little below the City called Nutten [Governor's] Island where they have been intrenching all Night and are now at work, and have got a good Breast Work there raised which will cover them from the fire of the Ships; and it is directly in the Way of the Ship coming up to the Town.   The Asia has fallen down out of Gun Shot from this Place and it deprives the Ships of the only Watering Place they have here without going down toward the Hook." [1]   There was something of the Bunker Hill flavor about this move, and it was Prescott's Bunker Hill regiment that was first stationed [2] on the Island, which subsequently became one of the strongest posts of the position.   At the same time another party occupied Red Hook, [3] on Long Island, which commanded the channel between the Hook and Governor's Island.

The occupation by Putnam of these two points, which was clearly necessary for a more effective defence of the East River, required, or at least resulted in, the modification of Lee's plan, and the adoption of a new line on Long Island.   It was now decided to hold the Brooklyn peninsula with a chain of works thrown up across the neck from Wallabout Bay to the Gowanus Marsh; and it was in this vicinity that the encampment for Greene's brigade

[1] MS. letter from Colonel Silliman to his wife, in possession of Mrs. O. P. Hubbard, New York City.

[2] General Orders, April 16th, 1776 : . . . "Colonel Prescott's Regiment is to encamp on Governour's Island as soon as the weather clears. They are to give every assistance in their power to the works erecting thereon." . . .

[3] "Monday night 1000 Continental troops stationed here went over and took possession of Governor's Island and began to fortify it ; the same night a regiment went over to Red Hook and fortified that place likewise." *New York Packet, April* 11, 1776.

was marked out by Mifflin, the quartermaster-general, and afterwards approved by Washington.[1] By the fortunate recovery of the daily orders issued by General Greene on Long Island, and also of original sketches of the site, it has become possible to fix the location of this line and the names of the works with almost entire accuracy.

To defend the approach between the bay and marsh, the engineers laid out three principal forts and two redoubts, with breastworks connecting them. The site occupied was a favorable one. On the left rose the high ground, now known as Fort Greene Place or Washington Park, one hundred feet above the sea-level; and on the right, between the main road and the marsh, were lower elevations on lands then owned by Rutgert Van Brunt and Johannes Debevoise. The flanks were thus well adapted for defence, and they were near enough each other to command the ground between them. Two of the works were erected on the right of the road, and received the names of Fort Greene and Fort Box; three were on the left, and were known as the Oblong Redoubt, Fort Putnam, and the redoubt "on its left." In view of the fact that local historians heretofore have put but three fortifications on this line, where, it is now well established, there were five, a more particular description of them becomes necessary. Extending from right to left, they were laid out as follows:[2]

[1] General Orders, April 25th, 1776: "The encampment of the Third Brigade to be marked out in like manner, upon Long Island, on Saturday morning. The chief engineers, with the quartermasters, etc., from each regiment, to assist the quartermaster-general in that service. As soon as the general has approved of the encampments marked out, the troops will be ordered to encamp. . . ."

[2] Consult map accompanying this work, entitled "Plan of the Battle of Long Island, and of the Brooklyn Defences in 1776;" also the note in regard to it under the title "Maps," in Part II.

FORT BOX.—It has been supposed that the fort by this name occupied an independent site southwest of the main line, with the object of defending Gowanus Creek where it was crossed by a mill-dam. That it stood, however, on the right of the line is beyond question. Thus the letter of a spectator of the battle[1] says: "Our lines fronted the east. On the left, near the lowest part of the above-described bay [Wallabout], was Fort Putnam, near the middle Fort Greene, and towards the creek Fort Box." In his order of June 1st, General Greene directs five companies to take post "upon the right in Fort Box;" and on August 16th a fatigue party is detailed "to form the necessary lines from Fort Box to Fort Putnam," clearly indicating that the two were on the same continuous line. To confirm the correctness of this locality, we have the fort and its name distinctly indicated on the outline map sketched by President Stiles, of Yale College, in his Diary of Revolutionary Events. By reference to the fac-simile of the sketch here presented, it will be seen that although there are errors in the drawing, the relative position of the principal works is preserved, and the site of Fort Box finally determined. It stands nearest Gowanus Creek, and on the right of the other forts. The work appears to have been of a diamond shape, and was situated on or near the line of Pacific Street, a short distance above Bond.[2]

[1] "Memoirs of the Long Island Historical Society," vol. ii., p. 494. "Battle of Long Island." By Thomas W. Field.

[2] As the British demolished all the Brooklyn works very soon after their capture, it would be difficult to fix the exact site of some of them, but for data which have been preserved. That they were destroyed is certain. Baurmeister, the Hessian major, states that Howe directed the Hessian division to level the "Brocklands-Leinen," but recalled the order when General De Heister represented that "this could not be done by soldiers without compensation, especially as it would be the work of four weeks." According

As to its name, we must assume that it was called Fort Box in honor of Major Daniel Box, Greene's brigade-major (an office corresponding to the present assistant adjutant-general), whose services were then highly appreciated. Box first appears as an old British soldier, who had been wounded in the French war, and afterwards as an organizer and drill-master of Independent companies in Rhode Island, which subsequently furnished many fine officers to the Continental army.[1] In a letter to Colonel Pickering in 1779, Greene speaks of him in flattering terms, as having been invaluable in the earlier years of the war. That he was something of an engineer,

---

to tradition, the inhabitants levelled them by Howe's orders. General Robertson testified in 1779 that "there were no vestiges of the lines soon after they were taken." Cornwallis on the same occasion said that, being detached to Newtown after the battle, he had "no opportunity of going to Brooklyn till the lines were nearly demolished." But with the assistance of Lieutenant Ratzer's accurate topographical map of New York and Brooklyn of 1766–7, the Hessian map published in vol. ii. of the Society's *Memoirs*, the plan of the lines thrown up in the 1812 war, and other documents, the forts of 1776 can readily be located. Ratzer's map shows all the elevations where works would naturally be put ; and the Hessian map, which is a reduction of Ratzer's, adds the works. The accuracy of the latter, which heretofore could not be proved, is now established by the fact that the position of the forts corresponds to the location assigned them relatively in Greene's orders. There can be little doubt that this map was made from actual surveys soon after the battle, and that the shape as well as the site of the works and lines is preserved in it. Another guide is the 1812 line as marked out by Lieutenant Gadsden, of the Engineer Corps. A copy of the original plan of this line, furnished by the War Department, shows a close correspondence with the Hessian draft. The same points are fortified in each case. Fort "Fireman" of 1812 occupies the site, or very nearly the site, of Fort Box ; Fort "Masonic," that of Fort Greene ; Redoubt "Cummings," that of the Oblong Redoubt ; and "Fort Greene," that of Fort Putnam. The site of the "redoubt on the left" was inclosed, in 1812, in the outer intrenchment which was carried around the brow of the hill. Although the British obliterated all marks of the Brooklyn defences of 1776, we thus find nature and the records enabling us to re-establish them to-day.

[1] MS. letter of General Greene to Colonel Pickering, August 24, 1779, in possession of Prof. Geo. Washington Greene, East Greenwich, L. I.

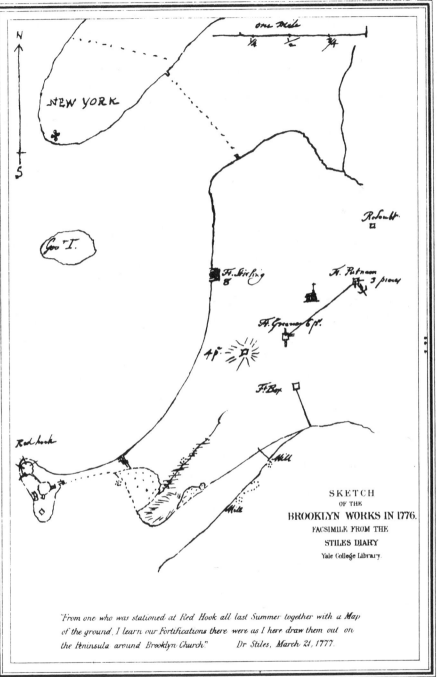

one Mile

N

S

NEW YORK

Geo I.

Ft. Stirling
8

Ft. Greene 6 p.

4 p.

Ft. Box.

Red hook

Mill

Mill

Redoubt.

Ft. Putnam
3 piece

SKETCH
OF THE
BROOKLYN WORKS IN 1776.
FACSIMILE FROM THE
STILES DIARY
Yale College Library.

"From one who was stationed at Red Hook all last Summer together with a Map
of the ground, I learn our Fortifications there were as I here draw them out on
the Peninsula around Brooklyn Church." Dr Stiles, March 21, 1777.

J. Bien Photo. Lith. N.Y.

as well as an excellent brigade-major, is evident from the fact that he assisted in marking out the lines around Boston in 1775, and later superintended the construction of Fort Lee, on the Jersey side. No doubt he had much to say about the building of the Brooklyn lines, and of the work in particular which bore his name.

FORT GREENE.—About three hundred yards to the left of Fort Box, a short distance above Bond Street, between State and Schermerhorn, stood Fort Greene, star-shaped, mounting six guns, and provided with a well and magazines. Colonel Little, its commander, describes it as the largest of the works on Long Island; and this statement is corroborated by the fact that its garrison consisted of an entire regiment, which was not the case with the other forts, and that it was provided with nearly double the number of pikes. It occupied an important position on one of the small hills near the centre of that part of the line lying southwest of Washington Park, and its guns commanded the approach by the Jamaica highway. Being the principal work on the line, the engineers, or possibly Little's regiment, named it after their brigade commander.

OBLONG REDOUBT.—Still further to the left, and on the other side of the road, a small circular redoubt, called the "Oblong Redoubt," was thrown up on what was then a piece of rising ground at the corner of De Kalb and Hudson avenues. The reason of its name is not apparent. Greene's orders refer to it as the "Oblong Square" and the "Oblong Redoubt." Major Richard Thorne, of Colonel Remsen's Long Island militia, speaks of being on guard at "Fort Oblong" all night a short time before the battle.[1] This redoubt had very nearly direct command

---

[1] "*Force*," Fifth Series, vol. ii., p. 202.

of the road, and in connection with Fort Greene was depended upon to defend the centre of the line.

FORT PUTNAM.—From the Oblong Redoubt, the line ascended northeasterly to the top of the hill included in Washington Park, where the fourth in the chain of works was erected. This was Fort Putnam. Star-shaped like Fort Greene, it was somewhat smaller than the latter, and mounted four or five garrison guns. Its strong natural position, however, made it the salient point of the line, and it became, as will be seen, the main object of attack by the British during and after the battle.[1] The fort may have taken its name, as usually supposed, from Major-General Israel Putnam; but it is altogether more probable that it was named after Colonel Rufus Putnam, the chief engineer, who marked out many of the works on Long Island as well as in New York, and who must have frequently crossed to give directions in their construction.

REDOUBT ON THE LEFT.—At the eastern termination of the hill, a short distance from Fort Putnam, and on a lower grade, stood the last of the works, which is identified in the orders and letters of the day as the "redoubt on the left." It was a small affair, and occupied a point at about the middle of the present Cumberland Street, nearly midway between Willoughby and Myrtle avenues; but in 1776 the site was twenty feet higher, and appeared as a well-defined spur extending out from Fort Putnam. As

---

[1] Mr. Field states that the site of Fort Putnam was unfortunately overlooked by the high ground east of it, Greene and his engineers probably not noticing the fact until after the woods were cut down. The official surveys of the ground, made before it was levelled, show no such commanding elevation, the Fort Putnam Hill being as high as any *within range;* nor can we credit Greene or his officers with fortifying a point which was untenable, or with not observing that it was untenable. As the engineers of 1812 occupied the same site, it could be safely concluded, were no surveys preserved, that it was entirely defensible.

it was commanded by the latter, its capture by the enemy would bring them no advantage, while as an American defence it could materially assist in protecting the left.

Between these five works a line of connecting intrenchments was laid out, while on the right it was to be continued from Fort Box to the marsh, and on the left from the Fort Putnam Hill, "in a straight line," to the swamp at the edge of Wallabout Bay. Anticipating their construction, we may say that each work became a complete fortification in itself, being surrounded with a wide ditch, provided with a sally-port, its sides lined with sharpened stakes, the garrison armed with spears to repel storming parties, and the work supplied with water and provisions to withstand a siege if necessary. The greater part of the line was picketed with abattis, and the woods cut down to give full sweep to the fire of the guns. As every thing depended upon holding this front, the necessity of making it as strong as possible was fully realized, and at the time of the engagement in August it was considered a sufficient barrier to the enemy's advance.[1]

[1] Some important and interesting information relative to the main line at Brooklyn was brought out in 1779 at the examination of Captain John Montressor, before the Parliamentary Committee which investigated Howe's conduct of the war. Montressor was a British army engineer, acting as Howe's aid on Long Island. Being one of the general's witnesses, he naturally made out the American position as strong as possible, but the main facts of his testimony are to be accepted. The examination was in part as follows :

" Q. Can you give a particular account of the state of those [Brooklyn] lines ?

A. Yes—the lines were constructed from Wallabout Bay, on one side to a swamp that intersects the land between the main land and Read Hook, which terminates the lines. The lines were about a mile and a half in extent, including the angles, cannon proof, with a chain of five redoubts, or rather fortresses, with ditches, as had also the lines that formed the intervals, raised on the parapet and the counterscarp, and the whole surrounded with the most formidable abbaties.

FORT COBBLE HILL.—Passing to the remaining works on Long Island, we find a redoubt on the crest of a cone-shaped hill, which stood alone near the intersection of the present Court and Atlantic streets, and which was known by the Dutch inhabitants as *Punkiesberg*. As it does not appear to have been called Cobble Hill before this date, the reasonable inference may be drawn that it was so named by Greene's troops because of its close resemblance to the Cobble Hill which formed one of the fortified points in the siege of Boston, but a short distance from Winter Hill, where Greene's brigade was posted. In the orders of the day, the. redoubt is known as " Smith s

Q. Were those lines finished on every part, from the swamp formed by the Wallabout on the left, to the swamp on the right ?

A. Yes.

Q. Do you know the particulars of the left part of the line towards the Wallabout ? Have you any reason for knowing that?

A. The line runs straight from the rising ground where Fort Putnam was constructed, in a straight line to the swamp that terminates itself at the bottom of Wallabout Bay.

Q. Was there a possibility of a single man's passing round the left part of the line?

A. There was not. After entering the lines, Sir William Howe, on the enemy's evacuating, followed the road to the point, to examine and see if he could get out at that part, which he could not do, and we were obliged to return and go out of a sally port of the lines. . . .

Q. Can you say of your own knowledge, that the right redoubt of the lines at Brooklyn had an abattis before it ?

A. I have already said that the whole had an abattis before it.

[He produces an actual survey of the lines.] . . . .

Q. If any one of these redoubts were taken, did not they flank the line in such a manner to the right and left that the enemy could not remain in the lines ?

A. I have already said, that they could not be taken by assault, but by approaches, as they were rather fortresses than redoubts."—*A View of the Evidence Relative to the Conduct of the American War under Sir William Howe*, etc.; second edition ; London, 1779. *Manual of the Corporation of the City of New York*, 1870, p. 884.

The maps in the early London editions of Gordon's and Stedman's histories of the war, each put *five* fortifications on the line from the Wallabout to Gowanus Creek.

barbette," Captain William Smith, the engineer whom Lee brought with him, having it in charge. The work mounted four guns, and, from its central interior position, could have prevented the enemy from securing a foothold on the peninsula in the rear or flank of the main line in case they effected a landing back of Red Hook or crossed Gowanus Creek above. This hill was long since cut away.[1]

REDOUBT AT THE MILL.—Near the corner of the present Degraw and Bond streets, a small battery or breastwork, in the form of a right angle, mounting one gun, was thrown up to cover the narrow passage over a mill-dam which here crossed Gowanus Creek. It stood at the extremity of a long low sand-hill, and the dam connected this point with a tongue of land on the opposite side, on which two mills were built, known as the upper or yellow, and lower mills. The upper mill was immediately opposite the redoubt, and it was here that the Port Road came down to the edge of the creek.

RED HOOK—FORT DEFIANCE.—This work, already referred to, was originally a single water battery, mounting four eighteen-pounders, *en barbette*, to prevent the passage of ships east of Governor's Island, as well as to keep the enemy from landing at the southern extremity of the peninsula. Washington speaks of it in May as being "a small, but exceedingly strong" fort. Lieutenant Samuel Shaw, of Knox's artillery, who was stationed there most of the

---

[1] One of Greene's orders refers to this fort as follows: "*Camp on Long Island, July* 19, 1776.—The works on Cobble Hill being greatly retarded for want of men to lay turf, few being acquainted with that service, all those in Colonel Hitchcock's and Colonel Little's regiments, that understand that business, are desired to voluntarily turn out every day, and they shall be excused from all other duty, and allowed one half a pint of rum a day." Two guns fired from Cobble Hill were to be the signal that the enemy had landed on Long Island.

summer, states that it was named " Fort Defiance," and subsequently strengthened by additional works, which, from the Hessian map and the Stiles draft, appear to have consisted of a second and larger redoubt connected with the first by an intrenchment or inclosed way.[1] On the 5th of July, Greene wrote to Washington that he regarded Red Hook as " a post of vast importance," and proposed stationing a considerable force there permanently, as in that case the commanding officer would be " more industrious to have every thing in readiness, and obstinate in defence" when the attack came; and on the 8th we find the order for " Col. Varnum's regiment to remove their encampment to Red Hook, and do the duty of that post."

FORT STIRLING.—The first work laid out on Long Island, as we have seen, was Fort Stirling, which, in connection with batteries on the New York side, was designed to command the East River channel. Its exact site has been a point of dispute. Several writers and old inhabitants associate the name with the remains of a large fortification which stood at the corner of Henry and Pierrepont streets as late as 1836. It is clear, however, that this was a work erected by the British during the latter part of the Revolution. General Robertson, acting as Governor of New York in 1780, wrote to Lord Germaine, May 18th, that, among other works thrown up to make New York more secure against an attack by the Americans, " a large square fort is built at Brooklyn Heights."[2] The traveller Smyth, writing in the same year, says, " The town [New

---

[1] " Our fort [Defiance] is much strengthened by new works and more troops, and it is in so good a posture of defence, that it would be almost impossible to take it either by attack or surprise. To guard against the latter, each man is every other night on duty."—*Memoir of Samuel Shaw*, p. 17.

[2] *Documents, Col. Hist. of New York*, vol. viii., p. 792.

York] is entirely commanded by a considerable eminence in Long Island, directly opposite to it, named Brookland Heights, on which a strong regular fort with four bastions has lately been erected by the British troops." This exactly describes the work in question.[1] The corner of Henry and Pierrepont streets, moreover, being a thousand feet back from the river's edge, could not have been selected at that time as the site for a strictly water battery intended for effective resistance. The fort must be looked for nearer the edge of the bluff, and there we find it. Both the Stiles and the Hessian maps place it directly on the bank of the river—the latter, a little north of what was then known as the Bamper House, or at about the intersection of Clark and Columbia streets.[2]

The fort was a strong inclosed work, mounting eight guns. Ward's men broke ground for it about the 1st of March, and continued digging, as their major, Douglas, writes, through " cold, tedious weather," until other troops took their place.[3]

Greene's soldiers, whose experience around Boston had

[1] The recollections and incidents preserved by Stiles and Furman go to show that this was not an American-built fort.—*Stiles' Brooklyn*, vol. i., pp. 314, 315.

[2] A return of the batteries around New York, March 24th, describes Fort Stirling as opposite the "Fly Market" in Maiden Lane [*Force*, Fourth Series, vol. v., p. 480]. Clark, Pineapple, and Orange streets, Brooklyn, can all be called " opposite" Maiden Lane in New York. The Hessian map puts the fort nearest the line of Clark.

[3] The work, which was to be known as the *Citadel*, was in all probability the " redoubte commencé," or unfinished fort, indicated on the Hessian map in the rear and to the south of Fort Stirling. The site corresponds with that of the British fort of 1780, corner of Henry and Pierrepont streets, which was then, as it still is, the highest point on Brooklyn Heights, and hence the natural position for a citadel or commanding fortification. Stirling, in his letter to the President of Congress of March 14, says : " The work [Fort Stirling] first begun on Long Island opposite to this city is almost completed, and the cannon carried over. The grand citadel there

made them veterans, at least in the use of the spade, now
went to work to throw up these lines. He reminded them
early of the importance of the post, and the necessity of
preparation and vigilance. " As the security of New
York greatly dependeth on this *pass*," runs his order of
May 5th, " while these works are constructing, the general hopes the troops will carefully forward the same as
fast as possible ;" and this he followed up with the caution
that if any soldier left his work without liberty, he should
do fatigue duty for a whole week. Orders from head-
quarters in New York at the same time directed General
Greene to report " all extraordinaries" to the commander-
in-chief; the officers at Red Hook and Governor's Island
to do the same ; and the officer commanding the riflemen
on Long Island to " constantly report all extraordinaries to
General Greene." Although no enemy had yet appeared,
every regiment in the army was ordered to mount a picket
every evening, to lie on their arms, and be ready to turn
out at a moment's notice.

It is possible to follow the troops on Long Island in their
routine of camp life all through the tedious summer

will be marked out to-morrow, and will be begun by the inhabitants of
King's County and Colonel Ward's Regiment."

The list of batteries, March 24th, contains a note to the effect that a citadel covering five acres, called the *Congress*, was to be built in the rear of
Fort Stirling.   Major Fish writes, April 9th: "There are *two* fortifications on Long Island opposite this city, to command the shipping."   One of
these was Fort Stirling—the other, undoubtedly, the citadel then in process
of construction.   The latter, though not in as favorable a position for the
purpose as the former, could still fire on ships entering the river.

The position of these two works, taken in connection with Lee's plan of
forming an intrenched camp on Long Island, fortified with a chain of redoubts, which, according to one of his letters, were to be three in number,
indicates quite clearly that this general intended to hold simply the heights
along the river.   The facts fail to bear out the supposition that the lines, as
finally adopted on Long Island, were of Lee's planning.   Work on the
citadel was probably discontinued, because his plan was so much enlarged
as to make that fortification unavailable.

they were to spend on this ground. Digging was the main thing at first, and they had so much of this that the officers complained of their inability to keep the men in clothes, they wore them out so fast, and they made themselves so begrimed with dirt at the trenches, that the allowance of soap would not clean them; all which moved Greene to write to Washington that it would be no more than "a piece of justice to the troops" to allow them a double quantity of soap. Their encampment, in the rear of the lines, appears to have been a pleasant one. The soldiers lived in bell-shaped tents with board floors, and varied their regulation fare with the produce of the Dutch farms; with the permission of their field-officers they could occasionally cross on a visit to the city. Their general, however, held them closely to duty, and we find in these early orders the beginnings of that strictness which subsequently made him known, with his other soldierly qualities, as a thorough disciplinarian. No enemy being near them, the men, when put on guard, perhaps relaxed even ordinary vigilance; but they were soon brought up sharply by the general, with the direction that every part of camp duty must be done with as much exactness as if the British were in their front, for bad habits once contracted, they are told, "are difficult to get over, and doing duty in a slovenly manner is both disgraceful and dangerous to officers and men." They were sure of being watched, too, by Lieutenant-Colonel Cornell, of Hitchcock's regiment, whose habit of reprimanding the men for every neglect had won for him the title of "Old Snarl" throughout the camp;[1] but his subsequent promotion to offices of responsibility showed that in other quarters his particular qualities were appre-

[1] *Letter from General Greene written at Fort Lee. Mrs. Williams' Life of Olney.*

ciated. As the warm season came on, Greene cautioned
his soldiers about their health. The "colormen" were to
keep the camps clean, and look after the hospitals. Many
soldiers being down with fever in July, the general recommends "the strictest attention to the cookery, and that
broiling and frying meat, so destructive to health, be prohibited;" going into the water in the heat of the day is
also forbidden. A neglect of these matters at this critical
season, Greene continues, "may be attended with dreadful consequences."

Occasionally it was found necessary to give the soldiers
a sharp reproof for insulting the inhabitants or trespass-
ing on their property. When the complaint was brought
to Greene that some of his men had been stealing water-
melons, he promptly issued an order that such practices
must be punished. "A few unprincipled rascals," he
said, "may ruin the reputation of a whole corps of virtuous men;" and on another occasion he called upon the
soldiers to behave themselves "with that decency and
respect that became the character of troops fighting for
the preservation of the rights and liberties of America."
Perhaps the offenders found an excuse for their conduct
in the Tory character of the complaints; but Greene,
though no friend himself to such people, could never
accept this as a provocation to justify a breach of military
discipline.

The Tory element in the population required other and
sterner treatment.[1] It had developed to such an extent

[1] A history of the Tories on Long Island and in New York—the trouble
they gave in the present campaign, and the measures taken for their suppression—properly forms a subject by itself. The scope of the present
work admits of but brief allusions to them. However honest this class of
the population may have been in taking sides with the British, and whatever sympathy may be expressed for them in their trials, losses, and en-

in Kings and Queens counties as to require its suppression by the civil and military power combined. The refusal of the majority of the voters in Queens to send delegates to the New York Provincial Convention in 1775 indicated not only a confidence on their part that the Home Government would succeed in crushing the rebellion, but a secret intention as well to give the British troops upon their arrival all the aid and comfort in their power. As they provided themselves with arms and the British fleet with provisions, the Continental Congress took up the matter, ordered the arrest of the leaders, and dispatched Colonel Heard, of New Jersey, with a regiment of militia to execute the business. Arrests were made, but the complete suppression of the loyalists here was never effected.

While Lee was in command he saw no solution of the problem other than to remove the entire Tory population to some other quarter where they could do less mischief in the event of active operations; but Congress, to the regret of Washington, could not sanction so radical a method. Greene did his best to root out this element, but we may imagine that it was uncongenial work, and that he took far more interest in the progress of his redoubts than in chasing suspected persons on the island.[1]

forced dispersion during and at the end of the war, there was obviously no course left to the Americans, then in the midst of a deadly struggle, but to treat them as a dangerous and obstructive set. The New York Provincial Congress, in the fall of the year and later, dealt with them unsparingly; and no man wished to see the element rooted out more than John Jay—a fact to be borne in mind by those who condemn Lee and other American officers for attempting to banish the Long Island Tories, as a military precaution, in the early part of the year.

[1] What General Greene thought of the Tories, and what treatment he proposed in certain cases, appears from a report on the subject signed by Generals Heath, Spencer, Greene, and Stirling, and submitted to Washington towards the close of June : "With regard to the disaffected inhabitants

6

By the 1st of June the works around Brooklyn appear to have so far progressed as to admit of the mounting of some of the cannon, and on the evening of that date the troops were ordered to parade with arms and man the lines. On the 17th the general assigned them to permanent positions as follows:

"Colonel Varnum's regiment is to take Fort Box and the Oblong Redoubt for their alarm-posts—Fort Box, six companies; Oblong Redoubt, two companies. Captain Wolverton's Independent Company[1] to join those in the redoubt, and to receive orders from Colonel Varnum.

Colonel Hitchcock's regiment to take Fort Putnam and the fort or redoubt on the left of it for their alarm-posts.

Colonel Little's regiment to take Fort Greene for their alarm-posts."

To impress his soldiers with his own sense of the great importance of the Long Island front, Greene added the determined words: "In case of an attack, *all these posts are to be defended to the last extremity.*" And Colonel Little, who had proved his fitness to command the post

who have lately been apprehended," say these officers, "we think that the method at present adopted by the County Committee, of discharging them on their giving bonds as a security for their good behavior, is very improper and ineffectual, and therefore recommend it to your Excellency to apply to the Congress of this province to take some more effectual method of securing the good behavior of those people, and in the mean time that your Excellency will order the officers in whose custody they are to discharge no more of them until the sense of the Congress be had thereon."—*Journals of the N. Y. Prov. Congress*, vol. ii.

On this subject Colonel Huntington wrote to Governor Trumbull, June 6th, as follows: "Long Island has the greatest proportion of Tories, both of its own growth and of adventitious ones, of any part of this colony; from whence some conjecture that the attack is to be made by that way. It is more likely to be so than not. Notwithstanding the vigilance of our outposts, we are sure there is frequent intercourse between the Asia and the shore, and that they have been supplied with fresh meat. New guards have lately been set in suspected places, which I hope will prevent any further communication."—*Force*, 4th Series, vol. vi., p. 725.

[1] This was a company of New Jersey Minute-men from Essex County, which had been sent over to Long Island on May 17th.

assigned him by his cool and soldierly conduct at Bunker Hill, quietly resolved that if the enemy assaulted Fort Greene it should never be surrendered while he was alive.[1]

Guards were now stationed at the forts and greater vigilance enjoined about the camp. Even as early as May 25th, when the works were still far from complete, the orders were strict that none but a general officer should be admitted to them without special leave. The lines were to be manned every morning "between day and sunrise," and the troops exercised at parapet firing. The orders of July 1st directed the commanding officers of the regiments "to make a line round each of the forts and fortifications for the troops to begin a fire on the enemy if they attempt to storm the works, and the troops are to be told not to fire sooner than the enemy's arrival at these lines, unless commanded. The line should be about eighty yards from the parapet." The officers of the guards were to be accountable for every thing in the forts, but particularly for the rum lodged there for the use of the men in time of action. Provisions also were to be supplied to each alarm-post "in case of siege," and the water-casks kept constantly full of fresh water. To assure the effectiveness of the means of defence, one hundred spears were to be placed in Fort Greene, thirty in the works to the right, twenty in the Oblong Redoubt, fifty in Fort Putnam, and twenty to the left of it.

And so the work went on under Greene's eye, and by the middle of summer his troops[2] had inclosed them-

---

[1] Colonel Little to his son. Doc. No. 9.

[2] It is a somewhat singular fact, indicating perhaps the scantiness of our material heretofore, that none of the local accounts of operations on Long Island mention either Hitchcock's, Varnum's, or Little's regiments in any connection, whereas these, with Hand's, formed the permanent garrison on that side and threw up the greater part of the works.

selves on the Brooklyn peninsula, with lines which, though unfinished, were still of very respectable strength.

Recrossing the river to New York, we find the other brigades there at work as uninterruptedly as Greene's on Long Island. The many well-known "general orders" issued by the commander-in-chief during this season testify to the great amount of fatigue duty performed by the troops. Washington regretted that the necessity for it left so little opportunity for drilling and he urged his officers to make the most of what time they had for this purpose. But his chief anxiety was to have the defences pushed on, and by the middle of June the principal works were completed or well under way. The location and names of these are indicated in the orders and maps of the day.[1] Beginning on the North River side and continuing around the city, they were as follows:

[1] In locating the works in New York City, the writer follows the list of batteries reported March 24th, 1776 (Force, 4th Series, vol. v., p. 480) ; Putnam's order of May 22d, naming the several works ; Knox's artillery returns of June 10th, giving the number of guns in each ; and Hills' map of the fortifications, drawn at the close of the war. The first list shows the works as they stood at about the time the Boston troops came down, and which Lee had planned. There are alterations and additions in Putnam's and Knox's lists, which are to be followed where they differ from the list of March 24th. Although many other works were erected, no names appear to have been attached to them, those only being designated which occupied the most important points and were provided with guns and garrisons.

The Hills map is indispensable in this connection. John Hills, formerly a British engineer, surveyed the city and island of New York as far as Thirty-fourth Street in 1782, and in 1785 made a careful map of the same, which John Lozier, Esq., presented to the Common Council in 1847. This is still preserved, and is consulted at times for official purposes. In addition to giving all the streets, blocks, docks, and squares, Hills added all the works thrown up in and around the city during the Revolution, giving their exact location and shape. Part of the lines have a confused appearance, but they become clear on referring to the following memorandum on the map : " All the works colored yellow were erected by the Forces of the United States in 1776. Those works colored Orange were erected by Dº and repaired by the British Forces. Those works colored Green

GRENADIER BATTERY.—This was a "beautiful" circular battery, situated on the bank of the North River where it ran out into a well-defined bluff, at the corner of the present Washington and Harrison streets. Captain Abraham Van Dyck's Grenadier Company of New York City Independents built it while Lee and Stirling were in command, and received the thanks of Washington in general orders for the skilful manner in which they had executed their work. The fort mounted two twelve-pounders and two mortars. The grenadier company was organized by Stirling a few years before, when he lived in New York, and he watched the construction of the battery with considerable pride. The *Pennsylvania Gazette* of May 8th, 1776, contains a letter from Captain Van Dyck to Stirling, informing him of the completion of the work, and desiring " the approbation of their former captain." Stirling replied that he had frequently admired the battery, and reflected with " real satisfaction" on the hour when he formed the company.

JERSEY BATTERY.—A short distance below, on the line of Reade Street, just west of Greenwich, stood the Jersey Battery—a five-sided work, mounting two twelve and three thirty-two pounders. A line of intrenchments connected these two batteries, and, extending beyond on either side, made the position a particularly strong one. Their guns had the range of the bank up and down the river, and could enfilade an enemy attempting to land in that vicinity.

were erected by the British Forces during the War." In the map of New York accompanying the present work, Hills' "yellow" line has been followed, showing all the American forts. Their location corresponds precisely with that which Putnam gives, so far as he names them ; and by projecting the present streets over Hills' plan, it is possible to ascertain where they stood in the plan of our modern city.

McDOUGALL'S AND THE OYSTER BATTERY.—The works next below on the Hudson consisted of two batteries' situated on the high ground in the rear and to the south of Trinity Church. The one on the bluff near the church, or on the line of the present Rector Street, a little east of Greenwich, was known under Stirling as McDougall's Battery; but this name does not appear in the return of June 10th, and in its place in the order of the works we have the "Oyster" Battery. It is possible that this was the work a little south of McDougall's, at the intersection of the present Morris and Greenwich streets. Its location is described by Putnam in May as "behind General Washington's head-quarters."[1] It mounted two

[1] WASHINGTON'S HEAD-QUARTERS IN NEW YORK.—This reference creates some uncertainty as to the particular house occupied by Washington in New York during the first part of the campaign. If the site of the Oyster Battery were known exactly the house could be identified. On the other hand, if head-quarters, as generally supposed, were at the Kennedy Mansion, No. 1 Broadway, then the battery should have stood still lower down, at the corner of Battery Place and Greenwich Street; but the Grand Battery terminated there, and Hills' map shows no distinct battery at that point. Mr. Lossing states ("Field Book of the Rev.," vol. ii., p. 594, n.) that Washington, on his first arrival in the city, took up his quarters at 180 Pearl, opposite Cedar Street, his informant being a survivor of the Revolution, and that, on his return from a visit to Philadelphia, June 6th, he went to the Kennedy House. That Washington, however, spent the greater part of the summer at the "Mortier House," on Richmond Hill, is well known. He was there on June 22d and probably much earlier, as appears in *Force*, 4th Series, vol. vi., p. 1157, where one Corbie is described as keeping a tavern "to the south-east of General Washington's house, to the westward of Bayard's woods, and north of Lispenard's meadows." The house referred to was the Mortier. From Mr. Lossing's informant, and the reference in the orders of August 8th, which speaks of the "old head-quarters on the Broadway," we may conclude that Washington first put up at 180 Pearl Street; that if he then went to the Kennedy House at all, it was but for a short time; that it is more likely, from the position of the batteries, that the house he did occupy was one of the two or three next above it; and that in June he moved his quarters to the Mortier House, where he remained until September 14th, when he went to the Morris Mansion at Harlem Heights. The Kennedy House was Colonel Knox's artillery head-quarters during part if not all of the time, his wife being with him there up to July 12th. (*Drake's Life of Knox.*)

thirty-two-pounders and three twelve-pounders. In March, McDougall's Battery was provided with six guns.

FORT GEORGE AND THE GRAND BATTERY. — These works at the lower end of the city had been pronounced almost useless by Lee, but as it was of course necessary to include that point in the system of defence they were repaired and greatly strengthened under Washington. In Fort George were mounted two twelve-pounders and four thirty-two-pounders. The walls of the Grand Battery were banked up from within, and mounted thirteen thirty-two-pounders, one twenty-four-pounder, three eighteen-pounders, two twelve-pounders, one thirteen-inch brass mortar, two eight-inch and one ten-inch iron mortars.

WHITEHALL BATTERY.—A small work on the Whitehall dock on the East River, and practically a continuation of the Grand Battery. It carried two thirty-two-pounders.

WATERBURY'S BATTERY.—On the dock at the northeast angle of Catherine and Cherry streets, mounting, in June, two twelve-pounders.

BADLAM'S REDOUBT. — On the hill above, south of Market and between Madison and Monroe streets. It mounted seven guns in March, but appears not to have been occupied later in the season.

SPENCER'S REDOUBT.—This was either the horseshoe redoubt at the intersection of Monroe and Rutgers streets, or the larger star redoubt between Clinton and Montgomery, east of Henry Street.[1] It mounted two twelve-pounders and four field-pieces.

[1] Spencer's Brigade probably built both works, as it was stationed in the vicinity of both. Colonel John Trumbull, who was then Spencer's brigade major, and afterwards in the Canada army, says in the " Reminiscences"

JONES' HILL.—From Spencer's Redoubt a line of intrenchments extended around along the crest of the high land above Corlear's Hook to a circular battery on the northern slope of Jones' Hill, a little north of the intersection of Broome and Pitt streets, and was pierced for eight guns. During Stirling's command it was proposed to call this fortification "Washington," but it was known subsequently simply as Jones' Hill. From this battery the works continued along the line of Grand Street to the Bowery, and included two more circular batteries— one on Grand at the corner of Norfolk Street, and the other near the corner of Grand and Eldridge streets.

BAYARD'S HILL REDOUBT.—Upon this commanding site, west of the Bowery, where Grand and Mulberry streets intersect, was erected a powerful irregular heptagonal redoubt, mounting eight nine-pounders, four three pounders, and six royal and cohorn mortars. It had the range of the city on one side and the approach by the Bowery on the other. Lasher's New York Independent companies first broke ground for it about the 1st of March, and continued digging there as well as on the redoubt around the hospital until May 16th, when they were relieved, with Washington's "thanks for their masterly manner of executing the work on Bayard's Hill."[1] In the March return this battery is called the "Independent Battery," and it also received the name of "Bunker Hill," which was retained by the British during their occupation; but its proper name as an American fort was "Bayard's Hill Redoubt," this having been given to

of his own time: "The brigade to which I was attached was encamped on the (then) beautiful high ground which surrounded Colonel Rutgers' seat near Corlear's Hook."

[1] *Force*, 4th Series, vol. v., p. 492. Compare, also, Documents 38 and 41.

it officially in general orders; and it was so called in letters and orders repeatedly through the summer.

THOMPSON'S BATTERY.—This was the name given to
the work thrown up at Horn's Hook by Colonel Drake's
Westchester minute-men soon after Lee's arrival.   It
mounted eight pieces.[1]

GOVERNOR'S ISLAND.—The forts erected on this island
were among the strongest around New York.   According
to a letter from Colonel Prescott of July 3d, they consisted of a citadel with outworks, and were garrisoned
during the latter part of the summer by Prescott's and
Nixon's regiments.   The works mounted in June four
thirty-two and four eighteen pounders.

PAULUS OR POWLE'S HOOK.—The point of land on the
New Jersey side, opposite the city, and which is now the
site in part of Jersey City. Works were commenced here
about May 20th, and in June they mounted three thirty-
two-pounders, three twelve-pounders, and two three-
pounder field-pieces.[2]

In addition to these, several other redoubts were
erected north of the town, in which no cannon were
mounted, and which had no names. They were probably
thrown up to be ready for occupation in case the enemy

---

[1] This work stood at the foot of East Eighty-eighth Street.   See Document
41. Some ten years after the war, Archibald Gracie occupied this site, and it
became known as Gracie's Point.   The writer of a city guide-book in 1807,
referring to Mr. Gracie, says: " His superb house and gardens stand upon
the very spot called *Hornshook*, upon which a fort erected by the Americans
in 1776 stood till about the year 1794, when the present proprietor caused
the remains of the military works to be levelled at great expense, and
erected on their rocky base his present elegant mansion and appurte-
nances."—*The Picture of New York, etc.*, 1807, *New York*.

[2] The fortifications erected at the upper part of the island are noticed in
Chapter V. Mr. Lossing, it should be said, gives a very full list of the
Revolutionary works in and around New York (" Field Book of the Rev.,"
vol. ii., p. 593), from which the list as given here, based on Hills' map,
differs in several particulars.

succeeded in landing above the city. There was a circular battery at the corner of Broome and Forsyth streets; another in the middle of Broadway, opposite White Street; another, of octagonal shape, near the corner of Spring and Mercer streets; a half-moon battery above this, between Prince and Spring, on the line of Thompson Street; another on the northwesterly continuation of Richmond Hill, at McDougall and Houston streets; and still another on the river-bank, near the junction of Christopher and Greenwich streets. The hospital on Duane Street was strongly fortified, and breastworks were thrown up at numerous points between and around the forts. On June 10th the entire number of guns fit for service in and around New York was one hundred and twenty-one, thirty-three of which were held as a reserve for field service, "to be run where the enemy shall make their greatest efforts." The mortars were nineteen in number.

As for barricades, the city was full of them. Some were built of mahogany logs taken from West India cargoes. Not a street leading to the water on either side that was not obstructed in this manner; so that, had the enemy been able to gain a footing in the city under the fire of their ships, they would still have found it, to use Lee's expression, "a disputable field of battle." The City Hall Park was almost entirely inclosed. There was a barrier across Broadway in front of St. Paul's Church, another at the head of Vesey Street, and others at the head of Barclay, Murray, and Warren. On the Park Row or Chatham Street side a barricade stretched across Beekman Street; another, in the shape of a right angle, stood in Printing House Square, one face opposite Spruce Street, the other looking across the Presbyterian church-yard and Nassau Street;[1] another ran across Frankfort Street; another at the entrance of Centre Street; and still another near it, facing Chatham Street.

Another element in the defence was a motley little fleet, made up of schooners, sloops, row-galleys, and whale-boats, and placed under the command of Lieutenant-Colonel Benjamin Tupper,[2] who had distinguished himself by a naval exploit or two in Boston Harbor during the siege. Crews were drafted from the regiments and assigned to the various craft, whose particular mission was to scour the waters along the New Jersey and Long Island coast, to watch for the British fleets, and prevent communication beween the Tories and the enemy's ships already lying in the harbor. Tupper, as commodore, appears first in the sloop Hester as his flag-ship, and later in the season in the Lady Washington, while among his fleet were to be found the Spitfire, General Putnam, Shark, and Whiting. The gallant commodore's earliest cruises were made within the Narrows, along the Staten Island shore, and as far down as Sandy Hook, where he attempted the feat of destroying the light-house. But he found this structure, which the enemy had occupied since Major Malcom dismantled it in March, a hard piece of masonry to reduce. He attacked it confidently, June 21st, after demanding its surrender, but retired when he found that an hour's bombardment made no impression upon its walls.[3] He kept a good lookout along these waters, gathered information from desert-

---

[1] One side of this barricade ran in front of the *Times*, and the other in front of the *Tribune* building.

[2] This officer was Lieutenant-Colonel of Jonathan Ward's Massachusetts Regiment, and subsequently became colonel in the Massachusetts Continental Line.

[3] *Force*, 4th Series, vol. vi., p. 1011.

ers, and when reporting on one occasion that the enemy's fleet were short of provisions and the men reduced to half allowance, he added, with unction, "May God increase their wants!" A little later we meet again with the adventuresome Tupper and his flotilla.

As the soldiers went on with their exacting duties, the monotony of the routine was now and then relieved by some diversion or excitement. One day there is "Tory-riding"[1] in the city, in which citizens appear to have figured principally. Then the whole camp is startled by the report that a "most accursed scheme" had come to light, just "on the verge of execution," by which Washington and all his generals were to have been murdered, the magazines blown up, and the cannon spiked by hired miscreants in the army at the moment the enemy made their grand attack upon the city.[2] Again, on the 9th of

[1] "*Thursday, 13th June.*—Here in town very unhappy and shocking scenes were exhibited. On Munday night some men called Tories were carried and hauled about through the streets, with candles forced to be held by them, or pushed in their faces, and their heads burned; but on Wednesday, in the open day, the scene was by far worse; several, and among them gentlemen, were carried on rails; some stripped naked and dreadfully abused. Some of the generals, and especially Pudnam and their forces, had enough to do to quell the riot, and make the mob disperse."—*Pastor Shewkirk's Diary, Doc. 37.*

[2] The particulars of this plot need hardly be repeated; indeed, they were never fully known. It was discovered that an attempt had been made to enlist American soldiers into the king's service, who at the proper time should assist the enemy in their plans. They were to spike cannon, blow up magazines, and, as at first reported, assassinate our generals; but the latter design seems not to have been proved, though universally believed. Governor Tryon and Mayor Matthews, of the city, were suspected of furthering the plot and furnishing the funds. Matthews was arrested at Flatbush by a party of officers under Colonel Varnum, but the evidence against him was insufficient. Among the soldiers implicated was Thomas Hickey, of Washington's guard, who was tried by court-martial, found guilty of sedition, mutiny, and correspondence with the enemy, and executed in the presence of the army on June 28th. Something of the feeling excited by the discovery of the plot is exhibited in the letter from Surgeon Eustis of Colonel Knox's regiment (*Document* 39). This is better known as the "Hickey Plot."

July, the brigades are all drawn up on their respective parade-grounds, listen to the reading for the first time of the Declaration of Independence, and receive it, as Heath tells us, "with loud huzzas;" and, finally, to celebrate the event, a crowd of citizens, "Liberty Boys," and soldiers collect that evening at Bowling Green and pull down the gilded statue of King George, which is then trundled to Oliver Wolcott's residence at Litchfield, Ct., for patriotic ladies to convert into bullets for the American soldiers.[1]

But now occurred a much more stirring and important event to engage the attention of the army, and this was the arrival of the enemy. It was full time for them to make their appearance. Nearly three months and a half had elapsed since the evacuation of Boston; the spring and a whole month of summer had gone; the best season for active movements was passing rapidly; and unless the

---

[1] The following [memorandum, preserved among Governor Wolcott's papers, is of interest in this connection :

"An Equestrian Statue of George the Third of Great Britain was erected in the City of New York on the Bowling Green at the lower end of Broadway. Most of the materials were *lead* but richly *gilded* to resemble gold At the beginning of the Revolution this statue was overthrown. Lead being then scarce and dear, the statue was broken in pieces and the metal transported to Litchfield a place of safety. The ladies of this village converted the Lead into Cartridges for the Army, of which the following is an account.   O. W.

Mrs. Marvin,	Cartridges	.	.	6,058
Ruth Marvin,	"	.	.	11,592
Laura Wolcott,	"	.	.	8,378
Mary Ann Wolcott,	"	.	.	10,790
Frederick "	"	.	.	936
Mrs. Beach,	"	.	.	1,802
Made by sundry persons	"	.	.	2,182
Gave Litchfield Militia on alarm,		.	.	50
Let the Regiment of Col. Wigglesworth have				300

42,088 Cartridges."

British began operations soon, all hope of conquering
America "in one campaign" would have to be abandoned.
Rumors of their coming took definite shape in the last
week of June, when word reached camp that an American privateer had captured a British transport with more
than two hundred Highlanders as prisoners. On the
25th and 26th three or four large ships arrived off Sandy
Hook, one of which proved to be the Greyhound, with
Sir William Howe on board ; on the 29th a fleet of forty-
five sail anchored off the same point, and four days later
the number had increased to one hundred and thirty.[1]
This was the fleet from Halifax with Howe's Boston
veterans. Preparations were made to land them on the
Long Island coast near the Narrows; but on being informed that the Americans were posted on a ridge of hills
not far distant, Howe disembarked his troops opposite on
Staten Island,[2] and there went into camp to wait the arrival of the reinforcements from England under Admiral
Howe. The middle of July saw these also encamped on
the island, with the fleet increased to nearly three hundred transports and ships of war. On the 1st of August
there was an unexpected arrival in the shape of the dis-
comfited expedition under Generals Clinton and Cornwallis, that was to gain a foothold in the South;[3] and last

[1] "For two or three days past three or four ships have been dropping in,
and I just now received an express from an officer appointed to keep a
lookout on Staten Island, that forty-five arrived at the Hook to-day—some
say more ; and I suppose the whole fleet will be in within a day or two."—
Washington to Hancock, June 29th.

[2] Extract of a letter from an officer in the Thirty-fifth Regiment at Staten
Island, July 9th, 1776: "Our army consisted of 6155 effectives, on our embarkation at Halifax ; they are now all safe landed here, and our head-quarters are at your late old friend, Will Hick's Mansion house."—*London
Chronicle.*

[3] The expedition sailed from Cork for the Cape River in North Carolina,
where Clinton joined it. It was expected that the loyalists in the State

of all, on the 12th of August came the British Guards and De Heister's Hessians, after a tedious voyage of thirteen weeks from Spithead, completing Howe's force, and swelling the fleet in the Narrows to more than four hundred ships. England had never before this sent from her shores a more powerful military and naval armament upon foreign service.

The arrival of the enemy hastened Washington's preparations. The troops which Congress had called out to reinforce his army were coming in too slowly, and expresses were sent to governors, assemblies, and committees of safety, announcing the appearance of the enemy, and urging in the most pressing terms the instant march of the reinforcements to New York. To his soldiers with him the commander-in-chief issued both warning and inspiring orders. On the 2d of July, a few days after Howe arrived, he reminded them that the time was at hand which would probably determine whether Americans were to be freemen or slaves. "The fate of unborn millions," he said, "will now depend, under God, on the courage and conduct of this army. Our cruel and unrelenting enemy leaves us no choice but a brave resistance or the most abject submission. This is all we can expect. We have, therefore, to resolve to conquer or die. Our country's honor calls upon us for a vigorous and manly exertion, and if we now shamefully fail we shall become infamous to the whole world. Let us, therefore, rely

would rise in sufficient numbers to give the expeditionary corps substantial aid ; but not over eighteen hundred were mustered, and these under General McDonald were completely defeated by the North Carolina Militia under Colonels Caswell and Lillington at Moore's Creek Bridge on the 27th of February. The expedition then moved against Charleston, S. C., and there met with the famous repulse from Colonel Moultrie off Charleston Harbor on the 28th of June. Clinton and Cornwallis after this could do nothing but join Howe at New York.

upon the goodness of the cause and the aid of the Supreme Being, in whose hands victory is, to animate and encourage us to great and noble actions. The eyes of all our countrymen are now upon us, and we shall have their blessings and praises, if happily we are the instruments of saving them from the tyranny meditated against them. . . . . Any officer or soldier, or any particular corps, distinguishing themselves by any acts of bravery and courage, will assuredly meet with notice and rewards; and, on the other hand, those who behave ill will as certainly be exposed and punished: the general being resolved, as well for the honor and safety of the country as of the army, to show no favor to such as refuse or neglect their duty at so important a crisis."

The digging still went on; the troops were ordered to keep their arms in condition for immediate use; the officers cautioned to look after the health of their men, as the season was excessively warm and sickly; and every attention to necessary details enjoined.

In addition to their military and naval commands, the two Howes were invested by their government with extraordinary powers as civil commissioners. They were authorized to issue pardons, and to open up the question of reconciliation and a peaceable settlement of the troubles; but their first advances in a civil capacity completely failed, though not without furnishing an entertaining episode. On the 14th of July they dispatched an officer in a barge with a communication for General Washington. The barge was detained by one of Commodore Tupper's boats in the harbor until Washington's pleasure in regard to it could be known. Suspecting, by previous experience at Boston, that Howe would not recognize his military title, Washington consulted a few of his officers in the matter, and it was the unanimous opinion that should the communication be addressed to him as a private individual it could not, with propriety, be received. Colonel Reed, the adjutant-general, and Colonel Knox immediately went down the bay and met the British officer. The latter, with hat in hand, bowed politely and said to Colonel Reed, "I have a letter from Lord Howe to Mr. Washington." "Sir," replied Reed, "we have no person in our army with that address." "But will you look at the address?" continued the officer, at the same time taking out of his pocket a letter marked

"GEORGE WASHINGTON, Esq.,

NEW YORK.

HOWE."

"No, sir," said Reed, "I cannot receive that letter." "I am very sorry," returned the officer, "and so will be Lord Howe, that any error in the superscription should prevent the letter being received by *General Washington*." "Why, sir," replied Reed, whose instructions were positive not to accept such a communication, "I must obey orders;" and the officer, finding it useless to press the matter, could only repeat the sentiment, "Oh! yes, sir, you must obey orders, to be sure." Then, after exchanging letters from prisoners, the officers saluted and separated. The British barge had gone but a short distance when it quickly put about, and the officer asked by what particular title Washington chose to be addressed. Colonel Reed replied, "You are sensible, sir, of the rank of General Washington in our army." "Yes, sir, we are," said the officer; "I am sure my Lord Howe will lament exceedingly this affair, as the letter is quite of a civil nature, and not of a military

7

one. He laments exceedingly that he was not here a little sooner." Reed and Knox supposed this to be an allusion to the Declaration of Independence, but making no reply, they again bowed, and parted, as Knox says, "in the most genteel terms imaginable." [1]

But Howe was unwilling to have the matter dropped in this fashion, and on the 20th he sent his adjutant-general, Lieutenant-Colonel Patterson, to hold an interview with Washington in person, if possible, and urge him to receive the letter and also to treat about the exchange of prisoners. Patterson landed at the Battery, and was conducted to Colonel Knox's quarters at the Kennedy House, without the usual formality of having his eyes blindfolded. Washington, " very handsomely dressed "[2] and making " a most elegant appearance," received him with his suite, and listened attentively while Patterson, interspersing his words at every other breath with " May it please your Excellency," explained the address on the letter by saying that the etc. etc. appended meant every thing. " And, indeed, it might mean any thing," replied Washington, as Patterson then proceeded to say, among other things, that the benevolence of the king had induced him to appoint General and Admiral Howe his commissioners to accommodate the unhappy disputes ; that it would give them great pleasure to effect such an accommodation, and that he (Colonel Patterson) wished to have that visit considered as preliminary to so desirable an object. Washington replied that he himself was not vested with any authority

---

[1] *Colonel Knox to his wife.—Drake's Life of Gen. Knox*, p. 131.

[2] " General Washington was very handsomely dressed, and made a most elegant appearance. Colonel Patterson appeared awe-struck, as if he was before something supernatural. Indeed, I don't wonder at it. He was before a very great man, indeed."—*Ibid.* p. 132.

in the case; that it did not appear that Lord Howe could do more than grant pardons, and that those who had committed no fault wanted no pardons, as they were simply defending what they deemed their indisputable rights.[1] Further conversation followed, when Patterson, rising to leave, asked, " Has your Excellency no particular commands with which you would please to honor me to Lord and General Howe?" "Nothing," replied Washington, "but my particular compliments to both;" and, declining to partake of a collation prepared for the occasion, the British adjutant-general took his departure. Again the king's "commissioners" had failed, and Washington had preserved the dignity of the young nation and his own self-respect as the commander of its armies.

An incident, of greater moment as a military affair, and which disturbed Washington as much as the Patterson interview must have diverted him, was the easy passage, on the 12th of July, of two of the British men-of-war, the Rose and Phœnix, past all the batteries, unharmed, up the North River. Taking advantage of a brisk breeze and running tide, the ships with their tenders sailed rapidly up from the Narrows, and to avoid the fire of the batteries as much as possible kept near the Jersey shore. The American artillerists opened upon them with all their guns along the river, but could do them no serious damage, while by accident, in their haste to load the pieces, six of their own gunners were killed. The ships sent many shots into the city, some crashing through houses but doing no other injury, while the roar of the cannon frightened the citizens who had not already moved away,

[1] Memorandum of an interview between General Washington and Colonel Patterson.—*Sparks' Washington*, vol. iv., p. 510.

and caused more to go.[1]   At the upper end of the island, around Fort Washington, where the batteries and river obstructions were as yet incomplete, the ships suffered still less harm, and sailing by, anchored safely in the broad Tappan Bay above.   Their object was to cut off the supplies which came down the river to Washington's army, and, as supposed, to encourage the loyalists in the upper counties and supply them with arms.   Washington acknowledged that the event showed the weakness and inadequacy of the North River line of defences, and reported to Congress that it developed a possible plan of attack by the British upon his rear.   Measures were taken to annoy if not destroy the ships, and, on the 3d of August, Commodore Tupper, with four of his sloops and schooners, boldly attacked the enemy, but though, as Washington wrote, "our officers and men, during the whole affair, behaved with great spirit and bravery," neither side sustained serious damage.   On the night of the 16th two fire-rafts were directed against the ships, which were successful so far as to destroy one of the tenders; and on the 18th the enemy weighed anchor and returned to the Narrows as readily as they came up.

It was now apparent that the great struggle between the two armies could be postponed no longer, and no day after the arrival of the Hessians passed that the British attack was not looked for.   The orders of August 8th cautioned the men to be at their quarters, " especially

---

[1] On August 17th Washington requested the New York Convention to remove the women, children, and infirm persons, as the city was likely soon to be "the scene of a bloody conflict." He stated that when the Rose and Phœnix sailed past, "the shrieks and cries of these poor creatures, running every way with their children, was truly distressing." Pastor Shewkirk says: "This affair caused a great fright in the city. Women and children, and some with their bundles, came from the lower parts and walked to the Bowery, which was lined with people."

early in the morning or upon the tide of flood," when the enemy's fleet might be expected, and every preparation was made to resist the landing of the British at any point upon Manhattan Island.[1]

Upon Long Island General Greene and his men were still at work on the defences, and, since the arrival of the enemy, doubly vigilant. Hand's riflemen kept close watch at the Narrows and reported every suspicious movement of the fleet. Word was brought in on the 9th that a large number of regulars were drawn up at the Staten Island ferry, and Greene immediately sent around the order for "no officer or soldier to stir from his quarters, that we may be ready to march at a moment's warning, if necessary." Upon another alarm, when probably he himself was indisposed, he directed Colonel Little, the senior regimental officer present, to superintend the disposition of the troops. His hastily written letter, penned apparently not long after midnight, runs as follows:

THURSDAY MORNING [August 8 or 15 ?]

DEAR SIR—By Express from Col Hand and from Red Hook, and from on board the Sloop at Governor's Island it is very evident there was a General Imbarcation of the Troops last evening from Statten Island—doubtless they'l make a dessent this morning. Youl please to order all the troops fit for duty to be at their Alarm posts near an hour sooner than is common—let their flints arms and ammunition be examined and everything held in readiness to defend the works or go upon a detachment. A few minutes past received an Express from Head Quarters. Youl acquaint the Commanding officers of Col Hitchcock's Regiment and Col Forman's Regiment

---

[1] Captain Nathan Hale, the "Martyr-spy," says in a letter of the 20th of August: "Our situation has been such this fortnight or more as scarce to admit of writing. We have daily expected an action—by which means, if any one was going, and we had letters written, orders were so strict for our tarrying in camp, that we could rarely get leave to go and deliver them. For about six or eight days the enemy have been expected hourly, whenever the wind and tide in the least favored."—*Document* 40.

of this, and direct them to observe the same orders, also the Artillery officers.   I am ys,

N. GREENE.

[Addressed to Col. Little.] [1]

Greene had been promoted to the rank of major-general on the 9th, and his old brigade on Long Island given to Brigadier-General John Nixon, of Massachusetts, who was promoted from a colonelcy at the same time. A new arrangement of the army was effected, and Brigadier-General Heard's brigade of five New Jersey regiments was ordered to Long Island to reinforce Greene. His division, now consisting of these two brigades—Nixon's and Heard's—numbered, August 15th, two thousand nine hundred men fit for duty. Parts of two Long Island militia regiments under Colonels Smith and Remsen which joined him about this date, and Colonel Gay's Connecticut levies, who had been on that side since the 1st of August, increased this number to something over thirty-five hundred.

But Greene was not to be a participator in the approaching scenes. The prevailing fever which had prostrated so many officers and men seized him with all but a fatal hold, and he was obliged to relinquish his command. He clung to it, however, to the last moment in hopes of a change for the better. " I am very sorry," he wrote to Washington on the 15th, "that I am under the necessity of acquainting you that I am confined to my bed with a raging fever. The critical situation of affairs makes me the more anxious, but I hope, through the assistance of Providence, to be able to ride before the presence of the enemy may make it absolutely necessary;" and he assured the commander-in-chief that his

[1] Original in possession of Chas. J. Little, Esq., Cambridge, Mass.

men appeared to be "in exceeding good spirits," and would no doubt be able to render a very good account of the enemy should they land on Long Island. On the 16th there was no change for the better in his condition, but on the contrary Livingston, his aid, reported that he had "a very bad night of it;" and in a day or two he was removed to New York, to the house of John Inglis now the intersection of Ninth Street and Broadway where with rest and care he slowly passed the crisis of his illness.[1]

On the 20th Washington gave orders to General Sullivan, who had recently returned from Canada, to take the command upon Long Island, until General Greene's state of health should permit him to resume it.[2]

[1] *Greene's Life of Greene*, vol. i.

[2] *General Orders, August* 20, 1776.—. . . "General Sullivan is to take command upon Long Island till General Greene's state of health will permit him to resume it, and Brigadier Lord Stirling is to take charge of General Sullivan's division till he returns to it again."

CHAPTER III.

RIGHT here, before entering upon the details of the coming struggle, we may delay a moment to glance at the two armies as they lay in their opposite camps waiting to engage in the serious business before them. What was their composition and organization, what their strength, who their officers and leaders? In the case of the American troops particularly may these questions be asked, because to them and their services the country has long acknowledged its obligations, and so far bound itself to perpetuate their memory. Who were the men who stood with Washington in this first and critical year of our national life—who came to this vicinity to fight on strange ground for a common cause? We are called upon to remember them, not as soldiers simply, but as public-spirited citizens arming to secure themselves in their privileges, or perhaps as ancestors who had a thought for the peace and happiness of present generations.

The original army of the Revolution was that ardent though disjointed body of provincials which gathered around Boston immediately after the Lexington alarm, and came nominally under the command of General Artemas Ward, of Massachusetts. As a military corps it entirely lacked cohesion, as the troops from New Hampshire, Rhode Island, and Connecticut were under independent control, and yielded to General Ward's authority only by patriotic consent. The appointment of Washington as commander-in-chief of all the American forces relieved this difficulty, and the adoption by Congress of the Boston troops as a Continental army, under the orders and in the pay of Congress, gave that army more of a military character. But the terms of enlistment were short, and it became necessary to reorganize the entire body by new enlistments for a year's service from the 1st of January, 1776. This force thus recruited was the nucleus of the army which Washington mustered at New York in the present campaign. It consisted of twenty-seven battalions, or "regiments of foot," as they were styled, each divided into eight companies, and having a maximum strength of about six hundred and forty officers and men. With the exception of the First Regiment, or Pennsylvania Riflemen, all were from the New England States; and, as already stated, twenty-one of them, after the evacuation of Boston, marched to New York under the command of Generals Heath, Spencer, Sullivan, and Greene.

This force, diminished by the regiments sent to Canada, was quite inadequate for the purposes of the campaign, and on the 1st of June Congress issued a call for large reinforcements both for the New York army and that on the Canada border. For the former thirteen thousand eight hundred troops were voted necessary, and for the latter six thousand, while in addition it was resolved to establish a "flying camp" of ten thousand men, who could be sent wherever needed. The quota Massachusetts was to furnish for New York was two thousand; Connecticut, five thousand five hundred; New York, three thousand; and New Jersey, three thousand three hundred. For the flying camp, Pennsylvania was to recruit six thousand; Delaware, six hundred; and Maryland, three thousand four hundred. All these men were to be militia or State troops, but to serve under the orders of Congress and in its pay until at least the 1st of December following.

The necessity of these calls was impressed upon the country by urgent letters from the President and members of Congress and the leaders of the day. "The militia of the United Colonies," wrote Hancock, "are a body of troops that may be depended upon. To their virtue, their delegates in Congress now make the most solemn appeal. They are called upon to say whether they will live slaves or die freemen." To the governors and State assemblies he added: "On your exertions at this critical period, together with those of the other colonies in the common cause, the salvation of America now evidently depends. . . Exert, therefore, every nerve to distinguish yourselves. Quicken your preparations, and stimulate the good people of your government, and there is no danger, notwithstanding the mighty armament with which we are threatened, but you will be able to lead them to victory, to liberty, and to happiness." But the reinforcements came forward slowly, and it was not until the enemy had actually arrived that the peculiar dangers of the situation were appreciated and the militiamen hurried to Washington's assistance at his own pressing call for them. By the 27th of August, his army, which on July 13th numbered a little over ten thousand men fit for duty, had been increased in the aggregate to twenty-eight thousand; but so many were on the sick list during this month, that he could muster not quite twenty thousand effectives, officers and men, at the opening of active operations.

To this force the State of New York contributed thirteen regiments. Of her Continental battalions then in the service, three were in the Northern department under Schuy-

ler, part of another in the Highlands, and two, commanded
by Colonels Alexander McDougall and Rudolph Ritzema,
here with Washington, both of which were largely recruited from New York City. McDougall, colonel of the
first battalion, had identified himself early with the liberty party in the city, became a member of the Provincial
Congress, and by his zealous and energetic efforts in both
his civil and military capacity contributed much towards
preserving the honor and interests of the colony in the
present crisis. In August he was promoted to the rank
of brigadier-general in the Continental army, and rose to
the grade of major-general before the close of the war.
Nine of the other regiments from this State, chiefly militia, formed two brigades under Brigadier-Generals John
Morin Scott and George Clinton. In Scott's command
were two battalions which were credited to and represented the city distinctively. The oldest and largest was
the "First Independent Battalion," commanded by Colonel John Lasher, remembered as one of the substantial
citizens of the place. A man of property and influence,
with a taste for military affairs and evidently popular, he
had been elected colonel of the Independent Companies
during the colonial régime, and now, with most of his
officers and men, had taken up the Continental cause.[1]
The battalion was a favorite corps, composed of young
men of respectability and wealth, and when on parade

---

[1] In a letter to Peter Van Schaack, dated New York, February 23d,
1776, Fred. Rhinelander says : "We are going to raise a new battalion; Colonel Lasher and Gouverneur Morris are candidates for the command.
As both the gentlemen have great merit, it is hard to tell which will succeed." The reference here is probably to a plan formed by private citizens
in New York to raise a battalion of fifteen hundred men for nine
months, on condition that the projectors could appoint the officers. This
being refused by the Provincial Congress the plan was abandoned.—*Life
of G. Morris*, vol. i. p. 89, n.

was doubtless the attraction of the city. Its companies bore separate names, and the uniform of each had some distinguishing feature. There were the " Prussian Blues," under Captain James Alner; the " Oswego Rangers," under Captain John J. Roosevelt; the " Rangers," under Captain James Abeel; the " Fusileers," under Captain Henry G. Livingston; the " Hearts of Oak," under Captain John Berrian; the " Grenadiers," under Captain Abraham Van Dyck; the " Light Infantry," under Captain William W. Gilbert; the " Sportsmen," under Captain Abraham A. Van Wyck; the " German Fusileers," under Captain William Leonard; the " Light Horse," under Captain Abraham P. Lott; and the " Artillery," under Captain Samuel Tudor. As reorganized in the summer of 1776, the regiment had for its field officers Colonel John Lasher, Lieutenant-Colonel Andrew Stockholm, and Major James Abeel. The Second New York City Battalion was originally commanded by Colonel William Heyer, and among its companies were the " Brown Buffs," " Rifles," " Grenadiers," " Hussars," and " Scotsmen," the latter of whom were commanded by Captain Robert Smith, of New York, who, after doing good service at various times during the war, settled in Philadelphia, where for nearly half a century after he filled offices of public and private trust.[1] In 1776, in the reappointment of field officers, William Malcom, formerly first major, became colonel; Isaac Stoutenburgh, lieutenant-colonel; and James Alner, major.[2] The two remaining regiments of Scott's brigade

---

[1] See Biographical Sketches, Part II.

[2] The New York Congress voted that the City and County of New York should furnish twelve hundred men as their quota of the three thousand recently called for, and these were to consist of " the two independent battalions." They were composed of ten companies each, which, however, never reached their maximum strength. In September Lasher's total was 510; Malcom's, 297.

were commanded by Colonel Samuel Drake, of Westchester, and Colonel Cornelius Humphrey, of Dutchess
County. Scott himself was a man of the highest public
spirit. A history of the progress of the revolutionary
sentiment in the Colony of New York would be incomplete without a record of his career. An able lawyer and
speaker, he early resisted the pretentions and arbitrary
policy of the home government, and when war became
inevitable, he spared no energy to provide for the crisis.
In 1775 and 1776 he was one of the most active and useful
members of the Provincial Congress and the Committee
of Safety. " Nothing from the other side of the water,"
he wrote to a friend in November, 1775, " but a fearful
looking for of wrath. But let us be prepared for the
worst. Who can prize life without liberty? It is a bau-
ble only fit to be thrown away." He served through the
present campaign, and then continued in the public service as Secretary of the State of New York and afterwards member of the Continental Congress.

Two other acquisitions to the army in this campaign
were the brothers James and George Clinton, of Ulster
County, N. Y., both destined to be prominent charac-
ters in the Revolution. James Clinton, as colonel of one
of the Continental regiments, superintended the construction of fortifications in the Highlands, and in August was
promoted to the rank of brigadier-general in the Continental service. George was member of Congress, and after
voting for the Declaration of Independence returned to
command a militia brigade which the State called out
during the summer, and which joined Washington's army
just before the battle of Long Island. These troops were
commanded by Colonel Levi Paulding, of Ulster County; Colonels Morris Graham and James Swartwout, of

Dutchess ; Colonel Isaac Nichol, of Orange ; and Colonel Thomas Thomas, of Westchester. Before this, in November, 1775, an attempt was made to raise three regiments of militia in New York City to be commanded respectively by Henry Remsen, John Jay, and Abraham P. Lott; but the enlistment of men into other corps made it impossible to organize them.[1] In this campaign, too, we first meet with young officers from this State who subsequently rose to distinction in the service. Here Alexander Hamilton appears ; and we read that upon the certificate of Captain Stephen Badlam, that he had examined Hamilton and found him qualified for a command, the New York Convention appointed him, March 14th, Captain of the " Provincial Company of Artillery of the Colony." Among others were Lieutenant-Colonel Henry B. Livingston, Majors Nicholas Fish and Richard Platt, and Hugh Hughes, teacher of a classical school, who, as assistant Quartermaster-General, rendered, at least on one occasion, a most important service to the army.

Long Island was represented in the New York quota by two regiments of militia and two small companies of " troop." The Suffolk County regiment, at the eastern end, was commanded by Colonel Josiah Smith, of South Haven parish, and that from King's County by Colonel Rutgert Van Brunt. But the militia, especially in dissaffected Kings and Queens counties, could be mustered, as volunteers, with difficulty ; and early in August the New York Provincial Congress ordered a draft to be made from these counties, and the troops so raised to be commanded by Colonel Jeronimus Remsen, of Queens,

[1] Lewis Morris, one of the Signers of the Declaration, was appointed brigadier-general of the Westchester County militia, but he remained in Congress until later in the fall, when he took the field for a short time with New York militia in the Highlands.

with Nicholas Cowenhoven, of Kings, for lieutenant-colonel, and Richard Thorne, of Queens, for major. Colonel Smith's lieutenant-colonel at this time was John Sands, and his major, Abraham Remsen. The two regiments—Smith's and Remsen's—did not report to Greene until August 15th and after, and mustered together probably less than five hundred men. The troopers, not over fifty in all, were a few horsemen from Brooklyn under Captain Adolph Waldron and Lieutenant William Boerum; and others, representing King's County, under Captain Lambert Suydam. About the middle of August, Nathaniel Woodhull, of Mastic, brigadier-general of the Long Island militia, and now President of the State Convention, dropping his civil functions, repaired to the Island to render whatever aid the situation might demand. A man of the purest motives and capable of doing good service, an unhappy, although a soldier's fate, awaited him.

New Jersey at the outbreak of the war met an obstacle to hearty co-operation with the other colonies in the conduct of William Franklin, her royal governor. Little sympathy had he with the revolutionary movement, and his influence was powerful in keeping men out of it, until the aroused State legislature ordered his arrest. In William Livingston, her new governor, New Jersey found a patriot and civil leader of the right stamp for the emergency. Part of the year he acted in a military capacity, and directed the movements of the militia in the vicinity of Amboy and Elizabeth. As the Tory element was very considerable here, the State found the same difficulty experienced by New York in raising troops for the army; but she furnished a good proportion. Her three Continental regiments under Colonels Dayton, Maxwell, and Winds, were in the Canada army during the present campaign.   In the spring and summer the State sent several detachments of militia, under Lieutenant-Colonels Ward and Cadmus and other officers, to assist in fortifying New York.   In answer to the last call of Congress, the legislature voted to raise a brigade of five battalions, to be known as "new levies," to serve until December 1st, and to each man that would enlist a bounty of three pounds was offered.   The command of the brigade was given to Colonel Nathaniel Heard, of Woodbridge, now promoted to a State brigadier.   The colonels were Philip Van Cortland, whose regiment was recruited in Bergen, Essex, and Burlington counties; David Forman, with four companies from Middlesex and four from Monmouth; Ephraim Martin, with four from Morris and four from Sussex; Philip Johnston, with three from Somerset and five from Hunterdon; and Silas Newcomb, with men from Salem, Gloucester, Burlington, and Cumberland. In September the command numbered seventeen hundred and sixty-two enlisted men, and one hundred and sixty officers.[1]   We shall find these troops figuring in the movements on Long Island.

Pennsylvania was well represented in this campaign. Her troops participated in nearly every engagement, and had the opportunity in more than one instance of acquitting themselves with honor.   Besides her large body of "associators," or home guards, many of whom marched into New Jersey, the State sent four Continental regiments under Colonels Wayne, St. Clair, Irvine, and De Haas, to Canada, and eight other battalions, three of them Continental, to the army at New York.   Of these, the oldest was commanded by Colonel Edward Hand, of

[1] *List of the Officers and Men from New Jersey who served in the Revolution.* By Adjutant-General W. S. Stryker.

Lancaster. It was the first of the Continental establishment, where it was known as the "rifle" corps. Enlisting in 1775, under Colonel Thompson, it joined the army at the siege of Boston, re-enlisted for the war under Colonel Hand in 1776, and fought all along the Continent from Massachusetts to South Carolina, not disbanding until the peace was signed in 1783. Hand himself, a native of Ireland, and, like many others in the service, a physician by profession, had served in the British army, was recognized as a superior officer, and we find him closing his career as Washington's adjutant-general and personal friend. The two other regiments, raised on the Continental basis, were commanded by Colonels Robert Magaw, formerly major of Thompson's regiment, and John Shee, of Philadelphia. The remaining battalions were distinctively State troops, and formed part of the State's quota for the Flying Camp. Colonel Samuel Miles, subsequently mayor of Philadelphia, commanded what was known as the First Regiment of Riflemen. Unlike any other corps, it was divided into two battalions, which on their enlistment in March aggregated five hundred men each. The lieutenant-colonel of the first was Piper; of the second, John Brodhead. The majors were Paton and Williams. Another corps was known as the First Regiment of Pennsylvania Musketry, under Colonel Samuel John Atlee, of Lancaster County, originally five hundred strong, and recruited in Chester and the Piquea Valley. Atlee had been a soldier in his youth in the frontier service, afterwards studied law, and in 1775 was active in drilling companies for the war. Mercer, who knew a good soldier when he met him, wrote to Washington that Atlee was worthy his regard as an officer of "experience and attention," and his fine conduct on Long Island proved his title to this word of commen-

8

dation from his superior. How much of a man and soldier he had in his lieutenant-colonel, Caleb Parry, the events of August 27th will bear witness. The three other battalions were incomplete. Two were composed of Berks County militia, under Lieutenant-Colonels Nicholas Lutz and Peter Kachlein. Lutz's major was Edward Burd, and their colonel was Henry Haller, of Reading, who did not join the army until after the opening of the campaign. Another detachment consisted of part of Colonel James Cunningham's Lancaster County militiamen, under Major William Hay.

Delaware furnished more than her proportion to the flying camp. The "Lower Counties," as this little State had been known in colonial times, had shown no haste to break with the mother country. Her people were chiefly farmers of a peaceable disposition, who used herbs for tea and felt no weight of oppression. But Delaware had her public-spirited men, who, when the crisis came, felt that the "counties" must take their place by the side of the colonies in the pending conflict. Among these were Thomas MacKean and Cæsar Rodney. Rodney's right-hand man in his patriotic efforts was John Haslet, born in Ireland, once a Presbyterian minister, now a physician in Dover, "tall, athletic, of generous and ardent feelings." The news of the adoption of the Declaration of Independence Haslet celebrated with "a turtle feast;" and he did more. Already he had begun to raise a regiment for the field, and five weeks before the opening battle it left Dover eight hundred strong, composed of some of the best blood and sinew Delaware had to offer.[1]

Maryland raised as her contingent for this campaign four regiments and seven independent companies; but of

[1] *Delaware's Revolutionary Soldiers.* By William G. Whiteley, Esq., 1875.

COLONEL FIRST REGIMENT OF FOOT (PENN. RIFLEMEN).
BRIGADIER GENERAL 1777

these, Smallwood's battalion and four of the companies alone had joined the army when hostilities commenced. Though forming part of the State's quota for the flying camp, this was far from being a hastily-collected force. It stands upon record that while Massachusetts was preparing for the contest in the earlier days, there were men along the Chesapeake and the Potomac who took the alarm with their northern brethren. Mordecai Gist, Esq., of "Baltimore town," was among the first to snuff the coming storm, and the first to act, for he tells us that as early as December, 1774, at the expense of his time and hazard of his business, he organized "a company composed of men of honor, family, and fortune," to be ready for any emergency. The Lexington news, four months later, found the best part of Maryland ready to arm. In Baltimore, William Buchanan, lieutenant of the county, collected a body of the older citizens for home defence, while their unmarried sons and others organized themselves into two more companies, donned "an excellent scarlet uniform," and chose Gist for their leader. When the State called for troops at large many of these young men responded, and in the spring of 1776 made up three companies, which, with six other companies that gathered at Annapolis from the surrounding country, formed the first Maryland battalion of "State regulars." William Smallwood, living on the banks of the Potomac, in Charles County, was chosen colonel; Francis Ware, lieutenant-colonel; and Mordecai Gist, first major. On the day it left for the field, July 10th, it numbered, inclusive of Captain Edward Veazey's large independent company from the Eastern Shore, seven hundred and fifty men. The State sent no better material into the service. Without cares, patriotic, well drilled, well led, priding themselves in their soldierly appearance, both officers and men were a notable and much needed acquisition to Washington's army.

Men from Virginia, too, were to take an active part in this campaign, but not until after it had opened. The State had nine regiments organized for service, five of which, under Colonels Weedon, Reed, Scott, Elliott and Buckner, joined the army during the fall. There were several Virginia officers on the ground, however, as early as July and August, one of whom was a host in himself. This was General Hugh Mercer, who had been a surgeon in the Pretender's army on the field of Culloden ; who afterward coming to America figured as a volunteer in Braddock's defeat, and then settled down to practice as a physician in Fredericksburg. Appointed a Continental Brigadier, Washington intrusted him with the important command of the New Jersey front, where he kept a constant watch along the shore opposite Staten Island. He had at various times from three to six thousand troops under him, composed of Pennsyvania and New Jersey home guards and militia, but which were never enrolled as a part of Washington's army.[1]

From New England, as we have seen, came the troops sent on from Boston by Washington, which formed the nucleus or basis of the force gathered at New York. These were all Continental or established regiments, and were reinforced from this section during the summer by militia and State troops.

Massachusetts furnished the Continental battalions commanded by Colonels William Prescott, of Pepperell ;

---

[1] Durkee's Continentals garrisoned Powle's Hook, and Bradley's Connecticut regiment was at Bergen, both being returned on Washington's rolls, but otherwise under Mercer's orders.

John Glover, of Marblehead ; Moses Little, of Newburyport ; John Nixon, of Framingham ; Jonathan Ward, of
Southboro ; Israel Hutchinson, of Salem ; Ebenezer
Learned, of Oxford ; Loammi Baldwin, of Woburn ;
John Bailey, of Hanover ; Paul Dudley Sergent, of
Gloucester, and Joseph Read. In August, Brigadier-
General John Fellows, of Sheffield, brought down three
regiments of militia under Colonels Jonathan Holman,
of Worcester County, Jonathan Smith, of Berkshire,
and Simeon Cary, with men from Plymouth and Bristol
counties. The State also sent the only artillery regiment [1]
then in the service, under Colonel Henry Knox, of
Boston.

Many of these officers named had already made something of a record for themselves. Prescott will be forever associated with Bunker Hill. With him there were
Nixon, who was severely wounded, Ward, Little, Sargent, and not a few of the officers and men who were
here in the present campaign. Many of them were
representative citizens. Little, of Newburyport, whose
name we have seen associated with the defences of Long
Island, had been surveyor of the king's lands, owned
large tracts in his own right, and was widely known as
a man of character and influence. As an officer he was
distinguished for his judgment and great self-possession
in the field. His lieutenant-colonel, William Henshaw,
of Leicester, belonged to the line of Henshaws whose
ancestor had fallen in the English Revolution in defence
of popular rights and privileges. A man of the old
type, with cocked hat and provincial dress, modest and

---

[1] At New York, the artillery was increased by Captain Alexander Hamilton's company, and soldiers were detached from the several regiments to act
as gunners in consequence of Knox's inability to furnish enough from his
own regiment to man all the points.

brave, he writes home to his wife one day that he finds it difficult to stop profanity among the troops ; another day he hopes his children are improving in all the graces ; and then he is heard of in the heat of some engagement. He was the first adjutant-general of the provincial army around Boston in 1775, and served in that capacity with the rank of colonel until relieved by General Gates. The services rendered by Colonel and afterwards General Glover in this as well as in other campaigns is a well-known record. Learned and Nixon became Continental brigadiers. Shepherd, Brooks, Jackson, Winthrop Sargent, and many other officers from this State, distinguished themselves in the later years of the Revolution. But perhaps no man proved his worth more in this campaign than Colonel Rufus Putnam, of Brookfield, Washington's chief engineer. He succeeded Colonel Gridley at Boston ; and at New York, where engineering skill of a high order was demanded in the planning and construction of the works, he showed himself equal to the occasion. That Washington put a high estimate on his services, appears from more than one of his letters.[1]

Rhode Island at this time had two regiments in the field. In 1775 they were around Boston ; in 1776 they were here again with the army—Varnum's Ninth and Hitchcock's Eleventh Continentals. A third regiment from this State, under Colonel Lippett, did not join the army until September. Varnum and Hitchcock were rising young lawyers of Providence, the former a graduate of Brown University, the latter of Yale. Hitchcock's lieutenant-colonel was Ezekiel Cornell, of Scituate, who sub-

---

[1] Document 43, Part II., contains interesting and important extracts from Colonel Putnam's Journal, now published for the first time.

sequently served in Congress and became commissary-general of the army. Greene, Varnum, Hitchcock, and Cornell were among those Rhode Islanders who early resisted the pretensions of the British Ministry. In the discipline and soldierly bearing of these two regiments Greene took special pride, and not a few of their officers subsequently earned an honorable reputation. Varnum was created a brigadier; Hitchcock, as will be seen, closed his career as a sacrifice to the cause; Colonels Crary and Angell and the Olneys served with the highest credit; and the men of the regiments, many of them, fought through the war to the Yorktown surrender.

In proportion to her population, no State contributed more men to the army in 1776 than Connecticut, nor were all ranks of society more fully represented. Fortunately the State had in Trumbull, its governor, just the executive officer which the times demanded. A man of character and ability, greatly respected, prompt, zealous, ardent in the cause, his words and calls upon the people were seldom unheeded; and the people were generally as patriotic as their governor. In the present crisis Connecticut sent to New York six Continental battalions, seven of " new levies," and twelve of militia. Her Continentals were commanded by Colonels Samuel Holden Parsons,[1] of Lyme; Jedediah Huntington, of Lebanon; Samuel Wyllys, of Hartford; Charles Webb, of Stamford; John Durkee, of Bean Hill, near Norwich; and Andrew Ward,[2] of Guilford. The " levies" were the troops

---

[1] On his promotion to a brigadier-generalship in August, Parsons was succeeded by his lieutenant-colonel, John Tyler.

[2] This was the same officer who came down with Lee in the spring. When his regiment returned home he was put in command of another raised on the continental basis. He joined the army in August, but did not cross to Long Island.

raised in answer to the last call of Congress, and were commanded by Colonels Gold Selleck Silliman, of Fairfield ; Phillip Burr Bradley, of Ridgefield ; William Douglas, of Northford ; Fisher Gay, of Farmington ; Samuel Selden, of Hadlyme ; John Chester, of Wethersfield ; and Comfort Sage, of Middletown. Among these names will be recognized many which represented some of the oldest and best families in the State. Wyllys was a descendant of one of the founders of Hartford. His father held the office of Secretary of State for sixty-one years ; his grandfather had held it before that, and after the Revolution the honor fell to the colonel himself. The three held the office in succession for ninety-eight years. Three members of this family, which is now extinct, were in the army during this campaign, and two served with honor through the war. From Lebanon came Colonel Jedediah Huntington and his two brothers, Captains Joshua and Ebenezer. They were sons of Jabez Huntington, who like Trumbull was a type of the patriotic citizen of the Revolution. Although his business and property, as a West India merchant, would be greatly endangered if not ruined by the war, he and his family cheerfully ignored their personal interests in their devotion to the common cause. The three brothers and their brother-in-law, Colonel John Chester, served through the present campaign as they had in the previous one, and two of them, Jedediah and Ebenezer, fought to the end of the struggle. Parsons, who subsequently rose to the rank of a Continental major-general, Wyllys and Webb, were among those who pledged their individual credit to carry out the successful enterprise against Ticonderoga in 1775. In his section of the State few men were more influential than Colonel Silliman, of Fairfield, where, before the war, he had held the office of king's attorney. After the present campaign, in the course of which he was more than once engaged with the enemy, he was appointed a State brigadier, rendered further service during the British forays into Connecticut, and marched with troops to the Hudson Highlands upon Burgoyne's approach from Canada. Colonel Douglas, of Northford, engaged heart and hand in the struggle. Joining Montgomery's command in 1775, he served in the flotilla on Lake Champlain, and was subsequently appointed commodore by Congress; but accepting a colonelcy of Connecticut levies he marched to New York in 1776, after first advancing the funds to equip his regiment. With Silliman he enjoyed the confidence and good opinion of the commander-in-chief, and both were appointed to command regiments to be raised for the Connecticut Continental Line. Another of those citizen-soldiers who came from the substantial element in the population was Colonel Selden. A descendant of the Seldens who were among the first settlers in the Connecticut Valley, fifty years of age, possessing a large estate, incapacitated for severe military duty, the father of twelve children, he nevertheless answered the governor's call for troops, and joined the army at New York, from which he was destined not to return. Durkee, Knowlton, Hull, Sherman, Grosvenor, Bradley, afterwards a Continental colonel, and many others, were men from Connecticut, who gave the country their best services. The militia regiments from this State turned out at the governor's call upon the arrival of the enemy. Of the fourteen he designated to march, twelve reported at New York before August 27th, each averaging three hundred and fifty men, with Oliver Wolcott as their brigadier-general,[1] than

[1] The original letter from Trumbull to Wolcott, among the latter's papers,

whom no man in Connecticut had done more to further the public interests of both the State and the nation. Signing the Declaration in 1776, he was to be found in the following year fighting Burgoyne in the field, and afterwards constantly active in a military or civil capacity until the success of the cause was assured.

Pass these men in review, and we have before us not a small proportion of those "fathers" of the Revolution, to whose exertions and sacrifices America owes her independence. It was a crude, unmilitary host, strong only as a body of volunteers determined to resist an invasion of their soil. Here and there was an officer or soldier who had served in previous wars, but the great mass knew nothing of war. The Continental or established regiments formed much less than half the army, and some of these were without experience or discipline ; very few had been tested under fire. As to arms, they carried all sorts—old flint-locks, fowling-pieces, rifles, and occasionally good English muskets captured by privateers from the enemy's transports. Not all had bayonets or equipments. Uniforms were the exception ; even many of the Continentals were dressed in citizens' clothes.[1] The mili-

informing him of his appointment, states that the fourteen regiments had been called out upon "the most pressing application of General Washington." The governor adds : "Having formed raised expectations of your disposition and ability to serve your country in this most important crisis, on which the fate of America seems so much to depend, I trust you will cheerfully undertake the service," etc. General Wolcott proceeded at once to New York, and was with the militia in the city during the fighting on Long Island, and for some time after. As to the number of the regiments that came down, see Colonel Douglas' letter of August 23d (Document 22), where he says twelve were on the parade the day before.

[1] When it was proposed to put the Boston army on the new Continental basis on January 1st, 1776, Washington evidently hoped to have it all uniformed. Thus his orders of December 11th, 1775, read : "As uniformity and decency in dress are essentially necessary in the appearance and regularity

tiamen, hurriedly leaving their farms and affairs, came down in homespun, while some of the State troops raised earlier in the spring appeared in marked contrast to them, both in dress and discipline. Smallwood's Marylanders attracted attention with their showy scarlet and buff coats. The Delawares, with their blue uniform, were so nearly like the Hessians as to be mistaken for them in the field. Miles' Pennsylvanians wore black hunting shirts ; and Lasher's New York battalion perhaps appeared in the various uniforms of gray, blue and green worn by the independent companies. The general and regimental officers in the army were distinguished by different-colored cockades and sashes. For regimental

of an army, his Excellency recommends it earnestly to the officers to put themselves in a proper uniform. . . . The general by no means recommends or desires officers to run into costly or expensive regimentals ; no matter how plain or coarse, so that they are but uniform in their color, cut, and fashion. The officers belonging to those regiments whose uniforms are not yet fixed upon had better delay making their regimentals until they are." The orders of January 5th, 1776, say : " The regimentals, which have been made up, and drawn for, may be delivered to the respective Colonels, by the Quartermaster-General, to the order of those Colonels, who drew them at such prices as they have cost the continent, which is much cheaper than could otherwise be obtained. As nothing adds more to the appearance of a man than dress, and a proper degree of cleanliness in his person, the General hopes and expects that each regiment will contend for the most soldierlike appearance." These " regimentals" were of a brown color. That Little's and Hitchcock's men, or most of them, were in uniform when they came to New York, appears from General Greene's Providence order of April 4th (*ante*, p. 62). A description of the colors of Colonel Joseph Read's Massachusetts Continental regiment refers to the " uniform of the regiment ;" so doubtless most of the Boston army was in uniform. But whether they were kept supplied with uniforms may be doubted. The men wore out their clothes fast while throwing up the works, and Washington speaks of the " difficulty and expense" of providing new ones. (Orders, July 24th, 1776.) At this date he does not insist on uniforms, but recommends the adoption of the hunting shirt and breeches as a cheap and convenient dress, and as one which might have its terrors for the enemy, who imagined that every rebel so dressed was " a complete marksman." A valuable article on " The Uniforms of the American Army" may be found in the *Magazine of American History*, for August, 1877, by Professor Asa Bird Gardner, of the West Point Military Academy.

colors, each battalion appears to have carried those of its own design. One of the flags captured by the Hessians on Long Island was reported by a Hessian officer to have been, a red damask standard, bearing the word " Liberty" in its centre. Colonel Joseph Read's Massachusetts Continentals carried a flag with a light buff ground, on which there was the device of a pine-tree and Indian-corn, emblematical of New-England fields. Two officers were represented in the uniform of the regiment, one of whom, with blood streaming from a wound in his breast, pointed to children under the pine, with the words, " For posterity I bleed." [1]

Had this force acquired the discipline and been hardened by the service which made Washington's troops later in the war a most trusty and effective body, the campaign of 1776 would have shown another record. But not the less are we to respect it, with all its failings and defeats. If not all the men were " patriots ;" if some lost faith in the cause ; if others deserted it entirely and joined the enemy ; if some entered the army from mercenary motives and proved cravens in the field ; if still others who were honest enough in their intentions were found to be wretched material for the making of good soldiers—this was only the common experience of all popular struggles. As a body, it fairly represented the colonists in arms ; and as an army, it did its share in bringing about the final grand result.

To recapitulate : Washington's army, at the opening of the campaign on August 27th, consisted of seventy-one regiments or parts of regiments, twenty-five of which were Continental, aggregating in round numbers

[1] *Force*, 5th Series, vol. ii., p. 244.

twenty-eight thousand five hundred officers and men.
Of these, Massachusetts furnished seven thousand three
hundred; Rhode Island, eight hundred; Connecticut, nine thousand seven hundred; New York, four
thousand five hundred; New Jersey, one thousand
five hundred; Pennsylvania, three thousand one hundred; Delaware, eight hundred; and Maryland, nine
hundred. Between eight and nine thousand were on the
sick-list or not available for duty, leaving on the rolls not
far from nineteen thousand effectives, most of them levies
and militia, on the day of the battle of Long Island.[1] As
officered and brigaded at this date the army stood as follows :

---

[1] The last official return of the army before the battle, published in *Force's
Archives*, bears date of August 3d ; the next about September 12th.   The latter
is the proper basis for making an estimate of the numbers for August 27th, as
it includes all the regiments except Haslet's known to be then present, and
no more.   On September 12th the total of rank and file on the rolls, not including the absent sick, was 24,100.   To these add 1800 commissioned officers and 2500 sergeants, drums and fifes, and the total strength is 28,400.
On the same date, rank and file, *fit for duty*, numbered 14,700.   Add to these
1000 lost on Long Island and 3500 officers, sergeants, drums and fifes fit for
duty, and we have, all told, between 19,000 and 20,000 effectives on August
27th ; and these figures correspond with Washington's statement of September 2d : " Our number of men at present fit for duty is under 20,000."   The
army suffered greatly from sickness during August and September.   General
Heath writes in his *Memoirs*, under date of August 8th : " The number of
sick amounted to near 10,000 ; nor was it possible to find proper hospitals or
proper necessaries for them.   In almost every farm, stable, shed, and even
under the fences and bushes, were the sick to be seen, whose countenances
were but an index of the dejection of spirit and the distress they endured."
On the 4th of August, Colonel Parsons wrote to Colonel Little : " My Doctor
and Mate are sick.   I have near Two Hundred men sick in Camp ; my
neighbours are in very little better state."   And he asks Little to consent to his
surgeon's mate remaining with him until his own surgeons were better.
[MS. letter in possession of Charles J. Little, Esq.]

GEORGE WASHINGTON,

COMMANDER-IN-CHIEF.

AIDES-DE-CAMP.

Colonel William Grayson, of Virginia; *Lieutenant-Colonel* Richard Cary, Jr., of Massachusetts; *Lieutenant-Colonel* Samuel B. Webb, of Connecticut; *Lieutenant* Tench Tilghman, of Pennsylvania.

SECRETARY.

Lieutenant-Colonel Robert Hanson Harrison, of Virginia.

ADJUTANT-GENERAL.

Colonel Joseph Reed, of Philadelphia.

QUARTERMASTER-GENERAL.

Colonel Stephen Moylan, of Pennsylvania.

COMMISSARY-GENERAL.

Colonel Joseph Trumbull, of Connecticut.

PAYMASTER-GENERAL.

Colonel William Palfrey, of Massachusetts.

MUSTER-MASTER-GENERAL.

Colonel Gunning Bedford, of Pennsylvania.

DIRECTOR OF THE GENERAL HOSPITAL.

Doctor John Morgan, of Pennsylvania.

CHIEF ENGINEER.

Colonel Rufus Putnam, of Massachusetts.

PUTNAM'S DIVISION.

MAJOR-GENERAL ISRAEL PUTNAM.

AIDES-DE-CAMP.

Major Aaron Burr, Major ————————.

CLINTON'S BRIGADE.

BRIGADIER-GENERAL JAMES CLINTON.[1]
Brigade-Major, David Henly.

Colonel Joseph Read, Massachusetts			505[2]
"	Ebenezer Learned,	"	521
"	John Bailey,	"	503
"	Loammi Baldwin,	"	468

SCOTT'S BRIGADE.

BRIGADIER-GENERAL JOHN MORIN SCOTT.
Brigade-Major, Nicholas Fish.

Colonel John Lasher,	New York		510
"	William Malcom,	"	297
"	Samuel Drake,	"	459
"	Cornelius Humphrey,	"	261

FELLOWS' BRIGADE.

BRIGADIER-GENERAL JOHN FELLOWS.
Brigade-Major, Mark Hopkins.

Colonel Jonathan Holman, Massachusetts			606
"	Simeon Cary,	"	569
"	Jonathan Smith,	"	551
"	John Glover,[3]	"	365

HEATH'S DIVISION.

MAJOR-GENERAL WILLIAM HEATH.
AIDES-DE-CAMP.
Major Thomas Henly, Major Israel Keith.

---

[1] General Clinton being absent all summer in the Highlands, the brigade was commanded first by Colonel Read, and afterwards by Colonel Glover.

[2] The figures given here represent the total number of enlisted men on the rolls on September 12, absent sick included. In the case of some of the regiments, especially from the flying camp, under Lutz, Kachlein, and others, only an estimate can be formed. The strength of these is noted in connection with the losses on Long Island in the next chapter. The Connecticut militia regiments are credited with 350 men each, as Washington gives the figures.

[3] Glover's regiment did not join the army at New York until August. It as assigned on the 12th to Stirling's brigade. and on the 15th to Fellows'.

MIFFLIN'S BRIGADE.

BRIGADIER-GENERAL THOMAS MIFFLIN.

Brigade-Major, Jonathan Mifflin.

Colonel Robert Magaw, Pennsylvania.................... 480
"   John Shee,   "   496
"   Israel Hutchinson, Massachusetts.................. 513
"   Paul Dudley Sargent,[1]   "   527
"   Andrew Ward, Connecticut....................... 437

CLINTON'S BRIGADE.

BRIGADIER-GENERAL GEORGE CLINTON.

Brigade-Major, Albert Pawling.

Colonel Isaac Nichol, New York....................... 289
"   Thomas Thomas,   "   354
"   James Swartwout,   "   364
"   Levi Paulding,   "   368
"   Morris Graham,   "   437

SPENCER'S DIVISION.

MAJOR-GENERAL JOSEPH SPENCER.

AIDES-DE-CAMP.

Major William Peck, Major Charles Whiting.

PARSONS' BRIGADE.

BRIGADIER-GENERAL SAMUEL HOLDEN PARSONS.

Brigade-Major, Thomas Dyer.

Colonel Jedediah Huntington, Connecticut............... 348
"   Samuel Wyllys,   "   530

---

[1] Sargent's and Ward's reported on the ground in August. They were *probably* in Mifflin's brigade.

Colonel John Durkee, Connecticut...................... 520

"   John Tyler,   "   569

"   Jonathan Ward, Massachusetts................... 502

WADSWORTH'S BRIGADE.

BRIGADIER-GENERAL JAMES WADSWORTH.

Brigade-Major, John Palsgrave Wyllys.

Colonel Gold Selleck Silliman, Connecticut................ 415

"   Fisher Gay,   "   449

"   Comfort Sage,   "   482

"   Samuel Selden,   "   464

"   William Douglas,   "   506

"   John Chester,   "   535

"   Phillip Burr Bradley,   "   569

SULLIVAN'S DIVISION.

MAJOR-GENERAL JOHN SULLIVAN.

AIDES-DE-CAMP.

Major Alexander Scammell, Major Lewis Morris, Jr.

STIRLING'S BRIGADE.

BRIGADIER-GENERAL LORD STIRLING.

Brigade-Major, W. S. Livingston.

Colonel William Smallwood, Maryland................... 600

"   John Haslet, Delaware......................... 750

"   Samuel Miles,   Pennsylvania.............. 650

"   Samuel John Atlee,   "   300

Lieutenant-Colonel Nicholas Lutz, "   200

"   "   Peter Kachlein, "   200

Major Hay,   "   200

9

McDougall's Brigade.

BRIGADIER-GENERAL ALEXANDER McDOUGALL.

Brigade-Major, Richard Platt.

Late McDougall's, New York 428
Colonel Rudolph Ritzema, New York................... 434
    "   Charles Webb, Connecticut.................... 542
    "   Jonathan Brewer (Artificers).................... 584

Greene's Division.

MAJOR-GENERAL NATHANIEL GREENE.

AIDES-DE-CAMP.

Major William Blodgett, Major William S. Livingston.

Nixon's Brigade.

BRIGADIER-GENERAL JOHN NIXON.

Brigade-Major, Daniel Box.

Colonel Edward Hand, Pennsylvania.................... 288
    "   James Mitchell Varnum, Rhode Island............ 391
    "   Daniel Hitchcock,   "   368
    "   Late Nixon's, Massachusetts.................... 419
    "   William Prescott,   "   399
    "   Moses Little,   "   453

Heard's Brigade.

BRIGADIER-GENERAL NATHANIEL HEARD.

Brigade-Major, Peter Gordon.

Colonel David Forman,   New Jersey.................... 372
    "   Phillip Johnston,   "   235
    "   Ephraim Martin,   "   382
    "   Silas Newcomb,   "   336
    "   Phillip Van Cortlandt, "   269

CONNECTICUT MILITIA.

BRIGADIER-GENERAL OLIVER WOLCOTT.

Colonel Thompson,	Connecticut	......	350
" Hinman,	"	......	"
" Pettibone,	"	......	"
" Cooke,	"	......	"
" Talcott,	"	......	"
" Chapman,	"	......	"
" Baldwin,	"	......	"
Lieutenant-Colonel Mead,	"	......	"
" " Lewis,	"	......	"
" " Pitkin,	"	......	"
Major Strong,	"	......	"
" Newberry,	"	......	"

LONG ISLAND MILITIA.

BRIGADIER-GENERAL NATHANIEL WOODHULL.[1]

Brigade-Major, Jonathan Lawrence.

Colonel Josiah Smith,	Long Island	......	250
" Jeronimus Remsen,	"	......	200

ARTILLERY.

Colonel Henry Knox, Massachusetts..................... 406

As appears from a document among the papers of General Knox, the encampments and posts of these brigades, before the advance of the enemy, were fixed as follows : Scott's, in the city ; Wadsworth's, along the East River,

---

[1] These regiments were nominally under General Woodhull, but actually under Greene and Sullivan. At the time of the battle of the 27th both were doing duty with Nixon's brigade. (Sullivan's orders, August 25th. *Document* 2.) Their strength can only be estimated, but it is probably correct to say that together they were less than five hundred strong.

in the city ; Parsons', from the ship-yards on the East
River to Jones' Hill, and including one of the redoubts to
the west of it ; Stirling's and McDougall's, still further
west as a reserve near Bayard's Hill ; Fellows', on the
Hudson, from Greenwich down to the " Glass House,"
about half-way to Canal Street ; and James Clinton's,
from that point down to the " Furnace," opposite the
Grenadier Battery.   These brigades, forming Putnam's,
Spencer's, and Sullivan's divisions, with the Connecticut
militia, were retained within the city and its immediate
vicinity.   Of Heath's division, Mifflin's brigade was
posted at Fort Washington, at the upper end of the isl-
and, and George Clinton's at King's Bridge.   Greene's
division—Nixon's and Heard's brigades—with the exception of Prescott's regiment and Nixon's, now under his
brother, Lieutenant-Colonel Thomas Nixon, which were
on Governor's Island, occupied the Long Island front.[1]

A far more perfect and formidable army was that
which lay encamped on Staten Island, seven miles down
the bay.   It was the best officered, disciplined, and equipped that Great Britain could then have mustered for
any service.   The fact that she found it difficult to raise
new troops to conquer America only made it necessary to
send forward all her available old soldiers.   The greater
part of Howe's army, accordingly, consisted of experienced regulars.   He had with him twenty-seven regiments
of the line, four battalions of light infantry and four of
grenadiers, two battalions of the king's guards, three
brigades of artillery, and a regiment of light dragoons,
numbering in the aggregate about twenty-three thousand
officers and men.   The six thousand or more that came

[1] See Appendix to Drake's *Life of General Knox.*

from Halifax were the Boston "veterans." These had been joined by regiments from the West Indies; and among the reinforcements from Britain were troops that had garrisoned Gibraltar and posts in Ireland and England, with men from Scotland who had won a name in the Seven Years' War.[1] Howe's generals were men who showed their fitness to command by their subsequent conduct during the war. Next to the commander-in-chief ranked Lieutenant-Generals Clinton, Percy, and Cornwallis; Major-Generals Mathews, Robertson, Pigot, Grant, Jones, Vaughan, and Agnew; and Brigadier-Generals Leslie, Cleveland, Smith, and Erskine.

The Hessians or "foreigners" formed more than one fourth of the enemy's strength. They numbered eight thousand officers and men, which, added to the distinctively British force, raised Howe's total to over thirty-one thousand. His total of effectives on the 27th of August was something more than twenty-four thousand.[2]

[1] The "Highlander" regiments were the Forty-second and Seventy-first. In *Stewart's Highlanders*, vol. i., p. 354, as quoted in the *Memoir of General Graham*, the following passage appears: "On the 10th April, 1776, the Forty-second Regiment being reviewed by Sir Adolphus Oughton, was reported complete, and so unexceptionable that none were rejected. Hostilities having commenced in America, every exertion was made to teach the recruits the use of the firelock, for which purpose they were drilled even by candle-light. New arms and accoutrements were supplied to the men; and the colonel of the regiment, at his own expense, supplied *broadswords and pistols*. . . . . . The pistols were of the old Highland fashion, with iron stocks. These being considered unnecessary except in the field, were not intended, like the swords, to be worn by the men in quarters. When the regiment took the field on Staten and Long Island, it was said that the broadswords retarded the men by getting entangled in the brushwood and they were therefore taken from them and sent on board the transports."

[2] General Clinton, quoting from Howe's returns on this date, says he had " 24,464 effectives fit for duty"; a total of 26,980, officers not included, who, when added, amount to 31,625 men." See General Carrington's *Battles of the Revolution*, p. 199. To the British force should be added two or three companies of New York loyalists.

Drawn up in complete array upon the field this army would have confronted Washington's in the following order :[1]

ORDER OF BATTLE FOR THE BRITISH.

[SIR WILLIAM HOWE.]

COMMANDER-IN-CHIEF.

LIEUT GENLL CLINTON.

BRIGADIER GENLL LESSLIE.

2^d Bat^n Lt. Infty.   3^d Brigade[2] Lt. Infty.   1st Bat^n Lt. Infty.

Major of Brigade Lewis.

BRIGADIER GENLL CLEVELAND.

2nd Brig. of Art'lly.   3^d Brigade of Art.   1st Brigade of Art.

Major of Brigade Farrington.

---

[1] The list that follows is copied from what appears to have been the roster-book of Adjutant Gilfillan of the Fifty-fifth Regiment. The book was captured by Captain Nathaniel Fitz Randolph, of New Jersey (see *Document* 56), and is now in the possession of Captain John C. Kinney, of Hartford, a great-grandson of the latter. There is no date attached to the "Order of Battle," but from the few dates that follow it was probably made out in the first part of August, 1776. The list gives the full British strength, and is interesting as naming the majors of brigade, represented by the abbreviation M. B.

[2] An error, evidently, for Battalion.

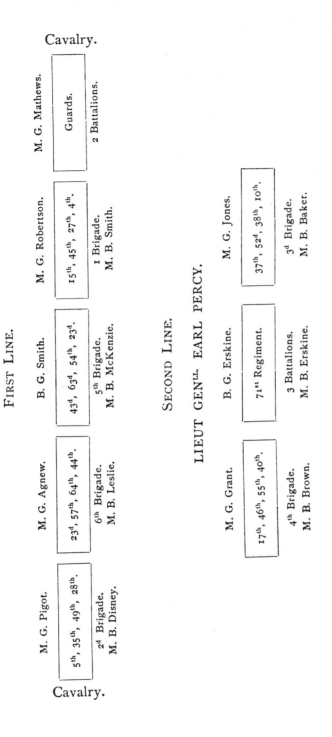

Cavalry.

FIRST LINE.

M. G. Mathews. — Guards. | 2 Battalions.

M. G. Robertson. — 15th, 45th, 27th, 4th. | 1 Brigade. M. B. Smith.

B. G. Smith. — 43d, 63d, 54th, 23d. | 5th Brigade. M. B. McKenzie.

M. G. Agnew. — 23d, 57th, 64th, 44th. | 6th Brigade. M. B. Leslie.

M. G. Pigot. — 5th, 35th, 49th, 28th. | 2d Brigade. M. B. Disney.

Cavalry.

SECOND LINE.

LIEUT GENLL. EARL PERCY.

M. G. Jones. — 37th, 52d, 38th, 10th. | 3d Brigade. M. B. Baker.

B. G. Erskine. — 71st Regiment. | 3 Battalions. M. B. Erskine.

M. G. Grant. — 17th, 46th, 55th, 40th. | 4th Brigade. M. B. Brown.

CORPS DE RESERVE.

LIEUT GENLL EARL CORNWALLIS.

Major Genll Vaughan.

2 B. Grend[rs] 4th B. Grend[rs] 3 Batt. Grend[rs] 1st Battln Grend[rs]
42 Regmt.   33[d] Regt.

HESSIAN DIVISION.[1]

LIEUT-GENERAL DE HEISTER.

MIRBACH'S BRIGADE.

MAJOR GENERAL VON MIRBACH.

REGIMENTS.

Kniphausen.   Rall.   Lossberg.

STIRN'S BRIGADE.

MAJOR-GENERAL VON STIRN.

REGIMENTS.

Donop.   Mirbach.   Hereditary Prince.

DONOP'S BRIGADE.

COLONEL VON DONOP.

GRENADIERS.

Block.   Minegerode.   Lisingen.

YAGERS.

[1] The arrangement of the Hessian troops, as here given, is compiled from Von Elking's work, Baurmeister's Narrative, and the Hessian map in vol. ii. of the Long Island Historical Society's *Memoirs*.

LOSSBERG'S BRIGADE.

COLONEL VON LOSSBERG.

REGIMENTS.

Von Ditfurth.   Von Trumbach.

When and where, now, will these two armies meet?
Or rather, the question was narrowed down to this:
When and where will the British attack? With Washington there was no choice left but to maintain a strictly
defensive attitude. The command which the enemy
had of the waters was alone sufficient to make their
encampment on Staten Island perfectly secure. As to
assuming the offensive, Washington wrote to his brother,
John Augustine, on July 22d: "Our situation at present, both in regard to men and other matters, is such as
not to make it advisable to attempt any thing against
them, surrounded as they are by water and covered with
ships, lest a miscarriage should be productive of unhappy
and fatal consequences. It is provoking, nevertheless, to
have them so near, without being able to give them any
disturbance." Earlier in the season an expedition had been
organized under Mercer, in which Knowlton was to take
an active part, to attack the enemy's outposts on Staten
Island from the Jersey shore, but the weather twice interfered with the plan. All that the Americans hoped to
do was to hold their own at and around New York.
Washington tells us that he fully expected to be able to
defend the city.[1] Even the passage of the Rose and
Phœnix did not shake his faith. None of his letters written during the summer disclose any such misgivings as

[1] "Till of late I had no doubt in my own mind of defending this place."
—*Washington to Congress*, September 2d, 1776.

Lee expressed, respecting the possibility of maintaining this base, and in attempting to hold it he followed out his own best military judgment.

What occasioned the principal anxiety in the mind of the commander-in-chief was the number of points at which the British could make an attack and their distance from one another. They could advance into New Jersey from Staten Island ; they could make a direct attack upon the city with their fleet, while the transports sailed up the Hudson and the troops effected a landing in his rear ; they could cross to Long Island and fall upon Greene in force ; or they could make landings at different points as feints, and then concentrate more rapidly than Washington, as their water carriage would enable them to do, and strike where he was weakest.[1]

The summer and the campaign season were passing, and still the uncertainty was protracted—when and where will the enemy attack ?

---

[1] " Before the landing of the enemy in Long Island, the point of attack could not be known, nor any satisfactory judgment formed of their intentions. It might be on Long Island, on Bergen, or directly on the city."— *Washington to Congress*, September 9th, 1776.

CHAPTER IV.

THE BATTLE OF LONG ISLAND.

AT length, upon the twenty-second of August, after days of expectation and suspense in the American camp, the British moved forward. Thoroughly informed of Washington's position, the strength of his army, and the condition of his lines at every point,[1] Lord Howe matured his plan of action deliberately, and decided to advance by way of Long Island. An attack from this quarter promised the speediest success and at the least cost, for, should he be able to force the defences of Brooklyn, New York would be at his mercy ; or, failing in this, he could threaten Washington's flank from Hell Gate or beyond, where part of the fleet had been sent through the Sound, and by a push into Westchester County compel the evacuation of the city. Preparations were accordingly made to transport the troops from Staten Island

---

[1] The Tories gave Howe all the information he needed. One Gilbert Forbes testified at the "Hickey Plot" examination that a Sergeant Graham, formerly of the Royal Artillery, had told him that he (the sergeant), at the request of Governor Tryon, had surveyed the works around the city and on Long Island, and had concerted a plan of attack, which he gave to the governor (*Force*, 4th Series, vol. vi., p. 1178). On his arrival at Staten Island, Howe wrote to Germaine, July 7th : "I met with Governor Tryon, on board of ship at the Hook, and many gentlemen, fast friends to government, attending him, from whom I have had the fullest information of the state of the rebels, who are numerous, and very advantageously posted, with strong intrenchments, both upon Long Island and that of New York, with more than one hundred pieces of cannon for the defence of the town towards the sea," etc. —*Force*, 5th Series, vol. i., p. 105.

across to the Long Island coast and debark them at
Gravesend Bay, a mile to the eastward of the Narrows.
A thunder-storm of great violence on the previous evening, which had fallen with fatal effect on more than one of
Washington's soldiers, threatened to delay the movement, but a still atmosphere followed, and the morning
of the 22d broke favorably.[1] At dawn the three frigates Phœnix, Greyhound and Rose, with the bomb-
ketches Thunder and Carcass, took their stations close
into the Bay as covering ships for the landing, while
Sir George Collier placed the Rainbow within the
Narrows, opposite De Nyse's Ferry, now Fort Hamilton,
to silence a battery supposed to be at that point. Upon
the Staten Island shore fifteen thousand British and Hessian troops, fully equipped, and forty pieces of artillery
had been drawn up during the day and evening before,
and a part of them embarked upon transports lying near
at anchor. At the beach were moored seventy-five flat-
boats, eleven batteaux, and two galleys, built expressly
for the present service, and manned by sailors from the
ships of war, which, with the rest of the naval armament,
were placed under the direction of Commodore Hotham.

As soon as the covering frigates were in position, the
brigade of light infantry and the reserves of grenadiers
and foot, forming an advance corps four thousand strong
and headed by Sir Henry Clinton and Lord Cornwallis,
entered the flotilla and were rowed in ten divisions to the
Gravesend landing, where they formed upon the plain

---

[1] This storm, which is mentioned by Colonel Douglas, Captain Hale, Chaplain Benedict, and others, hung over the city from seven to ten in the evening, and is described by Pastor Shewkirk as being more terrible than that
which "struck into Trinity Church" twenty years before. Captain Van
Wyck and two lieutenants of McDougall's regiment and a Connecticut soldier
were killed by the lightning.

without opposition.[1]   Then followed the remaining troops
from the transports, and before noon the fifteen thousand, with guns and baggage, had been safely transferred
to Long Island.   All who witnessed this naval spectacle
that morning were the enemy themselves, a few Dutch
farmers in the vicinity, and the pickets of Hand's riflemen,
who at once reported the movement at camp.

The landing successfully effected, Cornwallis was immediately detached with the reserves, Donop's corps of
chasseurs and grenadiers, and six field-pieces, to occupy
the village of Flatbush, but with orders not to attempt the
" pass" beyond, if he found it held by the rebels ; and the
main force encamped nearer the coast, from the Narrows
to Flatlands.   As Cornwallis advanced, Colonel Hand and
his two hundred riflemen hurried down from their outpost camp above Utrecht, and, keeping close to the enemy's front, marched part of the way " alongside of them,
in the edge of the woods," but avoided an open fight in
the field with superior numbers.[2]   Captain Hamilton and

[1] The landing-place was at the present village of Bath.   No opposition by
the Americans would have availed and none was attempted.   Washington
wrote to Hancock, August 20th : " Nor will it be possible to prevent their
landing on the island, as its great extent affords a variety of places favorable for
that purpose, and the whole of our works on it are at the end opposite to the
city.   However, we shall attempt to harass them as much as possible, which
will be all that we can do."   To the same effect Colonel Reed's letter of August 23d : " As there were so many landing-places, and the people of the island
generally so treacherous, we never expected to prevent the landing."   General
Parsons says (*Document* 5) : " The landing of the troops could not be prevented at the distance of six or seven miles from our lines, in a plain under
the cannon of the ships, just within the shore."   An American battery had
gone down to De Nyse's, earlier in the summer, to annoy the Asia, but there
was none there at this date.   The particulars of the debarkation and of subsequent movements of the enemy appear in the reports and letters of the two
Howes and Sir George Collier.   (*Force*, 5th Series, vol. i., pp. 1255—6 ;
and *Naval Chronicle*, 1841.)

[2] " On the morning of the 22d of August there were nine thousand British
troops on New Utrecht plains.   The guard alarmed our small camp, and we
assembled at the flagstaff.   We marched our forces, about two hundred in

twenty men of the battalion fell back on the road in advance, burning grain and stacks of hay, and killing cattle,
which, says 'Lieutenant-Colonel Chambers, he did '' very
cleverly.'' Among the inhabitants along the coast, confusion, excitement, and distress prevailed,[1] and many
moved off their goods in great haste to find refuge in the
American lines or farther east on the island ; while others
remained to welcome the enemy, for whose success they
had been secretly praying from the outset.

The section of Long Island which the enemy now occupied was a broad low plain, stretching northward from
the coast from four to six miles, and eastward a still
further distance. Scattered over its level surface were
four villages, surrounded with farms. Nearest to the
Narrows, and nearly a mile from the coast, stood New
Utrecht ; another mile south-east of this was Gravesend ;
north-east from Gravesend, nearly three miles, the road
led through Flatlands, and directly north from Flatlands,
and about half-way to Brooklyn Church, lay Flatbush.
Between this plain and the Brooklyn lines ran a ridge of
hills, which extended from New York Bay midway
through the island to its eastern extremity. The ridge
varied in height from one hundred to one hundred and fifty
feet above the sea, and from the plain it rose somewhat
abruptly from forty to eighty feet, but fell off more gradually in its descent on the other side. Its entire surface
was covered with a dense growth of woods and thickets,

---

number, to New Utrecht, to watch the movements of the enemy. When we
came on the hill we discovered a party of them advancing toward us. We
prepared to give them a warm reception, when an imprudent fellow fired, and
they immediately halted and turned toward Flatbush. The main body also
moved along the great road toward the same place.''—Lieutenant-Colonel
Chambers, of Hand's riflemen, to his Wife, September 3d, 1776. *Chambers-
burg in the Colony and the Revolution.*

[1] *Strong's History of Flatbush.*

and to an enemy advancing from below it presented a continuous barrier, a huge natural abattis, impassable to artillery, where with proportionate numbers a successful defence could be sustained.

The roads across the ridge passed through its natural depressions, of which there were four within a distance of six miles from the harbor. The main highway, or Jamaica Road—that which led up from Brooklyn Ferry—after passing through Bedford, kept on still north of the hills, and crossed them at the "Jamaica Pass," about four miles from the fortified line. From this branched three roads leading to the villages in the plain. The most direct was that to Flatbush, which cut through the ridge a mile and a half from the works. Three quarters of a mile to the left, towards the Jamaica Pass, a road from Bedford led also to Flatbush ; and near the coast ran the Gowanus Road to the Narrows. Where the Red Lion Tavern stood on this road, about three miles from Brooklyn Church, a narrow lane, known as the Martense Lane, now marking the southern boundary of Greenwood Cemetery, diverged to the left through a hollow in the ridge and connected with roads on the plain. To clearly understand succeeding movements on Long Island, it is necessary to have in mind the relative situation of these several routes and passes.

When word of the enemy's landing reached Sullivan and Washington the troops were immediately put under arms. The commander-in-chief had already been prepared for the intelligence by a dispatch from Governor Livingston, of New Jersey, the night before, to the effect that he had certain information from the British camp that they were then embarking troops and would move to

the attack on the following day.[1]   As the report came in
that the enemy intended to march at once upon Sullivan,
Washington promptly sent him a reinforcement of six
regiments, which included Miles' and Atlee's from Stirling's brigade, Chester's and Silliman's from Wadsworth's, and probably Lasher's and Drake's from Scott's,
numbering together some eighteen hundred men.   They
crossed with light spirits, and were marched to alarm-
posts.   Miles' two battalions went on to the Bedford
Pass; Silliman was ordered down into "a woody hill
near Red Hook, to prevent any more troops from landing thereabout."[2]   Hand's riflemen, supported by one

---

[1] Livingston sent a spy to Staten Island on the night of the 20th, who
brought word that the British were embarking, and would attack on Long
Island and up the North River.   Washington received the information during
the storm on the following evening, and immediately sent word to Heath at
King's Bridge that the enemy were upon "the point of striking the long-
expected stroke."   The next morning, the 22d, he wrote again instructing
Heath to pick out "eight hundred or a thousand, light, active men, and good
marksmen," ready to move rapidly wherever they were most needed; and he
promised to send him some artillery, "if," he continues, "we have not other
employment upon hand, which General Putnam, who is this instant come
in, seems to think we assuredly shall, this day, as there is a considerable embarkation on board of the enemy's boats." (*Mass. Hist. Soc. Coll.*, volume
for 1878.   The Heath correspondence.)   On the same date Washington wrote
to Hancock : "The falling down of several ships yesterday evening to the
Narrows, crowded with men, those succeeded by many more this morning,
and a great number of boats parading around them, as I was just now informed, with troops, are all circumstances indicating an attack, and it is not
improbable it will be made to-day.   It could not have happened last night,
by reason of a most violent gust." (*Force*, 5th Series, vol. i., p. 1110).   On
the 21st, Colonel Hand at the Narrows reported three times to General Nixon
that the British transports were filling with men and moving down, and the
reports were sent to Washington.   These facts show how closely the enemy
were watched.   The embarkation was known at head-quarters early on the
morning of the 22d, before the landing was made on Long Island.

[2] Washington wrote to Heath the next day : "Our first accounts were that
they intended by a forced march to surprise General Sullivan's lines, who commands during the illness of General Greene ; whereupon I immediately reinforced that post with six regiments."   Miles, Silliman, and Chester's adjutant, Tallmadge, state that their regiments were among the first to cross after

of the Eastern regiments, watched and annoyed the Hessians under Donop at Flatbush, and detachments were sent to guard the lower roads near the Red Lion. Within the Brooklyn lines the troops stood to their alarm-posts. Colonel Little, expecting that "morning would bring us to battle," and remembering his promise to defend Fort Greene to the last extremity, enclosed his will to his son, and directed him in a certain event to take proper charge at home.

The morning of the 23d, however, brought no battle, nor did the enemy attempt any advance for three days. Washington made Sullivan an early visit, saw the situation there for himself, and during the day issued another of his fervent orders to the army. He formally announced the landing of the British, and again reminded his troops that the moment was approaching on which their honor and success and the safety of the country depended. "Remember, officers and soldiers," he said, "that you are freemen, fighting for the blessings of liberty ; that slavery will be your portion, and that of your posterity, if you do not acquit yourselves like men. Remember how your courage and spirit have been despised and traduced by your cruel invaders ; though they have found by dear experience at Boston, Charleston, and other places what a few brave men, contending in their own land and in the best of causes, can do against base hirelings and mercenaries." He urged them, too, to be cool, but determined ; not to fire at a distance, but wait for the word from their officers ; and gave express orders that if any

the enemy landed. Sullivan's orders of the 25th and other records seem to indicate that Atlee's, Lasher's, and Drake's were the other three battalions sent over at the same time.

[1] See Sullivan's orders, Silliman's letters, Miles' Journal (Part II.), and Chambers' letter.

10

man attempted to skulk, lie down, or retreat, he must be instantly shot down as an example. Those who should distinguish themselves for gallantry and good conduct were assured that they might depend upon being honorably noticed and suitably rewarded. Strict orders as to other matters were also issued. The commissary-general was to have five days' baked bread on hand for distribution; the men were to have constantly ready with them two days' hard bread and pork, and the officers were to see not only that they had it, but kept it. The officers of the newly arrived militiamen were instructed also to see that the cartridges fitted their soldiers' muskets, and that each man had twenty-four rounds and two flints.

On the Long Island front, Sullivan was alert, and kept his division in readiness for the attack, which was now hourly expected. He ordered his command that afternoon, the 23d, to prepare two days' provisions and turn out the next morning at three o'clock. For the night, he assigned Hitchcock's and Little's regiments to guard the Flatbush Pass, Johnston's and Martin's to the coast road, and Remsen's Long Island militia to support Miles on the Bedford Road. They were all to be at their posts at six o'clock, and the regiments they relieved were to return to their encampments and, like the rest, "get two days' provisions dressed, and be ready for action."

Meanwhile some brisk skirmishing occurred in front of Flatbush. In the afternoon of this day, the enemy, as Sullivan reported, formed, and attempted to pass the road by Bedford, but meeting a warm reception from the riflemen, some "musketry" sent to their support, and two or three of our field pieces, they fell back. "Our men," wrote Sullivan to Washington, "followed them to the house of Judge Lefferts (where a number of them had taken lodgings), drove them out, and burnt the house and a number of other buildings contiguous.   They think they killed a number ; and, as evidence of it, they produced three officers' hangers, a carbine, and one dead body, with a considerable sum of money in pocket.   I have ordered a party out for prisoners to-night." [1]   The enemy returned in force, and the American skirmishers, having but two wounded, withdrew to the hills ; but their conduct in the affair was so highly appreciated by Sullivan, that he issued a congratulatory order in the following terms :

"The general returns his thanks to the brave officers and soldiers who, with so much spirit and intrepidity, repulsed the enemy and defeated their designs of taking possession of the woods near our lines.   He is now convinced that the troops he has the honor to command will not, in point of bravery, yield to any troops in the universe.   The cheerfulness with which they do their duty, and the patience with which they undergo fatigue, evince exalted sentiments of freedom and love of country, and gives him most satisfactory evidence that when called upon they will prove themselves worthy of that freedom for which they are now contending." [2]

[1] Referring evidently to this skirmish, Lieutenant-Colonel Chambers says : "Strong guards were maintained all day on the flanks of the enemy, and our regiment and the Hessian yagers kept up a severe firing, with a loss of but two wounded on our side.   We laid a few Hessians low, and made them retreat out of Flatbush.   Our people went into the town and brought the goods out of the burning houses.   The enemy liked to have lost their field-pieces. Captain Steel acted bravely.   We would certainly have had the cannon had it not been for some foolish person calling retreat.   The main body of the foe returned to town, and when our lads came back they told of their exploits."

[2] Little's Order Book, *Document* 2.   But it seems that Remsen's Long Island militiamen were seized by a panic, either during this skirmish or at a later hour, on the Bedford Road, and ran from their posts.   Sullivan rebuked

On the 24th, Washington was still in doubt as to the intentions of the enemy. Reports represented their numbers on Long Island at not more than eight thousand, whereas they were double this estimate; and it was suspected at head-quarters that their landing might only be a feint to draw off our troops to that side, while the real attack should be made on New York. But the imprudence of running any risks on the Brooklyn side was obvious, and Washington sent over a further reinforcement of four regiments, which appear to have been Wyllys's, Huntington's, and Tyler's of Parsons' brigade (his entire command was there on the next day) together with the Pennsylvania detachments under Lieutenant-Colonel Lutz and Major Hay. On this date Brigadier-General Lord Stirling crossed over, where more than half his brigade had preceded him; and Brigadier-General John Nixon, whose name now first appears in connection with the operations on Long Island, was detailed as field officer of the day, with orders to take command of the outer line and post his men "in the edge of the woods next the enemy." [1]

But the principal event of the 24th was the change made in the chief command on Long Island. Sullivan was superseded by Putnam. There were now on that side the whole of Nixon's and Heard's brigades (the two regiments on Governor's Island excepted), the larger part of Stirling's and Parson's, and half of Scott's and Wadsworth's. As this roster included one third of the army's effective force, the command could properly be assigned

them sharply in his orders of the 24th (*Document* 2), and confined them thereafter to "fatigue" duty. This proved to be only the first of several militia panics experienced in this campaign.

[1] Sullivan's Orders, August 24th. *Document* 2.

to Putnam as the senior major-general present ; but it does not appear that the question of his rank entered into the reasons for the change.   In a letter to Governor Livingston from Colonel Reed, the adjutant-general, dated August 30th, 1776, the statement is made that Washington, " finding a great force going to Long Island, sent over Putnam ;" leaving the inference to be drawn that, apart from his rank, Putnam was considered the proper officer, or an officer competent, to command such a force.   Reed states further that some movements had been made on Long Island of which the commander-in-chief did not entirely approve, and this also called for a change.   Sullivan, too, was wholly unacquainted with the ground ; although, as to this, Putnam's knowledge of it was not extensive, as he had been over it only " occasionally."   That Sullivan was a brave, zealous, and active officer, his military career abundantly proves.   Appointed a brigadier-general from New Hampshire, he commanded a brigade under Lee throughout the Boston siege, and had been sent, as already stated, in the spring of this year to help repair the misfortunes attending our force on the Canada border ; but success was not to be met with there, and Sullivan, finding Gates promoted to the chief command in that quarter, returned, after visiting Congress, to the New York army.   Like most of our general officers at that date, he as yet lacked military experience, especially in an independent capacity, for which his ambition to succeed was not a sufficient equivalent.   How far Putnam was more competent to assume the command on Long Island, is a point which the issue there, at least, did not determine.   His record before this was all in his favor.   A veteran of the old war, a man of known personal courage, blunt, honest, practical, and devoted to the

American cause, he had the confidence of at least the older part of the army, with which he had been identified from the beginning of the struggle. As he had never been tried in a separate department, Washington could not say how he would manage it, but he could say, from his experience with him at Boston, that Putnam was " a most valuable man and fine executive officer," [1] and such he continued to prove himself through the present campaign. He seconded Washington heartily and efficiently in all his plans and preparations, and when he was sent to Long Island the commander-in-chief had reason to feel that whatever directions he might give as to operations there, Putnam would follow them out to the letter. But if Putnam took the general command across the river, Sullivan continued in active subordinate control, as second in command. [2]

---

[1] Washington to Congress, January 30th, 1776.

[2] In regard to the change in the command, the adjutant-general's statement in full is this : " On General Greene's being sick, Sullivan took the command, who was wholly unacquainted with the ground or country. Some movements being made which the general did not approve entirely, and finding a great force going to Long Island, he sent over Putnam, who had been over occasionally ; this gave some disgust, so that Putnam was directed to soothe and soften as much as possible." (*Sedgwick's Life of Livingston,* p. 201.) What movements were referred to, unless it was the random firing of the skirmishers and the burning of houses at Flatbush by some of our men, or how Putnam was to reconcile Sullivan to the change, as he was directed (this evidently being the meaning of Reed's last phrase), does not appear. From subsequent occurrences, the inference is justified that Putnam did not disturb Sullivan's arrangements, but left the disposition of the troops to him. What Sullivan himself says is given in a note further along in the chapter. That Putnam went over on the 24th, and in the forenoon, is evident from a letter from Reed to his wife of that date, in which he says : " While I am writing, there is a heavy firing and clouds of smoke rising from the wood [on Long Island]. General Putnam was made happy by obtaining leave to go over— the brave old man was quite miserable at being kept here." (*Reed's Life of Reed.*) This firing, as Washington wrote to Schuyler on the same date, occurred in the morning. Putnam had been engaged during the summer, principally, in looking after the defences in the city and the river obstructions.

On the 25th, Putnam received written instructions from Washington. He was directed to form a proper line of defence around his encampment and works on the most advantageous ground ; to have a brigadier of the day constantly upon the lines that he might be on the spot to command ; to have field-officers go the rounds and report the situation of the guards ; to have the guards particularly instructed in their duty ; and to compel all the men on duty to remain at their camps or quarters and be ready to turn out at a moment's warning. The wood next to Red Hook bordering Gowanus Creek was to be well attended to, and the woods elsewhere secured by abattis, if necessary, to make the enemy's progress as difficult as possible. The militia, or troops which were least disciplined and had seen the least service, were to man the interior lines, while the best men were " at all hazards" to prevent the enemy's passing the woods and approaching the works. He disapproved also of the unmeaning picket firing and the burning of houses, and warned the general finally that when the attack came it was certain to be " sudden and violent." [1]

For brigadier for the day, General Lord Stirling was assigned to duty on this date.[2]

He had charge, also, of the water transportation, boats, pettiaguers, etc. His division was in the city or close to it. Had the enemy, accordingly, attacked the city directly, it would have fallen largely to Putnam to conduct the defence ; and this is doubtless the reason why, as Reed says, he was " kept here." But as it now seemed certain that the British were concentrating on Long Island, he evidently wished to be with the troops there, where that morning there was " a heavy firing" going on, and obtained leave to cross. Finding a change desirable, Washington, probably at the same time, gave Putnam the command and " sent" him over.

[1] Mr. Davis, in his Life of Aaron Burr, who was Putnam's aid at this time, states that after crossing to Long Island and making the round of the outposts, he (Burr) urged his general to beat up the enemy's camp, but that Putnam declined, on the ground that his orders required him to remain strictly on the defensive.

[2] Sullivan's Orders, August 25th. *Document* 2.

In the skirmishing that continued from the 24th to the 26th the Americans showed skill and bravery, although at times indulging in desultory firing. The riflemen, supported by field-pieces, made occasioned dashes upon the enemy and picked off their men with almost no loss to themselves. Among the troops on picket near Flatbush, on the 25th, were Colonel Silliman and his Connecticut battalion ; and from the colonel, who wrote from there, on a drum-head, to his wife, we get a glimpse of the situation at that point during his tour of duty. " I am now posted," he says, " within about half a mile from the Regulars with my Regt. under the covert of a woody hill to stop their passage into the country. There are a number of Regts. posted all around the town within about the same distance and for the same purpose. The Regulars keep up an almost constant fire from their Cannon and Mortars at some or other of us, but neither shott nor shell has come near my Regt. as yet and they are at too great a distance to fire muskets at. I have a scouting party going out now to see if they can't pick up some or get something from them. . . . They have wounded in all of our men in 3 days skirmish about 8 or 9, one or two mortally, which is not half the number that we have killed for them besides wounded." On the 26th a considerable party with artillery attacked the Hessians and drove them in, killing several men belonging to the Von Lossberg regiment, which later in the day advanced in turn and compelled our skirmishers to fall back. In this affair Colonel Ephraim ¦Martin, of New Jersey, was severely wounded.

On the morning of the 26th, Washington again crossed to Long Island, where he remained until night. The records are quite silent as to how he passed the most of his time, but judging from his letter to Congress of this date, in which he expressed his belief that the enemy had landed nearly all their force on that side, and that it was there they would make their " grand push," it was doubtless a busy, watchful, and anxious day with him. To suppose that he did not inform himself of all the preparations made to meet the enemy, that he did not know what number of men were posted on the hills and at what points, that he did not study the several modes and directions of attack possible for the enemy to adopt, and that he did not himself give personal directions, would be to charge that at the most important moment of the campaign he failed to exercise that care and attention to detail which he exercised on so many occasions both before and after. Indeed, although Putnam and Sullivan were in immediate command on Long Island, Washington never shifted the final responsibility from his own shoulders, and as a matter of fact was probably as well acquainted with the ground as either of these generals. Towards evening, in company with Putnam, Sullivan, and other officers, he rode down to the outposts near Flatbush and examined the position of the enemy. How long he remained, or what information he was able to gather, does not appear ; but both the other generals, Putnam and Sullivan, made a detour of the pickets either at this time or at an earlier hour in the day, visited Miles and Brodhead on the extreme left, took their opinion as to the movements and intentions of the British, so far as one could be formed by them, and then rode off to the right " to reconnoitre the enemies lines." [1]

[1] Several writers, Mr. Sparks among them, make the statement that neither Washington nor Putnam went outside of the Brooklyn lines. It would be impossible to credit this without absolute proof of the fact. Washington always reconnoitred the position of the enemy whenever they were near each

On this day also, the 26th, additional regiments were sent over. Two of these were the remainder of Stirling's brigade—Haslet's Delaware battalion, the largest in the army, as we have seen, and Smallwood's Marylanders, one of the choicest and best equipped. Either on this or one of the two previous days, Lieutenant-Colonel Kachlein's incomplete battalion of Pennsylvania riflemen, with two or three independent companies from Maryland, crossed ; and among the last to go over were one hundred picked men, the nucleus of the " Rangers," from Durkee's Connecticut Continentals at Bergen, with Lieutenant-Colonel Thomas Knowlton at their head.[1] These additions raised the force on Long Island on the night of the 26th to a total of about seven thousand men fit for duty.[2]

other ; in the last scenes of the war at Yorktown he was among the first at the outposts examining the British works. Undoubtedly he rode out to the Flatbush Pass on the 26th, as stated by the writer of the letter to the *South Carolina Gazette* (Document 19), who says : " The evening preceding the action, General Washington, with a number of general officers, went down to view the motions of the enemy, who were encamped at Flatbush." A letter from a survivor of the Revolution, present on Long Island, published in a newspaper several years since, well authenticated, and preserved in one of Mr. Onderdonk's scrap-books in the Astor Library, New York, confirms this statement. The soldier recollects that he saw Washington and others looking at the enemy with their glasses.

[1] Statement of Colonel Thomas Grosvenor to the late David P. Hall, Esq., of New York, who knew Grosvenor well, and preserved many facts in writing in regard to his military career. Knowlton's captains were Grosvenor and Stephen Brown, of Pomfret, Conn. The detachment was on duty at the outposts on the night of the 26th. The soldier whose letter is referred to in the note preceding this was one of the " Rangers," and he states that their number was about one hundred. That Smallwood's and Haslet's regiments crossed on the 26th, we have from Smallwood himself.—*Force*, 5th Series, vol. ii., p. 1011.

[2] The regiments were Little's and Ward's, from Massachusetts ; Varnum's and Hitchcock's, from Rhode Island ; Huntington's, Wyllys's, Tyler's, Chester's, Silliman's, and Gay's, and Knowlton's " Rangers," from Connecticut ; Lasher's and Drake's, from New York ; Smith's and Remsen's, from Long Island ; Martin's, Forman's, Johnston's, Newcomb's, and Cortland's, from New Jersey ; Hand's, Miles', Atlee's, Lutz's, Kachlein's, and Hay's, detachment from Pennsylvania ; Haslet's, from Delaware ; and Smallwood's, from

Following in turn after Nixon and Stirling, Briga-dier-General Parsons was detailed as field officer of the day[1] for the next twenty-four hours—the day of the engagement.

At about the time that Washington started to return to his headquarters at New York, on this evening, Sir William Howe began to set his columns in motion for the attack, and on the next morning, at the passes in the hills and along their inner slopes, was fought what is known in our Revolutionary history as the battle of Long Island.

Fortunately, a point so essential to the comprehension of the progress of any engagement, the position of both armies on Long Island, just before the attack, is now known nearly to the last detail. The record here is clear and satisfactory. On the night of the 26th, the various regiments and detachments on guard at the American outposts numbered not far from twenty-eight hundred men. At the important Flatbush Pass, supporting the two or three gun battery there, and with strong pickets thrown out to the edge of the woods nearest the enemy, were posted Hitchcock's and Little's Continental regi-ments, and Johnston's New Jersey battalion, the two for-mer being commanded by their lieutenant-colonels, Cor-nell and Henshaw. To this point, also, Knowlton and his rangers appear to have been sent. The battery or redoubt here stood about where the Flatbush and narrow

Maryland. Among other artillery officers on that side were Captains Newell and Treadwell, Captain-Lieutenants John Johnston and Benajah Carpenter ; Lieutenants Lillie and " Cadet" John Callender. This list is believed to in-clude all the battalions and detachments on Long Island at the time the British attacked.

[1] Parson's own statement, letter of October 5th : " On the day of the sur-prise I was on duty."—*Document* 5.

Port Road united, and was apparently no more than a plain breastwork, with felled trees in front of it, thrown up across the road, and perhaps extending to the rising ground on the left.[1] At the coast road, around and beyond the Red Lion, the guards consisted of Hand's riflemen, half of Atlee's musketry, detachments of New York troops, and part of Lutz's Pennsylvanians under Major Burd. At the Bedford Pass, to the left of the Flatbush Road, were stationed Colonel Samuel Wyllys's Connecticut Continentals, and Colonel Chester's regiment from the same State, under Lieutenant-Colonel Solomon Wills, of Tolland, who had seen service in the French war and at Havana. Still further to the left, Colonel Miles was now encamped a short distance beyond, in the woods. Between these several passes, sentinels were stationed at intervals along the crest of the ridge, to keep communication open from one end of the line to the other.[2]

[1] The site of this breastwork is now within the limits of Prospect Park, and it stood across what is known as " Battle Pass." Dr. Stiles in his History of Brooklyn, and Mr. Field in vol. ii. of the L. I. Hist. Society's *Memoirs*, put a well-constructed redoubt at this point on a hill-top to the left of the road. The account in the *South Carolina Gazette* says that the Flatbush Pass guards were posted " near a mile from the parting of the road [*i.e.*, a mile from where the Flatbush Road branched from the Jamaica Road] where an *abattis* was formed across the road, and a breastwork thrown up and defended by two pieces of cannon." In the original sketch of the " engagement," made by John Ewing, who was Hand's brother-in-law, and with him on the spot, there is this reference : " F. Where a considerable Number of our people were stationed with several Field-pieces & Breast-works made with Trees felled across the Road to defend themselves when attacked." (*Document* 15.) Colonel Miles speaks of "a small redoubt in front of the village [Flatbush]" (*Document* 20.) The breastwork across the road was doubtless the principal defence here, and this was merely temporary.

[2] The number of men at each of the three passes was about eight hundred, and on the left of these were Miles' two battalions, with perhaps five hundred men on duty. Sullivan's orders of August 25th give the detail which was to mount for picket on the following morning. This detail, therefore, was the one on duty on the night of the 26th. The order runs : " Eight hundred [men] properly officered to relieve the troops on Bedford Road to-morrow

As far, then, to the left as Miles' position the hills were as well guarded as seemed possible with the limited force that could be spared, and at the passes themselves a stout resistance could have been offered. But it was still an attenuated line, more than four miles long, not parallel but oblique to the line of works at Brooklyn, and distant from it not less than one and a half, and at the farthest posts nearly three miles. Should the enemy pierce it at any one point, an immediate retreat would have been necessary from every other. The line could have been defended with confidence only on the supposition that the British would not venture to penetrate the thick woods, but advance along the roads through the passes.

It will be noticed that in this disposition no provision was made for holding the fourth or Jamaica Pass far over

---

morning, six field officers to attend with this party. The same number to re-lieve those on Bush [Flatbush] Road, and an equal number those stationed towards the Narrows. A picket of three hundred men under the command of a Field Officer, six Captains, twelve subalterns to be posted at the wood on the west side of the creek every night till further orders." (See also *Documents* 5, 18, 19.) That Miles was on the extreme left, we well know ; that Wyllys was at the Bedford Pass, appears from both Miles' and Brodhead's accounts ; that Chester's regiment was with him, appears from an extract quoted below—Chester's lieutenant-colonel being Solomon Wills ; that Johnston was at the Flatbush Pass, appears from the same and other authorities ; that Henshaw with Little's regiment was there, he himself states ; that Cornell was also there with Hitchcock's Rhode Islanders, appears from Captain Olney's narrative as given in *Mrs. Williams' Life of Olney*, and from the lists of prisoners ; that Hand was at the lower road, until relieved, and Major Burd also, the major himself and Ewing's sketch both state ; the New York detachment there was probably a part of Lasher's regiment. The extract referred to is from the *Connecticut Courant*, containing a letter from an officer engaged in the battle, which says : "The night before August 27th, on the west road, were posted Colonel Hand's regiment, a detachment from Pennsylvania and New York ; next east were posted Colonel Johnson, of Jersey, and Lieutenant-Colonel Henshaw, of Massachusetts ; next east were posted Colonel Wyllys and Lieutenant-Colonel Wills, of Connecticut. East of all these Colonel Miles, of Pennsylvania, was posted towards Jamaica, to watch the motion of the enemy and give intelligence."

to the left. That the enemy could approach or make a diversion by that route, must have been well understood. But the posting of a permanent guard there would obviously have been attended with hazard, for the distance from the lines to this pass was four miles, and from the Bedford Pass two miles and a half through the woods. The position was thus extremely isolated, if the troops stationed there were expected to make the fortified line their point of retreat. None were stationed there during the five days since the British landed, and it nowhere appears that any were intended or ordered to be so stationed by either Sullivan, Putnam, or the commander-in-chief. There was but one effective way of preventing surprise from that quarter, and that was to have squads of cavalry or troops constantly patrolling the road, who on the appearance of an enemy could carry the word immediately and rapidly to the outposts and the camp. But in all Washington's army there was not a single company of horsemen, except the few Long Island troopers from Kings and Queens counties, and these were now engaged miles away in driving off stock out of reach of the enemy. The duty, accordingly, of looking after the open left flank fell, in part, upon Colonel Miles' two battalions. Lieutenant-Colonel Brodhead leaves it on record that it was "hard duty." The regiment sent out scouting parties every day a distance of four or five miles ; one hundred men were mounted for guard daily, and thirty more with a lieutenant were kept on duty on the left, evidently in the direction of the Jamaica Road. General Parsons reports that "in the wood was placed Colonel Miles with his Battalion to watch the motion of the Enemy on that part, with orders to keep a party constantly reconnoitering to and across the Jamaica road.'' Should he discover the enemy at any time, it would have been expected of him to report the fact at once, oppose them vigorously, and retreat obstinately in order to give time for the other detachments to govern their movements accordingly.

One other circumstance is to be noticed in regard to this Jamaica Pass. General Sullivan, subsequently referring to his connection with this battle, claimed that while he was in sole command he paid horsemen out of his own purse to patrol the road, and that he predicted the approach of the enemy by that road. Whatever inferences may be drawn from this is not now to the point ; but we have the fact that upon the evening of the 26th he exercised the same authority he had exercised in making other details, and sent out a special patrol of five commissioned officers to watch the Jamaica Pass. Three of these officers belonged to Colonel Lasher's New York City battalion—Adjutant Jeronimus Hoogland and Lieutenants Robert Troup and Edward Dunscomb ; and the other two were Lieutenant Gerrit Van Wagenen, a detached officer of McDougall's old regiment, and a Lieutenant Gilliland, who with Van Wagenen had crossed to Long Island, as a volunteer. What part this patrol played in the incidents of the following morning will presently appear.

Thus on the night of the 26th the American outposts stretched along the hills from the harbor to the Jamaica Pass, with unguarded intervals, a distance of more than six miles, while in the plains below lay the enemy, nearly ten times their number, ready to fall upon them with '' a sudden and violent'' shock. During the night one change was made in the picket guard. Colonel Hand's riflemen, who had been on almost constant duty since the arrival of the British, were relieved at two o'clock in the morning by a detachment from the flying camp, which may have been a part of Hay's and Kachlein's men, and returning to the lines, dropped down to sleep.[1]

If we leave our outposts now upon the hills and pass into the enemy's camp on the plain below, we shall find them on the eve of carrying out a great plan of attack. The four days since the 22d had been given to preparation. On the 25th, Lieutenant-General De Heister crossed from Staten Island with the two Hessian brigades of Von Stirn and Von Mirbach, leaving behind Von Lossberg's brigade, with some detachments and recruits, for the security of that island. With this addition, Howe's force on Long Island was swelled to a total of about twenty-one thousand officers and men, fit for duty and in the best condition for active service.[2] As disposed on the 26th, the army lay with the Hessians and the reserves under Cornwallis at Flatbush, the main body under Clinton and Percy massed at Flatlands, and Grant's division of the fourth and sixth brigades nearer the Narrows.

Outnumbering the Americans three to one on the island, Howe could lay his plans with assurance of almost absolute success. He proposed to advance upon the "rebels" in three columns. Grant was ordered to move p from the Narrows along the lower road, and De Heister was to engage the attention of the Americans at the

[1] Hand's letter of August 27th: "I escaped my part by being relieved at 2 o'clock this morning." (Document 12.) See John Ewing's letter and sketch.

[2] Extract from a British officer's letter dated, *Statton Island, August* 4, 1776: . . . . "We are now in expectation of attacking the fellows very soon, and if I may be allowed to judge, there never was an army in better spirits nor in better health, two very important things for our present business."—*Hist. Mag.*, vol. v., p. 69.

Flatbush Pass, while Clinton, Percy, and Cornwallis, with Howe himself, were to conduct the main body as a flanking force around the American left by way of the Jamaica Pass. A previous reconnoissance made by Clinton and Erskine, and information gathered from the Tories, showed the practicability of this latter movement.[1] Grant and De Heister were simply to make a show of an attack until they were assured by the sound of the firing that the flanking column had accomplished its design, when their demonstrations were to be turned into serious fighting. It was expected that by this plan the Americans stationed at the hills and passes would be entirely enveloped and thoroughly beaten if not captured in a body. With what nice precision this piece of strategy was executed, events will show.

The first collision was ominous. Grant's advance-guard, marching up from the Narrows, struck the American pickets in the vicinity of the Red Lion about two o'clock on the morning of the 27th. Whether because they were all new troops, a part of whom had but just come upon the ground, and were alarmed by the night attack, or because they were surprised at their posts and put in danger of capture, or whatever the reason, our picket guard at that point retreated before the enemy without checking their march. There was hardly more than an exchange of fire with Major Burd's detachment, as the major himself writes, and in the confusion or dark-

---

[1] Stedman, the British historian, who served as an officer under Howe, says : " Sir Henry Clinton and Sir William Erskine, having reconnoitred the position of the enemy, saw that it would not be a difficult matter to turn their left flank, which would either oblige them to risk an engagement or to retire under manifest disadvantage. This intelligence being communicated to Sir William Howe, he consented to make the attempt."

ness he, with many others probably, was taken prisoner. This was an unfortunate beginning, so far as our men had abandoned one of the very posts which it had been proposed to hold ; but otherwise, there being other positions available, it was not necessarily fatal to the plan of defending the hills.[1]

Word of the attack was quickly carried to General Parsons at his quarters and to General Putnam in camp. Parsons, as the brigadier on duty, rode at once to the spot, and found "by fair daylight" not only that the guards had "fled," but that the enemy were through the woods and already on this side of the main hills. Hastily collecting some twenty of the scattered pickets, he made a show of resistance, which temporarily halted the enemy's column.[2] At the same time Putnam, whose instructions were to hold the outposts "at all hazards" with his best men, called up Stirling and directed him in person to take the two regiments nearest at hand and march down to meet the enemy.[3] Stirling promptly

[1] Hardly more than a general statement can be made in regard to the attack on the pickets at the lower road. A part of them watched Martense Lane, where, it would appear from Ewing's sketch, Hand's riflemen were posted before being relieved. Major Burd's detachment, on the same authority, was probably on the direct road to the Narrows, both parties communicating with each other at the Red Lion Tavern, which stood near the fork of the roads. Grant's main column advanced by the Narrows Road, and possibly a party of the enemy came through the Martense Lane at about the same time. The skirmish Major Burd speaks of occurred in the vicinity of Thirty-eighth and Fortieth streets, on the Narrows Road, where former residents used to say the Americans had a picket guard stationed. When the enemy came up firing took place and some men were killed ; and this firing " was the first in the neighborhood." The pickets retreated, though General Parsons was misinformed when he wrote that they did so " without firing a gun." There was firing, but no stand made.

[2] *Parsons' Letters.* Part II., Document 5.

[3] *Stirling to Washington, Aug. 29th :* " About three o'clock on the morning of the 27th I was called up, and informed by General Putnam that the enemy were advancing," etc.—*Force,* 5th Series, vol. i., p. 1245.

turned out Haslet's and Smallwood's battalions and marched down. Colonel Atlee, who was also ordered forward, was on the road before him, with that part of his regiment, about one hundred and twenty men, not already on picket ; and Huntington's Connecticut Continentals, under Lieutenant-Colonel Clark (Huntington himself being sick),[1] and Kachlein's Pennsylvania riflemen were soon after started in the same direction. Meanwhile, within the lines, the alarm-guns were fired, the whole camp roused, and the troops drawn up at the forts and breastworks. Hand's riflemen, who had but just lain down, "almost dead with fatigue," were turned out to take post in Fort Putnam and the redoubt on its left.[2]

' When Stirling reached a point within half a mile of the Red Lion he found, as Parsons had before him, that the enemy had met with little opposition or delay at the outposts on that road, and were now on the full march towards the Brooklyn lines. As there were still good positions which he could occupy, he immediately made a

---

[1] "Col. Huntington is unwell, but I hope getting a little better. He has a slow fever. Maj. Dyer is also unwell with a slow fever. Gen'l Greene has been very sick but is better. Genls. Putnam, Sullivan, Lord Sterling, Nixon, Parsons, & Heard are on Long Island and a strong part of our army."— *Letter from Col. Trumbull, Aug. 27th, 1776. Document 7.*

[2] See references on Ewing's sketch, Document 15 : " H. Fort Putnam where part of Col⁰. Hand's men commanded by Lieut C. [Lieutenant-Colonel] Chambers were detached from the Regt. to man the fort.—I. A small upper Fort where [I] was with the Col⁰ the Day of the Engagement." Lieutenant-Colonel Chambers says : " We had just got to the fort, and I had only laid down, when the alarm-guns were fired. We were compelled to turn out to the lines, and as soon as it was light saw our men and theirs engaged with field-pieces." Nearly all the accounts put Hand and his battalion at the Flatbush Pass during the battle on the 27th. This, as we now find, is an error. The battalion was worn out by its continued and effective skirmishing since the landing of the enemy, and required rest ; but of this it was to get very little, even within the lines.

disposition of his force to offer resistance.　The road here ran in a winding course along the line of the present Third Avenue, but a short distance from the bay, with here and there a dwelling which together constituted the Gowanus village or settlement.　Where the present Twenty-third Street intersects the avenue there was a small bridge on the old road which crossed a ditch or creek setting up from the bay to a low and marshy piece of ground on the left, looking south ; and just the other side of the bridge, the land rose to quite a bluff at the water's edge, which was known among the Dutch villagers as " Blockje's Bergh."　From the bluff the low hill fell gradually to the marsh or morass just mentioned, the road continuing along between them.[1]　Right here, therefore, the approach by the road was narrow, and at the corner of Twenty-third Street was confined to the crossing at the bridge.

According to his own account, and from our present knowledge of the topography, Stirling evidently came to a halt on or just this side of " Blockje's Bergh."　Seeing the British not far in his front, and taking in the situation at a glance, he ordered Atlee to post his men on the left of the road and wait the enemy's coming up, while he himself retired with Smallwood's and Haslet's to form line on a piece of " very advantageous ground " further back.　Atlee reports this preliminary move as follows : " I received orders from Lord Stirling to advance with my battalion and oppose the enemy's passing a morass or swamp at the foot of a fine rising ground, upon which

---

[1] The writer is indebted to the Hon. Teunis G. Bergen, of Bay Ridge, L. I., for an accurate description and sketch of the Gowanus Road, as it lay at the time of the battle.　His survey is followed in the " Map of the Brooklyn Defences," etc., Title, Maps.　Part II.

Jed Huntington

COLONEL SEVENTEENTH REGIMENT OF FOOT (CONN.)
BRIGADIER GENERAL 1777.

Steel Engr. F.von Egloffstein N.Y.

they were first discovered, and thereby give time to our brigade to form upon the heights. This order I immediately obeyed, notwithstanding we must be exposed without any kind of cover to the great fire of the enemy's musketry and field-pieces, charged with round and grapeshot, and finely situated upon the eminence above mentioned, having entire command of the ground I was ordered to occupy. My battalion, although new and never before having the opportunity of facing an enemy, sustained their fire until the brigade had formed ; but finding we could not possibly prevent their crossing the swamp, I ordered my detachment to file off to the left and take post in a wood upon the left of the brigade." [1] General Parsons says : " We took possession of a hill about two miles from camp, and detached Colonel Atlee to meet them further on the road ; in about sixty rods he drew up and received the enemy's fire and gave them a well-directed fire from his regiment, which did great execution, and then retreated to the hill."

This advantageous site, where Stirling had now drawn up his brigade to dispute Grant's progress, was the crest of the slope which rose northerly from the marsh and low ground around " Blockje's Bergh," and which to-day is represented by about the line of Twentieth Street. [2]   Here

---

[1] *Atlee's Journal. Force*, 5th Series, vol. i., p. 1251.

[2] Probably the earliest of modern attempts to identify the site where Stirling formed his line was that made in 1839 by Maj. D. B. Douglass, formerly of the United States Army. Greenwood Cemetery, says Mr. Cleveland in his history of *Greenwood*, owes its present beautiful appearance largely to this officer's " energy and taste," Douglass having been one of the first surveyors of the ground. He located Stirling's position on what was then known as Wyckoff's hill, between Eighteenth and Twentieth streets ; and tradition and all the original documents confirm this selection. This was a lower elevation in the general slope from the main ridge towards the bay. Stirling simply drew his men up in a straight line from the road towards the hill-tops, and beyond him on the same line or more in

was an elevation or ridge favorable for defence, and here Stirling proposed to make a stand. On the right, next to the road, he posted Smallwood's battalion, under Major Gist; further along up the hillside were the Delawares, under Major MacDonough;[1] and on their left, in the woods above, Atlee's men formed after falling back from their attempt to stop the enemy.

When Kachlein's[2] riflemen came up, the general stationed part of them along hedges near the foot of the hill in front of the Marylanders, and part in front of the woods near Atlee. The line had hardly been formed before it was observed that the enemy threatened to overlap it on the left, and Parsons was accordingly ordered to take Atlee's and Huntington's regiments and move still further into the woods to defeat the designs on that flank.

Finding Stirling thus thrown across their path, the British also drew up in line and disposed their force as if intending to attack him at once. About opposite to the Marylanders, possibly on Blockje's Bergh, Grant posted the sixth brigade in two lines, while the fourth brigade was extended in a single line from the low ground to the top of the hills in Greenwood Cemetery.

Here, then, was a regular battle formation—Grant and Stirling opposing each other—and we may regard it with interest not only as the only line of battle preserved, on

advance, was Parsons. The map in Sparks' *Washington* putting Stirling down near the Narrows is erroneous.

[1] The colonels and lieutenant-colonels of both these regiments were detained at New York as members of the court-martial which tried Lieutenant-colonel Zedwitz, of MacDougall's regiment, charged with treasonable correspondence with the enemy. They joined their regiments after the battle.

[2] This name appears in other accounts as Kichline or Keichline. It is properly Kachlein, being so spelled by other members of this officer's family.

the American side at least, during this day's struggle, but as being the first instance in the Revolution where we met the British in the open field.   Before this it had been fighting under different conditions—the regulars mowed down at Bunker Hill, Montgomery attempting to storm Quebec, or Moultrie bravely holding a fort against a fleet ; now the soldiers on either side stood face to face, and the opportunity seemed at hand to fairly test their native courage.   Greatly disproportionate, however, was the strength of these two lines.   Stirling's, all told, contained not more than sixteen hundred men ; while Grant's, which besides the two brigades included the Forty-second Highlanders and two companies of American loyalists, was little less than seven thousand strong. But if we find here a threatening attitude, let us not expect any desperate fighting.   It was not Grant's object to bring on an engagement at this early hour, now seven o'clock in the morning, for he wished to keep Stirling where he was until the other movements of the day were developed.   He contented himself with appearing to be on the point of attack, and Stirling could do no more than prepare for a stubborn defence of his ground.

The first move of the British was to send forward a small body of light troops from their left, which advanced to within one hundred and fifty yards of Stirling's right. This would bring them not far from the little bridge on the road, where, from behind hedges and apple-trees, they opened fire on our advanced riflemen, who replied with spirit.

In the mean time, Stirling was reinforced by a two-gun battery from Knox's artillery, under Captain-Lieutenant Benajah Carpenter, of Providence, R. I., which was at once placed on the hillside to command the road, and, according to Stirling, "the only approach for some hundred yards," which must have been that part of the road running over the bridge. The skirmishing was kept up at a lively rate for about two hours, and occasionally, it would appear, our entire line engaged in the fire. Of the particular incidents which occurred at this point we have almost nothing ; but perhaps, from one or two mere references that have been preserved, the whole scene can be imagined. "The enemy," writes one of the Maryland soldiers, "advanced towards us, upon which Lord Stirling, who commanded, drew up in a line and offered them battle in true English taste. The British then advanced within about 200 yards of us, and began a heavy fire from their cannon and mortars, for both the Balls and Shells flew very fast, now and then taking off a head. Our men stood it amazingly well ; not even one of them shewed a Disposition to shrink. Our orders were not to fire until the Enemy came within fifty yards of us, but when they perceived we stood their fire so cooly and resolutely they declined coming any nearer, altho' treble our number." [1] Colonel Haslet, although not with his regiment, reported to his friend Cæsar Rodney that "the Delawares drew up on the side of a hill, and stood upwards of four hours, with a firm, determined countenance, in close array, their colors flying, the enemy's artillery playing on them all the while, not daring to advance and attack them;" [2] and his ensign, Stephens, pointed with pride to the standard "torn with shot" while held in his hands.

Galled perhaps by the fire of Carpenter's battery, the British light troops retired to their main line, and the

---

[1] *Extracts from the Stiles Diary* in vol. ii., p. 488, of the Long Island Historical Society's *Memoirs*.

[2] *Haslet to Rodney. Force*, 5th Series, vol. ii., p. 881.

firing from this time was continued chiefly by the artillery. On their left they advanced one howitzer to within three hundred yards of Stirling's right, and in front of his left they opened with another piece at a distance of six hundred yards, and until about eleven o'clock the cannonading was vigorously sustained. Here was an engagement begun, and for four hours Stirling's men were encouraged with the belief that they were holding back the invaders. Their general inspired them with his own resolution and bravery, both by word and example; and their good conduct in this their first experience under fire, exposed without cover to cannon and musket shot, indicated that Grant could not have pushed them back without suffering severely. The casualties had not been large, but the nerves of the men were none the less tested by the ordeal. Among the Marylanders, Captain Edward Veazey, who commanded one of the independent companies, doing duty with Smallwood's regiment, fell " early in the engagement ;" and either here, or on the retreat at a later hour, also fell Captain Carpenter, whose battery had been doing good work on Stirling's line. Of the Delawares, Major MacDonough and Lieutenants Anderson and Course were slightly wounded. Accounts agree that few of the men in either Smallwood's, Haslet's, or Kachlein's battalions were killed or wounded while holding this position.

The three regiments immediately under Stirling thus not only appeared to be doing well, but had actually proved themselves the best of soldiers, both by keeping an unwavering line when the British light troops advanced, as if to be followed by the main column, and in maintaining their ranks and discipline when subjected to the subsequent fire of the artillery.

Nor were these the only men who did themselves credit. That little party composed of Atlee's and Huntington's battalions, under General Parsons, which had gone into the woods to protect Stirling's left, must not be forgotten. Our published accounts heretofore fail to particularize the service it did; but it was of no small account, as Parson's and Atlee's independent testimony and the returns of the British losses clearly show. The party, not much over three hundred strong, filed off to the left, and soon came in sight of "a hill of clear ground" about three hundred yards distant, which was judged to be the proper situation from which to watch the enemy.[1] The direction Parsons' men took, the distances mentioned, and the fact that tradition associates the site with part of the fighting on that day, can leave no doubt but that the hill referred to here was one of the two or three distinct elevations in the north-western section of Greenwood Cemetery, and to one of which has since been given the commemorative title of "Battle Hill." A spot fitly named, for around it some brave work was done! As the detachment neared the hill, the British flanking troops were also observed to be marching to seize it. Atlee seeing this hurried his men to reach it first, but the enemy were there before him and poured a volley into his battalion. Fortunately, not being well aimed, this did trifling damage, but under the shock a part of his men, with two companies from the Delaware regiment, which had been ordered to join them, wavered. Rallying the most of them, Atlee soon ordered an advance up the hill, telling the men at the same time "to preserve their fire and aim aright;" and they all pushed forward with so much

---

[1] *Atlee's Journal. Force*, 5th Series, vol. i., p. 1251.

resolution, and apparently with such an effective discharge
of their pieces, that the enemy fell back, leaving behind
them twelve killed and a lieutenant and four privates
wounded.   In this encounter Atlee lost his " worthy
friend " and lieutenant-colonel, Caleb Parry, who fell dead
upon the field without a groan, while cheering on the battalion.   Ordering four soldiers to take the remains of " the
hero" back into the Brooklyn lines, Atlee halted his
" brave fellows" on the hill, and all Parsons' command
here took post to await the further movements of the
British on this flank.   The force they had met and
repulsed consisted of the Twenty-third and Forty-
fourth and a part of the Seventeenth regiments, by
whom they were soon to be attacked again.   In half an
hour after the first affair the enemy formed for another
effort to seize the hill, but again Atlee's and Huntington's
men opened upon them, and for a second time compelled
their retreat, with the loss of Lieutenant-Colonel Grant, a
brave and valued field-officer of the Fortieth Regiment,
whose fall gave ground for the report, credited for some
days after in the American army, that Major-General
Grant, the division commander, was among the enemy's
killed in the battle of Long Island.   Parsons' men by this
time had fired away all their ammunition (Atlee says that
his battalion, at least, had entirely emptied their cartridge-
boxes), and had used what charges could be got from the
enemy's dead and wounded, when Huntington's ammunition cart " very luckily" came on the ground, and the men
were re-supplied for still a third attack, which was threatened with the assistance of the Forty-second Highlanders ; but the British this time kept a safe distance, and
Parsons and Atlee remained on the hill, where they collected the enemy's dead and placed their wounded under

the shelter of the trees. Thus bravely and effectively had this small body of Americans protected Stirling's flank and dealt the enemy the severest blows they suffered at any one point during the day, and this, as in the case of Stirling's men, with but small loss to themselves. From behind fences and trees, and, if tradition is correct, from the tops of trees as well, and from open ground on the hill, they kept up their destructive fire and successfully accomplished what they had been called upon to do.[1] That the British did not intend at this hour to drive Parsons and Atlee from their post is no detraction from the spirited fight made by these officers and their men, who knew nothing of the enemy's intentions, and who actually won the field from the troops they met. All along this front, from Stirling holding the road on the right to Parsons holding the left, with a long gap between them, the fighting thus far had resulted most favorably to the American side. The main line, as already stated, had lost not more than two officers killed and three or four wounded, with a small number of men; while Parsons and Atlee both report that in addition to the death of Lieutenant-Colonel Parry they lost only one or two men wounded. But, on the part of the British, Grant's two brigades, with the Forty-second Highlanders and the

---

[1] Parsons' reference to this affair at or near "Battle Hill" in Greenwood is as follows: "I was ordered with Col. Atlee and part of his Reg't, and Lt. Col. Clark with Col. Huntington's Reg't to cover the left flank of our main body. This we executed though our number did at no time exceed 300 men and we were attacked three several times by two regiments, y[e] 44th and 23[d] and repulsed them in every attack with considerable loss. The number of dead we had collected together and the heap the enemy had made we supposed amounted to about 60. We had 12 or 14 wounded prisoners who we caused to be dressed and their wounds put in the best state our situation would admit."—*Document* 5.

See Colonel Atlee's journal in *Force's Archives* for a full account of the part his battalion took in this fighting.

two companies of New York loyalists, lost, according to Howe's official report, two officers killed and four wounded, and among the men twenty-five killed and ninety-nine wounded. The four regiments alone which at different times encountered Parsons—the Seventeenth, Twenty-third, Forty-fourth, and Forty-second—lost in the aggregate eighty-six officers and men killed and wounded.

While, now, Stirling and Parsons seemed to be effectually blocking the advance of the British by the lower road and the Greenwood hills, what was the situation at the other passes?

Up to eight o'clock, some five hours after Grant's appearance at the Red Lion, no determined attack had been reported from either the Flatbush or Bedford roads. The Hessians had made some show of advancing from Flatbush at an early hour, but they had not as yet driven in our pickets, although approaching near enough for the guns at the breastwork on the road to fire upon them. No word had come from Miles; nothing had been heard from the patrol of officers at the Jamaica Pass. Whatever tactics the enemy were pursuing, it was evident that at this hour they had not developed indications of a simultaneous advance "all along the line." Were they making their principal push against Stirling? Were they waiting for the fleet to work its way up to co-operate? or would they still attempt to force the passes and the hills at all points and overcome the American out-guards by sheer weight of numbers? Whatever theory our generals may have entertained at this time as to the intentions of the British—a point which we have no means of determining —it is certain that at about half-past eight or nine o'clock Major-General Sullivan rode out from the Brooklyn lines to the Flatbush Pass, with the evident purpose of examining the situation at that and other points, and of obtaining the latest information respecting the enemy's movements. We have this substantially from his own pen : "I went," he says, "to the hill near Flatbush to reconnoitre the enemy."[1] Nothing more natural, and nothing more necessary ; the situation at that hour required that some responsible general officer should be in this vicinity to direct the disposition of the troops the moment the enemy uncovered their plan. Stirling on the lower road had his hands full, and it became some one's duty to see that he was not put in danger by any possible mishap elsewhere on the hills. Sullivan, therefore, the second in command, went out to "examine" and to "reconnoitre." He had been out the evening before, making the rounds with Putnam ; to him Miles had reported the situation of affairs on the extreme left ; and it was by his general orders that the last detail of guards had been made for each of the passes. He was accordingly familiar with the plan of the outer defence, and upon reaching the Flatbush Pass, where, as Miles states, he took his station at the redoubt or barricade on the road, he seems to have given certain directions on the strength of the information he had obtained. If we may credit the writer of one of the letters published at the time, the general was

[1] Most of our writers are led into the error of supposing that Sullivan was already at the Flatbush Pass, and that when he went to reconnoitre he started from this point. The general says : "I went to the Hill near Flatbush to reconnoitre the enemy, and with a picket of four hundred men was surrounded by the enemy," etc. He went to the hill—where from ? The main camp, necessarily. We already had our pickets well out in front, and had Sullivan gone beyond these he would have come upon the Hessians. Besides his position fully overlooked Flatbush, and no reconnoissance was necessary. Miles states that the general remained at the redoubt. The quotation above means no more than that Sullivan went out from the Brooklyn lines, and afterwards was surrounded and fought with four hundred of the guard who were there at the Pass with him.

told that the main body of the enemy were advancing by the lower road, " whereupon he ordered another battalion to the assistance of Lord Stirling, keeping 800 men to guard the pass." [1] It is not difficult to accept this as a correct statement of what actually occurred, because it is what we should expect would have taken place under the circumstances. That Sullivan took out any additional troops with him when he went to the pass does not appear, but doubtless some were sent there. But as to this Flatbush Pass, the most that can be said with any degree of certainty is, that at about nine o'clock in the morning the Hessians still remained comparatively quiet at the foot of the hills below ; that our guards and pickets stood at their different posts, not in regular line, but detached on either side of the road, the commander of each party governing himself as necessity required ; that they were expected to hold that point stubbornly, if for no other purpose now than to secure Stirling's line of retreat ; and that if attacked they were to be reinforced. At the hour Sullivan reached the pass the situation at all points appeared to be satisfactory.

But little did the Americans suspect that at the very moment their defence seemed well arranged and their outguards vigilant they were already in the web which the enemy had been silently weaving around them during the night. That flanking column ! Skilfully had it played its part in the British plans, and with crushing weight was it now to fall upon our outpost guards, who felt themselves secure along the hills and in the woods. Cross again into the opposite camp and follow the approach of this unlooked-for danger. First, Lord Howe withdrew Corn-

[1] *Document* 19.

wallis from Flatbush to Flatlands towards evening on the 26th, and at nine o'clock at night set this flanking corps in motion. Sir Henry Clinton commanded the van, which consisted of the light dragoons and the brigade of light infantry. Cornwallis and the reserve immediately followed ; and after him marched the First Brigade and the Seventy-first Regiment, with fourteen pieces of field artillery. These troops formed the advance corps, and were followed at a proper interval by Lord Percy and Howe himself, with the Second, Third, and Fifth brigades, the guards, and ten guns. The Forty-ninth Regiment, with four twelve-pounders, and the baggage with a separate guard, brought up the rear. All told, this column was hardly less than ten thousand strong. With three Flatbush Tories acting as guides, it took up the march and headed, as Howe reports, "across the country through the new lots" towards the Jamaica Pass, moving slowly and cautiously along the road from Flatlands until it reached Shoemaker's Bridge, which crossed a creek emptying into Jamaica Bay, when the column struck over the fields to the Jamaica Road, where it came to a halt in the open lots a short distance south-east of the pass, and directly in front of Howard's Halfway House.[1]

Here now occurred one of those incidents which, though insignificant in themselves, sometimes become fatalities that turn the scale of battle. The five American officers whom General Sullivan had sent out the evening before to patrol this pass had stationed themselves at this time, now between two and three o'clock on the morning of the 27th, a short distance east of Howard's house, apparently waiting for sounds of the enemy on the line of the road.

[1] Consult map of the battle-field, Part II.

Evidently they had no thought of his approach "across lots" from the direction of Flatlands, or they could not have left the pass unwatched by one or more of the party. For most of them, this was the first tour of military duty of so responsible a nature, and whatever mistakes they made may be referred to their inexperience or ignorance of the relative situation of the roads in that vicinity. Who had charge of the party does not appear. So far as known, only one of them, Lieutenant Van Wagenen, had seen any considerable service ; but although something of a veteran, having entered the army in 1775 and charged with Montgomery upon Quebec, he could have known nothing of the country he was now patrolling. Lieutenants Troup and Dunscomb were young Columbia College graduates of two years' standing, who had eagerly taken up the cause of the colonists in the midst of adverse associations. Gilliland may have once been an officer in McDougall's regiment, and Hoogland was adjutant of Colonel Lasher's battalion. Had these officers, who without doubt were all mounted, been patrolling at the pass or nearer the lines, the events of the 27th might have worn a far different aspect. As it was, the British by coming into the road at Howard's had put themselves in the rear of the patrol, and its capture was quickly effected. Captain William Glanville Evelyn, " a gallant officer" of the Fourth Infantry, or King's Own, and a descendant of the eminent John Evelyn, of England, led the British advance this night, and it fell to his fortune to surround and capture all five American officers and send them immediately to Clinton, who commanded the leading column. Here was a blow inflicted upon us by the British, the real importance of which they themselves even were ignorant of, for they had made prisoners of the only patrol that was

12

watching the Jamaica route from the pass down to the very lines themselves !

Clinton "interrogated" the prisoners upon the spot, and ascertained from them that the pass had not been occupied by the Americans. He then attempted to obtain information of the position at Brooklyn and the number of troops now there, by pressing the officers with questions, when Dunscomb, indignant at the advantage he was taking of their situation, replied to Clinton that "under other circumstances he would not dare insult them in that manner." For this the young lieutenant was called "an impudent rebel," and the British officers threatened to have him hanged. Dunscomb's courage was equal to the occasion, and, scouting the threat, declared that Washington would hang man for man in return, and that as for himself he should give Clinton no further information. But stoutly as Dunscomb and his fellows maintained their rights and honor as prisoners, their capture was one of the fatal turns that brought misfortune to the American army.[1]

[1] Hardly one of our modern accounts refers to this patrol or its capture. The incident, however, affected the situation gravely. Howe mentions it in his report as follows : " General Clinton being arrived within half a mile of the pass about two hours before daybreak, halted, and settled his disposition for the attack. One of his patrols falling in with a patrol of the enemy's officers took them ; and the General learning from their information that the Rebels had not occupied the pass, detached a battalion of Light Infantry to secure it." Gordon says this : " One of his [Clinton's] patrols falls in with a patrol of American officers on horseback, who are trepanned and made prisoners." The letter in the *South Carolina Gazette* (*Document* 19) is to similar effect : " Five officers were also sent out on horseback to patrol the last-mentioned road and that leading to Jamaica, . . . and were all made prisoners." Still stronger is the testimony of a letter to be found in the *Autobiography and Correspondence of Mary Granville, Mrs. Delany, with Interesting Reminiscences of George III. and Queen Charlotte, &c.*, London, 1862. " The Hon. Mrs. Boscawen to Mrs. Delany.—*Glan Villa*, 17th Oct. 1776. . . . To compleat the prosperity of my journey I found on my return to y⁰ inn the most delightful news of our success on Long Island so

Upon learning that the pass was unguarded, Clinton, as Howe reports, ordered one of the light infantry battalions to occupy it, and soon after the main column followed. It would appear, however, that he still moved cautiously, and that the battalion, or the troops that followed, avoided a direct approach, and reached the Jamaica Road on the other side of the pass by a roundabout lane known as the Rockaway Path. The innkeeper Howard was waked up, and with his son compelled to

that I had a most agreeable supper and drank health to the noble brothers [the two Howes]. We have had a letter from Capt. Evelyn from the field of battle ; he was in y⁰ brigade of light infantry, and took 5 officers prisoners who were sent to observe our motions. He mentions Dr. Boscawen's son being well, for whom we were in great care, being the only child. O ! to compleat this by good news from N. York and then peace !" We know who these officers were from several sources, the most authoritative and important being the documents left by one of the party himself, Lieutenant Van Wagenen, and now in the possession of his grandson, Mr. Gerret H. Van Wagenen, of Brooklyn. This officer had been sent down to Philadelphia in charge of prisoners from Canada. At this point his deposition states that " on his return to New York he found the enemy landing upon Long Island, and being a supernumerary he went to Long Island and offered his services to Gen'l Sullivan, who requested him, and four other officers, namely, Robert Troup, Edward Dunscomb, William Guilderland and Jeromus Hooghland, to go and reconnoitre the enemy, who were observed to be in motion, and in the various advances on the enemy, fell in with a body of horse and infantry by whom he and his little party were made prisoners, and continued a Prisoner for about twenty-two months." Respecting the questioning of the officers by Clinton, there is good authority. Lieutenants Troup and Dunscomb, who afterwards rose to the rank of Lieutenant-colonel and Captain respectively, have daughters still living in New York, and from their own recollections and from papers in their possession, the account given in the text is collated. At the time of Captain Dunscomb's death one or more letters were published by friends who had the particulars of the incident directly from him. (See biographical sketches of these officers, Part II.) The sending out of officers on such duty as was required this night, was not unusual. The British scouts who preceded the expedition to Lexington in 1775 were officers in disguise. Similar instances during the war could be recalled as at Brandywine. Mr. Henry Onderdonk, Jr., of Jamaica, states, in his carefully compiled and valuable collection of *Revolutionary Incidents on Long Island*, that the patrol was captured under a tree east of Howard's House.

guide the British around to the road, where it was discovered, as the patrol had stated, that the pass was unguarded.   When the whole force had marched through
to the other side it was halted for a brief " rest and
refreshment," and then continued down the road to Bedford, where the van, consisting of dragoons and light infantry, arrived about half-past eight o'clock in the morning.   So this flanking corps had succeeded in making a
slow, difficult, and circuitous march of some nine miles
from Flatlands during the night, and had placed itself
directly in the rear of the left of the American outposts,
before its approach was known in the Brooklyn camp.   It
was now nearer the lines than were our picket guards at
either of the outposts on the hills, and by a swift advance
down the Jamaica Road and along the Gowanus Road to
its intersection with the Port Road, it could have interposed itself across every avenue of retreat from the hills
to the lines.   It was Howe's plan to cut off the American
retreat entirely, but while successful in reaching our rear
he fortunately failed to reap the fullest advantage of his
move.   The loss he was now able to inflict upon us was
hardly a third of what might have been possible.   But for
the Americans it was more than enough.   From this point
followed trial and disaster.   The day, which had opened
so promisingly on the lower road, had already, at early
dawn, been lost to them at the Jamaica Pass.

What next happened after the British reached Bedford ?   What, in the first place, had Miles been about in
the woods on the extreme left that the enemy should
gain his rear before he knew it ?   Fortunately we have
the colonel himself and his lieutenant-colonel, Brodhead,
to tell us much if they do not explain all.   Miles then
puts it on record that, on the day before the engagement,

General Sullivan came to his camp, to whom he reported his belief that when the enemy moved they would fall into the Jamaica Road, and he hoped there were troops there to watch them.   On the following morning, at about seven o'clock, firing began at the redoubt on the Flatbush Road, and he immediately marched in that direction, but was stopped by Colonel Wyllys at the Bedford Pass, who informed him that he could not pass on, as they were to defend the Bedford Road.   "Colonel Wyllys bearing a Continental, and I a State commission," says Miles, "he was considered a senior officer, and I was obliged to submit; but I told him I was convinced the main body of the enemy would take the Jamaica Road, that there was no probability of their coming along the road he was then guarding, and if he would not let me proceed to where the firing was, I would return and endeavor to get into the Jamaica Road before General Howe.   To this he consented, and I immediately made a retrograde march, and after marching nearly two miles, the whole distance through woods, I arrived within sight of the Jamaica Road, and to my great mortification I saw the main body of the enemy in full march between me and our lines, and the baggage guard just coming into the road."

Had Miles been surprised?   This is one of the problems of the battle.   For four days he had been on the watch on this flank, and now the British were in his rear!   Would he have made that "retrograde" march this morning, when the strictest attention to one's particular orders was necessary, unless he had known that there were no troops on the Jamaica Road, and unless it was a part of his duty to reconnoitre in that direction?   But he was now making a stout effort to find and fight Howe, and before charging him with a blunder let us follow the battle to its close.

One of Miles' soldiers hurried into camp and reported to Putnam that infantry and cavalry were marching down from the Jamaica Pass;[1] but all too late, for right upon the heels of the information came the enemy! They pushed down the road from Bedford, and across the country, to attack the American outguards in the rear, while the Hessians were to come up in front. So, if we glance over the field again at about half-past nine or ten o'clock on this eventful morning, we find the whole aspect changed, and our entire force on the hills apparently caught in a trap. Stirling was still facing Grant upon the right, but his rear was in danger; while Sullivan and the picket guards at the other passes were wedged in between the two powerful columns under Howe and De Heister. What now was done? Who escaped?

Evidently Miles, way out in the woods on the left, had the least prospect of getting back to the Brooklyn lines. When he found the British on the road between him and camp he first proposed to attack their baggage guard and cut his way through to the Sound, but on consulting his officers (his first battalion alone being with him) he turned about, determined to attempt a retreat to camp. It was impossible for him to succeed, for he had a march of full three miles to make; and after encountering the enemy once or twice in the woods, he, with many of his men, was compelled to surrender. Brodhead, while marching through the woods in Indian file to join him, was also attacked and his men dispersed, though most of them, with the lieutenant-colonel himself, escaped

---

[1] *Force*, 5th Series, vol. i., p. 1195.

to the lines. The rout was speedily communicated to the guards at the two remaining points. At the Bedford Pass the detachments under Colonel Wyllys and Lieutenant-Colonel Wills appear to have realized their danger about the time the British reached Bedford village. Finding Miles' troops broken up and flying, they too, through fear of being intercepted, took up the retreat. Finally, at the Flatbush Pass—the last point in the outpost line to be attacked—the peril was still greater, for now the Hessians were moving up in front. Here, as we have seen, General Sullivan had just arrived to examine the situation. He had not long to wait, however, before the nature of that situation fully dawned upon him and the troops at the pass. While watching the Hessians at Flatbush they suddenly hear the rattle of musketry on the left of their rear, where British light infantry and dragoons are beginning to chase and fire upon Miles, Brodhead, and Wyllys, and their broken detachments. The Flatbush Pass was a point to be held, for it was the centre of the outpost line, and retreat therefrom would endanger Stirling ; but Sullivan and his men must act promptly if they would do no more even than save themselves, for the enemy by this time are much nearer the Brooklyn lines than they. Just what occurred at this juncture the records fail to tell us clearly. Did Sullivan, as one letter states, immediately send word to Stirling to retreat?[1]

[1] The supposition that Stirling commanded outside of the lines on Long Island is erroneous. He had command of the reserves in camp (Orders of August 25th), and was the proper officer to call upon to reinforce any part of the outer line in case of attack. Sullivan says, " Lord Stirling commanded the main body without the lines ;" by which is meant that he was with the principal force that went out, as he was. Until the attack, the general officer of the day was in charge of the outposts. Sullivan governed himself according to circumstances. He was to be second in command under Putnam within the lines, he writes ; but the situation soon required his presence outside, where he was also familiar with the dispositions.

This would have been the first and natural step. Whoever the commanding officer might be at the Flatbush Pass, it was for him to watch the situation at the outpost line and give orders to the right and left. All depended on what was done at that pass. If the guards there gave way all the others must give way instantly. Whether the word, therefore, reached Stirling or not, we must believe that Sullivan sent it, as he ought to have done, and is reported to have done. As for the general himself and his party, retreat was the only alternative. Leaving the advanced pickets to fall back before the Hessians, they turned towards the British in their rear. Very soon they encountered the light infantry and dragoons, who were now engaging in the attack with the highest dash and spirit. Reinforced by four companies of the guards, the latter captured three pieces of our artillery—the same, doubtless, which had just been playing upon the Hessians, but were now turned, in the retreat, upon the British—and which our gunners defended "heroically" to the last. Sullivan and his men fought well, and apparently in separate parties, until nearly all that had been stationed at the Flatbush Pass succeeded in breaking or making their way through to the lines.

Meanwhile the Hessians appeared. They came up from the Flatbush plains with drums beating and colors flying. Donop's grenadiers and yagers led, and immediately after them followed the veteran De Heister at the head of the brigades. Reaching the summit of the ridge, they deployed their lines, and putting their sharpshooters in advance, moved rapidly upon the position which our Flatbush Pass guard had just abandoned. They met with little opposition, for they had nothing before them but our scattered pickets. Soon, however, they fell in with the retreating groups which the British had cut off from the lines and had pushed back into the hills, and upon these they fell fiercely, and in many instances cruelly. Where they found a rifleman resisting too long, they pinned him with their bayonets, and to some of the wounded they showed no mercy. Most of the prisoners fell into their hands, for the reason that they had been driven towards the Hessians by the British ; but otherwise the day afforded no opportunity for fair fighting between these " foreigners" and our troops.[1]

Thus all along the hills, from the Flatbush Pass to the extreme left, our outer guards were in full retreat ! It was a flight and fight to reach the Brooklyn lines ! Ten o'clock—and Miles, Brodhead, Wyllys, Wills, Johnston, Henshaw, and Cornell, with two thousand men, were hurrying through the woods, down the slopes and across the fields, some singly, some in groups, some keeping together in companies, some in battalions, all aiming for

[1] The Hessians are usually credited with taking a prominent part in this battle, whereas the day was practically decided before they came up. Necessarily our guards at the Flatbush Pass knew that the British were in their rear as soon or sooner than the Hessians knew it. They therefore turned to meet this unexpected enemy. What Olney and Henshaw say settles this point. Olney states that Cornell marched towards the lines on hearing firing in his rear, leaving Olney to reinforce his pickets in front of the Hessians. Henshaw writes that, finding the enemy between him and the lines, and knowing no orders could come to retreat, he marched for camp. Cornell and Henshaw were old officers, knew the ground thoroughly, and saw at once that they must retreat. No mention is made of the Hessians. Lieutenant Olney was in front of the latter some time before he followed after his regiment. Howe reports that it was the *British* who took our guns in that part of the field. If there was any such severe fighting at that pass, as Von Elking makes out, would the Hessians have lost but two men killed—all that they lost during the day ? There are errors of fact in this writer's account. The most that the Hessians did was to chase, capture, and sometimes bayonet those of our soldiers whom the British had already routed. The real fighting of the day was done by Howe's English troops, and the very best he had, principally the light infantry, grenadiers, dragoons, and Highlanders.

one objective—the camp! Here they fought the light infantry; there they were charged upon by the dragoons; those who were intercepted fell into the hands or upon the bayonets of the Hessians. It was a trying and desperate situation from which there was no relief and for a long time the woods echoed with the shouts and cries of the contending parties. But upon the whole the loss to the Americans up to this time was not heavy, and could Stirling have been saved, the enemy would have had no great victory to boast of. Full half of Miles' two battalions reached the lines; Wyllys' and Chester's suffered but slightly; Henshaw and Cornell brought their men in without much loss, and in comparatively good order; the greatest blow to the Jerseymen was the death of their brave colonel, Johnston, their casualties otherwise being light; and Knowlton's hundred rangers just saved themselves from the dragoons, "with the utmost difficulty and on the full run." The artillerymen suffered more. General Sullivan himself, after showing good courage and avoiding capture until noon, endeavored to conceal himself, but was found and made prisoner by three Hessian grenadiers.[1]

The day was lost at the left and centre, and it only remains to return to Stirling on the right. This general stood his ground firmly, though the firing in his rear grew

---

[1] During this fighting by the British infantry, Cornwallis and the reserves moved straight down the Jamaica Road. The Thirty-third Regiment and the grenadiers in their pursuit of some of the American fugitives approached the fortified lines between Fort Greene and Fort Putnam, and showed such eagerness to storm them that, according to Howe's report, it required repeated orders to hold them back. On the part of the Americans, Little reports that the enemy "attempted to force our lines, but soon retreated, being met with a smart fire from our breastworks;" and Little, no doubt, was at Fort Greene, an eye-witness.

ominously distinct.   He refused to retreat, says Scott, for want of orders.   If Sullivan sent him orders, as we have assumed on one writer's authority that he did, they failed to reach him.   The time had come for the general to act on his own judgment, and finding his salvation dependent on an immediate retreat, he fell back from Grant's front between eleven and twelve o'clock, but only to discover that he too was surrounded.   The force which had anticipated him was Cornwallis with the Seventy-first Regiment and the Second Grenadiers, and they were holding his line of retreat on the Gowanus Road.   Stirling, realizing his danger, at once determined upon the only manœuvre that promised escape for any of his command.   Upon his left lay the Gowanus marsh and creek, where both were at their broadest, and where a crossing had never been attempted.   But now the attempt must be made, or every man is lost.   Upon the other side of the creek are the Brooklyn peninsula, the lines, and safety.   Stirling therefore ordered his men to make their way across as they could, while, to protect them as they forded or swam, he himself took Gist and half the Maryland battalion and proceeded to attack Cornwallis. Against all the misfortunes of the day this piece of resolution and true soldiership stands out in noble relief. The Marylanders followed their general without flinching, and were soon " warmly engaged " with the enemy, who had posted themselves at a house—the old " Cortelyou" house —above the upper mills near the intersection of the Port and Gowanus roads.   They rallied to the attack several times, as Stirling reports, and seemed on the point of dislodging Cornwallis, when reinforcements came up, and the British drove back the Marylanders into a piece of woods.   Here, with conspicuous courage and determination, they formed again for still another effort to break through. Stirling's example was inspiring. "He encouraged and animated our young soldiers," writes Gist, "with almost invincible resolution." But his handful of brave men had done all that was possible, and in their last charge they were met by great numbers and forced to retire again, "with much precipitation and confusion." [1] They broke up into small parties and sought escape. Nine only, among whom was Major Gist, succeeded in crossing the creek, the rest having retreated into the woods.[2] Stirling endeavored to get into the lines between the British and Fort Box, or by way of the mill-

[1] The conduct of the Marylanders was soldierly beyond praise. But some accounts subject them to a singular martyrdom, killing every man of the two hundred and fifty-nine reported missing. As there was but one officer wounded, or at the most one killed and one wounded in the party, according to the official returns, the proportion of men killed was doubtless small. The letter in *Force*, 5th Series, vol. i., p. 1232, referring to this attack, bears every evidence of having been written by Gist himself, and it is quoted as his in the text. In this letter Gist speaks of being surrounded on all sides, and then adds : "The impracticability of forcing through such a formidable body of troops rendered it the height of rashness and imprudence to risk the lives of our remaining party in a third attempt, and it became necessary for us to endeavor to effect our escape in the best manner we possibly could." This shows that there were many left to disperse. Their prudence was equal to their courage.

[2] Before Stirling's fight with Cornwallis took place, the mill and little bridge at the further end of the mill-dam across Gowanus Creek were burned down. Colonel Smallwood charged "a certain Colonel Ward" with the act, and claimed that the destruction of the bridge prevented the escape of Stirling and the Marylanders with him. Mr. Bancroft and Mr. Field repeat the charge. But Smallwood is contradicted both by Stirling and Gist, the former stating that he could not get by the British on the road full half a mile beyond the bridge, and the latter adding that he was driven back into the woods. The charge had no foundation, the bridge not having been set on fire until after the enemy took possession of the road above (see Ewing's sketch). The "Colonel Ward" was Colonel Jonathan Ward, of Massachusetts ; and the probability is that he and Colonel Tyler, both of whom lost some men during the day, had been sent out on the Port Road, but, finding Cornwallis there, retreated, burning mill and bridge to obstruct the latter's possible advance in that quarter.

dam, but finding this impossible, he turned, ran through their fire, and eluding pursuit around a hill, made his way to the Hessian corps and surrendered himself to General De Heister. He had sacrificed himself and party as prisoners, but his main object was accomplished. The rest of the command was saved! They crossed the marsh and creek with a loss of but two or three killed and six or eight drowned.

It was during this scene in the incidents of the day that Washington and his staff came upon the ground. They had remained at New York watching the fleet, when, finding that no danger was to be apprehended from that quarter, they crossed to Long Island. From the top of one of the hills within the lines, possibly Cobble Hill, the Chief witnessed Stirling's retreat and fight, and is said there to have been profoundly moved as he saw how many brave men he must inevitably lose. Colonel Smallwood, of the Marylanders, who had rejoined his regiment, petitioned for a force to march out and assist Stirling, but the general declined on account of the risks involved. Douglas's Connecticut levies, just coming up from the ferry,[1] were sent to the extreme right opposite the mouth of Gowanus Creek, where, with Captain Thomas' Maryland Independent Company and two pieces of artillery, they stood ready to prevent pursuit of the retreating party by the enemy.

Last of all, where were Parsons and Atlee? Had they been holding that hill in Greenwood all the morning, with a tenacity worthy of veterans, only to be swallowed

---

[1] The reinforcements that came over during the forenoon, besides Douglas's regiment, were Sage's and Selden's, which, with Douglas, completed Wadsworth's brigade on that side ; Charles Webb's, of McDougall's brigade ; and Scott, with Malcom and Humphrey's men, or the rest of his brigade.

up in the defeat and confusion of the day? Such was to be their fate. For some unexplained reason, when Stirling fell back, he failed to inform Parsons of his move. Both Parsons and Atlee state that no word reached them to join the general, and that it was greatly to their surprise when they found the line, whose flank they had been protecting, no longer there. Whatever the mistake, there was no time to lose, for the enemy were now pressing on this little force, and it must retreat as Stirling had done. But it soon found itself more effectually hemmed in than any party in the field. Cornwallis, after driving the Marylanders back, had complete command of the road, and as Parsons and Atlee came along they found it impossible even to reach the marsh. Some escaped, but the greater part turned into the woods and were all taken. Atlee, with twenty-three men, avoided capture until five o'clock in the afternoon; while Parsons, more fortunate, hid in a swamp, having escaped from the action and pursuit "as by a miracle," and with seven men made his way into our lines at daylight next morning.[1]

The battle was over. It had continued at intervals, at one point or another, over a range of five miles, from three o'clock in the morning until nearly two in the afternoon. Less than five thousand Americans at the passes, including Stirling's command and all others who had marched out during the morning, had been swept up or

---

[1] "Colonel Huntington's and the Maryland regiment suffered the most. General Parsons says that some of our men fought through the enemy not less than 7 or 8 times that day. He lay out himself part of the night concealed in a swamp, from whence he made his escape with 7 men to our lines about break of day the next morning."—*Letter from an Officer, Conn. Journal,* September 18th, 1776. "I came in with 7 men yesterday morning, much fatigued."—*General Parsons,* August 29th, 1776.

swept back by nearly twenty thousand British and Hessians. For our troops it was a total defeat. They had been forced to abandon the outer line of defence—the very line Washington wished should be held "at all hazards"—and had been driven into the fortified camp on the Brooklyn peninsula. This result would have inevitably come, sooner or later, but no one could have entertained the possibility of its coming in this sudden and disastrous shape.

Looking back over the day's work, the cause of the defeat is apparent at once : *We had been completely outflanked and surprised on the Jamaica Road.* Where the responsibility for the surprise should rest is another question. Evidently, if that patrol of officers had not been captured, but, upon discovering the approach of the enemy, had carried the word directly to Miles' camp and to headquarters, the enemy would not have gained the rear of our outposts without warning. Miles and Wyllys could have interposed themselves across their path, and held the ground long enough at least to put our troops at the other points on their guard. The surprise of this patrol, therefore, can alone explain the defeat. But as the officers appear to have been sent out as an additional precaution, the responsibility must be shared by Miles and his regiment, who were the permanent guard on the left. Brodhead, who wrote eight days after the event, distinctly asserts that there were no troops beyond them, and that, for want of videttes, that flank was left for them to watch. Parsons, as officer of the day, reports that Miles was expected to patrol across the Jamaica Road. But to charge the colonel personally with a fatal mistake or neglect is not warranted by the facts. His own patrols and pickets may have failed him.   The simple fact appears that this regiment was put upon our left, that our left was turned, and the battle lost in consequence.   As to the generalship of the day, if the responsibility falls on any one, it falls first on Sullivan, who sent out the mounted patrol in the first instance, and to whom it be-.onged to follow up the precautions in that direction. Putnam was in chief command, but nothing can be inferred from contemporary records to fasten neglect or blunder upon him any more than upon Washington, who, when he left the Brooklyn lines on the evening of the 26th, must have known precisely what disposition had been made for the night at the hills and passes.   And upon Washington certainly the responsibility cannot rest.[1]

[1] RESPONSIBILITY FOR THE DEFEAT.—According to some of our more recent versions of this battle, the disaster is to be referred to the wilful disobedience, criminal inattention, and total incapacity of General Putnam. Several writers make the charge so pointedly and upon such an array of fact, that the reader is left to wonder how all this should have escaped the notice of the commander-in-chief at the time, and why Putnam was not immediately court-martialled and dismissed the service, instead of being continued, as he was, in important commands. The charge is the more serious as it is advanced by so respectable an authority as Mr. Bancroft. Mr. Field, Mr. Dawson, and Dr. Stiles, following the latter, incline strongly in the same direction.

Mr. Bancroft first assails Putnam for sending Stirling out to the right when word came in that the enemy were advancing and our pickets flying. This is criticised as "a rash order," because it sent Stirling to a position which was "dangerous in the extreme," with the Gowanus marsh in his rear. But as to this, it only needs to be said that Putnam's written instructions from Washington were imperative to prevent the enemy from passing the hills and approaching the works. It would have been a clear disregard of Washington's intention had Putnam not sent Stirling out precisely as he did. The enemy were coming up from the Narrows and must be checked " at all hazards." Furthermore, the position Stirling took up at about Nineteenth Street was actually safer than any other on the outpost line. His right could not be turned, for it rested on the bay, and he could see every movement of the fleet. His left was well covered by Parsons, and no one could have imagined his rear in danger with the other outposts guarding it for more than three miles. As a matter of fact, Stirling was nearer the lines than either Miles or Wyllys.

Again, it is charged that when Putnam and Sullivan visited the extreme

What has been said of other defeats may be said with equal truth of this one : if it was a disaster, it was not a disgrace. Even the surprise upon the left discloses no

left on the 26th " the movements of the enemy plainly disclosed that it was their intention to get into the rear of the Americans by the Jamaica Road," yet nothing was done. The foundation of this is probably a statement of Brodhead's and another by Miles to the effect that these generals might have themselves observed that the enemy were preparing for the Jamaica move. But if the intentions of the latter were so obvious at that time, it is proper to ask why it was not equally obvious on the next morning that they were actually carrying out their intentions, and why Miles and Brodhead did not so report at an early hour. These officers were rightly impressed with the conviction that the enemy would come by way of Jamaica, but it is certain that the enemy made no observable move in that direction from Flatlands, where they had been for three days, until nine o'clock that night. So says Howe. It was clearly in the plan of the British to give our outposts no ground for suspecting a flanking manœuvre. Their movements were far from being " plainly disclosed." The quotation given by Mr. Bancroft in this connection, namely, that " Washington's order to secure the Jamaica Road was not obeyed," unfortunately appears as original in a " Review of the War" published in 1779 and written by some irresponsible individual in England, who could neither have known what Washington's orders were, nor whether any attempt was made to carry them out.

A further charge is this : " Early in the morning, Putnam was informed that infantry and cavalry were advancing on the Jamaica Road. He gave Washington no notice of the danger ; he sent Stirling no order to retreat." This is doubtless on the authority of a letter in *Force*, 5th Series, vol. i., p. 1195. But how early was Putnam informed ? The writer of the letter who brought the word was probably one of Miles' or Brodhead's men, for he tells us that his regiment was dressed in hunting-shirts, and he makes the very important statement that on his way back to his post he met the enemy ! The information came too late, for the British were now marching down towards the lines. Sullivan had gone to the Flatbush Pass, where he could understand the situation better than Putnam, and he was the proper officer to give directions to the outposts at that moment.

The charges made by Mr. Dawson have still less foundation. General Putnam is stated never to have reconnoitred the enemy's position. Brodhead, however, states distinctly that he did.   " It is also a well-established fact," says this writer, " that no general officer was outside the lines at Brooklyn on the night of the 26th." What is the authority for this ? Nixon, Stirling, and Parsons had been successively officers of the day, and presumably did their duty. Parsons, on the morning of the 27th, was on the lower road trying to rally the pickets before Stirling appeared with reinforcements. " The mounted patrols which General Sullivan had established, as well as the guards at some of the passes established by General Greene, were withdrawn." The

13

criminal misconduct. In the actual fighting of the day our soldiers stood their ground. Necessarily we suffered heavily in prisoners, but otherwise our loss was incon-

fact that all the passes were well guarded and a special patrol sent out, is a complete answer to this assertion, so far as the night of the 26th is concerned. In this light the general conclusion arrived at by Mr. Dawson, that " General Putnam paid no attention to the orders of General Washington," cannot be sustained.

With regard to General Sullivan, it is but just to give his own explanation. A year after the battle, he wrote : " I know it has been generally reported that I commanded on Long Island when the actions happened there. This is by no means true ; *General Putnam* had taken the command from me four days before the action. Lord Stirling commanded the main body without the lines ; I was to have command under General Putnam within the lines. I was very uneasy about a road through which I had often foretold the enemy would come, but could not persuade others to be of my opinion. I went to the Hill near Flatbush to reconnoitre the enemy, and, with a piquet of four hundred men, was surrounded by the enemy, who had advanced by the very road I had foretold, and which I had paid horsemen fifty dollars for patrolling by night, while I had the command, as I had no foot for the purpose, for which I was never reimbursed, as it was supposed unnecessary." In another letter he adds : " I was so persuaded of the enemy's coming the [Jamaica] route, that I went to examine, and was surrounded by the British army, and after a long and severe engagement was made prisoner." These letters were written when Sullivan was restless under charges brought against him in connection with the defeat at Brandywine—charges which were properly dropped, however—and are not conclusive as to the Long Island affair. His statements are no doubt strictly true, but they in no way affect the main point, namely, did we or did we not have a patrol out on the Jamaica Road *on the night of the* 26*th ?* We have seen that there was such a patrol, and probably the best that had yet been sent out, and sent out, according to Lieutenant Van Wagenen, by General Sullivan himself.

There are but few references to the question of responsibility in contemporary letters and documents. Gordon blames Sullivan as being over-confident. Miles and Brodhead leave us to infer that this general had much to do with the plan of action, and must be held at least in part responsible. Sullivan, on the other hand, according to Brodhead, blamed Miles for the defeat, as Parsons did. When these officers wrote, they wrote to defend their own conduct, and their testimony is necessarily incomplete so far as others are concerned. In brief, the case seems to be this : On the night of the 26th we had all the roads guarded. On the morning of the 27th Putnam promptly reinforced the guards on the lower road when the enemy were announced. The arrangements were such that if an attack was made at any of the other points he and Sullivan were to have word of it in ample time. No word came in time from the left, for the reason that those who were to bring it were captured, or sur-

siderable. All the light that we have to-day goes to establish the very important fact, originally credited and reported by Washington himself, but which hardly a single historical writer has since ventured to repeat, that at the battle of Long Island *the British and Hessians suffered a loss in killed and wounded equal to that inflicted upon the Americans.*[1] Howe reported his total casualties at three hundred and sixty-seven officers and soldiers. On the side of the Americans the total loss did not exceed one thousand. About eight hundred, including ninety-one officers, were taken prisoners ; not more than six officers and about fifty privates were killed ; and less than sixteen officers and one hundred and fifty privates wounded. No frightful slaughter of our troops, as sometimes pictured, occurred during the action. It was a field where the American soldier, in every fair encounter, proved himself worthy of the cause he was fighting for.

To those who fell in the engagement we may render here a grateful tribute, though something more than this is due. Their services and sacrifices are deserving of remembrance rather by a lasting memorial ; for men died

prised, or failed of their duty. Hence the disaster. The dispositions on Long Island were quite as complete as those at Brandywine more than a year later, where we suffered nearly a similar surprise and as heavy a loss. Suppose the very small patrols sent out by Washington and Sullivan to gain information before that battle had been captured, as at Long Island—we should have sustained a greater disaster than at Long Island.

Under this state of facts, to charge Putnam with the defeat of the 27th, in the terms which some writers have employed, is both unjust and unhistorical. That misfortune is not to be clouded with the additional reflection, that it was due to the gross neglect and general incapacity of the officer in command. No facts or inferences justify the charge. No one hinted it at the time ; nor did Washington in the least withdraw his confidence from Putnam during the remainder of the campaign.

[1] See note at the close of the chapter.

here who showed not less of individual worth and heroism than others who are immortalized on victorious fields. Thus at the Flatbush Road we find Philip Johnston, colonel of the Jersey battalion, which formed part of the guard there during the night. He was the son of the worthy Judge Samuel Johnston, of the town of Sidney in Hunterdon County. In his youth he had been a student at Princeton, but, dropping his books, he took up the sword for the colonies in the French war, from which he returned with honor. The troubles with Great Britain found him ready again to fight in defence of common rights and his native soil. Parting from his wife and child with touching affection, he took the field with his regiment, and when attacked on Long Island he showed all the qualities which mark the true soldier. A gentleman of high principle, an officer of fine presence, one of the strongest men in the army, he fought near Sullivan with the greatest bravery until he fell mortally wounded. That August 27th was his thirty-fifth birthday.

Equally glorious and regretted was the death of Lieutenant-Colonel Caleb Parry, of Atlee's regiment, which occurred, as already noticed, at an earlier hour and in another part of the field. He too was in the prime of life, and eager to render the country some good service. A representative colonist, descended from an ancient and honorable family long seated in North Wales, and a man of polish and culture, he stood ready for any sacrifice demanded of him at this crisis. Parry came from Chester County, Pennsylvania, leaving a wife and five children, and crossed with his regiment to Long Island four days before the battle. Under what circumstances he fell has been told. As they crossed the line of Greenwood Cemetery to take position at or near "Battle Hill," the little command was greeted with a sudden though harmless volley from the enemy. The men shrunk and fell back, but Atlee rallied and Parry cheered them on, and they gained the hill. It was here, while engaged in an officer's highest duty, turning men to the enemy by his own example, that the fatal bullet pierced his brow. When some future monument rises from Greenwood to commemorate the struggle of this day, it can bear no more fitting line among its inscriptions than this tribute of Brodhead's, " Parry died like a hero."

Captain Edward Veazey, of the Marylanders, belonged to the family of Veazeys who settled in Cecil County, on the eastern shore of that State, and who traced their lineage back to the Norman De Veazies of the eleventh century. The captain was fifty-five years of age, took up the colonial cause at the start, raised the Seventh Independent Company of Maryland troops, and was among the earliest to fall in Stirling's line.

Captain Joseph Jewett, of Huntington's Continentals, perhaps defending himself to the last, even when escape was impossible, was three times stabbed with British bayonets after surrendering his sword. Cared for by a humane surgeon, but still lingering in pain, he died on the morning of the 29th, and was buried in the Bennett orchard, near Twenty-second Street and Third Avenue. He left a family at Lyme, on the Connecticut, where he lived, and from where he went to join the army on the Lexington alarm. A soldier who fought on Long Island remembers him as " an officer much respected and beloved, of elegant and commanding appearance, and of unquestionable bravery."

The officers and men of the artillery, who fought the six pieces we had in the action, covered themselves with honor. They were "the flower" of Knox's regiment, picked for a field fight. Captain Carpenter, of Providence, fell in Stirling's command, leaving a widow to mourn him. Captain John Johnston, of Boston, was desperately wounded, but recovered under the care of Surgeon Eustis. The record which John Callender, of the same place, made for himself is a familiar story. To wipe out the stain of an undeserved sentence passed upon him after Bunker Hill, by which he was cashiered, he rejoined the artillery as a private soldier, and then, as a " cadet," fought his piece on Long Island until the enemy's bayonets were at his breast. Upon his exchange as prisoner a year later, Washington restored him to his rank as captain-lieutenant, and he served honorably to the end of the war. Harmanus Rutgers, one of the patriotic Rutgers brothers in New York, serving, it would seem, as a gunner, was struck in the breast by a cannon-shot, and fell dead at his post. The tradition preserved in his family is that he was the first man killed in the battle. Knox, hearing how well his men had done, wrote to his wife : " I have met with some loss in my regiment. They fought like heroes and are gone to glory."

Of three others known to have been killed during the day, and who probably complete the list of officers, we have no more than the fact that they fell. They were Lieutenant Joseph Jacquet, of Miles' first battalion, and Lieutenants David Sloan and Charles Taylor, of the second battalion—all apparently from Chester County, Pennsylvania. Hardly more than three or four names of the private soldiers who were killed have been preserved, owing doubtless to the fact that, if they were ever known, it was not until long after, when no rolls would show their fate.

To the roll of the dead must be added also the honored name of General Nathaniel Woodhull, of Long Island. On the day after the battle, a party of British light horse, under Oliver De Lancey, rode out on the Jamaica Road and surprised the general at an inn, where without provocation he was cruelly hacked in the head and arm, and carried off a prisoner. He survived until the 20th, when he died at New Utrecht. His loss was greatly regretted, for he was a man of energy and ability, and had the success of the Revolutionary cause most fervently at heart.[1]

This battle was regarded at the time as one of very great importance, and the result created a deep impression on both sides of the water. In England they had long been waiting for the news, and the king became depressed at the British delay in moving ; in addition, the first reports, coming by way of France, were unfavorable. But at last, at three o'clock on the morning of October 10th, Major Cuyler, of Howe's staff, reached the government with the official accounts of the victory. Immediately, as Walpole tells us, the Court was filled with " an extravagance of joy." The relief was so great that it was displayed with " the utmost ostentation." The king at once determined to send Howe " a red riband ;" and Lord Mansfield, who had thrown the weight of his great legal abilities against America, was created an earl. The Mayor and Corporation of York voted an address to his Majesty " on the victory at Long Island ;" at Leeds they

---

[1] Mr. Onderdonk, Mr. Thompson, and others have gathered and published all the known incidents respecting the fate of General Woodhull, which are doubtless familiar to those interested in the history of Long Island. See General Scott's brief reference to him in *Document* 6.

rang the bells, lighted windows, fired cannon, and started a huge bonfire which made the town " quite luminous ;" and at Halifax, Colne, Huddersfield, and many other places, similar rejoicings were held. At Limerick Lieutenant-Colonel Campbell ordered the garrison under arms, and fired three volleys " on account of the success of his Majesty's troops at Long Island ;" and, for the same reason, in the evening " a number of ladies and gentlemen were elegantly entertained at dinner by the bishop." From Paris Silas Deane wrote to Congress : " The want of instructions or intelligence or remittances, with the late check on Long Island, has sunk our credit to nothing." In Amsterdam, the centre of exchange for all Europe, English stocks rose ; but the Dutch, with characteristic shrewdness, failed to accept " our misfortune" as final, and took the opportunity to sell out. In London Tory circles they considered the American war as practically over, and some began to talk of new schemes of colonial government.

As for America, the defeat, coupled with the subsequent retreat, everywhere carried alarm and keen disappointment. Greene speaks of the " panic" in the country. But at the same time many brave voices were raised to counteract despondency. Parsons, in the army, wrote : " I think the trial of that day far from being any discouragement, but in general our men behaved with firmness." Bartlett, in Congress, sent word home to New Hampshire that he hoped the event would only make our generals more careful in their future operations. " We have lost a battle and a small island," said Dr. Rush, of Philadelphia, in one of the sessions a few days later, " but we have not lost a State. Why then

should we be discouraged? Or why should we be discouraged even if we had lost a State? If there were but
one State left, still that one should peril all for independence." "The panic may seize whom it will," wrote John
Adams; "it shall not seize me." But the grandest
words inspired by the pervading anxiety were those
penned by Abigail Adams, the noble wife of the Massachusetts delegate. "We have had many stories," she
wrote from Braintree, September 9th, "concerning
engagements upon Long Island this week, of our lines
being forced and of our troops returning to New York.
Particulars we have not yet obtained. All we can learn
is that we have been unsuccessful there; having many
men as prisoners, among whom are Lord Stirling and
General Sullivan. *But if we should be defeated, I think we
shall not be conquered. A people fired, like the Romans, with
love of their country and of liberty, a zeal for the public good,
and a noble emulation of glory, will not be disheartened or
dispirited by a succession of unfortunate events. But, like
them, may we learn by defeat the power of becoming invincible!*"

This was the true inspiration of the hour. It was this
that sustained Washington and the strong men of the
country through all the dark period that followed. The
disaster of the 27th was a disciplinary experience. It
was but the first of a series of blows that were to harden
us for future endurance. The event was accepted in this
spirit by all who had taken up the cause in earnest; and
in this light the memory of the day deserves to be forever celebrated and perpetuated. Here, on Long Island,
all was done that could be done, for we had met the
enemy at the sea. Here America made her first stand

against England's first great effort to subdue her ; and here her resolution to continue resistance was first tested and tempered in the fire of battle.

THE LOSSES AT THE BATTLE.—So many widely different estimates have been made as to the extent of the American loss on Long Island, that it becomes a matter of historical interest to fix the actual figures, if possible, beyond dispute.

The first official reference to the matter occurs in the letter which Washington directed Colonel Harrison, his secretary, to write to Congress on the evening of the battle. Nothing definite on this point being known at that hour, Harrison, after announcing the attack of the enemy, and the retreat of the troops into the Brooklyn lines, could only make the vague report that the American loss was " pretty considerable." On Thursday morning, the 29th, at " half after four A.M.," Washington himself wrote to Hancock that he was still uncertain how far the army had suffered. On Saturday, the 31st, he wrote again, and in this letter gave an estimate in figures. This was the only report he made to Congress in the matter, except indirectly. " Nor have I," he writes, " been yet able to obtain an exact account of our loss ; we suppose it from seven hundred to a thousand killed and taken." In subsequent public and private letters to his brother, to Governor Trumbull, General Schuyler, and the Massachusetts Assembly, Washington did not vary these figures materially (except to make the estimate closer, about 800), and they stand, therefore, as his official return of the casualties of that day.

Sir William Howe's report, on the other hand, presented altogether a different showing. It left no room for doubt as to the extent of the British victory. Dated September 3d, seven days after the affair, it contained all those particulars of events up to that time which a successful general is well aware will be received with special satisfaction by his government. The landing at Gravesend, the occupation of Flatbush, the skilful march of the flanking column, the bravery of the troops, and the complete success of the entire plan of action were mentioned in order ; while a detailed statement and estimate of the losses on either side, including a tabulated return of prisoners taken, only fortified the impression that a most damaging defeat had been served upon the Americans. Against Washington's estimate of a total of one thousand or less for his own loss, Howe reported that the enlisted men he captured alone numbered one thousand and six, and that in addition he took ninety-one commissioned officers, of whom three were generals, three colonels, four lieutenant-colonels, three majors, eighteen captains, forty-three lieutenants, eleven ensigns, one adjutant, three surgeons, and two volunteers ; and he " computed " that in killed, wounded, and drowned, the Americans lost two thousand two hundred more. On the part of the British, Howe reported five officers and fifty-six men killed, twelve officers and two hundred and fifty-five men wounded, and one officer and thirty men prisoners and missing. The Hessians lost two men killed, three officers and twenty-three men wounded. Howe's total loss, in a word, was made to appear at less than four hundred ; Washington's full three thousand three hundred.

The apparent exactness of this report has secured it, in general, against close analysis. English historians, almost without exception, quote it as it stands, while there are American writers who respect it so far as to pronounce Washington's report clearly, and even purposely, inaccurate. Thus the most recent English history of this period says : " The Americans fled in confusion, leaving upwards of three thousand killed, wounded, and prisoners, including their three generals of division ;" and in a note the writer adds : " Washington's estimate of the loss on both sides was grossly incorrect. In his letter to Congress of the 30th August, giving a very meagre and evasive account of the action, he says that his loss in killed and prisoners was from 700 to 1000 ; and that he had reason to believe the enemy had suffered still more. This would seem to be a wilful misrepresentation to prevent the public alarm which might have been caused by the knowledge of his real loss ; were it not that in a private letter to his brother, three weeks afterwards, he makes a similar statement. General Howe's returns of *prisoners*, and of his own killed and wounded, are precise." (*History of England during the Reign of George the Third.* By the Right Hon. William Massey, 1865.) Among Brooklyn writers, Mr. Field asserts that Washington concealed the actual extent of his loss, and Dr. Stiles accepts the British report as it stands. Marshall puts the American loss at over 1000 ; Irving, 2000 ; Lossing, 1650 ; Field, 2000 ; Sparks, 1100 ; Bancroft, 800 ; Carrington, 970. Stedman, the earliest British historian, gives 2000, while Adolphus, Jesse, and Massey, who cover the reign of George III., blindly follow Howe and give over 3000 for the American loss.

There is but one explanation of this wide discrepancy between the British and American returns, namely : Washington's original estimate at its largest limit—one thousand, killed, wounded, and prisoners—*was almost precisely correct.*

Of this there can be no question whatever, the proof being a matter of record. Thus, on the 8th of October, Washington issued the following order : " The General desires the commanding officers of each regiment or corps will give in a list of the names and the officers and men who were killed, taken, or missing in the action of the 27th of August on Long Island and since that period. He desires the returns may be correct, &c." (*Force*). A large number of these lists are preserved in *Force*, 5th series, vol. iii., and from these we obtain the losses of the following regiments : Hitchcock's, total loss, one officer and nine men ; Little's, three men ; Huntington's, twenty-one officers and one hundred and eighty-six men ; Wyllys', one officer and nine men ; Tyler, three men ; Ward, three men ; Chester, twelve men ; Gay, four men ; Lasher, three officers. Smallwood's lost, according to Gist, twelve officers and two hundred and forty-seven men ; Haslet, according to his own letters, two officers and twenty-five men ; Johnston's New Jersey, two officers and less than twenty-five men, the rolls before and after the battle showing no greater difference in the strength of the regiment ; Miles' two battalions, sixteen officers and about one hundred and sixty men (*Document* 61) ; Atlee, eleven officers and seventy-seven men. (*Ibid.*) No official report of the losses in Lutz's, Kachlein's, and Hay's detachments or the artillery can be found, but to give their total casualties at one hundred and fifty officers and men is probably a liberal estimate. Lutz lost six officers (all prisoners) ; Kachlein not more ; Hay, one ; the artillery, three. The regiments named in the foregoing list include all from which Howe reported that he took officers prisoners, from which it is safe to conclude that these were all that lost any. No others are mentioned as having been engaged. These figures show in round numbers a total of *one thousand*, and this was our total loss, according to official returns in nearly every case.

How many of these, in the next place, were killed and wounded ? If we are to credit certain Hessian and British accounts, as well as those of our own local historians, the battle-field on Long Island was a scene of carnage, a pen in which our men were slaughtered without mercy. The confused strife, says one writer, " is too terrible for the imagination to dwell upon." " An appalling massacre," says another, " thus closed the combat." "The forest," writes a Hessian officer, " was a scene of horror ; there were certainly two thousand killed and wounded lying about." Lord Howe himself, as we have seen, " computed " that the American loss in killed and wounded alone was two thousand three hundred. But a striking commentary on this computation is not only the total omission on his part to mention how many of this very large number he buried on the field, but the important admission he makes that not more than sixty-seven wounded American officers and soldiers fell into his hands ! Where were the twenty-two hundred other maimed and fallen rebels ? Obviously, and as Howe must have well known, the Americans could carry few if any of their dead with them on their precipitate retreat, nor could any but the slightly hurt of the wounded make their escape. Full two thousand, by this calculation, must have been left upon the field. Who buried them ? Were they the victims of the supposed frightful slaughter ? Did the British general purposely give an evasive estimate to cover up the inhumanity which would thus have forever stained the glory of his victory ? Far from it. That " computation " has no basis to stand upon ; but, on the contrary, our loss in killed and wounded was not greater than the enemy's, but most probably less.

This statement will bear close examination. On the 19th of September, after he must have been able to satisfy himself as to the extent of the defeat on Long Island, the commander-in-chief wrote to the Massachusetts Assembly that he had lost about eight hundred men, " more than three fourths of which were taken prisoners." He wrote the same thing to others. So Washington felt authorized to state positively that we lost in killed and wounded that day not over two hundred men and officers. " The enemy's loss in killed," he added, " we could never ascertain ; but have many reasons to believe that it was pretty considerable, and exceeded ours a good deal." General Parsons, who saw as much of the field as any other officer, wrote to John Adams two days after the battle : " Our loss in killed and wounded is inconsiderable." General Scott, writing to John Jay, a week later, could say : " What our loss on Long Island was I am not able to estimate. I think from the best accounts we must have killed many of the enemy." Colonel Douglas wrote, August 31st : "The enemy surrounded a large detachment of our army, took many, killed some and the ;rest got off. . . . By the best account we killed more of them than they did of us. But they took the most prisoners." Lieutenant-Colonel Chambers, who was in the way of gathering many particulars from the Pennsylvanians who escaped, says : " Our men behaved as bravely as men ever did ; but it is surprising that, with the superiority of numbers, they were not cut to pieces. . . . Our loss is chiefly in prisoners." Lieutenant-Colonel Brodhead, who had to retreat among the last over the very ground which others have marked out as the scene of the massacre, as the site where " lay nearly one thousand men, slain in the shock of battle, or by subsequent murder" (*Field*)—Brodhead says : " I retreated to the lines, having lost out of the whole battalion, about one hundred men, officers included, which, as they were much scattered, must be chiefly prisoners. . . . No troops could behave better than the Southern, for though they seldom engaged less than five to one, they frequently repulsed the Enemy with great Slaughter, and I am confident that the number of killed and wounded on their side, is greater than on ours, notwithstanding we had to fight them front and rear under every disadvantage." Colonel Silliman, of Connecticut, who appears to have made particular inquiries in the matter, wrote, September 10th : " I think upon the best information I can get that we are about 1000 men the worse for that action. The Enemy say they have about 800 of them prisoners. We have about 50 of them in the hospital wounded. Of the other 150 'tis said that in the engagement a considerable number of the riflemen deserted and went over to the enemy and some no doubt escaped towards the other end of the Island. On the whole I do not think we had 50 men killed in the action." (*MS. letter.*) These are statements made by officers who were present at the battle, and who wrote within a few days of the event. They all, with many others, reach the same conclusion that the enemy suffered in killed and wounded as much if not more than the Americans. Their testimony, moreover, is strengthened by what we know directly and indirectly from the returns and other sources. The loss in officers, of which we have exact figures, is one basis of calculation. Ninety-one, as already stated, were taken prisoners, of whom nine were reported wounded in Howe's return. Among these were General Woodhull, Colonel Johnston, and Captain Jewett, all three mortally wounded, and Captain Bowie and Lieutenant Butler, of the Marylanders ; Captain Johnston, of the artillery ; Captain Peebles, of Miles', and Lieutenant Makepeace, of Huntington's. [Colonel Johnston is usually mentioned as having been killed on the field. But Howe's return gives one New Jersey colonel prisoner, and Elking's Hessian account states that he was wounded after being made prisoner.] Among officers known to be wounded, not captured, were Major McDonough, Lieutenants Course and Anderson, of the Delawares ; Lieutenant Hughes, of Hitchcock's ; and Captain Farmer, of Miles'. Lieutenant Patterson, of Hay's detachment, was either killed or captured (Colonel

Cunningham's return). The officers killed were Lieutenant-Colonel Parry, Captain Carpenter, Captain Veazey, and Lieutenants Sloan, Jacquet, and Taylor. Various accounts state that Colonel Rutgers, Lieutenant-Colonel Eppes, Major Abeel (of Lasher's), Captain Fellows, and Lieutenant Moore (of Pennsylvania) were killed, but there is an error in each case, all these officers being reported alive at different dates after the battle. We have, then, twenty-one killed or wounded (six only killed on the field) among the American officers engaged in the action. If, as we have a right to assume, the same proportion held among the enlisted men, our total loss in killed and wounded could not have exceeded two hundred or two hundred and fifty, or more than one hundred less than the enemy's loss. Parsons and Atlee write that they lost but two or three. Miles says that in one of his skirmishes he lost a number of men, but nearly all were made prisoners. Little's regiment lost one killed; Hitchcock's the same. The five companies of Smallwood's battalion that attacked Cornwallis lost but one officer wounded, or at the most one killed and one wounded, and there is no reason to suppose that the men suffered very heavily. The loss among the Delawares was nearly all in prisoners. Lutz had six officers taken, but none killed or wounded; Hay lost one officer, either killed or prisoner. In Kachlein's detachment it is certain that the lieutenant-colonel, major, adjutant, three captains, and three lieutenants were not killed, which leaves little room for casualties in a party of not over four or five companies. So of all the other regiments engaged, they suffered but slightly in killed or wounded.

Howe's list of prisoners was undoubtedly swelled by captures among the Long Island militia and citizen Whigs after the battle. He includes General Woodhull and two lieutenants, for instance, who were not taken at the battle but on the day following, and who, as Washington says, were "never arranged" in his army.

The reports of the slaughter and massacre of our troops current in the enemy's camp at the time were greatly exaggerated. Some of our men were probably cut down most wantonly in the pursuit through the woods, both by British and Hessians, but the number was small. It is a noticeable and significant fact that the American accounts make no mention of any such wholesale cruelty, and certainly our soldiers would have been the first to call attention to it. That word "massacre" should have no place in any accurate description of the battle.

CHAPTER V.

THE situation at the Brooklyn lines was relieved on the 29th by the famous retreat of our army to New York. If Howe had surprised us by an unexpected manœuvre on the 27th, Washington was now to surprise the British with a different manœuvre, conducted with greater skill. "A fine retreat," says Jomini, "should meet with a reward equal to that given for a great victory." History assigns such a reward to Washington at Long Island.

This success—the extrication of the army from what was soon felt to be a dangerous position—was not to be achieved without a previous two days' experience of great hardship, trial, and despondency on the part of the troops; and unceasing anxiety and watchfulness on the part of the commander-in-chief. The night of the 27th had closed cheerlessly on the devoted Americans. The hills had been wrested from them; many of their best officers and soldiers were slain or prisoners; before them stood the whole British army, flushed with success, and liable at any hour to rush upon their works, and in their rear flowed a deep, wide river.

Washington realized the position the moment of the retreat from the passes, and immediately took measures to guard against further disaster. Satisfied that Howe had his whole force with him, and that an attack was not to be apprehended at any other point, he ordered forward more troops to replace his losses and strengthen the lines. Mifflin brought down from Harlem Heights the two well-drilled Pennsylvania regiments under Colonels Magaw and Shee, with some others; and Glover's Massachusetts was sent on from Fellows' brigade. These all crossed to Long Island early on the morning of the 28th. At the same time, the afternoon of the 27th, Washington sent word to General Mercer in New Jersey to march all the forces under his command "immediately to Powle's Hook;[1] they might be needed in New York, they might be needed on Long Island. By the morning of the 28th, the commander-in-chief had drawn to the Brooklyn lines all the troops that could be spared from other points, and all with which he proposed to resist the British if they attempted to carry his position by storm. He had on that side the largest and best part of his army. The whole of Greene's division was there, the whole of Spencer's, half of Sullivan's, one third of Putnam's, and a part of Heath's—in all not less than thirty-five regiments or detachments, which numbered together something over nine thousand five hundred men fit for duty.[2]

[1] This order was sent at two o'clock through General Wooster, then temporarily in New York, and Mercer received it in the evening near Newark. He sent word at once to the militia at Amboy, Woodbridge, and Elizabethtown to march to Powle's Hook. *Force*, 5th Series, vol. ii.

[2] A close analysis of the returns of September 12th, estimating all additions or reductions which should be made since the battle, shows that this was about the number on Long Island at this date and at the time of the retreat. The brigades now there were Nixon's, Heard's, Parson's, Wadsworth's, Stirling's, Scott's, two regiments of Mifflin's, one at least of McDougall's (Webb's), Glover's, and Fellows', the Long Island militia, artillery, rangers, and several independent companies. We know at what part of the lines some of these troops were posted. Greene's four old regiments doubtless occupied the forts. Varnum was at Red Hook; Little at Fort Greene;

Had all things been relatively equal, the Americans within the lines, according to military experience, should have been well able to hold that front. But there was a total inequality of conditions. The enemy were thoroughly equipped, disciplined, and provided for. They were an army of professional soldiers, superior to any that could be brought against them the world over. Thus far they had carried everything before them, and were eager to achieve still greater victories. Behind the Brooklyn works stood a poorly armed, badly officered, and for the most part untrained mass of men, hurriedly gathered into the semblance of an army. The events of the previous day, moreover, had greatly depressed their spirits. Not a few of those who had been engaged in or witnessed the battle were badly demoralized. To make matters worse, the very elements seemed to combine against them. The two days they were still to remain on the island were days of "extraordinary wet." It rained almost continuously, and much of the time heavily. No fact is better attested than this. August 28th, writes Colonel Little, "weather very rainy;" "29th, very rainy." Major Tallmadge speaks of the fatigue as having been aggravated by

---

Hitchcock at Fort Putnam, and Hand with him there and in the redoubt on the left. Forman's New Jersey had been at Fort Box. Three of Scott's battallions were assigned to the centre, where the breastworks crossed the Jamaica Road. Magaw, Shee, and Glover guarded the line from Fort Putnam to the Wallabout ; Silliman was at the "northern part" of the works, probably on the right of Fort Putnam ; Gay's was between Fort Box and the Marsh ; Douglas watched the extreme right in the woods at the mouth of Gowanus Creek ; and there was a "reserve," which perhaps included among others the remnants of Stirling's shattered brigade. Encircling them a mile or a mile and a half distant in the edge of the woods, lay the British army with tents already pitched in many places. North and south of the Jamaica Road, just below Bedford, was Howe's main column ; within and west of Prospect Park were the Hessians ; and on the right, Grant's division bivouacked along the Gowanus Road.

14

the "heavy rain." "The heavy rain which fell two days and nights without intermission, etc.," said the council which voted to retreat. Pastor Shewkirk in his diary notes the weather particularly : "Wednesday 28th," he writes, . . . "in the afternoon we had extraordinary heavy rains and thunder." The flashes of the cannons were intermixed with flashes of lightning. On the 29th, "in the afternoon, such heavy rain fell again as can hardly be remembered." To all this deluge our soldiers were exposed with but little shelter. Necessity required that they should be at the lines, and constantly on the watch, ready to repel any attempt to storm them. When they lay down in the trenches at brief intervals for rest, they kept their arms from the wet as they could. Cooking was out of the question, and the men were compelled to take up with the unaccustomed fare of hard biscuits and raw pork. Their wretched plight is referred to in more than one of the letters of the day. Writes General Scott : "You may judge of our situation, subject to almost incessant rains, without baggage or tents, and almost without victuals or drink, and in some part of the lines the men were standing up to their middles in water." Captain Olney puts it on record that "the rain fell in such torrents that the water was soon ankle deep in the fort. Yet with all these inconveniences, and a powerful enemy just without musket-shot, our men could not be kept awake." Captain Graydon, of Shee's Pennsylvanians, says in his well-known "Memoirs :" "We had no tents to screen us from the pitiless pelting, nor, if we had them, would it have comported with the incessant vigilance required to have availed ourselves of them, as, in fact, it might be said that we lay upon our arms during the whole of our stay upon the island. In the article of food we were little better off." Under the circumstances could Washington's force have withstood the shock of a determined assault by the enemy ?

In spite, however, of weather, hunger, and fatigue, there was many a brave man in the American camp who kept up heart and obeyed all orders with spirit. One thing is certain, the British were not permitted to suspect the distressed condition of our army. Our pickets and riflemen, thrown out in front of the works, put on a bold face. On the 28th there was skirmishing the greater part of the day, and in the evening, as Washington reports, " it was pretty smart." Writing from the trenches on the 29th, Colonel Silliman says : " Our enemy have encamped in plain sight of our camp at the distance of about a mile and a half. We have had no general engagement yet, but no day passes without some smart and hot skirmishes between different parties, in which the success is sometimes one way and sometimes another. We are in constant expectation of a general battle ; no one can be here long without getting pretty well acquainted with the whistling of cannon and musket shot." Scarcely any particulars of these encounters[1] are preserved, though one of them, at least,

[1] In vol. ii. of the L. I. Hist. Society's " Memoirs," the author, Mr. Field, devotes pages 254–258 to the skirmishing of some Connecticut soldiers on the extreme right on the other side of Gowanus Creek, which appears to him to have been rash and foolhardy, and strangely in contrast with what also appears to him to have been an exhibition of cowardice on their part the day before. The narrative from which the incidents are taken (Martin's) shows no such singular inconsistency in the conduct of these men. This was Colonel Douglas' regiment, and, as Martin himself says, it moved promptly under orders from the ferry to the right to cover Stirling's retreat. " Our officers," he writes, " pressed forward towards a creek, where a large party of Americans and British were engaged." They very properly did not halt to help a company of artillerymen drag their pieces along. The skirmish on the following day was nothing remarkable in its way. It was

appears to have been quite an important affair. The enemy had determined to approach the lines by regular siege rather than hazard an assault, and late in the afternoon of the 28th they advanced in some force to break ground for the first parallel. The point selected was doubtless the high ground between Vanderbilt and Clinton avenues, on the line of De Kalb. As to what occurred we have but the briefest account, and that is from the pen of Colonel Little. "On the morning of the 28th," he writes, "the enemy were encamped on the heights in front of our encampment. Firing was kept up on both sides from the right to the left. Firing on both sides in front of Fort Putnam. About sunset the enemy pushed to recover the ground we had taken (about 100 rods) in front of the fort. The fire was very hot; the enemy gave way, and our people recovered the ground. The firing ceased, and our people retired to the fort. The enemy took possession again, and on the morning of the 30th [29th] had a breastwork there 60 rods long and 150 rods distant from Fort Putnam." It was this move of the British, more than any incident since the battle, that determined Washington's future course.

During all these trying hours since the defeat on the 27th, the most conspicuous figure to be seen, now at one point and now at another of the threatened lines, was that of the commander-in-chief. Wherever his inspiring presence seemed necessary, there he was to be found. He cheered the troops night and day. All that the soldiers endured, he endured. For forty-eight hours, or the whole of the 28th and 29th, he took no rest whatever, and

---

just such brushes as the men engaged in that Washington, on Graydon's authority, encouraged. The regiment displayed no particular rashness on the 28th, nor any cowardice on the 27th—that is, if Martin is to be credited.

was hardly once off his horse. As he rode among the men in the storm he spoke to some in person, and everywhere he gave directions, while his aids were as tireless as their Chief in assisting him.

But circumstanced as the army was, it was inevitable that the question should come up : Can the defence of the Brooklyn front be continued without great hazard ? It could not have escaped the notice of a single soldier on that side, that if, with the river in their rear, the enemy should succeed in penetrating the lines, or the fleet be able to command the crossing, they would all be lost. There was no safety but in retreat ; and for twenty-four hours from the morning of the 29th, all the energies of the commander-in-chief were directed towards making the retreat successful.

To few incidents of the Revolution does greater interest attach than to this final scene in the operations on Long Island. The formal decision to abandon this point was made by a council of war, held late in the day of the 29th, at the house of Phillip Livingston, then absent as a member of the Continental Congress at Philadelphia. The mansion made historic by this event stood on the line of Hicks Street, just south of Joralemon.[1] There were present at the council, the commander-in-chief, Major-Generals Putnam and Spencer, and Brigadier-Generals Mifflin, McDougall, Parsons, Scott, Wadsworth, and Fellows. As far as known, Scott alone of these generals has left us any thing in regard to what transpired on the occasion beyond the final result. He preserves the interesting fact that when the proposition to retreat was presented it took him by surprise and he as sud-

[1] See *Document* 6, in which General Scott says : " I was summoned to a council of war at Mr. Phillip Livingston's house on Thursday, 29th ult., etc."

denly objected to it, "from an aversion to giving the
enemy a single inch of ground." It was the soil of his
own State. As a member of the New York Convention
and of the Committee of Safety, and now as a general
officer, he had spent months in uninterrupted preparations to defend that soil, and on the first impulse of the
moment the thought of yielding any more of it to the
invaders was not to be entertained. But he was soon
"convinced by unanswerable reasons," and the vote of
the council was unanimous for retreat. Eight separate
reasons were embodied in the decision. *First.* A defeat
had been sustained on the 27th, and the woods lost where
it was proposed to make "a principal stand." *Second.*
The loss in officers and men had occasioned great confusion and discouragement among the troops. *Third.*
The rain had injured the arms and much of the ammunition, and the soldiers were so worn out, that it was feared
that they could not be kept at the lines by any order.
Fourth. The enemy appeared to be endeavoring to get
their ships into the East River to cut off communication
with New York, but the wind as yet had not served
them. *Fifth.* There were no obstructions sunk in the
Channel between Long and Governor's Island, and the
council was assured by General McDougall, "from his
own nautic experience," that small ships could sail up
by that channel; the hulks, also, sunk between Governor's Island and the Battery were regarded as insufficient
obstructions for that passage. *Sixth.* Though the lines
were fortified by several strong redoubts, the breastworks
were weak, being "abattised with brush" only in some
places, and the enemy might break through them.
Seventh. The divided state of the army made a defence
precarious. *Eighth.* Several British men-of-war had

worked their way into Flushing Bay from the Sound, and with their assistance the enemy could cross a force to the mainland in Westchester County, and gain the American rear in the vicinity of King's Bridge. In view of these considerations a retreat was considered imperative.

This was the official record of the council's action as afterwards transmitted to Congress. It is not to be inferred, however, that retreat was not thought of, or that nothing was done to effect it until the council met. That Washington had foreseen the necessity of the move, that he discussed it with others, and that he had already begun the necessary preparations, is obvious both from the record and from all that occurred during the day. The council did no more than to coincide in his views and confirm his judgment.[1]

[1] ORIGIN OF THE RETREAT.—Precisely when and why Washington came to a determination in his own mind to retreat has been made the subject of a somewhat nice historical inquiry. Gordon gives one story ; Mr. William B. Reed, biographer of Colonel Reed, gives another ; and Mr. Bancroft, General Carrington, and others indulge in more or less extended criticisms on the point. Gordon's account is the most probable and the best supported.

Whatever Washington may have thought of the situation on Long Island after the defeat, it is enough to know that he immediately reinforced himself there, and that on the 27th and 28th he made no preparations to withdraw to New York. It far from follows, however, that he had concluded to stay and fight it out " on that line" at all hazards. He was acting on the defensive, and was necessarily obliged to guide himself largely by the movements of the enemy. On Long Island, therefore, he could only be on the watch, and, like a prudent general, decide according to circumstances. Up to the morning of the 29th he was still watching—watching not only the enemy, but his own army also. In his letter to Congress, written at "half after 4 o'clock A.M." of this date, he gives no intimation of a retreat, but rather leaves that body to infer that he proposed to remain where he was. He speaks, for instance, of expecting tents during the day to make the troops more comfortable. On the same morning Reed wrote : "We hope to be able to make a good stand, as our lines are pretty strong ;" and he doubtless reflected the views of his Chief at the time.

The two particular dangers now to which the army was exposed were the

The first thing necessary was to provide all the transportation available in order to accomplish the retreat in the shortest time possible after beginning it. There were

danger of having its communication with New York cut off by the ships, and the danger of being approached by the enemy in front by siege operations, which the army was not prepared to meet. The first danger had existed ever since the arrival of the enemy, and had been provided for. All the batteries on Governor's Island and on both sides of the East River had been built to guard against it. In addition, ships had been sunk in the channel. Washington accordingly must have thoroughly canvassed the risks he ran in regard to his communications. *These alone had not decided him to retreat.* On the morning of the 29th, however, he first became aware of the second danger. It was not until then that the enemy fully developed their intention of advancing by trenches. After working all night, as Howe reports, they had thrown up by morning, as Little reports, a parallel sixty rods long and one hundred and fifty rods distant from Fort Putnam. Reed wrote, " They are intrenching at a small distance.'' In twenty-four hours at the farthest they would have come within very close range, and the hazardous alternative would have been forced upon us to attempt to drive them out of their own works. Washington well knew that, in view of the condition of his men and the great disparity of numbers, this could not be done. When, therefore, he became assured of Howe's intentions he acted promptly—*he determined to retreat ;* and this determination he reached early on the morning of the 29th.

This is substantially the theory which Gordon presents as a fact, and it is most consistent with fact. Gordon's account is this : " The victorious army encamped in the front of the American works in the evening ; and on the 28th at night broke ground in form about 4 or 500 yards distant from a redoubt which covered the left of the Americans. The same day Gen. Mifflin crossed over from New York with 1000 men ; at night he made an offer to Gen. Washington of going the rounds, which was accepted. He observed the approaches of the enemy, and the forwardness of their batteries ; and was convinced that no time was to be lost. The next morning he conversed with the General upon the subject, and said, ' You must either fight or retreat immediately. What is your strength ? ' The General answered, ' Nine thousand.' The other replied, ' It is not sufficient, we must therefore retreat.' They were both agreed as to the calling of a Council of war ; and Gen. Mifflin was to propose a retreat. But as he was to make that proposal, lest his own character should 'suffer, he stipulated, that if a retreat should be agreed upon, he would command the rear ; and if an action the van."

The fact that Mifflin was given the command of the rear on the retreat, and the fact that he sent the order to Heath that morning to send down all the boats from King's Bridge, lend the highest probability to Gordon's version of the story. Parsons, who was one of the members of the council, mentions this particularly as one of the reasons for withdrawing, namely, that the enemy were

boats at the Brooklyn ferry and across at New York, but these were too few for the purpose. Accordingly, on the forenoon of the 29th, Washington sent an order through

" not disposed to storm our lines, but set down to make regular approaches to us." Reed also puts as much stress on this point as any other. Giving the reasons for the retreat to Governor Livingston, he said : " The enemy at the same time possessed themselves of a piece of ground very advantageous and which they had [fortified]. We were therefore reduced to the alternative of retiring to this place or going out with [troops] to drive them off." Washington, too, is to be quoted. In his letter to Trumbull, September 6th, he writes : " As the main body of the enemy had encamped not far from our lines, and as I had reason to believe they intended to force us from them by regular approaches, which the nature of the ground favoured extremely, and at the same time meant, by the ships of war, to cut off the communication between the City and Island, and by that means keep our men divided and unable to oppose them anywhere, by the advice of the General officers, on the night of the 29th, I withdrew our troops from thence without any loss of men and but little baggage."

William B. Reed's account (Reed's Life of Reed) is to the effect, briefly, that a heavy fog settled over Long Island on the 29th, and that during the day Colonel Reed, Colonel Grayson, and General Mifflin rode to Red Hook inspecting the lines. While at the Hook, " a shift of wind " cleared the fog from the harbor, enabling the officers to catch a glimpse of the fleet at the Narrows. From certain movements of boats they inferred that the ships would sail up with the favorable breeze if it held until the tide turned and the fog cleared off. They immediately hurried to Washington, informed him of the impending danger, and induced him to call a council and order a retreat. Mr. Bancroft, however, has shown very thoroughly that this account cannot be accepted, because the fog did not come up until the morning of the 30th, and no change of wind occurred. Colonel Reed himself says in the Livingston letter, written only the next morning, that the enemy's fleet were attempting every day to get up to town with " the wind *ahead*"—thus directly contradicting his biographer. The Reed account has several errors of detail, one being the statement that the Red Hook battery had been badly damaged by the guns of the Roebuck on the 27th. It would be nearer the truth to say that it was not hit at all. The fleet could do nothing that day ; as Admiral Howe reports, the Roebuck was " the only ship that could fetch high enough to the northward to exchange *a few random shot* with the battery on Red Hook."

In a word, Washington, after receiving Mifflin's report in regard to the approaches of the enemy, and probably other reports from Grayson, Reed, and others in regard to the general condition of the troops (for instance, Colonel Shee's uneasiness, referred to by Graydon), found that the moment had come for decision. That decision was to retreat that night ; and during the forenoon, several hours before the council met, he issued secret orders for the concentration of boats at the ferry, as described in the text.

Mifflin to General Heath at King's Bridge to the following effect:

LONG [ISLAND, August 29th, 1776.

DEAR GENERAL—We have many battalions from New Jersey which are coming over to relieve others here. You will please therefore to order every flat bottomed boat and other craft at your post, fit for transporting troops, down to New York as soon as possible. They must be manned by some of Colonel Hutchinson's men and sent without the least delay. I write by order of the General. I am Affectionately Yours

MIFFLIN.

At about the same time, Colonel Trumbull, the commissary-general, was directed to carry a verbal order to Assistant Quartermaster Hughes at New York, " to impress every kind of water craft from Hell Gate on the Sound to Spuyten Duyvil Creek that could be kept afloat and that had either sails or oars, and have them all in the east harbor of the City by dark." [1] These two orders were carried out with great energy, promptness, and secrecy by all who had any part in their execution. Heath "immediately complied " with what Mifflin had written, and sent down all his boats under Hutchinson's men from Salem, who, like Glover's from Marblehead, were, many of them, the best of sailors. He brooked the less delay, perhaps, because he saw at once that Washington's " real intention" was, not to be reinforced from New Jersey, but to retreat from Long Island. [2] Hughes, on his part, was untiring, and rendered the greatest service. He would have been mistaken this day rather for the master of a military school, than for what he had been—the master of a classical one. For twenty-two hours, as his

---

[1] Memorial of Colonel Hugh Hughes. Leake's Life of General Lamb.
[2] Heath's Memoirs.

biographer tells us, he never dismounted from his horse, but superintended the collection of the vessels from all points, and at evening had them ready for their purpose.[1]

The final withdrawal of the troops from the lines was effected under the cover of a plausible general order, which was the only one known to have been issued by the commander-in-chief while on Long Island.[2] This order now comes to light for the first time, and is important as serving to correct the improbable though stan-

---

[1] There is an interesting letter of Washington's preserved in the Hughes Memorial, which adds light on this point. Eight years after the event, when Hughes needed some official certificate showing his authority to impress all the craft he could find, the general replied to him as follows :

" My memory is not charged with the particulars of the verbal order which you say was delivered to you through Col. Joseph Trumbull, on the 27th, August, 1776, ' for impressing all the sloops, boats, and water craft from Spyhten Duyvel, in the Hudson, to Hell Gate, in the Sound.' I recollect that it was a day which required the utmost exertion, particularly in the Quarter-Master's department, to accomplish the retreat which was intended, under cover of the succeeding night ; and that no delay or ceremony could be admitted in the execution of the plan. I have no doubt, therefore, of your having received orders to the effect, and to the extent which you have mentioned ; and you are at liberty to adduce this in testimony thereof. It will, I presume, supply the place of a more formal certificate, and is more consonant with my recollection of the transactions of that day." It appears from this that Washington remembered that the *entire day* of the 29th was devoted to planning and preparing for the retreat, and this fits the theory advanced in the note on the " Origin of the Retreat." As to the delivery of the orders about boats, it is probable that Trumbull crossed to New York with Mifflin's letter to Heath and gave it to Hughes to forward. At the same time he gave Hughes his instructions verbally. Hughes received them, says his biographer, about noon. He then had eight hours to carry them out, which gave him time to send to Heath and for Heath to comply, while he and his assistants scoured the coast everywhere else for boats, from Hell Gate down. Among other sloops impressed was the Middlesex, Captain Stephen Hogeboom, while on its way to Claverack. " I was prevented from proceeding," says the captain, " by Coll Wardsworth and Commissary Hughes who ordered your memorialist over with the sloop to Long Island ferry where she was used to carry off the Troops and stores after the unfortunate retreat, &c."—*N. Y. Hist. MS.*, vol. i., p. 620.

[2] *Document* 3. " General Orders. Head-Quarters Long Island, Aug. 29, 1776. Parole, *Sullivan*, Countersign, *Greene*."—*Col. Douglas' Order Book.*

dard theory that the regiments were moved from their posts under the impression that they were to make a night attack upon the enemy.[1] The order as actually given was far more rational, and less likely to excite suspicion as to its true intent. In the first place, the sick, " being an encumbrance to the army " were directed to be sent to the hospital, their arms and accoutrements taken with them, and from there to be conveyed across to New York and reported to Surgeon-General Morgan. In the next place, the order announced that troops under General Mercer were expected that afternoon from New Jersey, with whom it was proposed to relieve a proportionate number of the regiments on Long Island, and " make a change in the situation of them." In view of the distressed condition of most of the troops at the lines, the propriety of such a " change" was obvious ; and in all probability Washington did originally intend to make the relief. And last, as it was apparently undecided what regiments were to be relieved, they were all, or the greater part of them, directed " to parade with their arms, accoutrements, and knapsacks, at 7 o'clock, at the head of their encampments and there wait for orders." On the evening of the 29th, accordingly, we find the troops ready at their camps and the lines to march off at a moment's notice, and all prepared for a retreat by the most natural arrangement that could have been devised to conceal the real design.[2]

[1] All our principal accounts follow Graydon, who states that the order to attack the enemy was given " regimentally." Colonel Hand, in his letter describing the night's incidents (Reed's Life of Reed), makes no allusion to such an order, but on the contrary states that he and the other colonels of the covering party were told that they were to retreat. An order to attack would have been a poor disguise for a retreat, for every man must have felt its utter rashness and at once suspected some other move.

[2] A letter from Tilghman, Washington's aid, shows that the troops re-

At dark, the withdrawal began. As one regiment moved away towards the ferry another would have its situation "changed" to fill the gap, or extended from right to left. Every move at first was conducted busily, yet quietly and without confusion. Colonel Little, referring to his part this night, leaves the simple record that the general ordered each regiment to be paraded on their own parades at seven o'clock P.M., and wait for orders. "We received orders," he says, "to strike our tents and march, with our baggage, to New York." Colonel Douglas writes: "I received orders to call in my guard *all*, and march immediately with the utmost silence." Hitchcock's Rhode Islanders carried their baggage and camp equipage to the boats on their shoulders "through mud and mire and not a ray of light visible." The embarkation was made from the ferry—the present Fulton Ferry—where General McDougall superintended the movements. Between seven and eight o'clock the boats were manned by Glover's and Hutchinson's men, and they went to work with sailor-like cheer and despatch. The militia and levies were the first to cross, though there was some vexing delay in getting them off. Unluckily, too, about nine o'clock the adverse wind and tide and pouring rain began to make the navigation of the river difficult. A north-easter sprang up, and Glover's men could do nothing with the sloops and sail-boats. If the row-boats only were to be depended upon, all the troops could not be ferried over before morning. Discouraged at the prospect, McDougall sent Colonel Gray-

ceived the impression that they were to be relieved. The retreat, he says, "was conducted with so much Secrecy that neither Subalterns or privates knew that the whole army was to cross back again to N. York ; they thought only a few regiments were to go back."—*Document* 29.

son, of Washington's staff, to inform the general as to how matters stood, but unable to find him Grayson returned, and McDougall went on with the embarkation in spite of its difficulties. Most fortunately, however, at eleven o'clock there was another and a favorable change in the weather. The north-east wind died away, and soon after a gentle breeze set in from the south-west, of which the sailors took quick advantage, and the passage was now "direct, easy, and expeditious." The troops were pushed across as fast as possible in every variety of craft —row-boats, flat-boats, whale-boats, pettiaugers, sloops, and sail-boats—some of which were loaded to within three inches of the water, which was "as smooth as glass."

Meanwhile nearly a fatal blunder occurred at the lines. Early in the evening, a force had been selected, consisting of Hand's, Smallwood's, Haslet's, Shee's, Magaw's, and Chester's regiments, to remain at the works to the last and cover the retreat. General Mifflin commanded the party. Smallwood's men were stationed in Fort Putnam, part of Hand's under Captain Miller in the redoubt on the left, and the rest at the lines on the right of the main road ; and the other regiments near them. Brooklyn Church was to be the alarm-post, where the covering party was to concentrate in case the enemy attacked during the night. About two o'clock in the morning, Major Scammell, one of Sullivan's aids now serving with Washington, mistook his orders and started Mifflin's entire command for the ferry. All the regiments had left the lines and were marching down the main road, when Washington, who seemed to be everywhere during the night, met them and exclaimed in astonishment that unless the lines were immediately re-manned "the most dis-

Jn.º Glover

COLONEL FOURTEENTH REGIMENT OF FOOT (MASS.)
BRIGADIER GENERAL 1777.

agreeable consequences" might follow, as every thing then was in confusion at the ferry. Mifflin's party promptly faced about and reoccupied their stations until dawn, when Providence again "interposed in favor of the retreating army." To have attempted to withdraw in clear daylight would have been a hazardous experiment for these regiments, but just before dawn a heavy fog began to settle over Long Island, and the covering party was safe. So dense was this "heavenly messenger," as Gordon happily describes it, that it effectually hid the American lines from the British pickets. When the final order, therefore, came about sunrise for Mifflin's men to retire to the ferry, they were enabled to do so under cover of the fog without exciting any suspicion of their movements in the enemy's camp.[1] "We kept up fires,

---

[1] Mr. Reed, the biographer, states that the fog rose on the 29th. Dr. Stiles, in his "History of Brooklyn," says : "At midnight a dense fog arose, which remained motionless and impenetrable over the island during the whole of the next day [the 29th]." "A dense fog," writes Mr. Field, "hung over the island and river, when the morning of the 29th dawned." Now nothing is more certain than that the fog did not rise until shortly before dawn of the 30th, full six hours after the retreat had begun. The 28th and 29th, as already seen, were days of rain-storms, not mist, nor fog, but storm, "torrents," such rain at times the like of which could "hardly be remembered." Contemporary writers who mention the rains say nothing of fog on the 29th, whereas they do notice its appearance the next morning. Major Tallmadge writes : "As the dawn of the next day approached, those of us who remained in the trenches became very anxious for our own safety, and when the dawn appeared, there were several regiments still on duty. At this time a very dense fog began to rise, and it seemed to settle in a peculiar manner over both encampments. I recollect this peculiar providential occurrence perfectly well ; and so very dense was the atmosphere that I could scarcely discern a man at six yards' distance." This officer's regiment was one of the covering party, and he adds that after leaving the lines by mistake, and receiving orders to return, "Col. Chester immediately faced to the right about and returned, where we tarried until the sun had risen, but the fog remained as dense as ever." "At sunrise a great fog came up," says a spectator (*Stiles' MS. Diary*). An officer or soldier of either Shee's or Magaw's regiment, also of the covering party, wrote a few hours after crossing : "We received orders to quit our station about two o'clock this morning, and had made our retreat almost to the ferry when Gen. Washington ordered us

with outposts stationed," says Lieutenant-Colonel Chambers, " until all the rest were over. We left the lines after it was fair day and then came off." As our soldiers withdrew they distinctly heard the sound of pickaxe and shovel at the British works.[1] Before seven o'clock the entire force had crossed to New York, and among the last to leave was the commander-in-chief. " General Washington," adds Chambers, " saw the last over himself."

By the army the retreat was welcomed as a great relief, a salvation from probable calamity. Not a few appreciated its completeness and success as a strictly military move. " This evacuation," writes one, " is a masterpiece." " That grand retreat from the Island which will ever reflect honour to our Generals," says another. " Considering the difficulties," is Greene's criticism, " it was the best effected retreat I ever read or heard of." " It was executed," says Scott, " with unexpected success." But in the country at large it was generally associated with the defeat of the 27th, and the skilfulness with which it was conducted little compensated for the fact that the retreat was forced upon us.

back to that part of the lines we were first at, which was reckoned to be the most dangerous post. We got back undiscovered by the enemy, and continued there until daylight. Providentially for us, a great fog arose, which prevented the enemy from seeing our retreat from their works which was not more than musket shot from us."—*Force*, 5th Series, vol. i., p. 1233. So also, Stedman, the British historian, referring to the events of the night of the 29th–30th, says : "Another remarkable circumstance was, that on Long Island hung a thick fog, which prevented the British troops from discovering the operations of the enemy." Washington did not, as often stated in popular accounts, take advantage of a fog to cover his retreat. More than half the army was over before the fog appeared ; but it protected the covering party, and saved us the loss of considerable baggage and other material.

[1] An English patrol under Captain Montressor discovered the retreat of the Americans very soon after the latter left the lines, and reported the fact at once. But for some unexplained reason pursuit was delayed until too late. One boat with four stragglers was taken by the enemy.

CHAPTER VI.

LONG ISLAND surrendered, could New York be held? Columbia Heights, where Fort Stirling stood, had been regarded by Lee as the "capital point," the key of the position. Greene called the Brooklyn front "the pass," on the possession of which depended the security of the city. Both pass and heights were now in the enemy's hands, and New York was at their mercy. "We are in hourly expectation," wrote Commissary Trumbull, September 1st, "that the town will be bombarded." Lieutenant Jasper Ewing, of Hand's riflemen, saw that the British could reduce the place to "a heap of ashes" in a day's time. Colonel Douglas looked for an immediate cannonade from Fort Stirling, "which," he says, "I have the mortification to think I helped build myself." But the enemy kept their guns quiet, as they wished neither to injure the city nor drive our army away. They contented themselves at first with stretching their troops along the water front from Red Hook to Hell Gate, Newtown, and Flushing on Long Island, and threatening to land at any point on Manhattan Island from the Battery to Harlem, or beyond on the Westchester shore.

As for Washington, the successful retreat had not in

15

the least relieved him from care or anxiety. He had escaped one trap : it was of the utmost consequence now to see that he did not fall into another. What he feared most was a sudden move upon his rear in Westchester County, for in that case he would be hopelessly hemmed in on Manhattan Island. "The enemy," continued Trumbull on the 1st, "are drawing their men to the eastward on Long Island, as if they intended to throw a strong party over on this island, near Hell Gate, so as to get on the back of the city. We are preparing to meet them." Haslet wrote August 31st : "I expect every moment orders to march off to Kingsbridge to prevent the enemy crossing the East River and confining us on another nook. . . If they can coop us up in N. York by intrenching from river to river, horrid will be the consequences from their command of the rivers." General Heath pressed the matter of watching the Westchester coast, and Washington, concurring with him "as to the probability of the enemy's endeavoring to land their forces at Hunt's Point," above Hell Gate, wrote him on the 31st : "In order to prevent such an attempt from being carried into execution I have sent up General Mifflin with the troops he brought from your quarters, strengthened by reinforcements. With this assistance I hope you will be able to defeat their intentions. I beg you will exert yourself to the utmost of your abilities on this momentous occasion." Several days passing without any demonstration by the enemy, Washington's suspense was only protracted, and on September 5th he wrote again to Heath as follows :

"As everything in a manner depends upon obtaining intelligence of the enemy's motions, I do most earnestly entreat you and General Clinton to exert yourselves to accomplish this most desir-

able end. Leave no stone unturned, nor do not stick at expense
to bring this to pass, as I never was more uneasy than on account
of my want of knowledge on this score.

" Keep, besides this precaution, constant lookouts (with good
glasses) on some commanding heights that look well on to the
other shore (and especially into the bays, where boats can be concealed), that they may observe, more particularly in the evening,
if there be any uncommon movements. Much will depend upon
early intelligence, and meeting the enemy before they can in-
trench. I should much approve of small harassing parties, stealing, as it were, over in the night, as they might keep the enemy
alarmed, and more than probably bring off a prisoner, from whom
some valuable intelligence may be obtained." [1]

To add to his burdens, the commander-in-chief found
the condition of his army growing worse instead of improving. The experiences on Long Island had disheartened many of the troops, and their escape had not revived their spirits.[2] The militia became impatient and
went home in groups and whole companies, and indeed
in such numbers as to materially diminish the strength of
the army. To restore order and confidence, Washington
exerted himself to the utmost. Tilghman, one of his aids,
speaks of " the vast hurry of business" in which the general was engaged at this time. " He is obliged," he
writes, " to see into, and in a manner fill every department, which is too much for one man." To Rodney,
Haslet wrote : " I fear Gen¹ Washington has too

---

[1] " The Heath Correspondence," Mass. Hist. Soc. Coll., 1878.

[2] Pastor Shewkirk notes in his diary that immediately after the retreat " a
general damp" seemed to spread over the army. " The merry tones on
drums and fifes had ceased, and they were hardly heard for a couple of
days." The wet clothes, accoutrements, and tents were lying about in front
of the houses and in the streets, and every thing was in confusion. But this
was to be expected. General Scott, referring evidently to expressions heard
among his own men, says that some declared that they had been " sold out,"
and others longed to have Lee back from the South.—*Scott's MS. Letter*, September 6th, 1776.

heavy a task, assisted mostly by beardless boys."[1] But fortunately for the country the general's shoulders were broad enough for these great duties, and his faith and resolution remained unshaken.

As soon as possible the army was reorganized and stationed to meet the new phase of the situation. Several changes were made in the brigades, and the whole divided into three grand divisions, under Putnam, Spencer, and Heath. Putnam's, consisting of five brigades, remained in the city and guarded the East River above as far as Fifteenth Street ; Spencer's, of six brigades, took up the line from that point to Horn's Hook and Harlem ; and Heath with two brigades watched King's Bridge and the Westchester shore. Greene had not sufficiently recovered from his illness, and his old troops, under Nixon and Heard, were temporarily doing duty with Spencer's command.[2] This disposition was effected by the 2d of September, and by it our army again occupied an extended line, endeavoring to protect every point on the east side from the battery to King's Bridge, or the entire length of the island, a distance of fourteen and a half miles.

The question of abandoning New York and all that part of the island below Harlem Heights was, meanwhile, under consideration. The city would obviously be untenable under a bombardment, and the island equally

---

[1] Washington's aids were most of them quite young men.

[2] A large number of changes were made in the organization of the army after the retreat. The Connecticut militia were divided up and formed into brigades with the levies under General Wadsworth, Colonel Silliman, Colonel Douglas, and Colonel Chester. A brigade was given also to Colonel Sargent, of Massachusetts. Putnam's division included Parsons', Scott's, James Clinton's (Glover's), Fellows', and Silliman's brigades ; Spencer's and Greene's divisions included Nixon's, Heard's, McDougall's, Wadsworth's, Douglas', Chester's and Sargent's brigades ; while Heath had his former brigades, with a change of some regiments, under Mifflin and George Clinton.

so if the British crossed into Westchester County. Yet Washington, strangely, we may say, expressed the conviction that he could hold both provided his troops could be depended upon.[1] Among his generals, Greene earnestly opposed any such attempt, and advocated the evacuation and destruction of the place. " The City and Island of New York," he wrote to his chief, September 5th, " are no objects for us ; we are not to bring them into competition with the general interests of America. . . . The sacrifice of the vast property of New York and the suburbs, I hope has no influence on your Excellency's measures. Remember the King of France. When Charles the Fifth, Emperor of Germany, invaded his Kingdom, he laid whole Provinces waste ; and by that policy he starved and ruined Charles's army, and defeated him without fighting a battle. Two-thirds of the property of the City of New York and the suburbs belong to the tories. We have no very great reason to run any considerable risk for its defence. . . . I would give it as my opinion that a general and speedy retreat is absolutely necessary, and that the honour and interest of America require it. I would burn the city." John Jay before this also proposed its destruction. Scott urged abandonment of the place for sound military reasons, though the move would ruin him. Washington, however, on the 2d, presented the whole question to Congress. Also convinced by the condition of the army, that the city must be evacuated, he asked, " If we should be obliged to abandon

---

[1] " Till of late I had no doubt in my own mind of defending this place, nor should I have yet, if the men would do their duty, but this I despair of. It is painful, and extremely grating to me, to give such unfavorable accounts; but it would be criminal to conceal the truth at so critical a juncture."— *Washington to Congress*, September 2d, 1776.

the town, ought it to stand as winter quarters for the enemy?'' Congress voted, in reply, that "it should in no event be damaged, for they had no doubt of being able to recover it, even though the enemy should obtain possession of it for a time." On the 7th, a council of war, inferring that Congress wished the place to be held, decided to retain five thousand troops in the city and concentrate the rest around and above Harlem ; but on the 12th the matter was reconsidered, and a second council voted to evacuate the city and retire to Harlem Heights. The removal of stores and the sick had already commenced ; and on the 14th, when the enemy appeared to be on the point of crossing from Montressor's, now Randall's, Island to the mainland, all the teams and wagons that could be found were impressed by the quartermasters to remove the remaining stores. In one day more the removal would have been complete and the troops all withdrawn to the heights. In the evening of the 14th Washington left the city, and established his head-quarters at the Morris Mansion, at One Hundred and Sixty-first Street, overlooking Harlem River and the plains.[1]

The enemy made no advance from Long Island until more than two weeks after the battle. Howe's preparations were delayed because dependent upon the co-operation of the fleet. On the night of the 3d of September, the frigate Rose, of thirty-two guns, sailed up the East

[1] Colonel Reed, the adjutant-general, wrote to his wife, September 14th, from New York : '' My baggage is all at King's bridge. We expect to remove thither this evening. I mean our headquarters.''—*Reed's Reed*. Washington, writing of the events of the 15th, says : '' I had gone the night before to the main body of the army which was posted on the plains and heights of Harlem.'' These references fail to confirm the common statement that Washington made the Murray House on Thirty-sixth Street his quarters for a short time after leaving the city.

River convoying thirty boats, and running through the fire of our guns at the Grand Battery, the ship-yards, and Corlears Hook, anchored close into Wallabout Bay, where on the 5th our artillerists "briskly cannonaded" her. After dark on the 12th, thirty-six additional boats passed our batteries to Bushwick Creek, and the night after forty more followed. Then towards sunset on the 14th, the frigates Roebuck, Phœnix, Orpheus, and Carysfort, with six transports, joined the Rose without receiving material injury from the heavy fire poured upon them by our gunners.

On the following morning, the 15th, the British moved against Manhattan Island, and in the afternoon New York City fell into their possession. What occurred beforehand during the day is known as the "Kip's Bay affair."[1]

[1] According to the Hessian major, Baurmeister, the 13th had been first named as the date for the attack. "On this day," he writes, "General Howe wished to land upon the island of New York, because 18 years ago on this day General Wulff [Wolfe] had conquered at Quebec, but also lost his life. The watchword for this end was 'Quebec' and the countersign 'Wulff,' but the frigates were too late for this attack as they only sailed out of the fleet at five o'clock on the evening of the 14th."

The sailing up of these ships is described as follows by the Hon. Joshua Babcock, one of the Rhode Island Committee who had come down to consult with Washington in regard to military matters : " Just after Dinner 3 Frigates and a 40 Gun Ship (as if they meant to attack the city) sail'd up the East River under a gentle Breeze towards Hell-Gate, & kept up an incessant Fire assisted with the Cannon at Governʳˢ Island : The Batteries from the City return'd the Ships the like Salutation : 3 Men agape, idle Spectators had the misfortune of being killed by one Cannon-Ball, the other mischief suffered on our Side was inconsiderable Saving the making a few Holes in some of the Buildings ; one shot struck within 6 Foot of Genˡ Washington, as He was on Horseback riding into the Fort."—*MS. Letter in R. I. Public Archives.* Also in *Force.*

Baurmeister preserves the incident that Washington was often to be seen at the East River batteries in New York, and on one occasion " provoked the Hessian artillery Captain Krug [on the Long Island side] to fire off 2 Cannon at him and his suite." " A third shot too would not have been wanting, if the horses of the enemy had been pleased to stay," adds the major.

Kip's Bay was the large cove which then set in from the East River at about the foot of Thirty-fourth Street. It took its name from the old Kip family, who owned the adjacent estate. From this point breastworks had been thrown up along the river's bank, wherever a landing could be made, down as far as Corlears Hook or Grand Street. Five brigades had been distributed at this front to watch the enemy. Silliman's was in the city; at Corlears Hook was Parsons' brigade, to which Prescott's Massachusetts men had now been added; beyond, in the vicinity of Fifteenth Street, on the Stuyvesant estate, Scott's New York brigade took post; above him, at about Twenty-third Street, was Wadsworth's command, consisting of Sage's, Selden's, and Gay's Connecticut levies; and further along near Kip's Bay was Colonel Douglas, with his brigade of three Connecticut militia regiments under Cooke, Pettibone, and Talcott, and his own battalion of levies.[1] Up the river a chain of sentinels communicated with the troops at Horn's Hook, and every half hour they passed the watchword to each other, "All is well."

Very early on the morning of the 15th, which was Sunday, the five British frigates which had anchored under the Long Island shore sailed up and took position close within musket-shot of our lines at Kip's Bay, somewhat to the left of Douglas. This officer immediately moved

[1] We know the position of the troops from the statements of their officers. Douglas says : "I lay with my brigade a little below Turtle [Kips] Bay where we hove up lines for more than one mile in length. Gen'l Wadsworth managed the lines on the right and I on the left." Brigade-Major Fish says of Scott's brigade that they were "marched to the lines back of Stuyvesant's," about the foot of Fifteenth Street. Parsons was below at Corlears Hook as appears from *Document* 32. Silliman himself says that he was in the city. Consult map of New York, Part II., where the position at the time of the British attack is given.

his brigade abreast of them. The ships were so near, says Martin, one of Douglas' soldiers, that he could distinctly read the name of the Phœnix, which was lying " a little quartering." Meanwhile, on the opposite shore, in Newtown Creek, the British embarked their light infantry and reserves, and Donop's grenadiers and yagers, all under Clinton and Cornwallis, in eighty-four boats, and drew. up in regular order on the water ready to cross to the New York side.[1] The soldier just quoted remembered that they looked like " a large clover field in full bloom." All along the line our soldiers were watching these movements with anxious curiosity — that night they would have been withdrawn from the position—when suddenly between ten and eleven o'clock the five frigates opened a sweeping fire from their seventy or eighty guns upon the breastworks where Douglas and his brigade were drawn up. It came like " a peal of thunder," and the militiamen could do nothing but keep well under cover. The enemy fired at them at their pleasure, from " their tops and everywhere," until our men soon found it im-

[1] " The first landing was of 84 boats with English infantry and Hessian grenadiers under command of Lieut-General Clinton. Commodore Hotham conducted this landing, under cover of 5 frigates anchored close before Kaaps [Kip's] Bay above Cron Point, and maintained a 3 hours cannonade on the enemy's advanced posts in the great wood. The signal of the red flag denoted the departure of the boats, the blue on the contrary the stoppage of the passage, and if a retreat should become necessary, a yellow flag would be shown."—*Baurmeister*. " Sunday morning at break of day, five ships weighed anchor and fell in close within a musket shot of our lines quite to the left of me. I then moved my brigade abreast of them. They lay very quiet until 10 o'clock and by that time they had about 80 of their boats from under Long Island shore full with men which contained about five or six thousand and four transports full ready to come in the second boats." —*Col. Douglas.*

Major Fish wrote September 19th that the enemy's ships of war were drawn up " in line of Battle parallel to the shore, the Troops to the amount of about 4000 being embarked in flat bottom Boats, and the Boats paraded." —*Hist. Mag.*

possible to stay in that position. "We kept the lines," says Martin, "till they were almost levelled upon us, when our officers, seeing we could make no resistance, and no orders coming from any superior officer, and that we must soon be entirely exposed to the rake of the guns, gave the order to leave." At the same time the flotilla crossed the river, and getting under cover of the smoke of the ships' guns, struck off to the left of Douglas, where the troops effected a landing without difficulty. Howe says : "The fire of the shipping being so well directed and so incessant, the enemy could not remain in their works, and the descent was made without the least opposition." The ordeal the militia were subjected to was something which in similar circumstances veteran troops have been unable to withstand.[1] Retreating from the lines, Douglas's men scattered to the rear towards the Post Road, and the enemy who landed and formed rapidly were soon after them. Douglas himself, who was an excellent officer, was the last to leave, and all but escaped capture.[2] There was no collecting the brigade, however,

---

[1] All accounts agree that it was next to impossible to remain under the fire of the men-of-war. Major Fish says that "a Cannonade from the ships began, which far exceeded my Ideas, and which seemed to infuse a Panic thro' the whole of our Troops, &c." Silliman speaks of the "incessant fire on our lines" with grapeshot as being "so hot" that the militia were compelled to retreat. Douglas's description is as quaint as it is expressive : "They very suddenly began as heavy a cannonade perhaps as ever was from no more ships, as they had nothing to molest them." Martin thought his head would "go with the sound." Lieutenant John Heinrichs, of the Hessian yagers, writes : "Last Sunday we landed under the thundering rattle of 5 men-of-war."

[2] The enemy's boats, says Douglas, "got under cover of the smoke of the shipping and then struck to the left of my lines in order to cut me off from a retreat. My left wing gave way which was formed of the militia. I lay myself on the right wing waiting for the boats until Capt. Prentice came to me and told me, if I meant to save myself to leave the lines, for that was the orders on the left and that they had left the lines. I then told my men to make the best of their way as I found I had but about ten left with me. They soon moved out and I then made the best of my way out."—See further in *Documents*, Part II., p. 71.

in any new position in the field, for the thought of being intercepted had created a panic among the militia, and they fled in confusion.

When the cannonade at Kip's Bay began, Washington was four miles distant, at Harlem. At the first sound of the guns he mounted his horse and rode with all possible despatch to the scene. At about the same time, General Parsons, probably by Putnam's order, directed Prescott's, Tyler's, and the remnant of Huntington's regiment, not over eighty strong, to march immediately to the assistance of the troops where the enemy were landing.[1] Fellows' brigade was also ordered along for the same purpose.

At about the corner of the present Thirty-sixth Street and Fourth Avenue stood at that time the residence of Robert Murray, the Quaker merchant, on what was known as "Inclenberg" heights, now Murray Hill. His grounds extended to the Post Road, which there ran along the line of Lexington Avenue. Just above him a cross-road connected the Post and Bloomingdale roads, which is repesented to-day by the line of Forty-second and Forty-third streets. On the south side of the cross-road where it intersected the Post Road was a large corn-field adjoining or belonging to Murray's estate. When Washington reached this vicinity he found the militia retreating in disorder along both the cross and the Post roads, and Fellows' brigade just coming on to the field. The general, with Putnam and others, was then on the rising ground in the vicinity of the present Forty-second Street reservoir. In a very short time Parsons and his regiments arrived by the Bloomingdale Road, and Wash-

[1] *Document* 32.

ington in person directed them to form along the line of
the Post Road in front of the enemy, who were rapidly
advancing from Kip's Bay. " Take the walls !" " Take
the' cornfield !" he shouted ; and Parsons' men quickly
ran to the walls and the field, but in a confused and disordered manner. Their general did his best to get them
into line on the ground, but found it impossible, they
were so dispersed, and, moreover, they were now beginning to retreat. The panic which had seized the Connecticut militia was communicated to Fellows' Massachusetts men, who were also militia ; and now it was to sweep
up Parsons' Continentals, including Prescott's men of
Bunker Hill. The latter brigade had been brought on
to the ground in bad shape through the fugitive militiamen, and when the British light infantry appeared they
broke and retreated with the rest.

To Washington all this confusion and rout seemed
wholly unnecessary and unreasonable, and dashing in
among the flying crowds he endeavored to convince them
that there was no danger, and used his utmost exertions
to bring them into some order. He was roused to more
than indignation at the sight, and in his letter to Congress on the following day denounced the conduct of
these troops as " disgraceful and dastardly." [1] Putnam,

---

[1] Washington's account of the panic is as follows :

" As soon as I heard the firing, I rode with all possible despatch towards
the place of landing, where to my great surprise and mortification I found the
troops that had been posted in the lines retreating with the utmost precipitation and those ordered to support them (Parsons' and Fellows' brigades) flying in every direction, and in the greatest confusion, notwithstanding the exertions of their generals to form them. I used every means in my power to
rally and to get them into some order ; but my attempts were fruitless and
ineffectual ; and on the appearance of a small party of the enemy, not more
than sixty or seventy, their disorder increased, and they ran away in the
greatest confusion, without firing a single shot."

There were several stories current after the affair which cannot be traced to

Parsons, Fellows, and others were equally active in attempting to stop the flight, but it was to no purpose. "The very demons of fear and disorder," says Martin, "seemed to take full possession of all and everything on that day." Nothing remained but to continue the retreat by the Bloomingdale Road to Harlem Heights.

During these scenes, Wadsworth's and Scott's brigades, which were below Douglas on the river lines, saw that their only safety lay, also, in immediate retreat, and falling back, they joined the other brigades above, though not without suffering some loss. The parties now in the greatest danger were Silliman's brigade and Knox with detachments of the artillery, who were still in the city three miles below. When Putnam, to whose division they belonged, found that no stand could be made at Kip's Bay or Murray's Hill, he galloped down through Wadsworth's and Scott's retreating troops, to extricate Silliman and the others.[1] Not a moment's time was to be lost, for should the British stretch out their troops west of the Bloomingdale Road to the North River, escape would be impossible. Silliman, meanwhile, had taken post with Knox in and to the right of Bayard's Hill Fort,

any responsible source. One was that the Commander-in-Chief was so "distressed and enraged" at the conduct of the troops that "he drew his sword and snapped his pistols to check them;" and that one of his suite was obliged to seize his horse's reins and take him out of danger from the enemy. Another account represents that he threw his hat on the ground and exclaimed whether such were the troops with which he was to defend America; another states that he sought "death rather than life." Mr. Bancroft has shown how far these statements are to be accepted.

[1] Hezekiah Munsell, a soldier of Gay's regiment in Wadsworth's brigade, says : "We soon reached the main road which our troops were travelling, and the first conspicuous person I met was Gen. Putnam. He was making his way towards New York when all were going from it. Where he was going I could not conjecture, though I afterwards learned he was going after a small garrison of men in a crescent fortification which he brought off safe."—*Hist. of Ancient Windsor*, p. 715.

from the top of which they could see the enemy occupying the island above them. At this juncture, Major Aaron Burr, Putnam's aid, rode up to the fort with orders to retreat. He was told that retreat was out of the question. Knox said that he should defend the fort to the last. But Burr, who knew the ground thoroughly, declared that he could pilot them safely to the upper end of the island, and Silliman's men set out for the attempt.[1] Putnam also had called in other guards, and the entire force then took to the woods above Greenwich, on the west side, and keeping under cover wherever it was possible, made their way along without opposition. But it proved to be a most trying and hazardous march. The day was "insupportably hot;" more than one soldier died at the spring or brook where he drank; any moment the enemy, who at some points were not half a mile away, might be upon them. Officers rode in advance and to the right to reconnoitre and see that the way was clear. Putnam, Silliman, Burr, and others were conspicuous in their exertions. Silliman was "sometimes in the front, sometimes in the centre, and sometimes in the rear." The men extended along in the woods for two miles, and the greatest precautions were necessary to keep them out of sight of the main road.[2] Putnam encouraged them con-

---

[1] Affidavits in Davis' "Life of Burr," vol. i.

[2] The line of Putnam's retreat appears to have been from Bayard's Hill Fort on Grand Street across the country to Monument Lane (now Greenwich Avenue), which led to the obelisk erected in honor of General Wolf and others at a point on Fifteenth Street, a little west of Eighth Avenue. (See Montressor's Map of New York in 1775, "Valentine's Manual.") The lane there joined with an irregular road running on the line of Eighth Avenue, known afterwards as the Abington or Fitz Roy road, as far as Forty-second or Third Street. There Putnam, under Burr's guidance probably, pushed through the woods, keeping west of the Bloomingdale Road, and finally taking the latter at some point above Seventieth Street, and so on to Harlem Heights. (See Map of New York, Part II.)

tinually by flying on his horse, covered with foam, wherever his presence was most necessary. " Without his extraordinary exertions," says Colonel Humphreys, who frequently saw Putnam that day, " the guards must have been inevitably lost, and it is probable the entire corps would have been cut in pieces." Much, too, of the success of the march was due to Burr's skill and knowledge. Near Bloomingdale, the command fell in with a party of the British, when Silliman formed three hundred of his men and beat them off. After making a winding march of at least " twelve miles," these greatly distressed troops finally reached Harlem Heights after dark, to the surprise and relief of the other brigades, who had given them up for lost.

Although skilfully conducted, this escape is to be referred, in reality, to Howe's supineness and the hospitality of Mrs. Robert Murray, at whose house the British generals stopped for rest and refreshment after driving back our troops. Instead of continuing a vigorous pursuit or making any effort to intercept other parties, they spent a valuable interval at the board of their entertaining hostess, whose American sympathies added flavor and piquancy to the conversation. " Mrs. Murray," says Dr. Thacher in his military journal, " treated them with cake and wine, and they were induced to tarry two hours or more, Governor Tryon frequently joking her about her American friends. By this happy incident, General Putnam, by continuing his march, escaped a rencounter with a greatly superior force, which must have proved fatal to his whole party. Ten minutes, it is said, would have been sufficient for the enemy to have secured the road at the turn and entirely cut off General Putnam's retreat. It has since become almost a common saying among our officers, that Mrs. Murray saved this part of the American army."

Of the Kip's Bay affair there is but one criticism to be made—it was an ungovernable panic. Beginning with a retreat from the water-line, it grew into a fright and a run for safer ground. Panics are often inexplicable. The best troops as well as the poorest have been known to fly from the merest shadow of danger. In this case, so far as the *beginning* of the rout is concerned, probably the militiamen did no worse than Washington's best men would have done. A retreat from the ship's fire could not have been avoided, though, with better troops, the subsequent rout could have been checked and the enemy retarded.

The incident was especially unfortunate at that time, as it served to increase existing jealousies between the troops from the different States, and so far impair the morale of the army. It excites a smile to-day to read that men from New York, Pennsylvania, and Maryland charged New Englanders generally with provincialism and cowardice, and that the charge was resented ; but such was the fact. The feeling between them grew to such an extent that Washington was obliged to issue orders condemning its indulgence. The Kip's Bay panic offered a favorable opportunity for emphasizing these charges, and the Connecticut and Massachusetts runaways came in for their full share of uncomplimentary epithets. The Connecticut men were remembered particularly, " dastards" and " cowards" being the terms which greeted their ears. All this of course could not but be ruinous to the discipline of the army, and it was an alarming fact to be dealt with.[1] The men south of New England were not without reason in making their harsh criticisms, for many of the New England regiments, the militia in particular, came upon the ground with an inferior military organization. They were miserably officered in many cases, and the men, never expecting to become soldiers as such, were indifferent to discipline. But in another view the criticisms were unfair, because the Pennsylvanians and others, in making comparisons, compared their best troops with New England's poorest. As two thirds of the army were from New England—more than one third from Connecticut—men from this section were necessarily represented largely in every duty or piece of fighting, and whenever any misconduct of a few occurred, it was made to reflect discredit upon the whole. There was no difference between the better drilled and officered regiments from the several States, just as there was little difference between their hastily gathered militia. Thus it may be mentioned as a notable and somewhat humorous coincidence that at the very moment the Connecticut militia were flying from the bombardment of the ships at Kip's

---

[1] This jealousy disappeared when the army was reorganized and the troops became proficient in discipline. The American soldier was then found to be equal to any that could be brought against him, regardless of the locality from which he hailed. But in the present campaign the sectional feeling referred to came near working mischief, especially as it was kept alive by so prominent an officer as Colonel Reed, the Adjutant-general. New England officers protested against the "rancor" and "malice" of his assertions, and represented their injurious influence to members of Congress. Washington, finding that the matter was becoming serious, took the occasion to send a special invitation to Colonels Silliman and Douglas to dine with him in the latter part of September, when he "disavowed and absolutely disapproved every such piece of conduct" which had been a grievance to these and other Eastern officers.—*Silliman's MS. Letter.* See also extracts in Gordon's history as to the condition of the army at this time.

16

Bay, New Jersey and Pennsylvania militia were flying with equal haste from the bombardment of other ships at Powle's Hook as they sailed up the North River to Bloomingdale on the same morning; and that while Reed, Tilghman, Smallwood, and others, were denouncing the Kip's Bay fugitives in unmeasured terms, the indignant Mercer was likewise denouncing the "scandalous" behavior of the fugitives in his own command.[1]

The events of the 15th naturally and justly roused the wrath of both Washington and Mercer, and their denunciations become a part of the record of the time. But in recording them it belongs to those who write a century later to explain and qualify. Justice to the men who figured in these scenes requires that the terms of reproach should not be perpetuated as a final stigma upon their character as soldiers of the Revolution. All military experience proves that troops who have once given way in a panic are not therefore or necessarily poor troops; and the experience at Kip's Bay and Powle's Hook was only an illustration in the proof. These men had their revenge. If the records of New Jersey and Pennsylvania were to be thoroughly examined, they would doubtless show that large numbers of Mercer's militia re-entered the service and acquitted themselves well. This is certainly true of many of the routed crowd whom Washington found it impossible to rally on Murray's Hill and in Murray's cornfield.

---

[1] "The militia of Pennsylvania and New Jersey, stationed on Bergen and at Paulus-Hook, have behaved in a scandalous manner, running off from their posts on the first cannonade from the ships of the enemy. At all the posts we find it difficult to keep the militia to their duty." (*Mercer to Washington*, Sept. 17th, 1776.) "I don't know whether the New Eng^d troops will stand there [at Harlem Heights], but I am sure they will not upon open ground," etc.—*Tilghman. Document 29.*

Some of those who ran from the Light Infantry on the 15th assisted in driving the same Light Infantry on the 16th. Prescott's men a few weeks later successfully defended a crossing in Westchester County and thwarted the enemy's designs. Not a few of the militia in Douglas's brigade were the identical men with whom Oliver Wolcott marched up to meet Burgoyne a year later, and who, under Colonels Cook and Latimer, "threw away their lives" in the decisive action of that campaign, suffering a greater loss than any other two regiments on the field. Fellows, also, was there to co-operate in forcing the British surrender. In Parsons' brigade were young officers and soldiers who formed part of the select corps that stormed Stony Point, and among Wadsworth's troops were others who, five years later, charged upon the Yorktown redoubt with the leading American Light Infantry battalion.[1]

When Washington found that the enemy had made their principal landing at Thirty-fourth Street, and that a retreat was necessary, he sent back word to have Harlem Heights well secured by the troops there, while at the same time a considerable force under Mifflin marched

[1] The Major of this battalion (Gimat's) was John Palsgrave Wyllys, of Hartford, who, as Wadsworth's Brigade-Major, was taken prisoner at Kip's Bay. Alexander Hamilton and Brigade-Major Fish, of New York, who were swept along in this retreat, also figured prominently at Yorktown. Two young ensigns in the Connecticut "levies," Stephen Betts and James Morris, were captains of Light Infantry in that affair. Lieutenant Stephen Olney, of Rhode Island, who barely escaped capture on Long Island by Cornwallis's grenadiers, led Gimat's battalion as captain, and was severely wounded while clambering into the redoubt; and there were probably a considerable number of others, officers and men, who were chased by this British general in the present campaign, who finally had the satisfaction of cornering him in Virginia in 1781. Scammeil, Huntington, Tilghman, Humphreys, and others, could be named.

down to the strong ground near McGowan's to cover the escape of troops that might take the King's Bridge road. Chester and Sargent evacuated Horn's Hook and came in with Mifflin. Upon the landing of more troops at Kip's Bay, Howe sent a column towards McGowan's, and in the evening the Light Infantry reached Apthorpe's just after Silliman's retreat. Washington had waited on the Bloomingdale Road until the last, and retired from the Apthorpe Mansion but a short time before the British occupied it. Here at Bloomingdale the enemy encamped their left wing for the night, while their right occupied Horn's Hook, their outposts not being advanced on the left beyond One Hundredth Street. The Americans slept on Harlem Heights, not quite a mile and a half above them.

" That night," says Humphreys, " our soldiers, excessively fatigued by the sultry march of the day, their clothes wet by a severe shower of rain that succeeded towards the evening, their blood chilled by the cold wind that produced a sudden change in the temperature of the air, and their hearts sunk within them by the loss of baggage, artillery, and works, in which they had been taught to put great confidence, lay upon their arms, covered only by the clouds of an uncomfortable sky." [1]

---

[1] The American loss in prisoners in the Kip's Bay affair was seventeen officers and about three hundred and fifty men, nearly all from Connecticut and New York. A very few were killed and wounded, Major Chapman, of Tyler's regiment, being among the former.

The officer of highest rank among the prisoners was Colonel Samuel Selden, of Hadlyme, Conn., mentioned on page 121. (See biographical sketches, Part II.) One of his officers was Captain Eliphalet Holmes, afterwards of the Continental line, a neighbor of the Colonel's. Being a man of great strength he knocked down two Hessians, who attempted to capture him, and escaped.

During the day, meantime, the British occupied the city. After the departure of the last troops under Silliman (Knox with others escaping to Powle's Hook by boats) a white flag was displayed on Bayard's Hill Redoubt by citizens, and in the afternoon a detachment from the fleet first took possession.[1] In the evening a brigade from Howe's force encamped along the outer line of works. The next forenoon, the 16th, "the first of the English troops came to town," under General Robertson, and were drawn up in two lines on Broadway. Governor Tryon was present with officers of rank and a great concourse of people. "Joy and gladness seemed to appear in all countenances;" while the first act of the victors was to identify and confiscate every house owned and deserted by the rebels. "And thus," says the now happy loyalist pastor Shewkirk, "the city was delivered from those Usurpers who had oppressed it so long."

Fortunately, the demoralizing effect of the panic of the 15th was to be merely temporary. Indeed, before the details of the affair had time to circulate through the camps and work further discouragement or depression, there occurred another encounter with the enemy on the following morning, which neutralized the disgrace of the previous day and revived the spirits of our army to an astonishing degree. So much importance was attached to it at the time as being a greatly needed stimulant for the American soldier that it becomes of interest to follow its particulars. It has passed into our history as the affair or

---

[1] *Baurmeister's Narrative. Shewkirk's Diary.*

BATTLE OF HARLEM HEIGHTS.[1]

'Never for a moment relaxing his watch over the enemy's movements, Washington, before daylight on the morning of the 16th, ordered a reconnoitring party out to ascertain the exact position of the British. The party consisted of the detachment of "Rangers,"[2] or volun-

---

[1] The centennial anniversary of this battle was celebrated in 1876, under the auspices of the New York Historical Society. The oration delivered on the occasion by the Hon. John Jay has been published by the Society, with an appendix containing a large number of documents bearing upon the affair, the whole making a valuable contribution to our Revolutionary history.

[2] THE RANGERS.—The small corps known by this name consisted, first, as already stated, of about one hundred men of Durkee's Connecticut Regiment (Twentieth Continentals), who appear to have accompanied Lieutenant-Colonel Knowlton, of that regiment, when he went on any special service. These he took with him to Long Island. After the battle there the Rangers were formally organized as a separate body, composed of volunteer officers and men from several of the New England regiments. These were borne on their respective regimental rolls as detached "on command." For captains, Knowlton had at least three excellent officers, men from his own region, whom he knew and could trust—Nathan Hale, of Charles Webb's regiment, and Stephen Brown and Thomas Grosvenor, of his own. The rolls in *Force* show that there were officers and men in the Rangers from Durkee's, Webb's, Chester's, Wyllys', and Tyler's Connecticut ; Ward's and Sargent's Massachusetts ; and Varnum's Rhode Island. For a time they received orders directly from Washington and then from Putnam, and were of great service to the army in watching the enemy along the Harlem front. They distinguished themselves on the 16th, and later in the season, when Colonel Magaw was in command of Fort Washington, he begged to have the Rangers remain with him, as he declared that they were the only safe protection to the lines. (Greene to Washington.) They remained and were taken prisoners at the surrender of the fort, November 16th. Though probably not over one hundred and fifty strong, their losses seem to have been heavy. Knowlton fell at Harlem Heights ; Major Coburn, who succeeded him, was severely wounded a few weeks later ; Captain Nathan Hale was executed as a spy ; and Captain Brown, a man as cool as Knowlton, was killed at the defence of Fort Mifflin near Philadelphia, in 1777, a cannon-ball severing his head from his body. Grosvenor served through the war, retiring as Lieutenant-Colonel commanding the Fifth of the Connecticut line. These facts are gathered from MS. Order Books, documents in *Force* and *Hist. Mag.*, and from MS. letter of the late Judge Oliver Burnham, of Cornwall, Conn., a soldier in Wyllys'

teers from the New England regiments, which had been organized for scouting service since the battle of Long Island, and placed under the command of Lieutenant-Colonel Thomas Knowlton, of Connecticut. No better man could have been found in the army to head such a corps, for he had proved his courage at Bunker Hill, and on more than one occasion since had shown his capacity for leadership. The detachment started out, not more than one hundred and twenty strong, and passing over to the Bloomingdale heights, marched for the Bloomingdale Road, where the enemy were last seen the night before.

The ground which Knowlton reconnoitred and which became the scene of the action remains to-day unchanged in its principal features. What was then known as Harlem Heights is that section of the island which rises prominently from the plain west of Eighth Avenue and north of One Hundred and Twenty-fifth Street. Its southern face extended from an abrupt point, called "Point of Rocks," at One Hundred and Twenty-sixth Street, east of Ninth Avenue, northwesterly to the Hudson, a distance of three quarters of a mile. At the foot of these heights lay a vale or "hollow way," through the centre of which now runs Manhattan Street, and opposite, at distances varying from a quarter to a third of a mile, rose another line of bluffs and slopes parallel to Harlem Heights. This lower elevation stood mainly in the Bloomingdale division of the city's out-ward, and is gen-

regiment and one of the Rangers, in which he says : "Soon after the retreat from Long Island, Colonel Knowlton was ordered to raise a battalion of troops from the different regiments called the Rangers, to reconnoitre along our shores and between the armies. Being invited by a favorite officer, I volunteered, and on the day the enemy took New York we were at Harlem and had no share in the events of that day."

erally known to-day as Bloomingdale Heights. In 1776 there were two farms on these heights, owned and occupied by Adrian Hogeland and Benjamin Vandewater, which were partly cultivated, but mainly covered with woods. The Bloomingdale Road, as stated in a previous chapter, terminated at Hogeland's lands about One Hundred and Eighth or Tenth streets, and from there a lane or road ran easterly by Vandewater's and joined the King's Bridge road near One Hundred and Twentieth Street. East of the Bloomingdale and south of Harlem Heights stretched the tract of level land called Harlem Plains.

After the retreat of the 15th, Washington's army encamped on Harlem Heights, with their pickets lining the southern slope from Point of Rocks to the Hudson. The British, as we have seen, lay at Bloomingdale and across the upper part of Central Park to Horn's Hook. An enemy, posted at the lower boundary of Harlem Plains, around McGowan's Pass, where the ground again rises at the northern end of the Park, might be easily observed from the Point of Rocks, and any advance from that quarter could be reported at once. Nothing, however, could be seen of movements made on the Bloomingdale Road or Heights, and it was in that direction that the "Rangers" now proceeded to reconnoitre at dawn on the 16th.

Knowlton, marching under cover of the woods, soon came upon the enemy's pickets, somewhere, it would appear, between Hogeland's and Apthorpe's houses on the Bloomingdale Road, more than a mile below the American lines. This was the encampment of the Light Infantry, and their Second and Third Battalions, supported by the Forty-second Highlanders, were immediately pushed forward to drive back this party of rebels who had dared to attack them on their own ground. Anticipating some such move, Knowlton had already posted his men behind a stone wall, and when the British advanced he met them with a vigorous fire. His men fired eight or nine rounds a piece with good effect, when the enemy threatened to turn his flanks, and he ordered a retreat, which was well conducted. In this brief encounter the Rangers lost about ten of their number, and believed that they inflicted much more than this loss upon the Infantry.[1]

At his head-quarters in the Morris Mansion, Washington, meantime, was writing his despatches to Congress. The unwelcome duty fell to him to report the scenes of the previous day which had so deeply stirred his indignation. He made a plain statement of the facts, described the retreat from New York, acknowledged the loss of

---

[1] The Rangers were thus engaged in a distinct skirmish before the main action of the day. Washington wrote to Congress early on the 16th: "I have sent some reconnoitring parties to gain intelligence, if possible, of the disposition of the enemy." A letter in the *Connecticut Gazette*, reprinted in Mr. Jay's documents, and which was probably written by Captain Brown, says: "On Monday morning the General ordered us to go and take the enemy's advanced guard; accordingly we set out just before day and found where they were; at day-brake we were discovered by the enemy, who were 400 strong, and we were 120. They marched up within six rods of us and there formed to give us Battle, which we were ready for; and Colonel Knowlton gave orders to fire, which we did, and stood theirs till we perceived they were getting their flank-guards round us. After giving them eight rounds apiece the Colonel gave orders for retreating, which we performed very well, without the loss of a man while retreating, though we lost about 10 while in action." Judge Burnham says substantially the same: "Colonel Knowlton marched close to the enemy as they lay on one of the Harlem Heights, and discharged a few rounds, and then retreated over the hill out of sight of the enemy and concealed us behind a low stone wall. The Colonel marked a place about eight or ten rods from the wall, and charged us not to rise or fire a gun until the enemy reached that place. The British followed in solid column, and soon were on the ground designated when we gave them nine rounds and retreated. . . . Our number engaged was only about 120."

baggage and cannon, and despondently expressed his misgivings as to the soldierly qualities of a majority of his
troops. "We are now," he wrote, "encamped with the
main body of the army on the Heights of Harlem, where
I should hope the enemy would meet with a defeat in case
of an attack, if the generality of our troops would behave
with tolerable bravery. But experience, to my extreme
affliction, has convinced me that this is rather to be
wished for than expected. However, I trust that there
are many who will act like men, and show themselves
worthy of the blessings of freedom." Not unfounded was
this trust, for at the very time the commander-in-chief
was writing the words, the Rangers were bravely fighting in the Bloomingdale woods, and many others soon
after, including one of the very regiments which fled from
Kip's Bay twenty-four hours before, were likewise to act
"like men" and prove their real worth in the open field.
Just as the letters were sent off word came in to head-
quarters that the enemy had appeared in several large
bodies upon the plains, and Washington rode down to
the picket-posts to make the necessary dispositions in case
of an attack. Adjutant-General Reed and Lieutenant
Tilghman, who had also been writing private letters describing Sunday's panic, and other members of the staff,
went to the front about the same time. Knowlton's men
had not yet come in, and their fire was distinctly heard
from the Point of Rocks, where the commander-in-chief
was now surveying the situation. Anxious to learn
whether the British were approaching in force on the
Bloomingdale Heights, no attack being threatened from
the plains, Colonel Reed received permission to go
"down to our most advanced guard," namely, to the
Rangers, whom he found making a momentary halt on

their retreat. The enemy soon came up again in large numbers, and the Rangers continued to retire. Colonel Reed, describing his experience at this point, states that the British advanced so rapidly that he had not quitted a house (which may have been Vandewater's) five minutes before they were in possession of it. " Finding how things were going," to use Reed's words, he returned to Washington " to get some support for the brave fellows who had behaved so well." Knowlton, however, fell back to our lines, and the enemy halted in their pursuit on the north-east edge of Bloomingdale Heights, opposite the Point of Rocks, where a part of them appeared in open sight, and " in the most insulting manner" sounded their bugle-horns as if on a fox chase. " I never felt such a sensation before," says Reed ; " it seemed to crown our disgrace." But the chase was not yet over.

Learning from Knowlton that the British Infantry who had followed him in were about three hundred strong, and knowing that they were some distance from their main army, Washington determined, if possible, to effect their capture. Knowlton's men, who had done nobly, were ready for another brush, and there were troops at hand who could be depended upon to behave well under any circumstances. The opportunity for a brisk and successful skirmish presented itself, and the general proposed to improve it. Accordingly he formed the plan of engaging the enemy's attention in their front, while a flanking party should attempt to get into their rear and cut off their escape. The troops that were stationed nearest to the Point of Rocks at this time appear to have been Nixon's brigade, of Greene's division, Weedon's newly arrived regiment of Virginians, General Beall's Marylanders, Colonel Sargent's eastern brigade, Clinton's and

Scott's brigades, and other regiments belonging to Putnam's and Spencer's divisions. For the flanking detachment, the general selected Knowlton's Rangers, to whom he added a reinforcement of three of the Virginia companies, about one hundred and twenty men, under Major Andrew Leitch.   These were directed to make their way or "steal around" to the rear of the enemy by their right flank.   To make a demonstration against the enemy in their front, while the flanking party effected its object, a detachment of volunteers was organized from Nixon's brigade, under Lieutenant-Colonel Archibald Crary, of Varnum's Rhode Islanders,[1] who marched down into the "hollow way" directly towards the British on the opposite ridge.   As Washington hoped, this move had the desired effect.   The British, seeing so small a party coming out against them, immediately ran down the rocky hill into an open field, where they took post behind some bushes and a rail fence that extended from the hill to the post road about four hundred yards in front of the Point of Rocks.[2]   This field was part of the old Kortwright farm,

---

[1] Captain John Gooch, of Varnum's regiment, wrote September 23d : "On the 16th the enemy advanced and took possession of a hight on our right flank about half a mile Distance with about 3000 [300?] men ; a party from our brigade of 150 men, who turned out as volunteers, under the command of Lieutenant-Colonel Crary, of the regm[t] I belong to, were ordered out if possible to dispossess them."—*Document* 30.

[2] Tilghman's reference to these movements is as follows : "The General rode down to our farthest lines, and when he came near them heard a firing, which he was informed was between our scouts and the outguards of the enemy.   When our men [Knowlton's] came in they informed the General that there was a party of about 300 behind a woody hill, tho' they only showed a very small party to us.   Upon this the General laid a plan for attacking them in the rear and cutting off their retreat, which was to be effected in the following manner : Major Leitch, with three companies of Col[o] Weedon's Virginia regiment, and Col[o] Knowlton with his Rangers, were to steal round while a party [Crary's] were to march towards them and seem as if they intended to attack in front, but not to make any real attack till they saw our men fairly in their rear.   The bait took as to one part ; as soon as

lying just west of the present Harlem Lane, above One
Hundred and Eighteenth Street, in which the line of
that fence had been established for more than half a century before this engagement, and where it remained the
same for more than half a century after.   It is possible to-
day to fix its exact position, for the march of modern im-
provements has not yet disturbed the site.

In order to keep the enemy engaged at that point,
Crary's party opened fire at long range, to which the
British replied, but not much execution was done on
either side.   Meanwhile Knowlton and Leitch moved
out to get in the rear.   Colonel Reed accompanied the
party, and as he had been over the ground he undertook
the lead, with the Virginians in advance.   It was probably his intention to march down under cover of the
bushes, cross the Kortwright farm unobserved some little distance below the enemy, and reach the top of the
Bloomingdale ridge before they were discovered.   Once
there, the British would be effectually hemmed in.
Unfortunately, however, some "inferior officers," as it
would appear, gave unauthorized directions to the flanking party; or the party forming the "feint" in front
pushed on too soon, in consequence of which Leitch and
Knowlton made their attack rather on the British flank
than in their rear.[1]   The latter now finding a retreat nec-

they saw our party in front the enemy ran down the hill and took possession
of some fences and bushes and began to fire at them, but at too great distance to do much execution," etc.—*Document* 29.   See also Washington's
letter to Congress, Sept. 18th, 1776.

[1] It is quite clear that Knowlton and Leitch did not form two parties, as
some accounts state, one moving against the right flank of the enemy and the
other against the left.   They acted as one body, the Virginians marching in
front, having been ordered on to "reinforce" Knowlton.   Thus Captain
Brown writes that after retreating they "sent off for a reinforcement," which
they soon received ; and Colonel Reed confirms this in his testimony at the

essary, left the fence and started back up the hill which they had descended. Our men quickly followed, Crary in front, Knowlton and Leitch on the left, and with the Virginians leading, joined in the pursuit with splendid spirit and animation. They rushed up the slope, on about the line of One Hundred and Twentieth Street, and, climbing over the rocks, poured in their volleys upon the running Light Infantry.

It was right here, now, just on the crest of the ridge, and when our gallant advance was turning the tide against the enemy, that we suffered the loss of those two noble leaders whose memory is linked with this day's action. In a very short time after the first rush, Leitch was severely wounded not far from Reed, having received three balls in his side in as many minutes ; and in less than ten minutes after a bullet pierced Knowlton's body, and he too fell mortally wounded. We can identify the spot where the fall of these brave officers occurred as on the summit of the Bloomingdale Heights below One Hundred and Nineteenth Street, and about half way between the line of Ninth and Tenth Avenues. The site is included within the limits of the proposed "Morningside Park," which will thus have added to its natural attractiveness a never-fading historical association.[1]

court-martial of a soldier who acted a cowardly part in the fight. " On Monday forenoon," he says, " I left Colonel Knowlton with a design to send him a reinforcement. I had accordingly ordered up Major Leitch, and was going up to where the firing was," etc. (*Force*, 5th Series, vol. ii. p. 500.) Reed's letters to his wife show that Leitch and Knowlton fell near him, within a few minutes of each other, which could not have been the case had they been on opposite flanks. The accounts of Tilghman, Marshall, the soldier Martin, and others, leave no doubt as to this point that there was but one flanking party, and that Knowlton commanded it.

[1] Judge Burnham refers to the flank attack briefly as follows : " Passing over we met the enemy's right flank which had been posted out of our sight on lower ground. They fired and killed Colonel Knowlton and nearly all

Leitch was borne to the rear to be tenderly cared for until his death at a later day. In after years the Government remembered his services by granting his widow a generous pension. Knowlton met his fate with a soldier's fortitude and a patriot's devotion. "My poor Colonel," writes an officer of the Rangers, who without doubt was Captain Stephen Brown, next in rank to Knowlton, "my poor Colonel, in the second attack, was shot just by my side. The ball entered the small of his back. I took hold of him, asked him if he was badly wounded? He told me he was; but says he, 'I do not value my life if we do but get the day.' I then ordered two men to carry him off. He desired me by all means to keep up this flank. He seemed as unconcerned and calm as tho' nothing had happened to him." Reed, on whose horse the colonel was carried to the lines, wrote to his wife on the following day: "Our loss is also considerable. The Virginia Major (Leitch) who went up first with me was wounded with three shot in less than three minutes; but our greatest loss was a brave officer from Connecticut, whose name and spirit ought to be immortalized—one Colonel Knowlton. I assisted him off, and when gasping in the agonies of death, all his inquiry was if we had drove the enemy." Washington spoke of him in his letters and orders as "a valuable and gallant officer," who would have been "an honor to any country."

Meanwhile the Rangers and Virginians kept up their attack under their captains, and Washington, finding that

that had reached the top of the height." This reference to the *top of the height*, taken in connection with Reed's statement that "our brave fellows mounted up the rocks and attacked them as they ran in turn," goes to confirm the selection of the spot where Leitch and Knowlton fell. Burnham states that he was within a few feet of the latter when he was shot.

the entire party needed support, sent forward three of the Maryland Independent companies, under Major Price, and parts of Griffith's and Richardson's Maryland Flying Camp.[1] At the same time, as Washington reports, some detachments from the Eastern regiments who were nearest the place of action, which included most of Nixon's and Sargent's brigades, Colonel Douglas's Connecticut levies, and a few others, were ordered into the field. Our total force engaged at this time, now about noon, was not far from eighteen hundred strong, and very soon a considerable battle was in progress. Besides Reed and other members of Washington's staff, Generals Putnam, Greene, and George Clinton accompanied the detachments, and encouraged the men by individual examples of bravery.[2] The troops now "charged the enemy with great intrepidity," and drove them from the crest of the heights back in a south-westerly direction through a piece of woods to a buckwheat field, about four hundred paces, as General Clinton describes it, from the ridge, or just east of the present Bloomingdale Asylum, where the Light Infantry, now reinforced by the Forty-second Highlanders, finally made a stand. The distance the latter troops had advanced and the sound of the firing had evidently warned Howe, at his head-quarters at Apthorpe's, that they needed immediate assistance, and he

[1] There appear to have been nine companies of Maryland troops engaged, three under Major Price, three under Major Mantz, and three others of Richardson's regiment. Among these were one or more companies of Colonel Ewing's as yet incomplete battalion. One of his officers, Captain Lowe, was wounded.—*Force*, 5th Series, vol. ii. p. 1024. Also Capt. Beatty's letter in Mr. Jay's Documents.

[2] Greene wrote at a latter date: "Gen. Putnam and the Adj. Gen. were in the action and behaved nobly." "I was in the latter part, indeed almost the whole of the action."—*Gen. Geo. Clinton*. (See his two letters in Jay's documents.) "Gen. Putnam and Gen. Greene commanded in the Action with about 15 to eighteen hundred men."—*Stiles's MS. Diary*.

promptly ordered forward the reserve with two field-pieces, together with the Yagers and Linsingen's grenadiers of Donop's corps. The field-pieces and Yagers came into action at the buckwheat field, and here a stubborn contest ensued for about an hour and a half.[1] But our troops pressed the enemy so hard at this point, and the Highlanders and Yagers having fired away their ammunition, the latter all again fell back, and the Americans pursued them vigorously to an orchard a short distance below, in the direction of the Bloomingdale Road. Here had been hard fighting in the open field, and the best British troops were beaten! At the orchard the result was the same, the enemy making little resistance, their fire "being silenced in a great measure," and the chase continued down one of the slight hills on Hogeland's lands and up another, near or quite to the terminus of the Bloomingdale Road. Beyond this third position our troops were not allowed to follow the enemy, whose main encampment was not far distant. The Fifth Regiment of Foot had been trotted up "about three miles without a halt to draw breath," reaching the ground at the close of the action. Linsingen's grenadiers appeared about the same time, while Block's and Minegerode's men were sent to McGowan's Pass, which had not yet been occupied. A large body of the enemy were put under arms, and within their camp every preparation was made for a general engagement; but this, above all things, Washington wished to avoid, and, quite content with the brilliant success of his troops thus far, he despatched

---

[1] " A very smart action ensued in the true Bush-fighting way in which our Troops behaved in a manner that does them the highest honor."—*Letter from Col. Griffith, of Maryland.* Lossing's *Historical Record*, vol. ii., p. 260.

17

Lieutenant Tilghman to the front to bring them off. Before turning from the field they had won so gloriously, they answered the bugle blast of the morning with a cheer of victory, and marched back in good order.[1]

---

[1] " The General fearing (as we afterwards found) that a large body was coming up to support them, sent me over to bring our men off. They gave a Hurra and left the field in good order."—*Tilghman's Letters*, Doc. 29.

THE BATTLE-FIELD.—Recently gathered material seems to settle all doubts as to the several points occupied by the British and Americans during the action. Where did it begin and where did it end? As to the first skirmish, it began near the British encampment at Bloomingdale. Here was Howe's left, and, as Howe reports, Knowlton approached his advanced posts under cover of the woods " by way of Vandewater's Height." This was what we call Bloomingdale Heights. The original proprietor of the greater part of this site was Thomas De Key. From him all or a large part of it passed to Harman Vandewater and Adrian Hogeland, as the deeds on record show. In 1784 the property was purchased by Nicholas De Peyster. The position of Hogeland's and Vandewater's houses as given on the accompanying map is taken from old surveys which mark the location and give the names. The Bloomingdale Road at that time stopped at these farms. That part of it above One Hundred and Tenth Street, running through Manhattanville and continuing until recently to the King's Bridge Road at One Hundred and Forty-sixth Street, did not exist during the Revolution, but was opened a few years later. (Hoffman's *Est. and Rights of the Corporation of New York*, vol. ii.) A lane or road running from Hogeland's by Vandewater's connected the Bloomingdale with the King's Bridge road at One Hundred and Nineteenth Street. Washington himself gives us the general line. Before the battle of Long Island he ordered Heath to have troops ready to march to New York as soon as called for, and he describes the proper route thus : " There is a road out of the Haerlem flat lands that leads up to the hills, and continues down the North River by Bloomingdale, Delancy's, &c., which road I would have them march, as they will keep the river in sight, and pass a tolerable landing-place for troops in the neighborhood of Bloomingdale." (*Heath Correspondence*, Mass. Hist. Coll. for 1878.) From this topography and the records the position becomes clear : Howe camped around Bloomingdale with his advance posts along the Bloomingdale Road, perhaps as far as its terminus near Hogeland's. They were last seen in this vicinity the night before. Knowlton, next morning, marches out from Harlem Heights, reconnoitres " by way of Vandewater's," and comes upon the British posts on and along the line of the Bloomingdale Road. Then he falls back under cover of the woods and over fences towards the Point of Rocks, the enemy following him.

As to succeeding movements, if we can fix Washington's station and the hill which all agree that the British descended, there is no difficulty in following them after. Point of Rocks was the extreme limit of Harlem Heights.

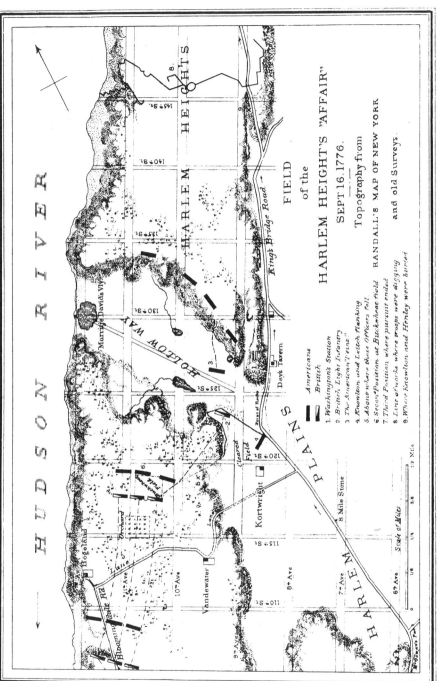

FIELD
of the
HARLEM HEIGHT'S "AFFAIR"
SEPT 16, 1776.
Topography from
RANDALL'S MAP OF NEW YORK
and old Surveys.

Americans
British

1. Washington's Station
2. British Light Infantry
3. The "American View"
4. Knowlton and Leitch flanking
5. Above where these Officers fell
6. Second Position at Buckwheat field
7. Third Position where pursuit ended
8. Line of works where troops were digging
9. Where Knowlton and Henley were buried

Scale of Miles
0   1/8   1/4   3/8   1/2 Mile

HUDSON RIVER

HARLEM HEIGHTS

HARLEM PLAINS

J. Bien Photo. Lith. N. Y.

This affair, as Washington wrote to Schuyler, "inspirited our troops prodigiously." The next day the general most heartily thanked the men "commanded by Major Leitch, who first advanced upon the enemy, and the others who so resolutely supported them ;" and once more he called upon all to act up to the noble cause in which they were engaged.

The British loss, according to Howe, was fourteen killed and about seventy wounded, but Baurmeister puts it much higher—seventy killed and two hundred wounded. The Americans lost not far from eighty, of whom at least

There were our advanced posts overlooking the country south. Washington states that he rode down to "our advanced posts" to direct matters. Where better could he do so than at Point of Rocks? And in a sketch of the field preserved in the Stiles Diary, and reproduced among Mr. Jay's documents, Washington is given just that station where an earthwork had [been thrown up. To confirm this and also to locate the next point, we have a letter from Major Lewis Morris (Jay documents), in which he says : "Colonel Knowlton's regiment was attacked by the enemy upon a height a little to the southwest of Days's Tavern, and after opposing them bravely and being overpowered by their numbers they were forced to retreat, and the enemy advanced upon the top of the hill opposite to that which lies before Days's door, with a confidence of success, and after rallying their men by a bugle horn and resting themselves a little while, they descended the hill," etc. In one of Christopher Colles's road maps (published in the N. Y. Corporation Manual for 1870, p. 778), Days's tavern is put directly opposite Point of Rocks on the King's Bridge Road, which fixes the hill occupied by the enemy as the north-east bluff of Bloomingdale Heights, or about One Hundred and Twenty-third Street, between Ninth and Tenth avenues. They ran down this bluff to fences and bushes at the edge of "a clear field." This was part of the Kortwright farm, and the farm lines of 1812 show the same northern boundary that surveys show in 1711. This northerly fence line is given in the accompanying map, and it will be noticed that it would be the natural line for the British Infantry to take in opposing Crary's party. The soldier Martin speaks of their taking a post and rail fence with a field in their rear. General George Clinton, who gives a clear description of the fighting from this point, also mentions this field and fence, but appears to have been mistaken in stating that the enemy were driven back to that position. They ran down the hill and took up that position. Then, when driven back, they retreated in the general direction of their first advance—that is, towards their camp, passing through a buckwheat field and or-twenty-five were killed or mortally wounded. The loss in officers, besides Knowlton and Leitch, included Captain Gleason, of Nixon's Massachusetts, and Lieutenant Noel Allen, of Varnum's Rhode Island, both of whom were killed. Captain Lowe, of Ewing's Marylanders, was wounded, also Captain Gooch, of Varnum's, slightly. The heaviest loss fell upon Nixon's and Sargent's brigades, namely: Nixon's regiment, four killed; Varnum's, four; Hitchcock's, four; Sargent's, one; Bailey's, five, and two mortally wounded. Colonel Douglas lost three killed. Among the Marylanders there were twelve wounded and three missing. The loss in the Virginia detachment and

chard to the Bloomingdale Road, and not, as generally stated, to the high ground in Central Park east of Eighth Avenue. General Clinton says they fell back from the orchard "across a hollow and up another hill not far distant from their own lines," which doubtless refers to undulations on Hogeland's place, and possibly to the then hilly ground about One Hundred and Seventh Street and Eleventh Avenue. One of the Hessian accounts states that the Yagers who were sent to support the Light Infantry came into "a hot contest on Hoyland's Hill"—a reference clearly to Hogeland's lands ; and this with the fact that the Yagers and Grenadiers afterwards bivouacked " in the wood not far from Bloomingdale," and that the British " encamped in two lines " at the same place, indicates the point where the action terminated —namely, near Bloomingdale, between Hogeland's and Apthorpe's.

In regard to the beginning of the action, General Clinton, in his account, starts with a locality called " Martje Davits Fly," and estimates distances from it. This name, more properly " Marrıtje David's Vly," strictly described the round piece of meadow at the western end of the Hollow Way close to the Hudson. It formed part of Harlem Cove. Old deeds, acts, and surveys give the name and site exactly. Clinton speaks of the " Point of Martje David's Fly " as if he had reference to a point of land in its vicinity, possibly the Point of Rocks, and from which he gives his distances.

The name of the battle appears perhaps most frequently in modern accounts as that of Harlem *Plains*. Greene and others speak of it as the action of Harlem *Heights* or the heights of Harlem. As the movements were directed by Washington from the Heights, and as the fighting was done practically in defence of the Heights, this seems to be the proper name to adopt. Heath says the fighting took place " on the Heights west of Harlem Plains," and Washington, Clinton, and others make similar references to the high ground, showing that the affair was not associated with the Plains.

the Rangers does not appear. General Clinton on the next day buried seventeen of our men on the field, and reported over fifty wounded. Lieutenant-Colonel Henshaw, of Little's regiment, simply writes to his wife in regard to the action, " I was there," and adds that our loss was one hundred. He puts the casualties in his brigade alone [Nixon's] at seventy-five. All the troops behaved well. Greene speaks with pride of the conduct of his Rhode Islanders, Varnum's and Hitchcock's. Captain Gooch wrote to a friend enthusiastically, " The New England men have gained the first Laurells;" while Tilghman wrote with equal enthusiasm, " The Virginia and Maryland troops bear the Palm." In reality, palm and laurel belonged to both alike.

Knowlton, on the 17th, was buried with the honors of war near the road on the hill slope, not far from the line of One Hundred and Forty-third Street, west of Ninth Avenue. Leitch died on the 1st of October, and is said to have been buried by Knowlton's side, where Major Thomas Henly, a Massachusetts officer, killed on Montressor's Island on September 23d, was also buried.[1] On

[1] Heath states that Henley was buried by Knowlton's side, and the spot is indicated in the orders of September 24th : " Thomas Henley will be buried this P.M. from the quarters of Maj. David Henley below the hill where the redoubt is thrown up on the road." During the action of the 16th, troops were throwing up intrenchments across the island at about One Hundred and Forty-fifth Street. This was the first and most southerly of the three lines constructed on the Heights. Sauthier's map, the authority in the case, shows this line with a battery across the King's Bridge Road, just at the top of what is known as Breakneck Hill. It was on the slope of this hill that Knowlton and Henley were buried. Mr. Lossing puts his grave in one of the redoubts on the second line, afterwards included in Trinity Cemetery ; but that line had not been thrown up when Knowlton died. (Silliman's letter of September 17th, P.M. Part II., page 55.) Mr. Jay and others have suggested the erection of a monument to Knowlton and Leitch. No finer site could be found than the spot where they fell in Morningside Park.

Respecting Major Henley, spoken of by Washington as " another of our best officers," see Glover's letter, *Document* 35.

the 22d, Captain Nathan Hale, "the martyr-spy," was executed in New York. Finding Washington anxious to have information of the enemy's numbers and designs, Hale volunteered to enter their camp in disguise. Captured at the last moment as he was on the point of escape, he frankly avowed his mission, and just before his execution, on the Rutgers farm, he told the spectators around him that he only regretted he had but one life to give for his country. The war saw no more courageous or unselfish sacrifice. Few worthier of a monument than he!

The battle of the 16th was followed by inactivity on the part of the British, and Washington securely established himself on Harlem Heights. The chief excitement was the occurrence of the great fire on the night of the 21st of September, which broke out near Whitehall Slip, in New York, and destroyed a fourth of the city. In addition to accounts of the calamity already published and generally familiar, the experiences of Pastor Shewkirk, as given in his diary in the present work, will be read with interest.

CHAPTER VII.

WHAT now remains to be noticed as coming within the scope of the present narrative are those incidents which led to the evacuation of Harlem Heights by our army, and the subsequent capture of Fort Washington, by which the British finally came into the possession of the whole of New York Island.

The American position at the Heights, strong by nature, was made still more so by defensive works. Three lines of intrenchments and redoubts were thrown across the island between One Hundred and Forty-fifth and One Hundred and Sixty-second streets ; batteries were built around King's Bridge, and at several points on the heights overlooking the Harlem ; and on the commanding site on the line of One Hundred and Eighty-third Street, two hundred and thirty feet above the Hudson, stood the powerful fortress called Fort Washington. Describing these works more in detail, the first of the three lines, that furthest south, was the one already referred to on which troops were digging during the action of Harlem Heights. It extended along the line of One Hundred and Forty-sixth Street. The second line, which was much stronger, was laid out a short distance above at One Hundred and Fifty-third Street. There were four redoubts in the line. Less than half a mile above, between One Hundred and Sixtieth and One Hundred and Sixty-second streets, and not extending east of Tenth Avenue, or the old Post Road, was the third line. It mainly commanded the depression in the heights which is now known as Audubon Park, and included no redoubts. In addition to this triple line, there were single breastworks and batteries at various points from Point of Rocks north, along the ridge. The high and rugged bank of the Harlem overlooking the present High Bridge was known as Laurel Hill, and at the northern extremity, at One Hundred and Ninety-second Street, there was an American battery, which the British afterwards named Fort George. On the west side, at One Hundred and Ninety-sixth Street, there was a small battery which became Fort Tryon. On the further side of Spuyten Duyvil Creek stood Fort Independence, commanding King's Bridge and its approaches. [1]

Fort Washington was a large, five-sided work with bastions, strong by virtue of its position, and important as commanding the passage of the Hudson in connection with Fort Lee (first named Constitution), opposite, on the summit of the Palisades on the Jersey side. Much labor had been expended upon it, and it was generally regarded as impregnable. The obstructions in the river consisted mainly of a line of vessels chained together, loaded with stone, and then sunk and anchored just below the surface

[1] The position of the various works at Harlem Heights appears on Sauthier's plan which seems to have accompanied Howe's report of the capture of Fort Washington. Good copies of it may be found in Stedman's history and in the *New York Revolutionary MS.*, vol. i. In 1812, when Randall surveyed the island, many of these works were still traceable. He gives parts of the second and third lines, Fort Washington and the others above, all of which agree with Sauthier's locations. Some of the works remain well preserved to-day.

of the river. It was expected that they would resist the passage of the British ships, which would thus be also brought to a stop under the guns from either shore, and made to suffer heavily. Both the Continental Congress and the Provincial Congress of New York had urged that no means or expense should be spared to make the obstructions effectual, in view of the serious results that would follow the enemy's possession of the river above.

Nearly a month now had elapsed since the retreat of our army to Harlem Heights, and the British had made no further progress. They had in the mean time thrown up a series of works across the island in front of their main camps at Bloomingdale and McGowan's Pass, which could be defended by a comparatively small force. On the 9th, however, they showed indications of taking the field again by sending two frigates up the Hudson. In spite of the sunken obstructions, the ships made their way through without difficulty. Then, on the morning of the 12th, Howe embarked the greater part of his army in boats, and passing through Hell Gate, under cover of a fog, landed on Throg's Neck, an arm of the Westchester coast, about six miles above. Percy was left to protect New York with three brigades. By this move the British general placed himself on Washington's flank in Westchester County, and threatened his communications. But the Neck was a poor selection for a landing-place.[1] It was practically an island, the crossings to the

[1] "Frog's Neck and Point is a kind of island ; there are two passages to the main which are fordable at low water, at both of which we have thrown up works, which will give some annoyance should they attempt to come off by either of these ways."—*Tilghman to William Duer*, October 13th, 1776. *MS. Letter.* On hearing that they had landed on the Neck, Duer replied from the Convention at Peekskill, on the 15th : " There appears to me an actual fatality attending all their measures. One would have naturally imagined from the Traitors they have among them, who are capable of giving them the

mainland being a causeway and fords, the opposite approaches of which were fortified by the Americans. Colonel Hand's riflemen had pulled up the planks on the bridges, and Prescott's Massachusetts were ready behind breastworks to resist any attempt on the part of the enemy to cross. Here the British wasted five days in collecting their stores, while the Americans kept a sufficient force to meet them at the causeway and vicinity. Among other regiments which relieved each other at this point were Nixon's, Varnum's, Malcom's, Graham's, and Ritzema's.

During and for some time before these movements an interesting correspondence was carried on between Washington's head-quarters and a committee of the New York Convention, a portion of which may be introduced in this connection. It gives us a glimpse of the deep interest and anxiety felt in the Convention in matters affecting the protection of the State, and the internal difficulties that had to be encountered. The correspondence was conducted mainly between Lieutenant Tilghman for head-quarters and Hon. William Duer for the Convention.[1] Thus, on September 20th, the latter writes to Tilghman as follows :

most minute description of the Grounds in the county of Westchester, that they would have landed much farther to the Eastward. Had they pushed their imaginations to discover the worst place, they could not have succeeded better than they have done."—*MS. Letter.*

[1] The Convention's Committee on Correspondence consisted of William Duer, R. R. Livingston, Egbert Benson, and two others. Nearly all of Tilghman's letters to the committee have been published either in Force or in the Proceedings of the N. Y. Provincial Congress. Of Duer's replies, however, but few are in print, the originals being in the possession of Oswald Tilghman, Esq., of Easton, Talbot County, Md., to whom the writer is under obligations for the favor of quoting the extracts given in the text. (See biographical sketch of Colonel Tilghman.)

" I can easily imagine that Gen¹ Howe must be both chagrined and disappointed at the Retreat of our Army from New York. I have no doubt but what he expected fully to have taken them in a net ; and he certainly would have succeeded had we pertinaciously persisted in the plan of defending the city. You observe that if the passage of the North River is sufficiently obstructed that our lines will keep the enemy from making any progress in front. This is certainly true ; but you must recollect that the Sound is, and must ever be, open ; and if they should succeed in landing a Body of Men in Westchester County, they might, by drawing lines to the North River, as effectually hem us in, as if we were in New York. From Sutton's Neck to the North River (if I am not mistaken) is not above twelve miles."

Again on the 2d of October, speaking of the possibility of the enemy's getting on our flank or rear, Duer says :

" I wish they would delay this attempt till Gen¹. Lee arrives, or till Mifflin comes from Philadᵃ. I am sensible that however great General Washington's abilities and vigilance are, he must stand in need of the assistance of such excellent officers. Is Gen¹ Greene with the Army, or is he still in Jersey ? If he could be spared from that quarter his presence, I think, would be of great consequence. I am much mistaken, if he is not possest of that Heaven-born Genius which is necessary to constitute a great General.—I can scarcely describe to you my feelings at this interesting Period —what, with the situation of our enemies in your quarter and the cursed machinations of our Internal Foes, the fate of this State hangs on a single battle of importance."

Again on the 8th :

" I am sorry to tell you (for the credit of this State) that the Committee I belong to make daily fresh discoveries of the infernal Practices of our Enemies to excite Insurrections amongst the inhabitants of the State. To-morrow one Company, actually enlisted in the enemy's service, will be marched to Philadelphia, there to be confined in jail, till the establishment of our Courts enables us to hang the Ringleaders."

And on the following day Robert R. Livingston added on this subject :

" Tho' we are constantly employed in the detection of treasons, yet plots multiply upon us daily, and we have reason every moment to dread an open rebellion. We have ordered troops to be raised but fear they will be too slow in coming, and that we shall be under the disagreeable necessity of asking a small and temporary aid from the Gen¹ ; but we shall defer this till reduced to the last extremity."

When the ships went up the river on the 9th, it was feared they had troops on board who might make an attempt on the Highlands, whereupon Duer wrote on the 10th :

" In this [attempt] they will undoubtedly be joined by the villains in Westchester and Duchess County ; it is therefore of the utmost consequence that a Force should be immediately detached from the main body of our army to occupy these posts. . . . By the Influence and Artifices of the capital tories of this State the majority of Inhabitants in those counties are ripe for a revolt."

But with a stout heart Duer continues :

" It is our Duty, however, to struggle against the tide of adversity, and to exert ourselves with vigour adequate to our circumstances. This, as an Individual, I am determined to do in the Capacity in which I am at present acting, and I have no doubt those friends I have in the military line will do the same. We are not to expect to purchase our Liberties at a cheaper rate than other nations have done, or that *our* soldiers should be Heaven born more than those of other nations. Experience will make us both have and win ; and in the end teach Great Britain that in attempting to enslave us she is aiming a dagger at her own vitals."

On the 12th, before he heard of the landing at Throg's Neck, he wrote to Tilghman :

" Notwithstanding the enemy had, agreeable to your last advices, sent no vessels up the Sound, depend upon it, they will endeavor to make an attack upon your Flanks by means of Hudson's and the East River. . . . If General Lee is returned from the Southward and arrived at your camp (which I suppose to be the case) I beg my affectionate compliments to him. I wish to Heaven I could come and see you, but I am so embarrassed with the Committee I am engaged in that I have not hardly an hour, much less a few days to spare. This morning we marched off a Company of men, who had been enlisted to join the Battalion to be raised by Major Rogers, to the City of Philadelphia. We have an admirable clue of their abominable conspiracies, and (however late this undertaking has been) I hope by spirit and perseverance we may baffle their wretched Plots of occasioning a revolt in this State." [1]

On the 13th, Tilghman wrote to Duer :

" When your favor of the 10th came to hand, I was attending his Excellency, who was obliged to ride up to West Chester upon the Alarm of the Enemy's Landing at Frog's Point. . . . From their not moving immediately forward, I imagine they are waiting for their artillery and stores, which must be very considerable if they seriously intend to set down in the country upon our rear. The grounds leading from Frog's Point towards our Post at King's bridge are as defensible as they can be wished. The roads are all lined with stone fences and the adjacent Fields divided off with stone [fences] likewise, which will make it impossible for them to advance their artillery and ammunition waggons by any other Rout than the great roads, and I think if they are well lined with troops, we may make a Considerable Slaughter if not discomfit them totally. Our riflemen have directions to at-

---

[1] As evidence of the estimation in which Lee was held at this time, Duer writes on the 15th to Colonel Harrison : " I beg my affectionate compliments to Gen¹ Lee, whom I sincerely congratulate on his arrival in camp—partly on account of himself as he will have it in his [power] to reap a fresh Harvest of Laurels, and more on account of his Country which looks to him as one of the brave asserters of her dearest rights."—*MS. Letter.*

Lee had just returned from South Carolina, and was associated by the army with the brave defence of Charleston harbor. The honor of that affair, however, belonged entirely to Moultrie.

tend particularly to taking down their Horses, which if done, will impede their march effectually. Our troops are in good spirits and seem inclined and determined to dispute every inch of Ground."

On the 15th he wrote to Duer again as follows, after informing him that the enemy had not moved from the Neck :

" From the number of vessels that have been continually passing up the Sound we conclude that they are transporting cannon and stores necessary to enable them to penetrate the country and set down in our rear. To hinder them from effecting this, Genl Lee, who arrived yesterday, has taken the command in that quarter. He will be posted in such a situation with a very considerable number of Light Troops that, let the Enemy advance by what road they will, they cannot elude him ; if they march in one great body he can easily draw his Divisions together ; if they divide and take different Routs, they will fall in with the different parties. He will have the Flower of the Army with him, as our lines in front are so strong that we can trust them to Troops who would not stand in the field."

Duer, on the 17th, replied :

" I expect daily to hear of some grand attempt made by the Enemy. . . . If one half of our army think as much of the Importance of the approaching Contest as you do, I shall entertain no Doubt of our success. May Heaven protect you, and all my Friends who are venturing their Lives in so great and good a cause."

On the same date Tilghman wrote :

" I have not time to describe the Disposition of our Army perfectly to you, but you may depend that every step is taken to prevent the enemy from outflanking us and at the same time to secure our Retreat in case of need. The Enemy have made no move from Frog's Point. . . . I don't know how it is, but I believe their design to circumvent us this time will prove as abortive as the former ones. If we can but foil Gen¹ Howe again, I think we knock him up for the Campaign. You ask if Gen¹ Lee is in Health and our people feel bold? I answer both in the affirmative. His appearance among us has not contributed a little to the latter. We are sinking the ships as fast as possible; 200 men are daily employed, but they take an immense quantity of stone for the purpose.''

To meet this move upon their flank and rear, the Americans were obliged to abandon their strong camp at Harlem Heights. On the 16th, while the British were still at Throg's Neck, Washington called a council of war, when it was agreed that they could not keep their communications open with the back country, if they remained where they were and the British advanced. At the same it was voted to hold Fort Washington. To be ready to counteract the next move of the enemy, a part of the army was stationed at advantageous points in Westchester County, the main camps being extended along the hills west of the Bronx River. Both Valentine's Hill and Miles Square were occupied and fortified.

On the 18th, Howe left Throg's Neck and transferred his army further eastward to Pell's Point below New Rochelle. The Light Infantry advanced from the coast, but were faced by Glover's brigade from behind stone walls, and made to suffer some loss.[1] Glover and his men were complimented for their conduct both by Washington and Lee. The enemy again delayed in the vicinity of East Chester and New Rochelle until the 22d.

Wishing exact information of the position of the enemy and of the topography of the country, the commander-in-

[1] In this skirmish Captain Evelyn, the British officer who captured the patrol of American officers on Long Island, was mortally wounded, and died soon after, much regretted. He is supposed to have been buried in New York.

chief, on the morning of the 20th, requested Colonel
Reed and Colonel Putnam, his engineer, to undertake a
reconnoissance in person. Setting out from King's
Bridge with a foot-guard of twenty men, these officers
proceeded to the heights at East Chester, where they
saw some of the enemy near the church, but could obtain no intelligence. The houses in the vicinity were
deserted. From this point Reed returned to attend to
his office duties, while Putnam, disguising his appearance as an officer by taking out his cockade, loping his
hat, and concealing his sword and pistols under his loose
coat, continued on alone in the direction of White Plains.
Learning from a woman at a house that the British were
at New Rochelle, he passed on to within three or four
miles of White Plains, where he met some " friends to the
cause" and ascertained the general situation. " I found,"
he writes, " that the main body of the British lay near
New Rochelle, from thence to White Plains about nine
miles, good roads and in general level open country, that
at White Plains was a large quantity of stores, with only
about three hundred militia to guard them, that the British had a detachment at Mamaroneck only six miles from
White Plains, and from White Plains only five miles to
the North River, where lay five or six of the enemies
ships and sloops, tenders, etc. Having made these discoveries, I set out on my return." Reporting this information to the commander-in-chief about nine o'clock in
the evening, Colonel Putnam retired to " refresh" himself and horse, only to receive orders soon after to proceed immediately to Lord Stirling's brigade,[1] now in

---

[1] Stirling, who with Sullivan had recently been exchanged as prisoner,
was now in command of Mifflin's brigade, Mifflin being absent in Philadelphia.

Spencer's division, which had already advanced on the road towards White Plains. He reached Stirling at two o'clock that night, and at dawn the general pushed on to White Plains, arriving there about nine o'clock on the morning of the 21st. Washington himself and Heath's division followed during the day, and the troops set to work throwing up lines at that important point. By delaying near New Rochelle, Howe had missed his opportunity. During the night of the 21st, Colonel Haslet, of Stirling's brigade, surprised and captured some thirty men belonging to the partisan Rogers' Scouts, and soon after Colonel Hand with his now veteran riflemen proved himself more than a match for an equal party of yagers encountered near Mamaroneck. In the first of these skirmishes, Major Greene, a fine Virginia officer, was mortally wounded.

Washington concentrated his army at White Plains, completed two lines of works, with his right on the river Bronx, and awaited the advance of the British. Howe had moved from New Rochelle to Scarsdale, and on the morning of the 28th marched against the Americans. A mile or more from White Plains, on the main road to New York, he fell in with General Spencer's advance parties under Colonels Silliman, Douglas,[1] and Chester, who offered resistance and lost some men, but they were driven back by superior numbers. On the left of the American position, across the Bronx, rose Chatterton's Hill, which offered a good site for the better defence of that flank. Colonel Putnam had just arrived on the hill to throw up works when the enemy made their appearance below.[2] Ac-

[1] See letters of these officers, *Documents* 17, 22. Also Tallmadge's account, *Document* 26.

[2] " October 29th [28th] the British advanced in front of our lines at White Plains about 10 o'clock A.M. I had just arrived on Chatterton Hill in order

18

cording to Haslet, the Delawares were the first troops to report on this hill, where they took post with one of General Lincoln's Massachusetts militia regiments, under Colonel Brooks, on their right. They were followed immediately by McDougall's brigade, consisting of what was lately his own battalion, which had no field officers, Ritzema's, Smallwood's, and Webb's. The troops formed along the brow of the hill, and stood waiting for the enemy. The two-gun battery brought up at the same time was Captain Alexander Hamilton's.

The British marched up in brilliant array towards Washington's position, but unexpectedly declined to make an attack in front, although the centre was our weakest point. Chatterton's Hill appeared to engage Howe's attention at once, and it became the first object of capture. The troops assigned for this purpose were the Second British brigade and Hessians under Donop, Rall, and Lossberg, in all about four thousand men. They crossed the Bronx, under cover of their artillery, and prepared to ascend the somewhat abrupt face of the hill on the other side. McDougall's men reserved their fire until the enemy were within short range, when they poured a destructive shower of bullets upon them. The British recoiled, but moved up again to the attack, while Rall came around

to throw up some works when they hove in sight; as soon as they discovered us they commenced a severe cannonade but without any effect of consequence. General McDougal about this time arriving with his brigade from Burtis's and observing the British to be crossing the Bronx below in large bodies in order to attack us, our troops were posted to receive them in a very advantageous position. The British in their advance were twice repulsed; at length, however, their numbers were increased so that they were able to turn our right flank. We lost many men, but from information afterwards received there was reason to believe they lost many more than we. The rail and stone fence behind which our troops were posted proved as fatal to the British as the rail fence and grass hung on it did at Charlestown the 17th of June 1775."—*Colonel Rufus Putnam, Document* 43.

more on the left, and after a brisk fight, in which the militia facing Rall failed to stand their ground, they succeeded in compelling McDougall to retreat. Had the militia held their own, the fight might have been another Bunker Hill for the enemy. As it was, Colonel Putnam. compared it to that engagement. In falling back, McDougall suffered some loss, but the whole force escaped to the right of our lines, with fewer casualties than they inflicted on the enemy. The latter lost about two hundred and thirty; the Americans something over one hundred and forty. Colonel Smallwood was wounded, and lost two of his captains, killed. Ritzema's New York Continentals suffered the most, having made a brave fight. Lieutenant-Colonel Samuel B. Webb, of Wethersfield, Ct., one of Washington's aids, who had shown his coolness under fire on Bunker Hill, was slightly wounded and had a horse shot under him while carrying orders.[1]

This affair on Chatterton's Hill is known as the Battle of White Plains. On the side of the Americans, not more than sixteen hundred troops were engaged, but the action was an important one, as it had the effect of changing the direction of future operations.[2]

On the following day, the 29th, Howe waited for reinforcements. On the 30th, the rain postponed an intended attack. On the 31st the weather proved fine about noon, but the British General "did not think proper to put his former intentions in execution." The next morning, November 1st, there was a further excuse for not attacking : Washington during the night had fallen back to the almost

[1] Statement of his son, General James Watson Webb, of New York.

[2] The details of the various movements in Westchester County would fill a long and interesting chapter ; but in the present connection not more than an outline can be attempted.

unassailable heights of North Castle, in his rear. Howe was thus again baffled in his attempt to bring the Americans to a decisive engagement, or to surround them, and he now turned his attention to another line of campaign. Stedman, the British historian, probably gives the correct reason why Washington was not followed. The American position, he says, was now " so advantageous that any attack on them must have proved unsuccessful, for the river Croton stretched along their front, and their rear was defended by woods and heights. Convinced that it was part of the enemy's system studiously to avoid an action, and that their knowledge of the country enabled them to execute this system with advantage, General Howe resolved to cease an ineffectual pursuit, and employ himself in the reduction of King's Bridge and Fort Washington." This accomplished, he could then push on to Philadelphia and close the year's operations with the occupation of that place. The capture of two cities, the successive defeats inflicted upon the Americans, and the good prospect of ending the rebellion in the next campaign, would be a brilliant military record with which to gratify the home government.

FORT WASHINGTON.

Howe broke up his camp near White Plains on November 5th, and marched west to the Hudson at Dobb's Ferry. Knyphausen, who had lately arrived with a second division of " foreigners," had already been despatched to King's Bridge. After various movements and delays, the entire British force also moved on the 12th to the immediate vicinity of the bridge, and dispositions were made to attack and capture Fort Washington. On the 15th, Howe sent a summons for the surrender of the fort, in which he intimated that a refusal to comply would justify the putting of the garrison to the sword.

The commander of Fort Washington was Colonel Robert Magaw, of Pennsylvania. In addition to his own regiment and Colonel Shee's, now under Lieutenant-Colonel Cadwallader, he had with him several detachments of troops from the Pennsylvania Flying Camp, under Colonels Baxter, Swoope, and others, together with a Maryland rifle battalion, under Colonel Rawlings, whose major was Otho Holland Williams, an officer distinguished later in the war. The artillery numbered about one hundred men, under Captain Pierce, and there were also the "Rangers," parts of Miles's and Atlee's old regiments, such as escaped the Long Island defeat, and about two hundred and fifty from Bradley's Connecticut levies, many of whom were to die in captivity. The whole force under Magaw numbered about twenty-eight hundred officers and men. The ground they were expected to hold was that part of Harlem Heights from the first of the three lines already described, northward to the end of Laurel Hill on the Harlem, and the hill west on the Hudson, a distance of two miles and a half.

At the lower lines at One Hundred and Forty-sixth Street, Cadwallader's men, the Rangers, and some others were posted ; at Laurel Hill, Colonel Baxter, and west of him, at the northern termination of the level summit of the ridge where Fort Washington stood, was Colonel Rawlings. Magaw remained at the fort to direct movements during the attack. The outer defences where the troops were stationed were to be held as long as possible, while the fort and the intrenchments immediately surrounding it were to be the point of retreat. Magaw believed he could hold the post against almost any force until December, and when the summons for a surrender reached him he returned the following spirited reply :

"15 NOVEMBER, 1776.

"SIR : If I rightly understand the purport of your message from General Howe communicated to Colonel Swoope, this post is to be immediately surrendered or the garrison put to the sword. I rather think it a mistake than a settled resolution in General Howe to act a part so unworthy of himself and the British Nation. But give me leave to assure his Excellency that actuated by the most glorious cause that mankind ever fought in, I am determined to defend this post to the last extremity.

"ROB'T MAGAW, Colonel Commanding.

"To the Adjutant-General of the British Army."

On the morning of the 16th, the enemy opened the attack from three directions.[1] The Hessians moved forward from King's Bridge against Rawlings' position, Rall on the right nearest to the Hudson, Knyphausen a short distance to his left nearer the King's Bridge road. Brigadier-General Matthews, supported by Cornwallis, came down the Harlem from the bridge in boats, and landed at the foot of Laurel Hill (One Hundred and Ninety-sixth Street), where Baxter was posted. These formed the attacking columns from the north side. On the south side Percy marched up from Harlem Plains and engaged Cadwallader at the lower lines.

At about the moment the cannonade began, Washington, Putnam, Greene, and Mercer were putting off from the Jersey shore at Fort Lee to make a final visit to Fort Washington, and determine whether to defend or evacuate the post. When they reached the island they

[1] Consult " Map of New York," etc., Part II.

found the threatened attack in actual progress, and evacuation then was out of the question. They saw Percy
making his dispositions, and could see nothing to modify
on their own side. All they could do was to await the
result. "There," says Greene, "we all stood in a very
awkward situation." Had they remained much longer it
would have been more than awkward. Putnam, Greene,
and Mercer felt that Washington at least ought not to
be exposed in a position which might become dangerous,
and they all urged him to return to Fort Lee, while each
in turn offered to stay and conduct the defence. But the
chief, who never wished to hold the fort as an isolated post,
foresaw the possible, if not the probable, result of the
British attack as clearly as his generals, and he advised
the return of the entire party. Entering their boat they
were rowed back to the Jersey side.[1]

The fighting began under a heavy fire from the enemy's
artillery posted at advantageous points, both on the island
and on the east side of the Harlem River. The several
columns pushed forward nearly at the same time. Rall
and Knyphausen encountered the most serious obstacles,
and met with the most obstinate resistance. Their course
lay through woods and underbrush and heavy abattis,
felled by the Americans. As they approached Rawlings,
his men received them with a destructive and determined
fire, which lasted a long time. Rall's force, including
the newly arrived Waldeckers, fought desperately, and, as
Cornwallis afterwards declared, "to the admiration of
the entire British army."[2] Knyphausen led his men and
tore down obstructions with his own hands. Matthews

[1] Read the letter Greene wrote to Knox on the following day.—*Document* 36.

[2] Testimony of Cornwallis before Parliamentary Committee on Howe's
case in 1779.

and Cornwallis climbed up the steep hill, and drove back Baxter's men ; but not before Baxter had fallen while fighting manfully. Percy, with whose column Lord Howe had taken his station, held Cadwallader's attention and made some progress in that direction, when Howe ordered a fourth column, consisting of the Forty-second Highlanders, under Lieutenant-Colonel Sterling, and two supporting regiments, to cross Harlem River, and attempt to land between Cadwallader and Fort Washington. This movement was successfully conducted under difficulties. The Highlanders rushed up the steep side of Harlem Heights just below the Morris Mansion, and captured over one hundred and fifty of the Americans whom Cadwallader and Magaw had detached to oppose them. Sterling's force, however, suffered considerably in making the landing. By this attack in flank, Cadwallader could maintain his position no longer, and his entire party retreated rapidly towards the fort.

Knyphausen and Rall, meanwhile, succeeded in driving back Rawlings, who had made the best resistance during the day, and the former soon reached Fort Washington, where all the Americans had now retreated. The German general at once sent in a summons for surrender, and Magaw finding that the fort was so crowded with his beaten troops, and that it was impossible to attempt further resistance without great sacrifice of life, agreed to a capitulation on favorable terms, officers and men to be guaranteed personal safety and allowed to retain private baggage.[1]

[1] Washington, who with his officers watched the fighting from Fort Lee, sent over Captain Gooch to tell Magaw to maintain himself until night, when an effort would be made to withdraw the garrison to New Jersey. The captain reached the fort, delivered his message, and, running through the fire of the enemy, got to his boat again and recrossed in safety.

By this surrender the Americans lost in prisoners two thousand six hundred and thirty-seven enlisted men and two hundred and twenty-one officers,[1] the greater part from Pennsylvania, and nearly half of them well-drilled troops. These were the men, with those taken on Long Island and at Kip's Bay, for whose accommodation the Presbyterian and Reformed churches in New York were turned into prisons, and who were to perish by hundreds by slow starvation and loathsome disease, which brutal keepers took little trouble to alleviate. The loss of the enemy in killed and wounded was something over four hundred and fifty, about two thirds of which fell upon the Hessians. The American casualties were four officers and fifty privates killed, and not over one hundred wounded.

Upon whom the responsibility for the loss of this post should rest is a question on which divided opinions have been expressed.[2] Greene had urged the retention of the

[1] Henshaw's copy of return of prisoners.—*Document No.* 59.

[2] Two weeks before the attack on the fort, Magaw's adjutant, William Demont, deserted to the enemy. This fact has lately been established by the recovery, by Mr. Edward F. de Lancey, of the New York Historical Society, of Demont's own letter confessing the desertion. It is dated London, January 16th, 1792, and is in part as follows:

"On the 2d of Nov'r 1776 I Sacrificed all I was Worth in the World to the Service of my King & Country and joined the then Lord Percy, brought in with me the Plans of Fort Washington, by which Plans that Fortress was taken by his Majesty's Troops the 16 instant, Together with 2700 Prisoners and Stores & Ammunition to the amount of 1800 Pound. At the same time, I may with Justice affirm, from my Knowledge of the Works, I saved the Lives of many of His Majesty's Subjects—these Sir are facts well-known to every General Officer which was there."

Mr. De Lancey makes this letter the text of a detailed and highly interesting account of the fall of Fort Washington (published in the *Magazine of American History*, February, 1877), in which the new theory is advanced that the disaster was due in the first instance to Demont's treason. It is quite probable, as the deserter claimed, that his information was of some

fort as necessary, both to command the passage of the river, and because it would be a threatening obstacle to the enemy's future operations. For them to advance into the country with such a fortification in their rear would be a hazardous move. These reasons were sound, and, as already stated, when the main army evacuated Harlem Heights, Washington's council voted to retain Fort Washington. But on the 7th of November, some British men-of-war again passed the obstructions without difficulty, and Washington wrote to Greene on the 8th from White Plains as follows :

" SIR : The late passage of the three vessels up the North River (which we have just received advice of) is so plain a proof of the inefficacy of all the obstructions we have thrown into it, that I cannot but think it will fully justify a change in the disposition which has been made. If we cannot prevent vessels passing up, and the enemy are possessed of the surrounding country, what valuable purpose can it answer to attempt to hold a post from which the expected benefit cannot be had ? I am therefore inclined to think it will not be prudent to hazard the men and stores at Mount Washington ; but as you are on the spot, leave it to you to give such orders as to evacuating Mount Washington as you judge best, and so far revoking the order given to Col. Magaw to defend it to the last."

General Greene on the following day replied that he did not think the garrison in any danger, and that it could

use to the British general in making his dispositions for the attack, but beyond this the incident could hardly have affected the situation on either side. Up to the night preceding the assault, Howe did not know whether the Americans would remain in the fort or not. Indeed, he gave them the opportunity to evacuate it by allowing a whole night to intervene between the summons to surrender and the attack. He could not, therefore, have changed his plans, as alleged, in the confident expectation of taking a large garrison prisoners and sending home word of another great victory. Fort Washington was simply in his way, and he would have moved against it under any circumstances, regardless of Demont and his treachery.

be drawn off at any time. He believed, too, that the stores could be removed at the last moment, in spite of an attack ; and again he called attention to the advantage of holding the post as an annoyance to the enemy. No further communications passed on the subject, but Washington rode to the Highlands, and, returning on the Jersey side of the Hudson, reached Greene's headquarters at Fort Lee on the 14th, to find no steps taken to withdraw men or stores from Mount Washington. Had the enemy in the mean time invested and captured the fort, it is pertinent to inquire whether Greene, having been acquainted with the distinct wishes of the commander-in-chief not to hazard the post, could not have been justly and properly charged with its loss. Washington's instructions were discretionary only so far as related to the details or perhaps the time of the evacuation ; and to leave Greene free, he revoked the order already given to Magaw to defend the fort to the last. Upon the arrival of Washington at Fort Lee, however, one phase of the question changed. By not renewing his instructions to evacuate the mount when he found that nothing had been done in the case, or not making the instructions peremptory, he entirely relieved Greene of the charge of non-compliance, which could have been brought against him before. The commander-in-chief was now present, and Greene was no longer under instructions, discretionary or otherwise. Washington accepted the situation as he now found it, and was reconsidering the propriety of a total evacuation. Finding Greene, of whose military judgment he had "a good opinion," strong in favor of holding the post, and others agreeing with him, among whom evidently were Putnam, Mercer, and Magaw, and knowing that Congress and the

country would not easily be reconciled to its abandonment, Washington hesitated for the moment to enforce
his own views and opinions. On the 14th and 15th, he
still'delayed a final decision. So says Greene. " His Excellency General Washington," he writes, " has been
with me several days. The evacuation or reinforcement
of Fort Washington was under consideration, but finally
nothing concluded on ;" and it was not until the morning of the 16th, just at the time of the attack, that they all
went over to the fort " to determine what was best to be
done." This clearly settles the fact that Greene was not
under instructions at the time of the surrender of the
post.

But at the same time, upon a review of all the circumstances, it is difficult to escape the conviction that but
for General Greene's earnest opposition to an abandonment of the fort, the disaster would not have occurred.
It was an error of judgment, an over-confidence in the
sufficiency of the preparations made for the defence, and
a belief that if matters came to the worst the garrison
could be withdrawn in spite of the enemy. That Greene
himself felt that he would be held largely accountable
for the loss of the post, is evident from his own expressions in the letter he wrote to Knox on the next day.
" I feel mad, vexed, sick, and sorry," are his words.
" Never did I need the consoling voice of a friend more
than now. Happy should I be to see you. This is a
most terrible event ; its consequences are justly to be
dreaded. Pray, what is said upon the occasion ?" [1]

[1] This is what Tilghman said upon the occasion : " The loss of the post is
nothing compared to the loss of men and arms, and the damp it will strike
upon the minds of many. We were in a fair way of finishing the campaign
with credit to ourselves and I think to the disgrace of Mr. Howe, and had
the General followed his own opinion the garrison would have been with-

There were those who censured Washington for not overruling Greene, but the chief kept his counsels to himself, and it was not until nearly three years later, in August, 1779, that he gave his version of the affair in a private letter to Colonel Reed. In that he frankly admits that Greene's representations and other reasons caused a "warfare" and "hesitation" in his mind, by which the evacuation was delayed until too late. But he indulged in no censures on Greene. His confidence in the latter remained steadfast. The disaster was one of those misfortunes which occur in the career of every great general, and become, indeed, a step by which he rises to greatness. Greene, more than any general of the Revolution, learned by experience. Every battle, whether a defeat or victory, was for him a training-school ; and at the close of the war we find him ranking hardly second to the commander-in-chief, in military talents, and enjoying nearly an equal reputation for his achievements.

This disaster at Fort Washington, the heaviest suffered by the Americans during the entire war, closed the campaign in the vicinity of New York. All the western part of Long Island, New York City, and all Manhattan Island, had fallen into the possession of the British, and their fleet came into undisturbed control of the Hudson, the East River, and the waters of the Sound. Every thing that Washington and his soldiers had sought to secure and defend was wrested from their hands. Their losses

drawn immediately upon the enemy's falling down from Dobb's Ferry ; but Gen'l Greene was positive that our forces might at any time be drawn off under the guns of Fort Lee. Fatal experience has evinced the contrary."
—*Correspondence in Proceedings of the N. Y. Provincial Congress*, vol. ii.

too, in men and material, were almost irreparable. Much the greater part of their artillery had been captured—two hundred and eighteen pieces of all calibres, according to the enemy's report. Three hundred and twenty-nine officers and four thousand one hundred men had been taken prisoners; nearly six hundred had been killed or wounded; and numbers had been swept off by disease. The enemy suffered more heavily, except in prisoners and cannon, in which their loss was nothing; but they had recovered territory, won victories, and they were now to find before them only a flying and dissolving body of rebels.

The situation at this point presented a gloomy prospect for America. But had the cause been then surrendered, we could still contemplate this struggle around New York and Brooklyn with respect, as a noble effort to gain an end worth fighting for. As success, however, was finally achieved, and achieved through the experience of these events, they challenge our deepest interest.

CHAPTER VIII.

TRENTON—PRINCETON—CLOSE OF THE CAMPAIGN.

To appreciate the full significance of what has been described in the preceding pages, follow the campaign in outline to its closing scenes.

Thus far the American army had met with nothing but defeat, retreat, sacrifice, hardship, and discouragement. First came the months of preparation, with England straining every nerve to conquer the colonies; then the first and disastrous collision on Long Island, on which so much depended; then the retreat, the loss of New York, the withdrawal to White Plains, and a battle which was not a victory for the Americans; and, finally, the heavy blow struck in the fall of Fort Washington. Much had been endured and learned alike by general and private soldier during these gloomy months, and both were now destined to profit by the trial. All this faith and patience had its legitimate reward, as we shall find if we now place ourselves in the last days of the year upon the banks of the Delaware.

What had occurred in the mean time was the evacuation of Fort Lee, a hasty retreat through New Jersey, the dwindling away of the army, the advance of the British towards Philadelphia, the removal of Congress to Baltimore, and an increase of despondency throughout the country.[1] Washington with the remnants of his army had taken post on the right bank of the Delaware, and, still strong in hope, was calling for militia to come to his assistance. At the same time he watched the opportunity to inflict upon the enemy some happy counter-stroke that might temporarily raise the spirits of his soldiers and the people. The opportunity came. The British delayed crossing the Delaware, and divided their force among different posts throughout New Jersey. At Trenton they stationed Colonel Rall with a body twelve hundred strong, composed chiefly of Hessians. This was the Rall who marched up with De Heister on Long Island, and figured in the capture of prisoners, who afterwards turned our right on Chatterton's Hill, at White Plains, and whose attack on Rawlings at Fort Washington was the brilliant feature of that day. He was every inch a soldier, except in possessing that reserve of caution which every commander is bound to exercise in the presence of

---

[1] After the battle of White Plains, Howe, we have seen, moved against Fort Washington. On the other hand, Washington, supposing that Howe would aim next for Philadelphia, prepared to cross part of his force into Jersey and endeavor to protect that city. He proposed to continue the policy of "wasting" the campaign. Heath was left to look after the Highlands ; Lee with another force remained at Northcastle, and Connecticut troops were posted at Saw Pits and the borders of that State. Washington took with him Putnam, Greene, Stirling, and Mercer, with less than four thousand men, and fell back before the British through Brunswick, Princeton, and Trenton. He wrote several times to Lee to join him, but Lee was full of excuses and utterly failed Washington at this crisis. While marching in no haste by a westerly route through Jersey, Lee was surprised at his quarters at Baskingridge on the morning of December 13th, and made prisoner by Lieutenant-Colonel Harcourt and a party of dragoons. (The account of the capture by Captain Bradford, Lee's aid, not heretofore published, is given in *Document* 46. In Wilkinson's *Memoirs* there is another account.) Sullivan then took command of Lee's troops and joined Washington, who at Trenton had crossed to the Pennsylvania side of the Delaware, removing all boats to delay the enemy, and had halted in camp a few miles above.

an enemy, however remote the probability of an attack. Rall despised Washington's troops, and would throw up no intrenchments around Trenton.

Washington resolved to make a sudden dash upon this Hessian. A surprise, an irresistible attack, the capture of a post with a thousand men, might work wonders in their moral effect. The soldiers with him were trusty men, twenty-four hundred of whom he proposed to lead himself on this enterprise. Many of the regiments we have already become familiar with, and their leaders are men who have led them from the first. Here are Greene, Sullivan, Stirling, Mercer, Glover, and Sargent, for division and brigade commanders ; and with them we meet new officers—Brigadier-Generals Adam Stephen, of Virginia ; Arthur St. Clair, of Pennsylvania, and De Fermoy, a French officer, lately commissioned by Congress. Here also are Hand's battalion, parts of Smallwood's and Haslet's, Knox and his artillerymen, Durkee's, Charles Webb's, Ward's, and parts of Chester's and Bradley's, from Connecticut ; Sargent's, Glover's, Hutchinson's, Baldwin's, Shepherd's, Bailey's, and Paterson's, of Massachusetts ; Stark's, Poor's, and Reed's, from New Hampshire, who, with Paterson's, have just arrived in camp from Ticonderoga ; the remnants of McDougall's and Ritzema's New York Continentals, and Weedon's, Scott's, Elliot's, Buckner's, and Reed's Virginians. How depleted are these battalions, many of them less than a hundred strong !

Washington's plan included a simultaneous move from several points. The body he was to lead was concentrated, on the night of December 24th, at McConkey's Ferry, nine miles above Trenton. The troops were to cross at night, reach the town at dawn, and take

19

its garrison by surprise. Lower down were two other bodies of troops. About opposite Trenton, General Ewing was posted with Pennsylvania militia and Nixon's Continental brigade, now commanded by Colonel Daniel Hitchcock, of Rhode Island. At Bristol, General Cadwallader commanded still another corps of Pennsylvanians, including many young men from the best families in Philadelphia. Ewing and Cadwallader were to cross and intercept the retreat of the Hessians from Trenton, or prevent Donop at Burlington from affording relief. Putnam was to make a demonstration from Philadelphia.

To his own force Washington issued minute and stringent orders. The troops he divided into two divisions, giving Sullivan the first, and Greene the second. Sullivan's brigades were Glover's, Sargent's, and St. Clair's ; Greene's were Stephen's, Mercer's, and Stirling's. De Fermoy was to follow in Greene's rear with Hand's riflemen and Hausegger's German battalion from Pennsylvania. To each brigade were attached from two to four pieces of artillery, eighteen guns in all, under Knox. Greene's division was to cross first, Stephen's in advance, provided with spikes and hammers to spike the enemy's guns, and with ropes to drag them off if that proved feasible. After the crossing, Captain Washington, of the Third Virginia, was to proceed with a guard on the road towards Trenton, and halt and detain any one who might be passing in either direction. Three miles from the ferry the road branched, making two lines of approach to the town. Greene's division was to take the upper road ; Sullivan's the lower one near the river. Stirling's and St. Clair's brigades were to act as reserves for their respective columns, and in case of necessity were to form separately or join forces, as the emergency required. The officers set their watches by Washington's. Profound silence was enjoined. Not a man to leave the ranks, read the orders, *under penalty of death.*[1]

The night of the 24th brought storm, snow, and sleet. Ewing and Cadwallader could do nothing on account of the ice in the river. But Washington was determined on the attempt. He called upon Glover's men to man the boats ; and these amphibious soldiers, who had transported the army on the retreat from Long Island, were ready again to strain every nerve for the plans of their chief. It was a long, tedious night as they pushed across the Delaware, through ice and chilling spray, and it was not until four o'clock in the morning that the force was ready to take up the march on the Jersey side. They could not surprise the Hessians before daylight, but a return was not to be thought of. The troops then marched on in the worst weather that could be encountered. " As violent a storm ensued of Hail & Snow as I ever felt," wrote Captain William Hull, of Webb's Continentals. The river was crossed, says Knox, " with almost infinite difficulty," the floating ice making the labor incredible. Fortunately the storm was against our backs, " and consequently in the faces of our enemy." The march was kept up swiftly and quietly. In Sullivan's column some of the soldiers could not cover their muskets from the wet, and word was sent to Washington of the unfitness of their arms. Washington promptly sent word back by his aid, Lieutenant-Colonel Samuel B. Webb, that if the men could not discharge their pieces they must use the bayonet, for the town must be taken.

At eight o'clock the two columns neared the enemy's

---

[1] Order of march to Trenton.—*Drake's Life of Knox.*

outposts—Sullivan striking them on the lower road but three minutes after Greene on the upper one. Greene's van was led by Captain Washington and Lieutenant James Monroe, the future President; Sullivan's by Stark's New Hampshire men. Surprising the Hessian outguards, our troops dashed after them " pell-mell" into Trenton, gave the enemy no time to form, cleared the streets with cannon and howitzers " in the twinkling of an eye," under Washington's own direction, dislodged them from the houses, drove them beyond into a plain, surrounded and forced them to surrender, with the loss of their commander Rall, who fell mortally wounded. A fine and remarkable exploit ! The turning-point of the campaign—if not, indeed, the decisive stroke of the war ! Gathering up their nine hundred and fifty prisoners, six brass field-pieces, standards, horses, and " a vast quantity of Plunder," the Americans marched back again, having lost not a man killed, and hardly more than two or three wounded.

In General Orders next day, Washington congratulated his soldiers in the warmest terms. He had been in many actions, in all of which he had seen misbehavior on the part of some ; but at Trenton, he told them their conduct was admirable, without exception. Among others he thanked Knox for his services in terms " strong and polite." " Providence seemed to have smiled upon every part of this enterprise." " What can't men do," said Hull, " when engaged in so noble a cause !" " That victory," writes Bancroft, " turned the shadow of death into the morning."

One more encounter with the enemy, one more success, and the campaign closes with final victory assured for America.

Convinced that inaction would be as demoralizing as defeat, Washington once more determined to try his fortunes in New Jersey, and at once prepared again " to beat up" the enemy's quarters. Crossing the Delaware as before, he marched on the 30th to Trenton, which the British had not reoccupied since Christmas. Hearing of this move, Cornwallis at Princeton gathered a force of seven thousand veterans, and on the 2d of January started for Trenton. Washington sent out detachments, and delayed his entry into the town until evening. At nightfall he took up position on the east bank of the Assanpink Creek, which ran along the east edge of the town and emptied into the Delaware. The British pursued our troops to the bridge, but were there repulsed by Knox's artillery. Cornwallis rested at Trenton, sent off for reinforcements, and expected the next morning to cross the Assanpink at the bridge or the fords above, and bring Washington to an engagement. Obviously the Americans were in a hazardous position. Should the British drive them back, there was no escape, for the Delaware flowed in their rear. They must save themselves that night. A council of war was called, and the situation discussed. From Trenton to Princeton ran a second roundabout road east of the main highway, along which Cornwallis had marched, and which it was possible for the Americans to take, and put themselves in the rear of Cornwallis, with lines of retreat open beyond to Morristown and the back country. Washington proposed escape by this route, and the council seconded him. Orders for a secret night march were given to the officers, and the regiments were silently withdrawn from their posts along the Assanpink, and set in motion along this back road towards Princeton. The camp-fires on

the banks of the creek were kept up by guards left behind for the purpose. Nothing occurred to excite suspicion of the movement in the minds of the British sentinels, nearly within musket-shot on the opposite bank.

Washington's troops reached a point within two miles
of Princeton about sunrise. The main column pushed
on for the village, while Mercer's brigade, consisting of
the remnants of Haslet's Delawares, Smallwood's Marylanders, and the First Virginia regiment under Captain
Fleming, turned to the left to break down a bridge on the
main road over Stony Creek, which the enemy would
have to cross on returning from Trenton, in pursuit of
Washington.

Three British regiments had been left at Princeton by
Cornwallis, but were now, on the morning of the 3d, proceeding under orders to join him. These were the Fifty-
fifth, the Fortieth, and Seventeenth, the latter commanded by Lieutenant-Colonel Mawhood. Mawhood
was a mile in advance of the others, and had just crossed
the Stony Creek bridge, when, looking across the country to his left and rear, he discovered Mercer's party on
its march. Surprised at the appearance of a force of
rebels where he least expected to see one, Mawhood,
nevertheless, with a soldier's instinct, promptly wheeled
about and proceeded to attack Mercer. They met on a
hill and exchanged fire, when Mawhood ordered a bayonet charge, and put the Americans to rout. Mercer,
on horseback, attempted in vain to rally his men, and was
mortally wounded with bayonet thrusts. Haslet, gallantly fighting on foot, and also trying to form the broken
brigade, fell dead with a bullet wound in his forehead.
Captain Fleming, of Virginia, suffered a like fate, as well
as Captain Neal of the artillery. This sudden and se-

rious reverse required instant attention, for Washington could not afford to be detained long in this position. Cadwallader's brigade, which had followed Mercer's, was accordingly brought up into line, while Washington attempted to rally the latter's force; but Mawhood was making a surprising fight, and he threw Cadwallader's militiamen into confusion as he had Mercer's. Matters now were worse, and the commander-in-chief made strenuous exertions, at great personal hazard, to bring the troops into some order. Meanwhile, he sent word for Hitchcock's brigade to advance upon the enemy, while Hand's riflemen endeavored to turn their left. The "gallant Hitchcock" promptly took his command into action—all that remained of it, five regiments together hardly five hundred strong—and formed in line. On the right was Lieutenant-Colonel Nixon, next Varnum's battalion, under Lieutenant-Colonel Crary, in the centre Colonel Lippett, with the largest number, one hundred and twenty-eight men, next Hitchcock's, under Major Angell, and on the left Little's battalion, under Lieutenant-Colonel Henshaw.[1] They opened fire at one hundred yards, and then, in conjunction with Cadwallader's men, whom Washington had rallied in part, they rushed upon Mawhood's force, recaptured the two guns we had lost, and joined in putting the enemy completely to rout.

No doubt these old troops experienced a glow of satisfaction over this brief and final work of the campaign, for they had endured hard service from the outset. Here was Greene's old brigade, which crossed with him to Long Island on the 1st of May—Varnum's, Hitchcock's, Little's, and, by a happy accident, Hand's, on the left—to

[1] *Stiles' MS. Diary.* Statement of Rhode Island officers engaged at Princeton.

assist in reversing the record of the year. These men had built the lines around Brooklyn ; Hitchcock's and Little's at the Flatbush Pass had been caught and all but captured in the surprise of August 27th ; they fought manfully, and suffered the most at Harlem Heights ; many of them responded to Washington's appeal to remain six weeks beyond their term of service, and now they had shared in the successful manœuvre at Princeton, which changed the whole aspect of affairs.

Hitchcock, who had temporarily succeeded Nixon in command of the brigade, received the thanks of Washington for himself and for his men in front of Princeton College for their aid and conduct in the action. But the colonel, a brilliant, promising officer, whose regiment built and guarded Fort Putnam in Brooklyn, was destined to only a brief career henceforth. Overcome by the fatigue and hardships of the campaign, he died in camp at Morristown, on the 13th of January, and was buried by the Philadelphia and Delaware Light Infantry companies, under Rodney, with all the honors of war. It was a fitting escort to the remains of the brave soldier, for Rodney and most of his men had behaved well at Princeton.

Sullivan's troops drove the other two British regiments out of Princeton towards Brunswick, and Washington's tired army then pushed on, and on the 6th went into camp at Morristown.[1] .

The effect of these two unexpected strokes at Trenton and Princeton was to baffle Howe, and utterly disconcert his plans. Expecting to march upon Philadelphia at his

---

[1] In connection with the battles of Trenton and Princeton, read the interesting letters from Knox, Haslet, Rodney, and Hull in Part II. They have all appeared since our general accounts were written.

leisure, he suddenly finds Washington turning about and literally cutting his way through the British posts, back to a point where he threatened Howe's flank and rear. The enemy were at once compelled to retire from all their positions below Brunswick, give up the thought of wintering in Philadelphia, and fall back to the vicinity of New York. When Horace Walpole heard of these movements, he wrote to Sir Horace Mann: "Washington has shown himself both a Fabius and a Camillus. His march through our lines is allowed to have been a prodigy of generalship. In one word, I look upon a great part of America as lost to this country." [1]

Here the campaign closed. Washington could not be dislodged from his strong mountain position, and Howe was satisfied to rest his troops and postpone further oper ations until the next season. Meantime the country took heart, Congress voted troops and supplies, and the army was recruited and organized on a better basis. "The business of war is the result of Experience," wrote Wolcott from Congress, with faith unshaken during the dakrest hours of the campaign; and experience was now put to good profit.

---

[1] In another letter Walpole says:

"It is now the fashion to cry up the manœuvre of General Washington in this action [Princeton] who has beaten two English regiments, too, and obliged General Howe to contract his quarters—in short, the campaign has by no means been wound up to content. . . . It has lost a great deal of its florid complexion, and General Washington is allowed by both sides not to be the worst General in the field."

Again, in a humorous vein:

"Caius Manlius Washingtonius Americanus, the dictator, has got together a large army, larger than our ally, the Duke of Wirtemberg was to have sold us; and General Howe, who has nothing but salt provisions in our metropolis, New York, has not twenty thousand pounds' worth of pickles, as he had at Boston."—*Walpole's Letters and Correspondence. Cunningham.*

The crisis was passed. Events proved decisive. Hard-ship and anxiety were yet to come during succeeding years of the war; but it was the result of this year's struggle that cleared away misgivings and confirmed the popular faith in final success. England could do no more than she had done to conquer America; while America was now more ready than ever to meet the issue. Independence was established in the present campaign—in the year of its declaration; and more than to any others we owe this political privilege to the men who fought from Long Island to Princeton.

NOTES.

OBSTRUCTIONS IN THE HUDSON.—The following letter from Mr. Duer to the Secret Committee of the New York Provincial Congress refers to the defence of the Hudson at Fort Washington:

"WHITE PLAINS, Sunday 21st July, 1776.

"DEAR GENTL:—I have just arrived at this place from New York where I have conversed with Genl. Washington on the Purport of the Letter from the Secret Committee.

"Gens. Putnam and Mifflen have made an exact Survey of the River opposite Mount Washington and find that the Depth in no Part exceeds seven Fathoms; the Width, however, of the Channel (which is from three to seven Fathoms) is not much less than 1800 Yards, the shallow Part of the River running in an oblique Direction. Genl. Washington expresses himself extremely anxious about the Obstruction of that Channel, and Measures are daily used for executing that Purpose. It is impossible to procure Vessels enough at New York, so that the Measure must be delayed till such Time as more Vessels can be brought through the Sound from Connecticut; however, I am not without Apprehensions that this Resource will be cut off, as I understand that some of the Enemy's Vessels have sailed out of the Hook with an Intention (probably) of cutting off our Communication with the Sound.

"It is, however an Object of so much Importance that no Difficulties, however great, ought to deter us from our Attempts to carry it into Execution ; *if we succeed, the Designs of the Enemy in this Campaign are effectually baffled*—if we fail, we cannot be in a more lamentable Situation than we are now.

"Exclusive of the great Advantage we should reap in obstructing the Channel so far to the Southward, it is, I fear, the only Place we can depend upon shallowing to the Southward of the Highlands, whilst the Men-of-War are in the River, for if proper Batteries are erected near the Water at Mount Washington, and on the opposite Side, mounted with Guns of 18, 24 and 32 Pounders, it will not be practicable for any Vessels to be so near as to prevent our working under the Cover of these Works. I have strongly urged Genl. Washington to send Gen. Mifflen some heavier Metal, and he seems half inclined. This necessary operation has not yet taken place.

"The Genl. is anxious to have either of you (as Members of the Secret Committee) to be with him in Town, and has authorized me to make the Offer to you of his House during your Residence. Let me entreat One of you immediately to come Down, and not to quit Genl. Washington till such Time as this Measure on which our Safety depends is effected. . . . .

"I am very sincerely, yours, etc.,

"WM. DUER.

"P. S.—For God's sake exert yourself to secure the Sea Vessels which are in the River."[1]

To hasten the completion of the obstructions General Putnam proposed the following plan of sinking ships, as appears in a letter from him to General Gates, dated July 26, 1776 (in Sparks') :

"We are preparing *Chevaux-de-Frize*, at which we make great Despatch by the Help of Ships, which are to be Sunk ; a Scheme of mine, which you may be assured is very simple, a Plan of which I send you. The two Ships' Sterns lie towards each other, about Seventy Feet apart. Three large Logs, which reach from Ship to Ship, are fastened to them. The two Ships and Logs stop the River two hundred and eighty Feet. The Ships are to be sunk, and, when hauled down on one side, the Picks will be raised to a proper Height, and they must inevitably stop the River, if the Enemy will let us sink them."

On the 21st of September, the New York Convention resolved :

"That the Secret Committee for obstructing the Navigation of Hudson's River be empowered and directed to purchase or impress for the Service of the State any Number of Vessels not exceeding six, which they shall think best calculated for the Purpose of completing the Obstructions in the Hudson's River opposite to Mount Washington. . . . .

"That the said Committee be directed to send all the Oak Plank which they may have in their Possession, to Mount Washington with the utmost Dispatch."

[1] From the Clinton papers as published in E. M. Ruttenber's *Obstructions to the Navigation of Hudson's River, etc. Munsell, Albany.*

GOVERNOR'S ISLAND.—The obstructions in the East River between Governor's Island and the Battery consisted of hulks sunk in the Channel. This was not done until a few days before the battle on Long Island. Colonel Douglas, as he states, sounded the river. The present Buttermilk Channel, between the island and Brooklyn, was not obstructed. Governor's Island was evacuated on the morning of the retreat from Long Island, but the enemy failed to take possession for two days. The interval was improved by the Americans in carrying off all except the heavy pieces to New York in the night-time.

BATTLE OF LONG ISLAND.—The prisoners named in *Document* 58 as having been captured by us at the battle of Long Island were a small party of marines, who mistook the Delaware regiment in Stirling's force for Hessians. They came too near and were taken by Lieut. Wm. Popham, who was ordered to march them into camp. He made them cross Gowanus Creek on Stirling's retreat, and brought all but one in safe. Popham afterwards became major and aid to General James Clinton, and settled in New York, where he lived to be over ninety years old. Was a member of the New York Cincinnati. During the battle the marines landed from the fleet, which could not make its way up above Gowanus Bay, and, according to one letter, Admiral Howe furnished Grant with ammunition while fighting Stirling. The Roebuck alone, as already stated, could work its way along far enough to send some harmless long-range shot at the Red Hook fort.

PART II.

—————◆—————

DOCUMENTS.

DOCUMENTS

[No. 1.]

GENERAL GREENE'S ORDERS

CAMP ON LONG ISLAND

[*Colonel Little's Order Book*]

GENERAL ORDERS.[1]

HEAD QUARTERS, April 30, 1776.

(Parole, SAWBRIDGE.)   (Countersign, OLIVER.)

. . . . Gen[l] Greene's Brigade is to encamp tomorrow at 10 A.M.. on the ground marked out on Long Island. . . .

GEN. GREENE'S ORDERS.

[NEW YORK] April 30, 1776.

The Q[r]. M[rs]. of the 9th, 11th, 12th regts. are to apply to the Q.. M. Gen[l]. for tents & camp utensils this evening to be in readiness to encamp agreeably to general orders to morrow morning—at 4 o'clock this P.M. Col. Varnum & Col. Hitchcock & Col. Little

[1] These orders are from the Order Book kept by Colonel Moses Little, of Greene's brigade, while encamped on Long Island during the months of May, June, July, and August, 1776, the original being in the possession of Benjamin Hale, Esq., of Newburyport, Mass. They cover the whole period of active operations there after the arrival of the main army at New York. The book also contains Washington's general orders from head-quarters, New York, General Sullivan's orders while in command on Long Island, Colonel Little's regimental orders, and scattering orders from Generals Lee, Spencer, Greene, and Nixon, in September and October, 1776. As all Washington's orders are to be found in Force's Archives, a few only are inserted here to preserve the connection. They are distinguished as. "General Orders." Sullivan's and the others are given separately.

are desired to attend at the General's quarters to go over to Long
Island & view the encampment marked out. A serg^t. & 20 men
are to parade at White Hall to morrow at 7 o'clock, to be under
the direction of Engineer Smith.

[LONG ISLAND] May 4th, 1776.

Captain Spurs is to draw out a party of carpenters to make
Bell tents, they are to apply to Col. Miflin for tools, boards & nails
to make them of. 300 men for fatigue to morrow. The Quarter
Master is to make an estimate of the necessary quantity of boards
to floor the tents & apply to the Quarter Master general for them.
The Cols. or commanding officers of each regiment is to give an
order for the boards, certifying the quantity wanted. A return is
to be made of the state of the cartridges now in possession of the
troops & the number wanted to make up each man's twenty
rounds.

REGIMENTAL ORDERS.

[*Col. Little's.*]

Officers for fatigue to-morrow, Cap. Gerrish, Lt. Kent, & Lt.
Atkinson.

GEN. GREENE'S ORDERS.

May 5th, 1776.

A fatigue party of 200 men to morrow morning properly officered.
No non-commissioned Officer or Soldier is to pass the ferries to
New York without permission from some of ye Field Officers.
Any of the troops attempting to pass over without permission will
be confined & tried for disobedience of orders. Any of the fatigue
parties that leave their work without liberty, shall do constant fatigue duty for a whole week. As the security of New York greatly
dependeth on this *pass*, when these works are constructing the
General hopes the troops will carefully forward the same as fast
as possible.

The inhabitants having entered a complaint that their meadow
ground was injured by the troops going upon it to gather greens,
they are for the future strictly prohibited going on the ground of
any inhabitants, unless in the proper passes to & from the encampments & the forts, without orders from some commissioned officer.
The General desires the troops not to sully their reputation by

any undue liberty in speech or conduct but behave themselves towards the inhabitants with that decency & respect that becomes the character of troops fighting for the preservation of the rights & liberties of America.

The General would have the troops consider that we came here to protect the inhabitants & their property from the ravages of the enemy, but if instead of support & protection, they meet with nothing but insult & outrage, we shall be considered as banditti & treated as oppressors & enemies.

GENERAL ORDERS.

HEAD QUARTERS May 7, 1776.
(Parole, DEVONSHIRE.)   (Countersign, CAVENDISH.)

Every regiment encamped in the lines & every reg^t. in the brigade on Long Island, exclusive of their quarter & rear guards, are to mount a picket every evening at retreat beating at sun set, consisting of one Capt. 2 Subs, 1 drum & 1 fife & 50 rank & file— they are to lay upon their arms, & be ready to turn out at a moments notice.

One Col. one L^t. Col. & one major are to mount every evening at sunset as Field Officers of the picket.

Immediately upon any alarm or order from the Brig. Genl. of the day, the pickets are to form in the front of their respective encampments, & there wait the orders of the Field Officer commanding the pickets, who is instantly to obey the orders of the Brig^r. Genl. of the Day.

A Brig. Genl. is to mount every morning at ten o'clock who will receive all reports, visit all the outguards in the day time & report all extraordinary occurrences to the Commander in Chief & the Brig^{de} Major of the day is constantly to attend head quarters to receive all orders, & distribute them immediately.

The Col. is to go the grand rounds, & the Lt. Col. & the major the visiting rounds of the Camp.

Brig. Genl. Greene will order the same picket to be mounted by the regiments in his brigade as are mounted in the grand Camp. He will also direct one field officer to mount daily to command them. Gen. Greene will report all extraordinaries to the Commander in Chief.

Col. Prescott or the officer commanding on Nutten's or Governor's Island & the officer commanding at Red Hook, are to report all extraordinaries to the Commander in Chief on any appearance of the enemy. The commanding officer at Red Hook will also dispatch a messenger to Gen¹. Greene.

The officer commanding the riflemen upon Long Island will constantly report all extraordinaries to Gen¹. Greene, & the officer commanding upon Staten Island will do the same to the Commander in Chief.

GEN. GREENE'S ORDERS.

May 8, 1776.

Field officers for the picket, Major Angell, Adj^t. for the day from Col. Hitchcock's regiment.

REGIMENTAL ORDERS.

Officers for picket tonight, Cap. Parker, L^t. Jenkins, L^t. Burnham, Ensign Story. Officers for fatigue to-morrow, Cap. Dodge, L^t. Jared Smith & Ensign Proctor.

GEN. GREENE'S ORDERS.

LONG ISLAND, May 10th 1776.

The Brig^{de} Major is to regulate the duty of the regiments, both officers & soldiers, by their number & not by regiments, some being much larger than others, & to establish a regular roster for the regulation of the same. A subaltern & 11 men are to guard the stores & ferries.

The officer commanding the guard is to receive his orders from Deputy Commissary Brown for the number of sentries necessary for securing the stores, to be relieved daily.

The Cols. or commanding officers of the ninth, eleventh, twelfth Reg^{ts} are to draw as many cartridges from the laboratory as will furnish each man 20 rounds; as many to be delivered out as the cartridge boxes will contain, the remainder to be tied up by the cap^t of companies, & every man's name written on his cartridges, that they may be delivered without confusion: All the bad cartridges now in the regiments are to be returned to the Laboratory. The Brig^{de} Major will send a party to the Q^r Mr Genl to draw tents for the establishment of the main guard, to consist of a subaltern and 21 men. An orderly sergeant from each regiment will attend at the general's quarters daily ; they are to bring their provisions with them.

The commanding officers of the 9th 11th & 12th Reg^{ts} are to make returns of the guns out of repair & the number wanted to furnish every non commissioned officer & soldier with a gun.

May 10th 1776.

A subaltern & 30 men are to parade immediately to fetch over 300 spears from the Q^r Mr Genl's store. The officer must pick those that are fit for use. He is also to bring over a grindstone to sharpen the spears on. Col. Hitchcock will send over the arms of his regiment that are out of order, to Mr. John Hillyard, foreman of a shop at the King's Works (so called) where they will be immediately repaired. Any soldier that has his gun damaged by negligence or carelessly injured, shall pay the cost of repairing, the cap^s & sub^s are desired to report all such.

May 11th 1776.

Field officer for picket tomorrow night Lt. Col. Henshaw, Adj^t from Col. Hitchcock's reg^t.

DETAIL.

	C.	S.	S.	C.	D.	F.	P.
Picket........	1	2	2	2	1	1	50
Fatigue.......	1	2	2	2	1	1	80
Main Guard...		1					8

REGIMENTAL ORDERS FOR THE 12th REG^t OF FOOT.

Those non commissioned officers & soldiers who have occasion to go over the ferry to New York will apply to Lt. Col. Henshaw for their permits.

A regimental Court Martial will sit today at 12 o'clock at Capt Wade's tent to try such prisoners as are contained in the Quarter Guard of the regiment. Cap. Wade, Pres. Lt. Hodgkins, Lt. Parsons, Lt. Knot & Ensⁿ Pearson, members.

GEN. GREENE'S ORDERS.

May 12th, 1776.

The 12th regiment exempt from fatigue tomorrow having to be mustered.

May 14, 1776.

Field officer for picket tomorrow night, Major Collins, adj^t. for the day from Col. Hitchcock's Reg^t.

REG^l. ORDERS FOR THE 12th REG^t. OF FOOT.

In Camp Long Island May 15, 1776.

The Col. desires hereby to remind the officers & soldiers of this regiment of the Rules & Regulations of the army, & of the general orders issued by the Commander in Chief agreable to them, especially that the Rules & Regulations be often read to the men that no one plead ignorance if he is called to account for the breach of any of them.

The Col. desires & orders that the officers pay particular attention that the Rules & Regulations be read to the men agreable to the resolves of Congress, likewise that the officers of each company, off duty, attend morning & evening to the calling of the roll & if possible that a report be made every day of such as be absent. The Col. is sorry to see so much inattention, of the officers & men to the duties of religious worship, & he desires as we are all engaged in the cause of God & our country, & are dependent on the Divine assistance for protection & success, & as it is a duty incumbent on all as far as possible in a social way to wait upon God in the way of his appointment, to implore pardon & forgiveness of all our sins, & to ask his guidance & direction in the prosecution of our affairs, that neither officers nor soldiers will unnecessarily absent themselves from the stated worship of God at the house of Prayer—or on the Sabbath day.

Commissioned officers for picket tonight Cap. Baker, L^t. Knot & Ensign Woodman. Commissioned officers for fatigue tomorrow, Capt. Parker, L^t. Silvanus Smith & L^t. Lamborn ; for main guard Ensign Mitchell.

GEN. GREENE'S ORDERS.

Brooklin May 16, 1776.

Col. Varnum's regiment to be off duty tomorrow morning in the forenoon, to parade on the regimental parade at 8 oclock, to be reviewed, & their arms examined. Every man in the regiment, that is well, is to be on parade with arms & accoutrements. No soldier is to borrow either arms or accoutrements from a soldier of either of the other regiments, as the true state of the regiment with respect to arms is wanted. Col. Hitchcock's reg^t. will be reviewed next day after tomorrow. Col. Little's the day after that will be reviewed in the same manner.

No soldier is to mount the picket guard without shoes.

May 16, 1776.

Tomorrow being the day appointed by the Continental Congress to be observed as a day of fasting & prayer & his Excellency Genl. Washington having ordered all duties to be discontinued except the necessary guard until next day after tomorrow, there are no fatigue parties to turn out tomorrow morning & the reviewing of Col. Varnum's regiment is put off until next day after tomorrow. the other regiments are to follow in order as in the morning orders. The general desires that the troops of the 9, 11 & 12 regiments (except those on duty) may be strict to attend the duties of the day in a devout & cleanly manner. Field officers for picket tomorrow night———— Adj^t. from Col. Varnum's regiment. Detail for Guard & fatigue as usual.

REGIMENTAL ORDERS FOR THE 12TH REG^T. OF FOOT.

James Holland, a fifer in Cap. Dodge's Company is appointed fife major to this regiment, & is to be obeyed as such.

Com^d officers for picket tonight L^t. Atkinson & L^t. Fiske.

GENERAL ORDERS.

HEAD QUARTERS, 17 May 1776.

(Parole, NEW CASTLE.)   (Countersign, WILMINGTON.)

Cap. Wolverton's Company of New Jersey is to join General Greene's Brigade. The Cap. is to take his orders from the General respecting his post. . . . .

GEN. GREENE'S MORNING ORDERS.

May 17, 1776.

A corporal & 6 men to be sent for a guard to fort Sterling to mount at 9 O'clock. This guard is to be sent every other day. The corporal to receive his orders from L^t. Randall of the train.

Field officer for picket tomorrow night L^t. Col. Henshaw, Adj^t. from Col. Varnum's regiment. Fatigue as usual.

May 19, 1776.

Field officer for picket tomorrow night Major Collins, Adj^t. from Col. Varnum's regiment. Detail as yesterday.

May 20, 1776.

Field officer for picket, Major Angell, Adj^t. from Col. Hitchcock's regiment.

May 21, 1776.

Field officer for picket tomorrow night, L^t. Col. Crary, Adj^t. from Col. Little's regiment.

May 23, 1776.

Field officer for picket to morrow night, L^t. Col. Henshaw, adjutant from Col. Hitchcock's regiment.

GENERAL ORDERS.

HEAD QUARTERS, May 25, 1776.

(Parole, MUGFORD.)   (Countersign, LEONARD.)

A working party consisting of nine hundred men to be ordered tomorrow morning from the different brigades, & the regiments.

Genl. Heath's { Colo^s. Leonard's & Bailey's / Colo^s. Read's & Baldwin's } To go to Powles Hook.

Genl. Spencer's. { Colo^s. Parson's & Wylly's—To go to Bayard's Hill. Colo^s. Huntington's to Red Hook. Arnold's to Fort Sterling. Col. Ward's—50 men with 4 days provisions to cut pickets . . . . The remainder of this regiment's working party—at Fort George.

Lord Stirlings. { Nixon's & Webb's Mc-Dougall's & Ritzema's. } On Governor's Island every day till further orders.

GEN. GREENE'S ORDERS.

May 25, 1776.

Cap. Silas Talbut of Col. Hitchcock's regiment, Cap^n. Frazier of Cap^n. (Col.) Wayne's regiment, L^t. Noel Allen of Col. Varnum's regiment & [L^t.] Samuel Huse of Col. Little's regiment are a Committee to inspect the provisions for the troops of this brigade. The commissaries & quartermasters are to apply to them to determine, which is merchantable and which is not. Such as they say are good the quarter masters are to receive and such as they condemn are to be refused.

No non commissioned officer or soldier is to be out of camp after retreat beating, & any that are discovered going out after that time are to be taken up & confined in the main guard, & any that are coming in, that have been out without leave from their officers are to be confined; any sentry that permits them to pass without examination will be punished for disobedience of orders.

L^t. Col. Cornell having reported great negligence among the guards, for the future they will be visited by day & night, by the field officer of the day. Every commissioned & non-commissioned officer that commands guards is to be reported, that has not his guard in good order. No soldier is to be absent from the guard without leave, & not more than 2 commissioned officers nor more than one non commissioned officer at a time. All guards except the picket are to mount at   o'Clock in the morning. The retreat is to beat half an hour after sunset. At guard mounting in the morning, the field officer of the day is to attend the parade & give to each respective officer a proper detail of his guard.

One man from each detached guard is to be sent to the grand parade to pilot the new guard to the relief of the old ones.

No person is to be admitted to any of the forts where there are cannon or ammunition except a General officer by day, without the leave of the officer commanding the guard, & a general officer after dark is not to be admitted without leave first obtained of the commanding (officer).

The officer commanding guards where there are cannon or ammunition, is to be very watchful & not to suffer by day or night any person to enter the forts unless they have business there, or are known to belong to the army, or are with some officer belonging to the army.

Adj^t. from Col. Varnum's.

GENERAL ORDERS.

(Parole, HANCOCK.)   (Countersign, TRUMBULL.)

· · · · The working party of Col. Nixon's regiment are to be ordered every day to Long Island, instead of Governor's Island as mentioned in yesterday's orders. · · · ·

GEN. GREENE'S ORDERS.

May 26, 1776.

Field officer for picket tomorrow night, Major Collins, Adj^t. from Col. Hitchcock's regiment.

May 29, 1776.

A garrison court martial to sit for the trial of prisoners now in the main Guard.

The commanding officer of the Ferry Guard is to permit the Ferry boats to pass until ten O'clock with common passengers, but no soldier is to pass after retreat beating, unless the Col. or commanding officer of the regiment, to which he belongs, certify the necessity. The troops are to be under arms at roll calling, morning & evening. Every soldier detected snapping his lock without orders from his officer, is to be immediately sent prisoner to the main guard, there to be confined two days & nights, & allowed nothing to eat or drink but bread & water.

All officers are desired to be more careful of discovering the countersign to persons that have no right to know it.

Any soldier on guard that discovers the countersign to any of his fellow soldiers, that are not on guard, is to be immediately confined. Every one that gives the countersign, is to give it as softly as possible so that if any person is listening, he may not hear it.

The sentries are not to suffer any person to stand near them, while they are on their posts after retreat beating.

The General wishes that every part of camp duty may be done with as much exactness, as if the enemy was encamped in the neighborhood, for bad habits once contracted are difficult to get over, & doing duty in a slovenly manner, is both disgraceful & dangerous to officers & men.

Field officer for picket tomorrow night, Major Smith, Adj^t. from Col. Hitchcock's regiment.

	C.	S.	S.	C.	D.	F.	P.
Fatigue	1	2	1	3	1	1	80
Guard			1	1	0	0	20
Picket	1	2	2	2	1	1	49

GENERAL ORDERS.

AFTER ORDERS, May 31, 1776.

Gen. Washington has written to Genl. Putnam[1] desiring him, in the most pressing form, to give positive orders to all the Col^s. to have colors immediately completed for their respective regiments.

GEN. GREENE'S ORDERS.

June 1st, 1776.

A sergeant & 20 men to parade immediately to clear out Mr. Livingston's Dock filled up by the Picket pealings. No pealings to be thrown into the dock for the future.

Six o'clock this evening the troops to be all under arms to man the works.

Five Co^s. of Col. Varnum's Regiment upon the right in fort Box. The other three upon the right of fort Green.

Col. Hitchcock's reg^t. to man fort Putnam & the redoubt upon the left of it. 5 Co^s. in the first & 3 in the Last.

Five Co^s. of Col. Little's regiment in Fort Green & 3 in the oblong square.

The independent Co. to be reserved in the rear of fort Green.

June 3^d, 1776.

150 men & officers wanted from Cols Varnum's Hitchcock's & Little's reg^{ts} with arms blankets & 2 days provisions cooked & ½ a pint of rum a man. To be ready to march at 3 o'clock to morrow morning every man to take his blanket & none to go but such as are decently dressed.

[1] General Washington was absent at Philadelphia from May 21st to June 6th, leaving General Putnam in command at New York.

CAMP LONG ISLAND, June 7, 1776.

Col⁵. of 9, 11, & 12 regiments to have all the arms in their regiments that need repairing sent to the armorers.

The pikes to be placed in the works in the following order—100 in fort Green, 30 in the works on the right of it, 20 in the oblong redoubt, 50 in fort Putnam & 20 in the works on the left of it. Every regᵗ. to clean the spears once a week at their alarm Post.

The officers at the Ferry guard to stop all arms coming over the Ferry to the island, & report immediately to the Genˡ. who has them & where they say they are going. 2 sentries to be posted at the church to stop all arms going eastward from the city, the names and place of abode of any person stopped with arms to be taken & reported immediately.

June 9ᵗʰ 1776.

Field officer for picket, Lᵗ. Col. Henshaw.

The 9, 11, 12 Regᵗˢ to parade tomorrow morning at 6 o'clock on the right of the encampment, every officer & soldier not on duty or unwell to join their respective regiments.

The Fatigue party not to turn out till after yᵉ regiments are paraded.

The officers of the 9ᵗʰ, 11ᵗʰ, 12ᵗʰ are desired to exercise together by regᵗˢ 4 days, & the whole of the officers of the three regiments to exercise together once a week to be exercised by the Col. of the Regᵗ. in turn or by some person appointed by the Col. whose turn it is. The Col⁵. of the 9, 11, 12, Regᵗˢ are desired to make returns of the state of the arms &c, agreably to yesterdays order tomorrow.

GENERAL ORDERS.

HEAD QUARTERS June 10, 1776.

(Parole, BEDFORD.)   (Countersign, CUMBERLAND.)

The Brig. Gens. are requested to make their different Brigades perfectly acquainted with their several alarm posts & to pay particular attention to the men's arms. . . .

GEN. GREENE'S ORDERS.

June 12, 1776.

A garrison court martial to sit to-day. . . .

The Col. or Commᵍ: officers of the 9, 11, 12 Regᵗˢ to certify to the Deputy Commissary from day to day the necessary supplies for the sick. The Surgeons to report every day the state and wants of the sick. Centries posted at Hospitals & armory not to demand the countersign of passengers unless they attempt to enter those places.

June 13, 1776.

The Camp Cullimen (?) of the 9. 11. 12 reg^{ts}. to keep the streets clean, remove the filth, cover the vaults every day & dig new ones once a week; they must attend the Hospitals, & give directions for having them kept in good clean order. Cols. are requested to appoint nurses. No soldier to purchase clothing of another without leave, many soldiers stealing and selling clothing.

June 14, 1776.

The 5 Co^{s}. of Col. Waynes reg^{t}. on Long Island are to be mustered to-morrow afternoon. A subaltern sergeant & 20 men to be detached from the picket guard every evening to mount guard at Red Hook Barbette battery to rejoin the picket in the morning.

In Camp Long Island, June 17, 1776.

The rank of the Captains in Col. Little's reg^{t}. being unsettled, a Court to day is to establish their rank. The members to be from Col. Varnum's & Hitchcock's Reg^{ts}.

Col. Varnum's Reg^{t}. is to take fort Box & the Oblong redoubt for their alarm posts, fort Box 6 cos., oblong redoubt 2 cos. Cap. Woolverton's Independent Co. to join those in the redoubt, & to receive orders from Col. Varnum.

Col. Hitchcock's Reg^{t}. to take fort Putnam & the fort or redoubt on the left of it for their alarm posts.

Col. Little's Reg^{t}. to take fort Greene for their alarm post.

In case of an attack all these posts are to be defended to the last extremity.

The lines to be manned every morning between day & sunrise & the troops to be exercised at parapet firing.

Camp Long Island June 18, 1776.

The picket to be discontinued till further orders, except guard at Red Hook.

300 men with their officers to parade at 8 O'clock tomorrow morning to receive orders from Engineer Smith.

GENERAL ORDERS.

(Parole, LONDON.)   (Countersign, MONTGOMERY.)

A working party of 900 men properly officered to parade tomorrow morning near the artillery park. . . . Brig. Gen. Greene & Col. Prescott will furnish 150 men each as a working party on Governor's Island. On the present emergency all working parties to work till 6 o'clock P.M. Those who go by water will leave work sooner if wind & tide make it necessary.

GEN. GREENE'S ORDERS.

June 20, 1776.

Field officer, L^t. Col. Cornell, Adj^t. from Col. Little's Reg^t.

Col. Hitchcock's & Col. Little's reg^{ts}. to furnish the fatigue party to Governor's Island tomorrow. The remainder furnished by those reg^{ts}. to be upon the " Abatee" between fort Putnam & the redoubt on the left of it, & the Cap. from fort Putnam to the half moon. L^t. Col. Johnson's 5 Co^s. of the 4th battalion of Pennsylvania Reg^t. (Wayne's) to furnish the fatigue party for Cobble Hill. Col. Varnum's Reg^t. to be employed on his alarm post. The Gen. disapproves of the report for the establishment of the rank of the 12th reg^t. & directs the same court to sit again day after tomorrow to examine the rank of the Cap^s. & to report how the court conceives they ought to rank, & how it may be most equitably established.

REGIMENTAL ORDERS.

June 21, 1776.

For guard L^t. Burnham, for Red Hook tomorrow night L^t. Collins.

GEN. GREENE'S ORDERS.

June 21, 1776.

L^t. Huse is requested to oversee the well-digging in fort Greene. 110 men for Governor's Island & 40 for Red Hook.

Those that are to go on the Island to be at S^t. George's Ferry by 8 o'clock. The others to march to Red Hook as soon as they have had their breakfasts.

June 28, 1776.

Picket guard to mount from the 9, 11, 12, Reg^{ts}. The 9 & 11 Reg^{ts} to lie in their alarm posts—the 12th to lie in the oblong redoubt.

GENERAL ORDERS.

HEAD QUARTERS, June 29.

. . . . The Commissary Gen. to lodge a fortnights provision on Governor's Island, Powles Hook & in all ye detached posts, Gen. Putnam furnishing him a list of the men.

All soldiers intrusted with the defence of any work will behave with coolness & bravery, & will be careful not to throw away their fire. The Gen. recommends them to load for their first fire with one musket ball & 4 or 8 buckshot according to the size and strength of their pieces. If the enemy are received with such a fire at not more than 20 or 30 yards distance, he has no doubt of their being repulsed.

Brig. Gen^{ls}. to order Chevaux de Freze & Fascines to close the sally ports of their respective works. 26000 musket cartridges to be sent Col. Prescott on Govr. Isl^d.

HEAD QUARTERS, June 30.

. . . . Upon the signal of the enemy's approach or on any alarm all fatigue parties are to repair to their respective corps ready for instant action. Working parties are not otherwise to be interrupted in finishing the defences. . . .

GEN. GREENE'S ORDERS.

IN CAMP LONG ISLAND, July 1, 1776.

Col^s. or comm^d. officers of 9th, 11th, 12th, Reg^{ts}. are desired to make a line round each of the forts & fortifications for the troops to begin a fire on the enemy if they attempt to storm the works & the troops are to be told not to fire sooner than the enemy's arrival at these lines, unless commanded. The line should be about 80 yards from the parapet.

Com^g. officers of the guards at Forts Green & Putnam to send a patrolling party to patrol about the $\frac{1}{4}$ of a mile to prevent a surprise by a partisan party.

The general thanks both officers & soldiers who turned out voluntarily to work upon the Little Cobble hill; such public spirit is laudable & shall not go unrewarded, if the gen^l. ever has it in his power to make a more suitable acknowledgement.

No officer below the rank of a field officer to lodge out of camp from their Co^s. on any pretence, sickness excepted. The General recommends the strictest discipline & daily attention to arms & ammunition. Brigade being sickly the Gen. recommends the strictest attention to the cookery & that broiling & frying meat so destructive to health be prohibited.

A picket of one hundred to go to Red Hook to night by order of a private message from his Excellency.

TUESDAY July 2^d, 1776.

A picket of 50 men in fort Putnam, 25 in fort Box, a serg^t. & 12 men at the milldam from the 9th, 11th, 12th Reg^{ts}. A picket of 20 men at fort Sterling & 25 at Smith's redoubt on Cobble Hill. Upon an alarm Col. Ward's reg^t. of Jersey militia to form in the rear of Fort Green, the sentries to be placed at the front of the redoubts. Major of Brigade to see to them. Patrols to be kept up from fort Putnam every hour.

July 4, 1776.

Officers of the guards at ye different posts to be accountable for everything in the forts but particularly for the rum lodged there for the people in time of action. Any one destroying the tools or taking the liquor without leave will be punished.

Every Reg^t. to furnish pickets for their alarm posts & to be credited therefor in the detail for duty. The 9th, 11th, 12th, Reg^{ts}. & the N. J. battalions under Col. Cadmus & Col. Ward to furnish a fatigue party of 250 men tomorrow morning. Garrison Court martial to sit tomorrow, Col. Little president. Cap^s. earnestly requested to examine the arms and ammunition of their Co^s. & have them ready for action at all times.

CAMP AT BROOKLIN, July 6, 1776.

The Ferry guard upon a night alarm are to repair to fort Sterling. The ground to be levelled from which Col. Hitchcock's Reg^t. moved. 233 men for picket from Col. Varnum's, Hitchcock's & Little's Reg^{ts}. 66 men from the same for guard.

July 8, 1776.

Col. Varnum's Reg^t. to remove their encampment to Red Hook, & do the duty of that post. Col. Forman's N. J. reg^t. to camp on the ground lately occupied by Col. Hitchcock's reg^t.

July 8, 1776.

Col. Forman's Reg^t. to occupy Col. Varnum's old alarm posts, namely, Fort Box and the Oblong redoubt. Brigade Major to lead the troops to the alarm Post at 7 A.M. The guard for the several works to be continued the same as before from the 11th & 12th of the old establishment & the Jersey new levies, that the new levies may have the benefit of the knowledge of the standing troops.

GENERAL ORDERS.

HEAD QUARTERS, July 9, 1776.

. . . . The Continental Congress impelled by the dictates of duty, policy and necessity have been pleased to dissolve the connection which subsisted between this country & G^t. Britain, & to declare the colonies of North America, Free & Independent States—the several Brigades are to be drawn up this evening on their respective parades at 6 o'clock when the declaration of Congress, showing the grounds and reasons of the measure is to be read with an audible voice. The Gen. hopes that this important *Point* will serve as a fresh incitement to every officer & soldier to act with courage & fidelity, as knowing that now the Peace & safety of this country depend (under God) solely on the success of our arms, & that he is now in the service of a state possessed of sufficient power to reward his merit & advance him to the highest honor of a free country.

The Brigade Majors are to receive copies of the declaration to be delivered to the Brig^{rs}. & Col^s.

GEN. GREENE'S ORDERS.

July 9, 1776.

Adj^t. for the day to carry the Parole & countersign to the guards at Red Hook, Smith's Barbette, Fort Box, Fort Green & forts Putnam & Sterling, & the ferry guard.

A fatigue tomorrow of 100 men for Smith's Barbette.

July 10, 1776.

Deputy Commissary, Mr. Brown, to issue provisions 3 times a week, Tu. Th. & Saturdays.

Putrid fevers prevailing among the troops, the troops are forbid going into the water only in the mornings and evenings, being dangerous in the heat of the day.

A fatigue party of 150 to be furnished from the 11th & 12th & Col. Forman's Regt. for Smith's Barbette to be continued till it is completed.

July 11, 1776.

Fatigue parties to be turned out to be at work on the Hill by five in the morning.

CAMP LONG ISLAND, July 16, 1776.

Prisoners sent to the main Guard by the Field officer of the day with or without arms, unless sooner released by him or the Gen. are only to be kept till the mounting of the new guard, unless a crime be delivered to the Cap. of the guard in writing against (the prisoners) by the person that committed them, with his name to it.

L^t. Col. Cornell & Cap. Warner are appointed to oversee the works at Smith's Barbette & complete them. They are to be excused from all other duty. Fatigue parties for the future are to work as long as the Col^s. think advisable every cool day. The general wishes the troops to be as industrious as possible, lest the enemy attack (the works) before they are done.

A subaltern's Guard to mount at Rapalyea's mill upon the point every night, to continue till sunrise.

GENERAL ORDERS.

HEAD QUARTERS, July 18 1776.

2 guns from fort Cobble Hill on Long Island to be a signal that the enemy have landed on that Island.

GEN. GREENE'S ORDERS.

July 18, 1776.

Field officer of the day tomorrow, L^t. Col. Henderson, Adj^t. from Col. Little's. . . . .

Patrolling parties to be sent out every hour to advance as silently as possible & to stop & listen every few rods, to discover spies lurking around the works.

CAMP ON LONG ISLAND, July 19 1776.

The works on Cobble Hill being greatly retarded for want of men to lay turf, few being acquainted with that service, all those in Col. Hitchcock's & Col. Little's Reg^{ts}. that understand that business, are desired to voluntarily turn out every day, & they shall be excused from all other duty, & allowed ½ a pint of rum a day.

Half the fatigue party to work tomorrow at fort Sterling in widening the ditch. L^t. Col. Cornell will detach the party & give the necessary instructions. Cap. Newell of the Train to mount an artillery guard on Smith's Barbette, on Cobble Hill, of a Sergeant & 6 men.

F. Officer of the day tomorrow Major Parker, Adj^t. from Col. Forman's Reg^t. (New Jersey).

July 22, 1776.

F. Off^r. tomorrow, Col. Forman, Adj^t. from his reg^t.

The Col^s. or C^g. Off^{rs}. of the 1st, 9th, 11th, 12th Regiments are requested to send in a return of vacancies, with a list of names to fill them, by tomorrow at 9 A.M. The 11th, 12th & Col. Forman's Reg^{ts}. are to parade on the regimental parade tomorrow A.M. instead of going to their alarm posts. Com^g. off. of each reg^t. will receive orders on the spot when & where to march.

The duties being exceedingly heavy on the men, the Genl. thinks proper to lessen the fatigue party ½ & reduce the guard in forts Green & Putnam ⅓, & a Serj^t. & 12 men to mount in fort Box, instead of the present guard.

July 24, 1776.

A fatigue party of 40 men & 1 sub. to cut fascines to parade this P.M. 4 days provisions to be provided. Passengers going into·

the city not to be stopped at the ferry unless there is reason to suspect them. No one to come out without a proper pass. Fatigue for home duty to be lessened as much as the number detached.

IN CAMP LONG ISLAND, July 28, 1776.

The success of the campaign must depend on the health of the troops; nothing should be neglected that contributes to it. Good Policy as well as humanity claims the attention of every officer to this object; our honor as well as our success depends on it.

The good officer discharges his duty not only in one but in every respect. It is a mistaken notion that the minutiæ of military matters is only an employment for little minds. Such an officer betrays a want of understanding and showeth a person ignorant of the necessary dependence and connection of one thing upon another. What signifies knowledge without power to execute? He who studies the Branches of military knowledge relating to Dispositions, & neglects to preserve the health of his troops will find himself in that disagreeable situation.

The general is pained to discover inattention to the digging and filling vaults for the reg^{ts}. & to the burial of filth and putrid matter. The general directs camp Columen (?) of the several reg^{ts}. to dig new vaults, and fill up old ones every 3 days, & that fresh dirt be thrown in every day to the vaults, & that all filth in and about the camp be daily buried. The sickly season coming on, & Putrid fevers prevailing, the Gen. recommends a free use of vegetables & desires the men may keep themselves & clothes clean, & cook their provisions properly; & little injury is to be dreaded. A neglect of these matters at this critical season may be attended with dreadful consequences.

Complaints are made of the troops stealing water mellons. Such practices must be punished. A few unprincipled rascals may ruin the reputation of a whole corps of virtuous men. The General desires the virtuous to complain of every offender that may be detected in invading people's property in an unlawful manner, whatever his station or from whatever part of the country he may come.

Aug. 1, 1776.

All the straw bunks & ———— in ye different reg^{ts}. occupied by the well to be collected for the sick of Col. Forman's reg^t. A sergeant & 8 men to be employed cutting wood for a coal pit for the armorers shop—apply to master armorers for orders.

IN CAMP LONG ISLAND, Aug. 4, 1776.

4 Co⁸. of Col. Gay's reg⁴. to take fort Sterling for their alarm post & 4—Cobble Hill.

The countersign having spread too generally in the camp, & amongst many that don't belong to the army, the Gen¹. orders every person to be punished who is base enough to discover it to those who have no right to it.

No person allowed to pass after 10 o'clock with or without the countersign within the limits of the camp or circle of the sentries, except Gen¹. & Field Officers, Brigade Majors & expresses. This order extends to inhabitants as well as the army.

A fatigue party from Col. Little's, Col. Forman's & Col. Gay's reg⁴ˢ. of 200 men, properly officered, to work at Fort Sterling tomorrow. Col. Gay or the com⁸. officer of his reg⁴. is directed to lead his troops into their alarm posts at 5 o'clock this afternoon. Officers are directed to acquaint themselves with the ground for miles about their camps.

MORNING ORDERS, Aug. 6, 1776.

Commanding Officers of fortifications are requested to pay particular attention to yᵉ provisions lodged at each alarm post for the support of the troops in case of seige, and also that yᵉ water casks & cisterns are filled & when the water is bad to have it pumped out & fresh water put in.

Aug. 6, 1776.

By a deserter from Sir Peter Parker's fleet we learn that the Hessians, from England, & Clinton's troops from S. Carolina are arrived & that the enemy meditate an attack on this Island & the city of New York. The Gen¹. wishes to have the troops provided with every thing necessary to give them a proper reception. Cap⁸. are directed to examine the arms of their co⁸. immediately.

Aug. 8, 1776.

A sub. & 20 men to parade immediately to march to Jamaica. Let the men be decently dressed, & the officers keep them from offering insolence or abuse to any person. They are to escort & assist L^t. Skinner & wait there for his directions.

Aug. 9, 1776.

A report from Col. Hand mentions a large number of regulars drawn up at Staten Island Ferry, & boats to embark in. No officer or soldier to stir from his quarters that we may be ready to march at a moment's warning if necessary.

Aug. 16, 1776.

Col. Smith (L. I. militia) to app^t an Adj^t., Q. M. & Serj^t Maj. & Q. M^r. Serj^t to his reg^t., & to have the troops in his reg^t not on duty exercised daily in learning the necessary manœuvres and evolutions.

Gen^{ls}. Nixon and Heard are to furnish a fatigue party from their brigades and to form the necessary lines from fort Box to fort Putnam. The gin shops and houses selling liquor, strictly forbidden to sell to soldiers, excepting near the two ferries.

The inhabitants of houses near the lines are immediately to move out of them, and they are to be appropriated to the use of the troops. The General is determined to have any soldiers punished that may be found disguised with liquor, as no soldier in such a situation can be fit for defense or attack.

The General orders that no sutler in the army shall sell to any soldier more than 1 gill of spirits per day. If the above orders are not adhered to, there shall no more be retailed out at all.

The Colonels of reg^{ts}. lately come in are immediately to make returns to the Genl. of their number of men & where they are quartered. Col. Hitchcock's and Smith's Reg^{ts} are to do duty in Genl. Nixon's brigade—Col^s. Van Brunt's and Gay's Reg^{ts}. to do duty in Genl. Heard's brigade. Cap^{ts} in the brigades are to be particularly careful that the Rolls are called 3 times a day & that the troops do not stray from quarters.

GENERAL ORDERS.

HEAD QUARTERS, Aug. 20, 1776.

. . . . General Sullivan is to take command on Long Island till Gen. Greene's state of health will permit him to resume it. Brig. Ld Sterling is to take charge of Genl Sullivan's division.

[No. 2.]

MAJOR GENERAL SULLIVAN'S ORDERS

CAMP ON LONG ISLAND

[*Colonel Little's Order Book*]

[LONG ISLAND,] August 20, 1776.

Field Off[r] of the Day tomorrow, Col. Phipps, (?) Adj[t] from Col. Little's reg[t].

August 21st, 1776.

Five hundred men to be on fatigue to-morrow to be on the works by 8 o'clock, to leave at 12, & begin at 2 o'clock, & work till half past 6. Nothing can be more disagreeable to the Gen[l]. than to call upon the men to be so constantly on fatigue, but their own salvation, and the safety of the country requires it. He hopes that in 2 or 3 days more the encampment will be so secure that he can release the men from fatigue and give them an opportunity to rest from their labors. Adj[t]. of the day to attend at the Gen[ls]. quarters every morning at 8, and an orderly from each brigade daily. Four men are to be drafted to row the Gen[ls] boat and do no other duty. The Brigade majors, upon receiving orders from Head Quarters are to call at Gen. Sullivan's quarters for his orders, or send adj[ts] to take them off.

Col. Johnson's and Newcomb's reg[ts] are to consider the woods on the west side of the creek as their alarm post, and repair there in case of an alarm. Gen. Nixon will show the ground this evening at 6 o'clock to the comm[g] officers of the Reg[ts].

Aug. 23, 1776.

The men not to turn out to their alarm posts this afternoon, (but) to get 2 days' provisions ready, & to be at their alarm posts to-morrow morning by 3 o'clock in order for action.

Col[s]. Miles & Ransom's (Remsen's of L. I.) reg[ts]. to take possession of the Bedford road this night—Col. Ransom's reg[t]. to march at 5 o'clock. Col. Miles' reg[t]. is on the spot. Col[s]. Little's & Hitchcock's Reg[ts] to possess the Flatbush road & Col[s]. Johnson's & Martin's to take possession of the road near the river.

All these reg^{ts}. to be at their posts by 6 o'clock.   Upon their arrival the troops now there are to retire to their encampments & get 2 days provisions dressed, & be ready for action.   The Gen. will never make a 3rd. requisition to the majors of brigade, to attend for orders.

LONG ISLAND Aug. 24 1776.

A return to be made to the Gen. this afternoon at 5 o'clock of all ye Light Horse & companies of troop within the lines.   The adj^t. of Col. Little's regiment is to attend at Gen^{ls}. quarters at 7 o'clock A.M. to-morrow.

The Genl. returns his thanks to the brave officers & soldiers who with so much spirit & intrepidity repulsed the enemy & defeated their designs of taking possession of the woods near our lines.   He is now convinced that the troops he has the honor to command, will not, in point of bravery, yield to any troops in the universe.   The cheerfulness with which they do their duty, & the patience with which they undergo fatigue evince exalted sentiments of freedom, & love of country gives him most satisfactory evidence that when called upon they will prove themselves worthy of that freedom for which they are now contending.

Col. Ramsons (Remsen's) Reg^t. to mount no guard except quarter guard of 12, but be considered a fatigue party, to which they are to attend from day to day.   The Genl. is sorry to find that Reg^t. flying from their posts, when timid women would have blushed to have betrayed any signs of fear at any thing this reg^t. discovered at the time of their flight.

Officers are requested to see that their men always keep at least 2 days provisions, ready dressed by them.   The Commissary is to deal out one gill of rum per man each day on this Island until further orders.   Soldiers are not to be out of their encampment but upon urgent business.   Gen. Nixon to take command of the lines next the enemy until further orders, to post his men in the edge of the woods next the enemy.   Brig^{de} Majors to attend punctually at the Genl's. quarters at 10 A.M.

LONG ISLAND Aug. 25 1776.

The following arrangement to take place on Long Island until further orders—Viz: Col. Mile's 2 battalions, Col. Atlee's, Col. Lutzs, Major Hayes, Col. Lashers and Drake's to be formed into one brigade under the command of Gen. L^d. Stirling. Col. Hand's, Prescott's, (Late) Nixon's, Varnum's, Hitchcock's, Little's, Smith's, & Ramson's to be under Gen. Nixon. Wylly's, Huntington's, Taylor's, (Tyler's) Silliman's, Chester's, & Gay's under Gen. Parsons; Johnson's, Courtlandt's, Martins, Newcombs & Freeman's (Forman's), under the command of Brig. Gen Hurd.

The General orders that the Brig^{rs}. attend at Head Quarters at 8 A.M. to-morrow for directions. Brig^{de} Major Box is appointed to act as Adj^t. Genl. for this department until further orders.

A Brig^r. Genl. of the Day to attend the Grand Parade at Guard mounting at 10 A.M., every day afterwards at 8, whose duty it shall be to see that the guards are regularly made up, & properly posted & duly relieved. No firing at the outposts *to be allowed* on any pretense, except by permission of the Com^g Gen. of the day, & none within the lines except by permission. This order not to extend to sentries on guard.

Brig^r. for the day Gen. L^d. Stirling.

The Gen. is surprised to find the soldiers strolling about, notwithstanding repeated orders, miles distant from the lines, at a time when the enemy are hourly expected to make an attack. The officers are enjoined to cause the arrest of any soldier who shall be found strolling without the lines unless they can show a written permit from their Cap. or Com^g. officer of the reg^t. or company. All the officers and soldiers are to keep within their quarters, unless ordered on duty.

All troops in this department are desired to wear a green bough or branch of a tree in their hats, till further orders.

Col. Ward's Regt. to be added to Gen. Parson's brigade. All the troops not[1]——

All other troops not mentioned and those which may be sent here

---

[1] The order breaks off at this point in Colonel Little's book, but it is fortunately preserved entire in an orderly book kept by Captain John Douglass, of Philadelphia. (Hist. Mag., vol. ii., p. 354.) The following order from General Lord Stirling also appears in Captain Douglass's book :

[LONG ISLAND] August 25th 1776.

" The Adjutants of each Corps of this Brigade are to attend Brigade Major Livingston at Gen. Sullivan's Quarters every morning at 9 o'clock to receive the orders of the day. The Weekly Returns are to be brought in this day. Such regiments as have tents are to encamp within the lines as soon as possible."

without a General Officer to command them are to be considered as a part of Lord Stirling's Brigade till further orders.

A return of the several Brigades to be made immediately. Eight hundred (men) properly officered to relieve the troops on Bedford Road to-morrow morning, six field officers to attend with this party. The same number to relieve those on Bush (Flatbush) Road, and an equal number those stationed towards the Narrows. A picket of three hundred men under the command of a Field Officer, six Captains, twelve Subalterns to be posted at the wood on the west side of the Creek every night till further orders.

It is a very scandalous practice unbecoming soldiers whose duty it is to defend the liberty and property of the Inhabitants of the country to make free with and rob them of that property; it is therefore ordered that no person belonging to this army do presume on any pretense whatever to take or make use of any Corn, Poultry or Provision, or anything else without the consent of the owners nor without paying the common price for them; any breach of this order will be severely punished. The Commanding Officer of each Regiment and Company is to see this order communicated to their respective corps and to see it carried into execution. . . . .

Brigadier Lord Stirling to command the front of our lines next Hudson's River and to command the reserve within the lines, and when either of the other Brigade Generals have the command of the Advance Lines Lord Stirling is to have command of his post in his absence. Each Brigadier General to assign the Alarm Posts to the several Regiments under their command.

[No. 3.]

GENERAL ORDERS

HEAD-QUARTERS LONG ISLAND Aug. 29, 1776.

Parole, SULLIVAN, }
Countersign, GREEN. }

As the sick are an encumbrance to the Army, & Troops are expected this afternoon from the flying camp in Jersey, under Gen¹ Mercer, who is himself arrived & room & cover is wanted for the troops, the commanding Officers of Regt's are immediately to have such sick removed. They are to take their Arms & Accoutrements & be conducted by an Officer to the Genl Hospital, as a rendezvous & then to cross to-gether under the directions of the Person appointed there, taking general Directions from Dr Morgan. As the above Forces under Genl Mercer are expected this afternoon, the General proposes to relieve a proportionate Number of Regiments & make a change in the situation of them.

The Commanding Officers of Regiments are therefore to parade their men with their Arms, Accoutrements, and Knapsacks, at 7 °Clock, at the Head of their Encampments & there wait for Orders.[1]

[From Ms. Order Book of Col. Wm. Douglas.]

HEAD-QUARTERS, NEW YORK, August 31, 1776.
(Parole, HARLEM.)   (Countersign, FLUSHING.)

. . . . Both officers and soldiers are informed that the retreat from *Long-Island* was made by the unanimous advice of all the General Officers, not from any doubts of the spirit of the troops, but because they found the troops very much fatigued with hard duty, and divided into many detachments, while the enemy had their main body on the Island, and capable of receiving assistance from the shipping. In these circumstances it was thought unsafe to transport the whole of an Army on an Island, or to engage them with a part, and therefore unequal numbers; whereas now our whole Army is collected together, without water intervening, while the enemy can receive little assistance from their ships. Their Army is, and must be, divided into many bodies, and fatigued with keeping up a communication with their ships; whereas ours is connected and can act together. They must effect a landing under so many disadvantages, that if officers and soldiers are vigilant, and alert to prevent surprise, and add spirit when they approach, there is no doubt of our success. . .

[Force, 5th Series, Vol. I., p. 1248.]

[1] The series of Washington's general orders in Force's Archives does not contain this order of August 29th, which throws light on the preparations made for the retreat. It is found, abridged, in both Col. Little's and Capt. Douglass's order books; in Col. Douglas's book it appears in the above form. Original in the possession of Benjamin Douglas, Esq., Middletown, Conn.

[No. 4.]

GEN. WASHINGTON TO THE MASSACHUSETTS ASSEMBLY

HEAD-QUARTERS, Colonel Roger Morris's House, ten miles from ⎰
New York, September 19, 1776. ⎱

GENTLEMEN : I was honoured the night before last with your favor of the 13th instant, and at the same time that I conceive your anxiety to have been great, by reason of the vague and uncertain accounts you received respecting the attack on *Long Island*, give me leave to assure you that the situation of our affairs, and the important concerns which have surrounded me, and which are daily pressing on me, have prevented me from transmitting, in many instances, the intelligence I otherwise should have conveyed.

In respect to the attack and retreat from *Long Island*, the publick papers will furnish you with accounts nearly true. I shall only add, that in the former we lost about eight hundred men ; more than three-fourths of which were taken prisoners. This misfortune happened in great measure, by two detachments of our people who were posted in two roads leading through a wood, in order to intercept the enemy in their march, suffering a surprise, and making a precipitate retreat, which enabled the enemy to lead a great part of their force against the troops commanded by Lord *Stirling*, which formed a third detachment, who behaved with great bravery and resolution, charging the enemy and maintaining their posts from about seven or eight o'clock in the morning till two in the afternoon, when they were obliged to attempt a retreat, being surrounded and overpowered by numbers on all sides, and in which many of them were taken. One battalion (*Smallwood's of Maryland*) lost two hundred and fifty-nine men, and the general damage fell upon the regiments from *Pennsylvania*, *Delaware* and *Maryland*, and Colonel *Huntington's*, of *Connecticut*.

As to the retreat from the Island, it was effected without loss of men, and with but very little baggage. A few heavy cannon were left, not being moveable on account of the ground's being soft and miry through the rains that had fallen.

The enemy's loss in killed we could never ascertain ; but have many reasons to believe that it was pretty considerable, and exceeded ours a good deal. The retreat from thence was absolutely necessary, the enemy having landed the main body of their army there to attack us in front, while their ships of war were to cut off the communication with the city, from whence resources of men, provisions, &c., were to be drawn. . . . .

I have the honour to be, &c.,

Go. WASHINGTON.

To the Hon. *Jeremiah Powell*, Esq., President, &c.

[Force, 5th Series, Vol. II., p. 399.]

[No. 5.]

BRIG. GEN. PARSONS TO JOHN ADAMS

PHILADELPHIA

LONG ISLAND 29 Aug 1776.

. . . . Before this reaches you the account of the battle of Tuesday last will arrive—'tis impossible to be particular in a narrative of the matter as many are yet missing, who we hope may come in. In the night of the 26th nine Regiments of the English troops perhaps about 2500 with Field artillery &c passed the Western road near the Narrows from the flat land, for our lines. We had a guard of 400 or 500 men posted in the wood, who about three o'clock Tuesday morning gave notice of the enemy's approach, a body of about 1500. We immediately marched down to oppose the progress of the enemy. We took possession of a hill about two miles from camp and detached Col Atlee with a Reg't of Delaware [Penn.] to meet them further on the road ; in about 60 rods he drew up & received the enemy's fire & gave them a well directed fire from his Reg't, which did great execution & then retreated to the hill; from thence I was ordered with Col Atlee & part of his Reg't & Lt Col Clark with Col Huntington's Reg't to cover the left flank of our main body.

This we executed though our number did at no time exceed 300 men & we were attacked three several times by two Regiments ye 44th & 23d and repulsed them in every attack with considerable loss. The number of dead we had collected together & the heap the enemy had made we supposed amounted to about 60. We had 12 or 14 wounded prisoners who we caused to be dress'd & their wounds put in the best state our situation would admit. About 10 o'clock we found a large body of the enemy had advanced on the other roads near our lines, but a constant fire was kept up on the enemy till about 12, when we found them fast advancing on our rear to cut off our retreat. Our little main body advanced boldly up to the enemy in the rear & broke through their lines and secured the retreat of most of the party; but it fared still harder with my little party who had three times repulsed the enemy in front and once in the rear; we had no notice of the retreat of the main body till it was too late for us to join them, the enemy having cut off our retreat on three sides & the main body having broke through the enemy's lines on the other side and left them between us. We had no alternative left but force through one line into a thick wood, which we attempted & effected with part of our men, the other part with Col. Clark being before sent into the wood. When we had made our way into the wood, I was accidentally parted from Col. Atlee & most of the men whom I have never seen since. I came in with 7 men yesterday morning much fatigued. Our loss is impossible to be ascertained. In my party a Lt. Col. Parry was killed and one wounded. Our loss in killed & wounded is inconsiderable, but many are missing among whom are General Sullivan & Lord Sterling. Colonels Miles, Atlee, Johnson, Lt. Col. Clark Maj. Wells & several other officers of distinction are yet missing. I think the trial of that day far from being any discouragement, but in general our soldiers behaved with firmness.

I am sir, with esteem & Regard

Yr. Humble Svt.

SAM'L H. PARSONS.

MORRISANIA Oct. 8, 1776.

DEAR SIR

Your's of the 2ᵈ inst I rec'd last night, for which I am obliged to you. If any information I can give will contribute to your satisfaction or my country's good I am happy in furnishing what falls in my observation. I agree fully with you that you were in the dark as to some facts relative to the transactions on Long Island & am fully satisfied you still remain so, or you could not suppose the surprise there was in the day time. To give you a clear idea of the matter, I must trouble you with a description of that part of the country where the enemy landed, and encamped, and the intervening lands between that and our lines. From the point of land which forms the east side of the Narrows, runs a ridge of hills about N. E. in length about 5 or 6 miles, covered with a thick wood which terminate in a small rising land near Jamaica ; through these hills are three passes only, one near the Narrows, one on the road called the Flatbush Road & one called the Bedford Road, being a cross road from Bedford to Flatbush which lies on the southerly side of these hills ; these passes are through the mountains or hills easily defensible being very narrow and the lands high & mountainous on each side. These are the only roads which can be passed from the south side the hill to our lines, except a road leading around the easterly end of the hills to Jamaica. On each of these roads were placed a guard of 800 men, and east of them in the wood was placed Col Miles with his Battalion to watch the motion of the enemy on that part, with orders to keep a party constantly reconnoitering to and across the Jamaica road. The sentinels were so placed as to keep a constant communication between the three guards on the three roads. South of these hills lies a large plain extending from the North River easterly to Rockaway Bay perhaps 5 miles & southerly to the sound bounded on the south by the sound and on the north by the hills. Those hills were from two to three miles and a half from our lines. The enemy landed on this plain & extended their camp from the River to Flatbush perhaps 3 or 4 miles. On the day of the surprise I was on duty, and at the first dawn of day the guards from the West road near the Narrows, came to my quarters & informed me the enemy were advancing in great numbers by that road. I soon found it true & that the whole guard had fled without firing a gun ; these (by way of retaliation I must tell you) were all New Yorkers & Pennsylvanians ; I found by fair daylight the enemy were through the wood & descending the hill on the North side, on which with 20 of my fugitive guard being all I could collect, I took post on a height in their front at about half a mile's distance—which halted their column & gave time for Lord Sterling with his forces to come up ; thus much for the West road—On the East next Jamaica Col. Miles suffered the enemy to march not less than 6 miles till they came near two miles in rear of the guards before he discovered & gave notice of their approach. This also was in the night & the guard kept by Pennsylvanians altogether—the New England & New Jersey troops being in the other two roads through which the enemy did not attempt to pass.

We were surprised—our principal barrier lost by that surprise, but as far as the cover of the night is an excuse we have it.—The landing of the troops could not be prevented at the distance of 6 or 7 miles from our lines ; on a plain under the cannon of the ships, just in with the shore. Our unequal numbers would not admit attacking them on the plain when landed.

When our principal barrier was lost, our numbers so much inferior to the enemy, they not disposed to storm our lines, but set down to make regular approaches to us—were part of the reasons which induced a retreat from thence and a consequent abandoning New York—. Our sentinels & guards in my opinion were well posted, they might have been better, too great security I thought prevailed with some leading officers, but I still am of opinion, if our guards on the West road & Col. Miles on East End of the hills had done their duty, the enemy would not have passed those important heights, without such very great loss as would have obliged them to abandon any further enterprise on the Island.   .   .

I am sir

Your Most Humble Sv't

SAM'L H. PARSONS.

[Originals in possession of Hon. Charles Francis Adams.]

[No. 6.]

BRIG. GEN. SCOTT TO JOHN JAY

WHITE PLAINS, N. Y.

NEW YORK Sept. 6, 1776.

DEAR SIR :

I received your letter about half an hour ago by the messengers of the honorable convention, in which you inform me that they are anxious to be informed of any transactions at this place that may be of use to the State, or otherwise of importance. My duty would have directed me to execute this task before the receipt of your letter, had I been possessed of the means of conveyance. I shall do it now as far as the want of good pen and ink, as scarce as almost every other necessary article, will permit.

I shall begin with our retreat from Long Island. For previous to that event the convention was so near the scene of action that they must have been acquainted with every occurrence. I was summoned to a Council of War at Mr. Philip Livingston's house on Thursday 29th ult. never having had reason to expect a proposition for a retreat till it was mentioned. Upon my arrival at the lines on the Tuesday morning before, and just after the enemy, by beating General Sullivan and Lord Stirling, had gained the heights *which in their nature appear to have been more defensible than the lines were*, it was obvious to me we could not maintain them for any long time should the enemy approach us regularly. *They were unfinished in several places when I arrived there*, and we were obliged hastily to finish them, and you may imagine with very little perfection, particularly across the main road, the most likely for the approach of the enemy's heavy artillery. *In this place three of my battalions* were placed, the traverse of the line in ground so low, that the rising ground immediately without it, would have put it in the power of a man at 40 yards' distance to *fire under my horse's belly* whenever he pleased. You may judge of our situation, subject to almost incessant rains, without baggage or tents and almost without victuals or drink, and in some part of the lines the men were standing up to their middles in water. The enemy were evidently incircling us from water to water with intent to hem us in upon a small neck of land. In this situation they had as perfect a command of the island, except the small neck on which we were posted, as they now' have. Thus things stood when the retreat was proposed. As it was suddenly proposed, *I as suddenly objected to it*, from an aversion to giving the enemy a single inch of ground ; but *was soon convinced by the unanswerable reasons for it*. They were these. Invested by an enemy of above double our number from water to water, scant in almost every necessary of life and without covering and liable every moment to have the communication between us and the city cut off by the entrance of the frigates into the East River between

(late) Governor's Island and Long Island; which General Mc-
Dougall assured us from his own nautic experience was very
feasible. In such a situation we should have been reduced to the
alternative of desperately attempting to cut our way [through] a
vastly superior enemy with the certain loss of a valuable stock of
artillery and artillery stores, which the continent has been collecting with great pains; or by famine and fatigue have been made
an easy prey to the enemy. In either case the campaign would
have ended in the total ruin of our army. The resolution therefore to retreat was unanimous, and tho' formed late in the day
was executed the following night with unexpected success. We
however lost some of our heavy cannon on the forts at a distance
from the water, the softness of the ground occasioned by the rains
having rendered it impossible to remove them in so short a time.
Almost everything else valuable was saved; and not a dozen men
lost in the retreat. The consequence of our retreat was the loss
of [late] Gov^{rs} Island which is perfectly commanded by the fort
on Red Hook. The enemy however from fear or other reasons
indulged with the opportunity of two nights to carry off all except
some heavy cannon. The garrison was drawn off in the afternoon
after our retreat under the fire of the shipping who are now drawn
up just behind [late] Gov^{rs} Island, and the fire of some cannon
from Long Island shore; but with no other loss than that of one
man's arm. What our loss on Long Island was I am not able to
estimate. I think the hills might have been well maintained with
5000 men. *I fear their natural strength was our bane by lulling
us into a state of security* and enabling the enemy to steal *a march
upon us.* I think from the best accounts we must have killed
many of the enemy. We are sure that late Colonel and afterwards
General Grant who was so bitter against us in Parliament, is among
the slain. General Parsons late Col. and promoted to the rank
of a general officer escaped from the action and pursuit as by a
miracle. I believe him to be a brave man. He is a Connecticut
lawyer. He told me that in the action he commanded a party of
about 250 men, with orders from Lord Stirling to cover his flank;
and that when the enemy gave way, he threw into a heap about
thirty of the enemy's dead, and that in advancing a little further
he found a heap made by the enemy at least as large as that which
he had collected. Lord Stirling had ordered him to maintain his
ground till receipt of his orders to retreat. However, finding

that no such orders came ; and finding the enemy by rallying to increase on his hands, he flew to the place where Lord Stirling was posted, leaving his party on the ground with strict orders to maintain it till his return, but he found his Lordship and his whole body of troops gone. There can be no doubt but Lord Stirling behaved bravely ; but I wish that he had retreated sooner. He would have saved himself and a great number of troops from captivity, but he refused to retreat for want of orders. We miss him much, he was a very active officer. General Sullivan who was also made a prisoner in the action on the heights went some day s ago on parole to Congress to endeavor to procure his exchange for Prescot. I have not heard of his return. Two or three days ago the Rose frigate went up between the islands and took shelter, after a severe cannonade from us, behind Blackwell's Island. She retreated yesterday as far as Corlear's Hook, where she was briskly cannonaded till night. I have not heard of her this morning. By the loss on Long Island and the running away of our militia, *especially those of Connecticut,* to their respective homes, our army is much diminished, and I am sure is vastly inferior to that of the enemy. . . . .

Poor General Woodhull with a lieutenant and four men were made prisoners on Long Island. I had a letter from him dated the first inst. but not dated from any place, nor does he tell me how he was taken. He has lost all his baggage and requested of me two shirts and two pairs of stockings, which I should have sent him had not the flag of truce been gone before I rec^d the letter. I shall comply with his request by the first opportunity. Commend me with all possible devotion to the honorable Convention.

I am, Sir,

Your most obedient servant

Jno. Morin Scott.

P. S. *The army badly paid & wretchedly fed.* 1100 men arrived from the southward. A deserter tells me be (?) 3000 foreign troops on Staten island. I know not what the flying camp is doing. He says the enemy on Long Island are 26,000. I believe this much exaggerated ; and 1000 in the shipping.

[Original in possession of Hon. John Jay, New York.]

[No. 7.]

COL. JOSEPH TRUMBULL TO HIS BROTHER

LEBANON, CONN.

NEW YORK 27th August 1776.

DEAR BROTHER

Since my last the enemy have landed their main force on Long Island near New Utrecht Church—between that & Flat Bush, our people and theirs have frequent skirmishes in all which our people have had the better of them. We have lost several men, killed and wounded—. Col. Martin of New Jersey badly wounded in the breast, but I hope not mortally. We just have received an account of a smart skirmish this morning at break of day—the particulars I don't yet know, if I can get them before the gentlemen go who bring this I will write you them. Col. Huntington is unwell, but I hope getting a little better. He has a slow fever. Maj. Dyer is also unwell with a slow fever. Gen'l Greene has been very sick but is better. Gens. Putnam, Sullivan, Lord Sterling, Nixon, Parsons & Heard are on Long Island and a strong part of our army. We have a fine ridge of hills and woods to meet them in on Long Island before they come near our lines.

I am dear Brother your Affectionate

JOS. TRUMBULL.

JON^A TRUMBULL JUN^R Esq.

P. S. It was true the enemy attacked in the morning—Several parties of them penetrated thro' the woods & the whole body are now thro' & within 2 miles of our lines. Some parties of them have been up to the lines but are drove back, or upon the Heights about 2 miles off from the lines. There has been some very brisk firing & smart engagements; what numbers are killed or wounded on either side—the firing ceases at present but expect it renewed again by & by. We have lost a Mr. Rutgers of this town, an artillery man & Lt. Col. Parry of Pennsylvania. These are all we know yet.

Your's as before.

[Original in possession of Henry E. Parsons, Ashtabula, O.]

[No. 8.]

COL. TRUMBULL TO HIS FATHER

LEBANON, CONN.

NEW YORK, Sept. 1ˢᵗ, 1776.

HONORED SIR,

. . . . We have been obliged to retreat from Long Island and Governor's Island, from both of which we got off without loss of men. We have left a great part of our heavy artillery behind. The field train is off. We are in hourly expectation that the town will be bombarded and cannonaded—and the enemy are drawing their men to the eastward on Long Island, as if they intended to throw a strong party over on this island, near Hell Gate, so as to get on the back of the city. We are preparing to meet them. Matters appear to be drawing near to a decisive engagement. Gen. Sullivan is allowed to come on shore, upon his parole, and go to Congress, on the subject of exchange of himself, Lord Sterling, and a large number who are prisoners; by the best accounts we yet have, we have lost, in last week's defeat, about 800 men killed and missing; how many of each, is not yet known. I rather expect that they will push in a body of troops between the town and our posts at and near King's bridge. If they do we shall have them between two fires, and must push them to the last extremity or be killed or taken prisoners. The event is in the hand of the Almighty, Disposer of all events. . . .

I am, honored Sir,

Your dutiful son,

JOS. TRUMBULL.

[Collections of the R. I. Hist. Soc., Vol. VI.]

[No. 9.]

COL. MOSES LITTLE TO HIS SON

NEWBURYPORT, MASS.

———

In Camp Long Island June 22ᵈ 76.

Dear Son—We still continue in Camp at this place. No arrivals since my last. Some hints this morning that the Torys had laid a plan to destroy the general officers of our army. The particulars I have not yet. The Regᵗ generally well.

July 6—1776.

About 160 ships and transports and other vessels are arrived with about 10000 soldiers—Numbers are landed on Staten Island. We expect 12000 more to join them. Camp very healthy. I have lost only one man since we left Prospect Hill (near Boston). Our men in good spirits. I am of opinion our hands will be full—hope we shall do well.

July 31, 1776.

Ten ships are added to the King's troops—part very large, can't say whether they are men of war or transports. This island is a place of great importance, & if possible must be defended. We are five *small* regᵗˢ, are scattered, & have 10 forts to defend. Col. Hand's Regᵗ is scattered over 5 miles in length. I am posted in fort Green which is the largest. I never desire to give it up, nor be taken while I am alive. I am of opinion my regᵗ. will stand fast in the cause of the United States.

August 9, 1776.

The enemy were seen to embark 30 boats full of men on 3 vessels & 100 boats full on the other transports. We expected an attack, but all is still & quiet.

Our enemies have been reinforced by the Hessians & Clinton's fleet. Deserters say the enemy are 30,000 strong & Genˡ. Greene judges them 20,000. I think them 16,000. We have only 1600 fit for duty on Long Island. I shall pay the Q. M. Gen[1]. the balance due him for cloathing my reg[t]. this day, which will square all accounts.

Aug. 22 1776.

I have thought fit to send you my will—you will take all charge necessary &c.

The enemy this day landed on this Island & marched within 3 miles of our camp. Three or four regiments lodge within 2 miles of the enemy. I expect morning will bring us to battle.

IN CAMP NEW YORK Sep. 1, 1776.

The enemy left Staten Island & landed on Long Island the 22[d]. Encamped on a large plain 5 or 6 miles across, at Flat Bush 4 miles distant. Our troops encamped in the edge of the woods in front of them. Our line extended about four miles on the night of the 27th. In the morning, at 2 o'clock, the enemy attacked our right wing (a smart engagement for some time).

The enemy also advanced on the left. Lord Stirling reinforced the right wing & defended himself till 12 o'clock when our wing gave way. My regt. was in the center on guard. The enemy's right wing almost encircled 2 or 3 regt's & as they were not together they were not able to defend themselves & retreated with about 20 wounded. Our people came in about 11 o'clock. The enemy at the same time with their light horse & English troops attempted to force our lines, but soon retreated being met with a smart fire from our breast works.

Two deserters informed us that the enemies dead & wounded was upwards of 500—I wish ours may not be more. On the morning of the 28th the enemy were encamped on the heights in front of our encampment. Firing was kept up on both sides, from the right to the left. Weather very rainy. 29th very rainy. Firing by both sides in front of Fort Putnam. About sunset the enemy pushed to recover the ground we had taken (about 100 rods) in front of the fort. The fire was very hot, the enemy gave way, & our people recovered the ground. The fire ceased, & our people retired to the fort. The enemy took possession again, & on the morning of the 30th had a breastwork there 60 rods long, & 150 rods distant from fort Putnam.

Two ships of war had got up the sound as far as Hell gate by this time. The general ordered each reg^t. to be paraded on their own parades at 7 O'clock P.M. & wait for orders. We received orders to strike our tents & march, with our baggage, to New York. Our lines were manned until day break.

The reason of the retreat was, that we should have had no chance to retreat if the ships came up. I am not certain we shall be able to keep the city of New York. You may hear of our being at King's Bridge. A great battle I think will be fought here, or near there.

I am in a good measure of health.

I am your affectionate father,

MOSES LITTLE.

To Mr. JOSIAH LITTLE.

IN CAMP FORT CONSTITUTION, Oct. 1, 1776.

I have been solicited by Genl. Green to remain in the service. I before declined, but he will not hear one word about my refusing to serve.

[Original in possession of Benjamin Hale, Esq.]

[No. 10.]

LIEUT. COL. WILLIAM HENSHAW TO HIS WIFE

LEICESTER, MASS.

LONG ISLAND 22^d June, 1776.

MY DEAR—

. . . . Last evening a Conspiracy of the Tories was discovered; their plan was to murder Genl. Washington, seize on the Persons of the other General officers, & blow up our Magazines, at the Instant of Time the King's Troops should Land. A number of our Officers rode last Night to Flat bush on this Island, & seiz'd the Mayor of the City, who is now in safe Custody &

suppos'd to be in the Conspiracy—several others are also taken & the Names of others we have, which I hope we shall soon be able to give a good account of.

In haste, I conclude

Yours affectionately,

WM. HENSHAW.

Aug'. 29th 1776.

I have but just time to inform you I am well, as I hope this will find you, our Family & Friends. You will undoubtedly hear, before you see this, that we have had an engagement with the Enemy—were surrounded, & had a Number Killed & Taken. I was with the Party who were Surrounded & through a kind Providence, got through their fire without being Wounded or Taken.—The Particulars of which I have not time to relate as the Enemy are close to us & we expect to be attacked every hour. I have wrote to Brother Josy by this conveyance which letter he will let you see.—May God Bless & preserve you from every disaster, is the unremitting wish of yours &c.

N. YORK Sep^t. 1st 1776.

Last Friday we left Long Island, (being unable to keep it any longer, without being made Prisoners) and came to New York. How long we shall stay here is uncertain—Our Public Enemies are numerous—Our private Ones not a few. Happy shall I esteem myself, if I live to see these Publick Calamities at an End, when we can live peaceably at home & Enjoy the Fruit of our Labors, the Sweets of Liberty, & none to molest us : 7 Regiments marched to King's Bridge Yesterday Afternoon. Lord Sterling & Gen. Sullivan are made prisoners by the Enemy. Sullivan was with us yesterday and is now gone to Philadelphia to Congress. Numbers of our People who were surrounded by the Enemy at Flat Bush, and we thought were Taken by them, have since got in—My Duty to Parents. Love to Sally, Bettsey, Ruthy & Josey, Brothers, Sisters & all Friends, with which I conclude,

Yours, &c.

White Plains, Octr. 31st, 1776.

In your last, you want to know whether I was in the Brush or Battle,[1] mentioned in my last.—I was there. In our Brigade was Kill'd & Wounded, 75—in the whole Kill'd & Wounded on our side, about 100—of the Enemy by the best Information we have about 500—since which we have had several Skirmishes. I was not in them, though I saw several of them. One of them last Week was fought by Reed's & Learned's Reg^ts., where we had six —kill'd & a number Wounded ; the Enemy had Kill'd & Wounded, about 200—the same Week, a Scouting Party came across the famous Rogers Scouts, with a scouting party of the Enemy, took 30 of them Prisoners, & kill'd a number of them— This Week we had some Battles with them. Monday the 28th Ins^t. about 2000 of them came on a height of Land on these Plains, Attacked our Picquet, & after some time, forced our People to give Back. The Loss on either side I cannot ascertain, but suppose we had Kill'd & Wounded near 100, as the Fire of Cannon & Small Arms was heavy for some time. The Day before, they Attacked our Lines near Fort Washington with two of their Brigades & some of their Ships—Their Ships were much damaged ; one of them they were obliged to Tow off ; Our People at the Lines reserv'd their Fire till the Brigades advanced pretty near, then gave them a heavy Fire which caused them to Retreat ; they form'd & advanc'd the second time, when our People gave them the second Fire ; they Retreated as before, & form'd the Third time, came up & Fired at the Lines, which was so warmly returned, that they Retreated. Our People then Jump'd over the Lines, and pursued them, & Kill'd many, but the Number is not ascertained.—should I have another Opportunity to write, can better inform you : we had but one Kill'd in this Battle. We took 14 Hessians one Day this Week, & one English Officer ; have had several Deserters come in this Week. The Enemy are now Encamp'd within Gun shot of us, so that there is a continual firing of Small Arms—We let two Hessians, which we took some time ago, return to the Enemy's Camp—We daily expect an engagement with the Enemy——

Brother Denny was here Yesterday to see me ; is well & station'd at Terry Town on the North River about 8 miles from

---

[1] Harlem Heights, Sept. 16.

this. Capt. Lincoln Parkman & our People in general, were well a few Days ago.

Should I live to see Peace restor'd & our Rights Secur'd, shall prize the Blessing more than ever. I have heard many rumors that it would be tedious to write. Last night we took Doc^t. Whitworth's son (of Boston) Prisoner. He was in some office with the Enemy.

[Originals in possession of Miss H. E. Henshaw, Leicester, Mass.]

[No. 11.]

DEPOSITION BY LIEUT. COL. HENSHAW

[Without date.]

PREVIOUS to the Campaign in 1776, there were 3 Reg^{ts} commanded by Lt. Colonels. General Washington offered me the command of either of them. I conversed with the Officers of these Regiments, & I found they were averse to a change; I informed Gen'l W. that if I accepted his offer, it would be injurious to the Service and declined it. He then said he hoped I would not leave the Service, but would take a Lt. Colonel's commission, which I did under Colonel Little, & in April we marched for New York in the Brigade commanded by Genl Green. Soon after Genl Washington came & ordered said Brigade to Long Island.

The latter part of August, I commanded in a picket guard at Flatbush, where the enemy was encamped, who marched by the East wing of the Pickets, and formed a line between us and our encampments, and knowing the Gen. could not send us orders to retreat we marched to reach our encampments. While marching in the rear of the enemy's line, they were holding a Council of War, whether to storm our lines, or take them by a regular siege. They chose the latter. Had they broke their lines and marched into our front, we must have been made prisoners; but they only turned on their heels and fired at us and we got in with little loss.

[Original in possession of Miss H. E. Henshaw, Leicester, Mass.]

[No. 12.]

COL. EDWARD HAND TO HIS WIFE

LANCASTER, PENN.

LONG ISLAND 27 August 1776 7 P.M.

DEAR KITTY:

Part of the enemy landed on the Island on the 22nd. they did not advance farther than Flatbush until last night—I have had a fatiguing time of it ever since—A number of our troops have been hemned in, but behaved well. Many have got clear and many are yet missing. Our Pennsylvanians were chiefly of the party.

I escaped my part only by being relieved at 2 o'clock this morning—Major Burd and Col. Atlee were out and are yet missing. Jessy and Jacky are yet with me

Adieu—May God preserve you

prays

Your affectionate

EDWARD HAND.

Mrs. KATHERINE HAND

Lancaster Pa.

[Original in possession of Mrs. S. B. Rogers, Lancaster, Penn.]

[No. 13.]

MAJ. EDWARD BURD TO JUDGE YEATES

LONG ISLAND 3rd Sept. 1776.

DEAR SIR.

I was taken prisoner at an advanced Post on the morning of ye 27th ulto after a skirmish, on the same day Capts. Herbert and Heister were both made prisoners. I was used with great Civility by General Grant & admitted to my Parole, Brigadier General Agnew and Major Leslie and Major Batt also treated me with great Politeness.

You must be sensible that hard money can only be of service in my present situation : The Politeness of several Gentlemen would have very fully supplied me with it, but I have only taken what will be immediately necessary for me. I should be much obliged to you if you could procure me a small Bill of Exchange in which perhaps Mr. Dundas of Reading could assist you, or Gold to the amount of about £20.

I can not learn the fate of poor Col° Hand or Jesse Ewing but believe they are not prisoners.

Col° Reed, the Adjutant Gen'l will be the only Person who can convey any thing to me, my Letter must be short, my Love to all the Family.

I am Dear Sir
Your Affect° Brother [in-law]
EDW. BURD.

JASPER YEATES Esqr.

[Original among the Yeates papers.]

[No. 14.]

LIEUT. JASPER EWING TO JUDGE YEATES

NEW YORK Aug. 30, 1776.

HONOURED SIR :

After a very fatiguing march we are all safely arrived. The Genl. yesterday gave orders for all the Regts on Long Island to hold themselves in readiness to march at the shortest notice, and evacuate our Lines for the enemy already had extended their advanced posts across the Island, & we were entirely surrounded, so that the only refuge he had left was New York—This morn'g a party about fifty men went a marauding and were surprised by the enemy, who after firing whole vollies secured one of the Boats, & then the Hessian Riflemen began to play upon them, so that our loss including that of the first engagement amounts to 500 men & upwards.

Lord Stirling & Genl. Sullivan are Prisoners, several officers are still missing amongst whom are Col. Miles and Atlee—The

4

militia from Berks County are almost cut off. The inhuman wretches thrust their bayonets through our wounded men and refused that mercy to us, which we granted to them. The situation of New York is very critical, the enemy being in possession of Long Island may reduce it to a Heap of ashes in a days time.

The loss of the enemy amounts to 1500 men amongst whom are a Brigadier Genl. and several Field Officers.—The Idea which we at first conceived of the Hessian Riflemen was truly ridiculous but sad experience convinces our people that they are an Enemy not to [be] despised, Several Companies of their Light Infantry are cloathed exactly as we are, in hunting shirts and trowers—Mr. Burd who commanded a detachment of 200 men is not yet returned, and sorry am I to say it, he is a Prisoner amongst them. —as this news must certainly afflict Aunt and the whole family, I have forewarned my Brother from making any mention of it.

Please to give my duty to Aunt, mammy, Kitty and my love to all the children,

I remain, Honrd Sir

Y^r dutiful & obliged Nephew

J. EWING.

To JASPER YEATES, Esqr.

[Original among the Yeates papers.]

[No. 15.]

JOHN EWING TO JUDGE YEATES

" *To Jasper Yeates Esq. at Fort Pitt.*"

LANCASTER Sept. 14, 1776.

HonRD Sir :

As it has pleased Divine Providence to spare my Life, I think it my Duty to send you as good an act. of the Engagement together with the enclosed Draught as lays in my power, as I had gone from Elizabeth Point New Jersey to Long Island to see my brothers I had an opportunity of seeing everything that occurred from the Time the Enemy landed on the Island untill a Day or two before we retreated from thence. Col. Hand's Regmt. had been on duty 2 days & the second Night were relieved between

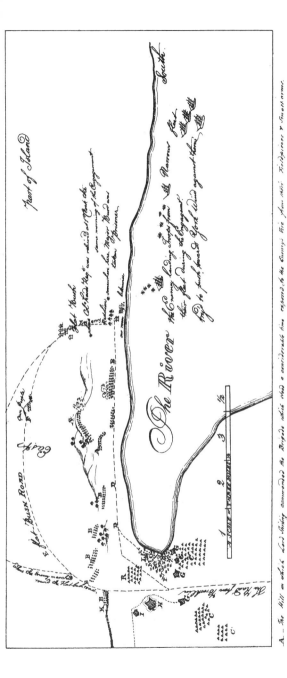

Front of Island

The River

South

Narrow flat

The Enemy Living Encampment their flat during the Engagement

Enemy to push forward York River against them

Flat-bush Road

East

Our People

When the Enemy marched round the Flat-bottom

The Mill Run Brooklin

Scale of three Miles   1   2   3   ½

A. — The Hill on which Lord Stirling commanded the Brigade which stopped a considerable time expecting the Enemy's Fire from Mills Kirkprairies & Great arms.

B. — Large B—Fire of the Enemy marching round our flank.

C.C.C. — Our Camp, with the Forts GGG in front of them.

D.D. — The Road to the Red Lion, where the Enemy marched from Flatbush along the River & got between our People and the Camp.

E. — Flat-bush Road.

F. — Where a considerable Number of our People were Taken with General Kirkprairies & Bryant Works made with Lines field across the Road & Island Manœuvre when attacked

H. — Fort Putnam where part of Col's Hand's men Commanded by Lieut C. Chambers were detected him the Regt. to man the Fort.

I. — A small Upper Fort where one was with the Cap't the Day of the Engagement, where we saw the whole Action at AAA.
Our People other standing their ground at the Hill, at last descended, and the was an incessant Fire of Small Arms for the best part of an Hour or longer with little or no intermission, till our Men Retreated by the Hill I, and in their Retreat O.O. Set fire to the house H, the Smoke of which prevented the Enemy of BBYX from seing them retreat & then they came over the March P where several brave Fellows were Drowned in the Creek P, in Deavering to get over.
We expected every Minute the Enemy would Storm the Forts & Lines IH, as they were not above 700 or 450 Yards from Fort I to Arm at XB, but our Cannon from Fort Putnam obliged them to lay close.

R. — The Enemy's Camp the Day after the Battle.

"Draught of the Engagement at Long Island. Aug. 27th 1776."

J. Bien Photo Lith. N.Y.

12 and 1 o'clock in the morning and about Two it is thought the
Enemy began their movements from Flat Bush to the Right, and
Left, and at between 7 & 8 o'clock in the morning we had the
mortification from our Lines to see our men commanded by Lord
Stirling almost surrounded by the Regulars, as they kept their
stand on a Hill without flinching an inch, The Regulars were firing
at them like Fury they at last descended then there was a continual peal of Small Arms for an Hour or better, our men at last
partly got off by the Marsh, as in the Draught inclosed, I have
been very Ill of a Fever which I got by being cloathed too thin
and lay at York about 2 Days before our People had made that
Grand Retreat from the Island which will ever reflect honour to
our Generals. from York I was removed to King's Bridge twelve
or fifteen miles from thence, after I had recovered, my Health suffered from Travelling. The Col⁰. was good enough to send me
Home in a Carriage which thank God I happily—and dont doubt
of recovering Health shortly—I am Sir

Your affectionate
Nephew
Jn⁰. Ewing.

P. S.

I shall refer you to the papers for our Loss in the Battle though
it is with infinite regret I must inform you of Major Burd's being
among the prisoners who Lord How treats them with great politeness. Time will not permitt my saying so much as I would wish
—I left the Col⁰. & all friends very well at King's Bridge where
the Regᵗ. is Stationed as I only left them this day week.

[Original among the Yeates papers.]

[No. 16.]

COL. JOHN HASLET TO HON. CÆSAR RODNEY

PHILADELPHIA

Hon'ble Sir,

I recᵈ. yours with pleasure because it was yours, all the Rest
was Indignation—We went over to Long Island, a Genˡ. Engagement ensued, the Southern Troops i. e Ld Stirlings Battalion bore

the Violence of the Attack & repulsed the Enemy but were out-numbered at least three to one, & obliged to retire; the Delaware Battalion have been complimented as the finest in the Service, they stood unmoved in firm Array four Hours exposed to the fire of the Enemy, nor attempted to retire till they received Orders from the Genl, then effected a most H'oble Retreat up to the mid-dle thro a Marsh of Mud & brought off with them 23 Prisoners— I fear we shall be outnumbered, expect every moment Orders to march off to Kingsbridge, to prevent the Enemy crossing the East River & confining us on another Nook, what the Event will be God knows—Lt. Stewart & Harney with 25 Privates fell in our Regiment—Ld. Stirling & Genl Sullivan Prisoners—Miles & Atlee the same Piper killed—250 of Smallmans (Swallwood's) missing—Atles cut to pieces—I fear Genl. Washington has too heavy a task, assisted mostly by Beardless Boys—if the Enemy can coop us up in N. York by Intrenching from River to River, horrid will be the Consequences from their command of the Rivers.

Between five & six thousand Dollars of Continental Money re-main in my hands, unknowing what to do with it, I have entrusted it to the care of Dr. Rogers & Chaplain Montgomery—if I fall, please to take Order in the Matter—I have not time to say one Word more, tis the first Letter I have had time to write—please to mention to some of your Friends below that I am well, by whose Means it may reach Mrs. Haslet—I am with

Great Esteem, Sir your Most Obed^t Humble Servant

JOHN HASLET.

Honble Genl RODNEY.

Camp at N. York Augt 31st 1776.

[Original in possession of Cæsar A. Rodney, Esq., Wilmington, Del.]

[No. 17.]

COL. GOLD S. SILLIMAN TO HIS WIFE

FAIRFIELD, CONN.

BROOKLINE ON L. I. Augst 24—1776
7 o'clock A.M.

. . . . . I never was in better Health and Spirits than now. On Thursday the enemy landed on Long Island at 3 o'clock P.M. We had intelligence that our Troops on the Island wanted to be reinforced. My Regiment and 3 more were ordered over for that purpose. My regt. was ordered down into a woody Hill near Red Hook to take Post that night to prevent any more troops from landing thereabout. We had the Heavens for our Covering and the Earth for my bed, wrapt in my blanket, when after posting my Sentries I slept finely. Was mighty well yesterday, and was then ordered here where I & my Regt. now are. The enemy are about 3 miles East of our troops, were a part of them skirmishing with them all day yesterday and are still on the same ground & have killed a number of the enemy. The enemy are said to be 8 or 9000 that are landed here. I am posted here at a fort & to see some breastworks compleated. By the blessing of Heaven I trust we shall be able to give a good acct of the enemy. . . . . My love to our Dear Sons & accept the same yourself from most affec. & loveing Husband

P. S. I refer you to Capt. Hawley for Particulars.

FLATT BUSH ON LONG ISLAND Aug. 25, 1776
2 o'clock P.M.

I wrote you yesterday morning from Brookline upon the Drum Head in the field as I do now, which I hope you will receive this day. . . . Have not so much as a bear skin to lie on, only my blanket to wrap me in, for our removals from place to place are so quick & sudden that we can have no opportunity nor means to convey beds &c, but go only with the cloaths on our backs & our blankets and a little ready-cooked victuals. I am now posted within about half a mile from the Regulars with my Regt. under the Covert of a woody hill to stop their passage into the Country. There are a number of Regts posted all around the town within about the same distance & for the same purpose. The regulars keep up an almost Constant Fire from their cannon & mortars at some or other of us, but neither shott nor shell has come near my Regt. yet and they are at too great a distance to fire muskets at as yet. I have a scouting party going out now to see if they can't pick up some or get something from them. I came to this post this day at 12 o'clock & shall remain here till this time to-morrow if God spares my life, with no other covering than the trees. I cant learn anything with respect to them different from what I wrote yesterday. The rest of the troops & their Ships lie at

Staten Island yet to wait the success of this part of their army, as I suppose before they make any other attempt. They have wounded in all of our men in 3 days skirmish about 8 or 9 men, one or two mortally, which is not half the number that we have killed for them beside wounded. . . .

NEW YORK (BROOKLYN) Aug 29 1776.

. . . Have been a stranger to a bed ever since last Wens'-day night till last night being relieved from manning a part of the lines with my regt. where I had been 36 hours I was invited by our mutual friend Major Mott to take part of his bed & have had a fine night indeed, the Night before there was a waggon near our Lines into which I got & wrapt myself in my Blanket after Twelve & half after One was waked & acquainted that the Enemy were coming up to force our Lines & we immediately took our Places in the Trenches & there remained untill after Sun Rise, but it proved a false Alarm, our Enemy have encamped in plain sight of our camp at the distance of about a mile & half, We have had no General Engagement yet, but no Day passes without some smart & Hot skirmishes between different Parties in which the success is sometimes One Way & sometimes another, We are in constant Expectation of a General Battle ; no one can be here long without geting pretty well acquainted with the whistleing of Cannon & musket shott.

HARLEM HEIGHTS Sep. 17th 1776.

. . . . On the morning of last Sabbath we had news that the regulars on Long Island were in motion as they would cross the East River & land about 3 miles above the city. At this place lay their ships close in with our shores & soon after the regulars marched in a large body down to the shore & embarked on Board the flat bottomed boats. Upon this their ships began a most incessant fire on our lines opposite to them with their grape shot from which they were distant but about 50 rods & behind which lay Gen[l]. Wadsworth's & Col. Douglass' Brigades until the fire was so hot from the ships that they were obliged to retreat. On this the regulars landed & fired upon them which completed their confusion & they ran away up here & are here now, but a part of them were out in yesterday's action & behaved nobly.

Now as to myself & my brigade we were left to guard the city until all the rest of the troops were drawn off & about half an hour or an hour after all the other troops were gone I was ordered with my brigade to march out of the city & man the lines on the East river opposite to Bayard's Hill fort. Then I marched & saw the regular Army land above me & spread across the Island from one river to another until my retreat seemed to be entirely cut off & soon after received an order to retreat if I could.

I attempted it along up through the woods by the North River when I came in sight of the enemy several times but kept my brigade covered in the woods so that I got thro' them to their uppermost guard & they pursued & fired on my rear & took a few of my men. I immediately formed about 300 of my men on an Hill to oppose them. On seeing this the regulars fled & I pursued my retreat & got my brigade safe here where I am now posted—a particular detail of the risks I ran must be deferred. It was supposed by everybody that I & my brigade were entirely cut off.

HARLEM HEIGHTS, 17 Sept. 1777. 2 o'cl P.M.

Yesterday at 7 o'clock in the morning we were alarmed with the sight of a considerable number of the enemy on the Plains below us about a mile distant.—Our Brigades which form a line across the Island where I am were immediately ordered under arms—but as the enemy did not immediately advance we grounded our arms & took spades & shovels & went to work & before night had thrown up lines across the Island—There was nothing before but three little redoubts in about a mile & we are at work this day in strengthening them. But yesterday a little before noon we heard a strong firing about half a mile below us in the woods near where we had two Brigades lying as an advanced guard. The enemy in a large body advanced in the woods a little before 12 o'cl & began a heavy fire on those two Brigades who maintained the fire obstinately for some time & then they were reinforced by several regiments & the fire continued very heavy from the musketry & from field pieces about two hours—in which time our people drove the regulars back from post to post about a mile & a half & then left them pretty well satisfied with their dinner since which they have been very quiet. Our loss on this occasion by the best information is about 25 killed & 40 or 50 wounded. The enemy by the best accounts have suffered much more than we.

A prisoner we have I am told says that Genl. Howe himself commanded the regular & Genl. Washington & Genl. Putnam were both with our Troops. They have found now that when we meet them on equal ground we are not a set of people that will run from them—but that they have now had a pretty good drubbing, tho' this was an action between but a small party of the army.

Camp at White Plains Oct. 29th 1776.

. . . . Yesterday about 10 o'clock in the morning we had news that the enemy were approaching, when I with my regiment & 3 others were ordered out about 1½ miles below our lines to take post on a hill to gall them in their march as they advanced. We accordingly took our post & mine & one other regiment had the advantage of a stone wall right in front at which we had been waiting but little time before the enemy came up within 6 or 8 rods,—when our men rose from behind the wall, poured in a most furious fire.

The enemy retreated & came on several times & were so hotly received every time that finally we drove them off from the hill. We killed some they did not carry off & some they did.

I had not one either killed or wounded. On this the enemy were coming upon us with a number of field pieces & as we had none there to meet them with, we were ordered to retreat over West on to another Hill & join another party of men & accordingly did it & formed a line of battle. We were I believe near 2000 on the Hill (Chatterton's). The enemy soon brought their main body opposite to us & formed them into three lines, one back of the other, & a large number of field pieces in their front & howitzers with which they threw small bombs on another Hill. Then they marched their first line off from the Hill where they stood, down into a deep Valley that lay between us & then they played on us most furiously with their artillery to keep us from meeting their people in the hollow & in short the shot & shells came like hail. I lay right in the heaviest of their fire. with my men by a fence & had two wounded there & were soon ordered to another post further on the line of battle up to which the enemy soon came as they did for a long way in lengths. We gave them a heavy fire which made them retreat but they soon returned when a most furious fire followed which continued for a few minutes when their numbers were increased so amazingly that we were obliged to retreat which we did thro' a most furious fire from the enemy for half a mile for so far there was nothing to cover us from it. . . . I have lost but 4 out of my reg't & can hear of only 10 or 12 wounded. We are all now within our line & the enemy are posted on a number of the neighboring hills & we expected they would have come on this morning when we should have had an engagement with both armies but they don't yet move & it is now about 12 o'clock."

[Originals in possession of Mrs. O. P. Hubbard, New York.]

[No. 18.]

COL. GOLD S. SILLIMAN TO REV. MR. FISH

STONINGTON, CONN.

NEW YORK Sep^r: 6th, 1776.

DEAR SIR Your Favour of the 1st Inst^t: I have this Morning received and ⁻am much obliged to you for it; in Order to answer your Inquiries I must necessarily give you some Account of our out Lines on Long Island before we left it, about 8 or Nine Miles below this Town is that Strait of Water commonly called the Narrows, from the upper end of it on the Long Island side a Bay puts into the Island on a Course about Northeasterly and runs into the Land about Two miles; from the Head of this Bay we had a line of Forts & Redoubts all connected by Breast Works and some part of it picketed, up Northeasterly and Northerly to a Bay on the Northwesterly part of the Island rather above the City; The British Troops landed below the Bay at the Narrows and marched to Flat Bush a Place on the Island about 6 or 7 miles from this city and 3 miles beyond our Lines. flat Bush stands near the Westerly Side of a large Plain which is 4 or 5 miles over and this plain is surrounded from the Southwest to the Northeast with a larg Ridge of Hills covered with Woods.

through this Ridge there are three roads into the Country, toward New York two of them ; and one out to a place called Bedford ; At each of these passes which were from 1 to 1½ Mile asunder we had strong Guards posted consisting of 600 or 700 Men, the other Forces which we had on the Island were posted within the Lines and in the Forts and once in 24 Hours relieved the Guards out at those advanced Posts toward the Enemy ; I was posted out on one of these Advanced Posts on Sabbath Day July (August) 25th, with my own Regimt and 2 more near by in order [to stop the Progress of the Enemy into the Country. I was relieved on Monday about half (past) Two & marched Back within the Lines to the Place where my Regiment was ordered for their Alarm Post in order to man the Lines there in case the Enemy advanced which was at the Northern Part of the Lines, and there was beside the Regiments that were ordered to man the Lines some Regiments as a Corps de Reserve to reinforce any Part of the Lines that might be attacked &c. Early on Tuesday Morning the Guards at all those Three Avenues were attacked (by) parties that vastly out numbered them, and soon were drove from their Posts and soon broken at the Same Time. . . . [The conclusion missing.]

[Original in possession of Mrs. O. P. Hubbard, New York.]

[No. 19.]

ACCOUNT OF THE BATTLE OF LONG ISLAND

The evening preceding the action, General Washington, with a number of general officers, went down to view the motions of the enemy, who were encamped at Flatbush. The enemy appeared to be striking their tents, and preparing for a march; whereupon it was ordered that 2400 men should be posted as guards, in the following manner, viz : 800 on the road that leads out of the Jamaica road by way of Yellow Hook to Flatbush ; these men were posted in a woods, at four miles distant from our lines, to oppose the enemy if they attempted that road, and to annoy them on their march : 800 more were posted in a woods upon the Middle road, which leads out of the Jamaica road to Flatbush, about a mile and a half from the lines ; these were posted at about half a mile distant from Flatbush, and near a mile from the parting of the road, where an *abatis* was formed across the road, and a breastwork thrown up and defended by two pieces of cannon : 800 more were posted at the Bedford road, which leads out of the Jamaica road, at about three miles distant from our lines ; this party was ordered to guard the Bedford road, and to patrol the road leading through the New Lots in the east of the Bedford road, from which it parts at the Halfway House, about six miles from the lines, and leads from it to Flatbush. Five officers were also sent out on horseback to patrol the last-mentioned road and that leading to Jamaica. At 10 o'clock at night about 5000 of the enemy marched by way of the New Lots, and arrived, near 2 in the morning, at Halfway House, without being discovered ; they took post in a field, and waited for daylight. The five officers sent to patrol fell into their hands, and were all made 'prisoners. About 3 in the morning a party of the enemy advanced into the Western road, leading by Yellow Hook, and attacked our guards ; the guards returned their fire, threw them into confusion, caused the whole to halt, and took one prisoner, who informed us that he belonged to the regiment which attacked our guards, and was by their fire thrown into confusion and forced to retreat, and that there were two brigades, of four regiments each, on their march in that road, commanded by Brigadier-General Grant. At daylight Lord Stirling was ordered with two battalions, into that road, to oppose the enemy. He took post on an eminence in front of the enemy whereupon a smart fight ensued, which lasted near an hour, and then abated. Two field-pieces were sent to Lord Stirling, which soon began to play upon the enemy, who returned the fire from four field-pieces. The two parties stood opposed to each other for near five hours, without either seeming to have the advantage, keeping up a continual fire from their field-pieces and musketry, with some intervals.—About 8 o'clock General Sullivan sent (went ?) down the flat (bush) middle (road) and inquired of the guards whether they discovered any movements of the enemy in either of the roads. He was informed that the whole body of the enemy had moved up the Yellow Hook road, whereupon he ordered another battalion to the assistance of lord Stirling, keeping 800 men to guard the pass.—About 9 o'clock, the enemy, who came by the Halfway House, advancing, began a fire in the rear of the party and advanced briskly to attack the men who guarded that Pass. General Sullivan hearing at the same instant that the enemy were passing through the woods to attack Lord Stirling in the rear, ordered 400 men to succor him, and sent him orders to retreat as soon as possible. The enemy then wheeled off to the right, and marched up to Fort Green in a column to attack.—Upon receiving a heavy fire from the lines, were forced to retire. They then fell back, and endeavored to cut off Lord Stirling's retreat by destroying his party. He, with a party of his troops' made an attempt on the enemy's left, commanded by Lord Cornwallis, and ordered the rest of the troops to retreat across the creek, which they did with some loss. The number of the enemy engaged was not less than 11,000 ; of ours not more than 3,000. The enemy's loss in killed was over 1,000, exceeding ours.

[From the *South Carolina and American General Gazette*, Charleston, Oct. 2, 1776, as reprinted in the *Brooklyn Advocate.*]

[No. 20.]

JOURNAL OF COL. SAMUEL MILES

In the Spring of 1776, I was appointed to the command of a regiment of riflemen, consisting of 1,000 men, formed in two battalions. . . . My regiment was soon ordered to join the army at New York. At that time General Washington had 24,000 men in his army, upwards of 7,000 of whom were returned sick and unfit for duty.

On the landing of the British army on Long Island, I was ordered over with my rifle regiment to watch their motions. I marched near to the village of Flat Bush, where the Highlanders then lay, but they moved the next day to Gen'l Howe's camp, and their place was supplied by the Hessians. I lay here within cannon shot of the Hessian camp for four days without receiving a single order from Gen'l Sullivan, who commanded on Long Island, out of the lines. The day before the action he came to the camp, and I then told him the situation of the British Army; that Gen'l Howe, with the main body, lay on my left, about a mile and a-half or two miles, and I was convinced when the army moved that Gen'l Howe would fall into the Jamaica road, and I hoped there were troops there to watch them. Notwithstanding this information, which indeed he might have obtained from his own observation, if he had attended to his duty as a General ought to have done; no steps were taken, but there was a small redoubt in front of the village which seemed to take up the whole of his attention, and where he stayed until the principal part of the British army had gotten between him and the lines, by which means he was made prisoner as well as myself. If Gen'l Sullivan had taken the requisite precaution, and given his orders agreeably to the attention of the Commander-in-Chief, there would have been few if any prisoners taken on the 27th of August, 1776. As Gordon in his history of the war has charged me indirectly with not doing my duty, I will here state my position and conduct.

I lay directly in front of the village of Flat Bush, but on the left of the road leading to New York, where the Hessians were Encamped. We were so near each other, that their shells they sometimes fired went many rods beyond my camp. The main body of the Enemy, under the immediate command of Gen'l Howe, lay about 2 miles to my left, and General Grant, with another body of British troops, lay about four miles on my right. There were several small bodies of Americans dispersed to my right, but not a man to my left, although the main body of the Enemy lay to my left, of which I had given General Sullivan notice. This was our situation on the 26th of August. About one o'clock at night Gen. Grant, on the right, and Gen. Howe, on my left began their march, and by daylight Grant had got within a mile of our entrenchments, and Gen. Howe had got into the Jamaica road about two miles from our lines. The Hessians kept their position until 7 in the morning. As soon as they moved the firing began at our redoubt. I immediately marched towards where firing was, but had not proceeded more than 1 or 200 yards until I was stopped by Colonel Wyllys, who told me that I could not pass on; that we were to defend a road that lead from Flatbush road to the Jamaica road. Col. Wyllys bearing a Continental, and I a State commission, he was considered a senior officer and I was obliged to submit; but I told him I was convinced the main body of the enemy would take the Jamaica road, that there was no probability of their coming along the road he was then guarding, and if he would not let me proceed to where the firing was, I would return and endeavor to get into the Jamaica road before Gen. Howe. To this he consented, and I immediately made a retrograde march, and after marching nearly two miles, the whole distance through woods, I arrived within sight of the Jamaica road, and to my great mortification I saw the main body of the enemy in full march between me and our lines, and the baggage guard just coming into the road. A thought struck me of attacking the baggage guard, and, if possible, to cut my way through them and proceed to Hell Gate to cross the Sound. I, however, ordered the men to remain quite still, (I had then but the first battalion with me, for the second being some distance in the rear, I directed Major Williams, who was on horseback, to return and order Lt. Col· Brodhead to push on by the left of the enemy and endeavor get into our lines that way, and happily they succeeded, but had to wade a mill dam by which a few were drowned,) and I took the adjutant with me and crept as near the road as I thought prudent, to try and ascertain the number of the baggage guard, and I saw a grenadier stepping into the woods. I got a tree between him and me until he came near, and I took him prisoner and examined him. I found that there was a whole brigade with the baggage, commanded by a general officer.

I immediately returned to the battalion and called a council of the officers and laid three propositions before them : 1st, to attack the baggage guard and endeavor to cut our way through them and proceed to Hell Gate and so cross the Sound ; 2nd, to lay where we were until the whole had passed us and then proceed to Hell Gate ; or, 3d, to endeavor to force our way through the enemy's flank guards into our line at Brooklyn. The first was thought a dangerous and useless attempt as the enemy was so superior in force. The 2nd I thought the most eligible, for it was evident that adopting either of the other propositions we must lose a number of men without affecting the enemy materially, as we had so small a force, not more than 230 men. This was, however, objected to, under the idea that we should be blamed for not fighting at all, and perhaps charged with cowardice, which would be worse than death itself. The 3d proposition was therefore adopted, and we immediately began our march, but had not proceeded more than half a mile until we fell in with a body of 7 or 800 light infantry, which we attacked without any hesitation, but their superiority of numbers encouraged them to march up with their bayonets, which we could not withstand, having none ourselves. I therefore ordered the Troops to push on towards our lines. I remained on the ground myself until they had all passed me, (the enemy were then within less than 20 yards of us,) and by this means I came into the rear instead of the front of my command. We had proceeded but a short distance before we were again engaged with a superior body of the enemy, and here we lost a number of men, but took Major Moncrieffe, their commanding officer, prisoner, but he was a Scotch prize for Ensign Brodhead, who took him and had him in possession for some hours, was obliged to surrender himself. Finding that the enemy had possession of the ground between us and our lines, and that it was impossible to cut our way through as a body, I directed the men to make the best of their way as well as they could; some few got in safe, but there were 159 taken prisoners. I was myself entirely cut off from our lines and therefore endeavored to conceal myself, with a few men who would not leave me. I hoped to remain until night, when I intended to try to get to Hell Gate and cross the Sound; but about 3 o'clock in the afternoon was discovered by a party of Hessians and obliged to surrender—thus ended the career of that day.

[Penn. Archives, Second Series, Vol. I.]

[No. 21.]

LIEUT.-COL. DANIEL BRODHEAD TO ———

CAMP NEAR KINGSBRIDGE, 5th Sep'r, 1776.

DEAR SIR,

I doubt not the Hon'ble the Convention of the State of Penn'a, is anxious to know the state of the Provincial Troops since the Battle on Long Island, and as I have now all the information to be expected concerning it for the present, will give them every circumstance that occurs to me. On the 26th of last month, Gen'ls Putnam, Sullivan and others came to our camp which was to the left of all the other posts and proceeded to reconnoitre the enemie's lines to the right, when from the movements of the enemy they might plainly discover they were advancing towards Jamaica, and extending their lines to the left so as to march round us, for our lines to the left, were, for want of Videttes, left open for at least four miles where we constantly scouted by Day, which beside mounting a Guard of one hundred men & an advance party of subaltern and thirty to the left of us, was hard Duty for our Reg't: during the night of the 26th, we were alarmed three Different times and stood to our Arms. As soon as it was light, Col. Miles, from the right of our first Batt^n, sent me orders to follow him with the second, to the left of our lines; when I had marched about half a mile, I was ordered to the right about to join Col. Willis's reg^t of New England troops, but by the time I returned to the camp, Major Williams on horseback, overtook me with orders from Col. Miles, to march Obliquely & join him, but could not say where I might find him; I Observed the orders and directed a Subaltern from the front of the Batt^n (which was march-ing in Indian file) with a small party to the left of the Batt^n, and desired Major Patton to send a Subaltern & small party from the rear to the right of the front of the Battalion, which he mistook and took the one-half of the Batt^n to the right, about two hundred yards, which immediately threw the half the Batt^n, so far to the rear as to render it very difficult to join without sustaining great loss, for presently after we left our camp we discovered the Enemie's horse & foot to the number of four or five Thousand in our front, and as we could discover nothing of the first Batt^n, the Enemy being vastly superior to us in Number, I immediately ordered the Batt^n to gain a Wood to the left and then formed, but seeing a Number of Artillerymen dragging a brass field-piece & Howit through a clear field in order to gain a wood a little to the left of our Front, and knowing the Enemy were also in our rear, I ordered that part of the Batt^n which was then with me, to proceed to the second wood, & cover the Artillery and make a stand, but the New England Reg^t aforementioned coming up with us, and running thro' our files broke them, and in the confusion many of our men run with them. I did all in my power to rally the musquetry & Riflemen, but to no purpose, so that when we came to engage the Enemy, I had not fifty men, notwithstanding which, we after about three Rounds, caused the Enemy to retire, and as the Enemy's main body was then nearly between us and the lines, I retreated to the lines, having lost out of the whole Battalion, about one hundred men, officers included, which, as they were much scattered, must be chiefly prisoners; during this time, four or five Reg'ts, among which were our musquetry & flying Camp, Delaware & Maryland Reg'ts, and some of our Riflemen who had joined them, were engaged to the left of us and right of the Lines. I had no sooner got into the Lines than the Enemy advanced up to them and kept up a brisk fire on us, but only one man killed in the Lines; as soon as we returned the fire with our rifles and musquetry, they retreated, and if we had been provided with a field piece or two, of which we had a sufficient number elsewhere, we might have killed the greater part of their advance party; as soon as the Enemy were beaten from the lines, I was ordered to a point about a mile and a-half to the right, to cover the retreat of the Delaware Battalion and the other Troops that might come over under the constant fire of the Enemie's field pieces and Howits; here I remained 'till almost night before I was relieved, notwithstanding the Generals there had a number of Reg'ts who were not engaged, and had had little or no fatigue. Upon the whole, less Generalship never was shown in any Army since the Art of War was understood, except in the retreat from Long Island, which was well conducted. No troops could behave better than the Southern, for though they seldom engaged less than five to one, they frequently repulsed the Enemy with great Slaughter, and I am confident that the number of killed and wounded on their side, is greater than on ours, notwithstanding we had to fight them front & rear under every disadvantage. I understand that Gen. Sullivan has taken the Liberty to charge our brave and good Col. Miles, with the ill success of the Day, but give me leave to say, that if Gen. Sullivan & the rest of the Gen'ls on Long Island, had been as Vigilant & prudent as him, we might, & in all probability would have cut off Clinton's Brigade; our officers & men in general, considering the confusion, behaved as well as men could do—a very few behaved ill, of which, when I am informed, will write you. . . . Col. Miles & Col. Piper are prisoners, and I hear are well treated, poor Atly I can hear

5

nothing of. Col. Parry died like a Hero. No allowance has as yet been made for the Lieutenant Coll's and Majors Table Expenses, in care of separate commands. I hope we shall be put upon as respectable a footing on that acc't as the Maryland officers are, our present pay being not more than half sufficient to support us according to our Rank in this Tory Country.

I am Dear Sir, in great Haste, your most H'ble Serv't

DANIEL BRODHEAD.

P. S. The Great Gen'l Putnam could not, tho' requested, send out one Reg't to cover our retreat.

[Penn. Archives, First Series, Vol. V.]

[No. 22.]

[COL. WILLIAM DOUGLAS TO HIS WIFE]

NORTHFORD, CONN.

[LONG ISLAND, Feb. 26 (?) 1776.] [1]

MY DEAR,

Our Regiment is now stationed on *Long Island* at and about the ferry. We shall soon begin a fortification on this side that will command the East River and the town. The troops in the City are fortifying in one of the Streets that will command the old fort, if the Enemy should get possession of it, (and are putting down the rear of the fort.) We have begun another Fort near " Hell Gate." The men of war have dropped down below the town and are very quiet, but supplied from the City by orders of this Congress. Our troops are very hearty and fare well as times will admit, most of the valuable articles are moved out of the City, and one third of the inhabitants. What are left behind look serious, as it is now a serious point with them. The destruc-

---

[1] At the time of writing this letter, Col. Douglas was Major of Ward's regiment which enlisted for six weeks' service under Lee, and which was stationed by him on Long Island. The fortification they were soon to begin was Fort Stirling.

tion of such a City as this would be a great loss, & I hope it will be prevented. It will be in vain for us to expect to keep the shipping out of the North River, unless we can fortify at the Narrows, where I intend to view as soon as the weather is good. The Fenoex now lays there in order to guard that place, but will not fire on us.

NEW YORK, July 20th, 1776.

You have likely heard before this that two ships passed this City yesterday week, through a warm fire from our batteries, our Gunners being in too much haste (I make no doubt,) was the occasion of our not doing them much damage ! and us the *loss* of 4 men in loading our Cannon. The Enemy did us no harm by their own shot and shells, which was warmly applied,—as soon as the fire had got pretty warm I receivd orders to march my Regt to the grand parade which brought us into Broadway, that leads along the North River, and as we were on our march in Broadway the tyrants did not fail to pelt at that part of the town smartly, but luckily for us the houses fended off the shot very well, &c. . . . My Regt is now quartered in *Broad Street.*

N. YORK the 27th July, 1776.

No new arrivals of the enemy. The ships that went up the River I believe would now be glad they were safe back to their old station (by their motion). I had the Honor to dine with his Excellency Genl. Washington day before yesterday at which time he had nothing new from any quarter. . . .

NEW YORK Aug. 10, 1776.

The enemy have a very formidable Army (some say more) but I suppose equal in number to ours, and from the best intelligence it is expected they will give us Battle soon, at which time I hope God in his infinite mercy will be on our side, and we shall have no occasion to dread their numbers, or experience. Our cause being so *just*, I cannot but hope for success. Our lines are very extensive. The Enemy are very compact, and together; at what place they will bend their fury is unknown, but is expected to be at this City, and Long Island. There sailed night before last, three Frigates and thirty transports from the Hook, supposed to be gone round the east end of Long Island, and are to come through the Sound, and land on the main to the Eastward of us, whilst the Shipping goes up the north river, and lands above us and endeavor to meet. If this be their plan I think we must most surely work them! I suppose they may possibly fire the town, as the buildings are many of them wood & very dry. But I do not believe they will fire the town until they grow dubious about the victory, and that will only serve to encourage us, and when the town is burned it will be much easier to defend ourselves than at present. If the "*Hessian*" troops are so lucky as to fall into our hands I am in hopes they will meet with such treatment as properly belongs to their Bloody crimes! For we have had no dispute with them but [they] have turned themselves out as murderers of the innocent.

N. YORK, 13ᵗʰ of Augˢᵗ 1776.

There was 43 large Ships came in yesterday—31 Ships, 10 Brigs & one Scow. I am now going to sound the channel to see if it will not do to sink some vessels against the fort.   .   .   .

NEW YORK, Augˢᵗ 23, 1776.

.   .   .   .   The Enemy landed yesterday on Long Island, at *Gravesend*, about nine miles from our lines; our flying parties are annoying them all the while. We have reinforced our side and I hope will be able to make a good stand. We expect the fleet up every tide, if the wind serves. Our fire ships in the North River have behaved manfully, have burnt one of their tenders. The rest of the enemy left the river the first opportunity afterwards. Our *Connecticut* Militia have come in *bravely ; twelve Regts* were on the grand parade yesterday at one time! Almost one half of the grand army now consists of *Connecticut Troops !*

NEW YORK, Saturday, Augˢᵗ 24, 1776.

.   .   .   .   Our men had yesterday two small brushes with the enemy on Long Island, and repulsed them both times. As yet things look well on our side ; a few days will now determine as the work is begun. Our troops are really in high spirits, and it is a general voice, let them come on as they *can* or dare ! There has been a heavy clashing of Arms on Long Island this morning, but have not yet heard the Consequence. . . .

N. YORK, Aug^st 26th 1776.

I am very well although many in the Reg^t are sick. We have not had any general action yet. The two Armies are intrenched on Long Island very near each other and very often exchange a few shots. We have had no considerable loss as yet. Col. Martin of the Jersey's is supposed to be mortally wounded. Both the lines are constantly reinforcing, and by all appearances a general action can't be far off ; we have got the advantage of the hills & woods, they of the plains. We shall not approach their lines, and if they do ours, it must cost them dear. The wind and tide served this morning, but they have not dared to give us battle in the City yet. The Lieut. Col. of the first battalion of York troops is now before a court marshall for treacherous behavior, and by the best accounts he will undoubtedly lose his life. I hope God in his providence will guard us from falling by our open enemy, and from all *traiterous wretches.* . . . . . It is expected that they mean to give battle at two places at one and the same time, that is Long Island, and this City.

N. YORK, Aug^st 31, 1776.

I take this as the first opportunity to acquaint you that on Tuesday last we got a severe flogging on Long Island. The enemy surrounded a large detachment of our army, took many, killed some, and the rest got off. Major Genl. Sullivan & Brig^r Genl. Lord Sterling, Col. Clark and several other field officers are prisoners. Col. Johnson was killed. By the best act's we killed more of them than they did of us. But they took the most prisoners. We took twenty one, which I am a witness to, as they came through my Reg^t as I was in the woods for a covering party, and to prevent the enemy from flanking our right wing. We were prevented from getting even one shot at them by a large creek which we could not cross. I remained at the most extreme part of the right wing of our Army in a thick wood to prevent their crossing a creek, where our sentry's could hail and often fire at each other, until night before last when I received orders to call in my guard *all*, and march immediately with the utmost silence, which was soon done, and the whole army retreated into this city, without the loss of any lives, except 4 or 5, which were late yesterday morning and were shot in a boat, as they were coming off. 'We have also evacuated Governor's Island where we have lost some Cannon. What is to be our next manouver I can't tell but I hope it is to make a good stand somewhere. I am well convinced that for us to try to defend Long Island, New York, and the Jersey's against their land forces & shipping will require *three armies* as large as theirs, as they have the water carriage to place their men when & where they please. Many people I suppose will wonder at our leaving Long Island. But I would have them suspend their judgment for a while, as they know not our situation or the *enemies !* The shipping lay now close by the city, and can in half an hour be abreast of it with the tide. I expect we [shall] soon have a cannonade from our own battery on Long Island, (Fort Sterling) which I have the mortification to think I helped build myself, in cold tedious weather ! They fired smartly from it yesterday at our boats passing from Governor's Island. . . .

Country Seat near Turtle Bay,
Septr 7th 1776.

Our Army is now in three grand Divisions. One at the City, which is our *right* wing, commanded by Genl. Putnam, one at and above Kings Bridge, commanded by Genl Heath, and one at and about Harlem, commanded by Genl Spencer, which is the Division that I belong to, and is called the Center Division. I have three Reg^{ts} of militia in my Brigade and they give me much fatigue & trouble. Col's. Cook, Pettibone, & Talcott are the commanders. We are encouraged by 1500 Troops which have come in from Maryland. I am sorry to say it but it is a truth, I do not believe that we have got in all our Army as many men as the enemy. I have heard that it has been said in the country that we should not have left Long Island, but salied out and drove the enemy off. We never were more than *one* to *three*, on the Island, neither was it so prudent to abandon other posts for that, as the shipping could & have since come up the East River and then our communication was gone, and the Army with it. We are now so as one part can get to the other, without water carriage, & think if we will only stand by each other, and not run home like cowards, with God's blessing, we may keep them off, which is a victory of itself! I have taken unwearied pains with the Militia, and I am afraid it is too much fatigue for me, as my cough is a little increased. But I hope it is only for a short time. . . . My expenses has been so large that my money falls a little short. I was obliged to entirely support the sick of my Reg^t for some time, but I suppose you have none to spare. I shall make out, but not so well as I could wish. . . .

IN THE FIELD AT THE LINES ON HARLAM HEIGHTS,
18th Sept 1776.

Since I wrote last we have had different scenes to go through. I lay with my brigade a little below Turtle Bay where we hove up lines for more than one mile in length. Gen'l Wadsworth managed the lines on the right and I on the left. We lay in the lines Friday and Saturday nights. Sunday morning at break of day, five ships weighed anchor and fell in close within a musket shot of our lines quite to the left of me. I then moved my brigade abreast of them. They lay very quiet until 10 o'clock and by that time they had about 80 of their boats from under Long Island shore full with men which contained about five or six thousand and four transports full ready to come in the second boats. They very suddenly began as heavy a canonade perhaps as ever was from no more ships, as they had nothing to molest them, but to fire on us at their pleasure, from their tops and everywhere—their boats got under cover of the smoke of the shipping and then struck to the left of my lines in order to cut me of from a retreat. My left wing gave way which was formed of the militia. I lay myself on the right wing waiting for the boats until Capt Prentice came to me and told me, if I meant to save myself to leave the lines for that was the orders on the left and that they had left the lines. I then told my men to make the best of their way as I found I had but about ten left with me. They soon moved out and I then made the best of my way cut. We then had a mile to retreat through as hot a fire as could well be made but they mostly overshot us. The brigade was then in such a scattered poster that I could not collect them and I found the whole army on a retreat. The regulars came up in the rear and gave me several platoons at a time when I had none of my men with me and I was so beat out that they would have had me a prisoner had not I found an officer that was obliged to leave his horse because he could not get him over a fence so as to get out of their way. I found myself gone if I could not ride. I went over the fence and got the horse over whilst they were firing, mounted him and rode off. We halted here at night and on Monday the enemy came on and we gave them a good drubbing. I have not time to give you the particulars of any part of our action. I have lost my major, a prisoner,—One sargeant or more killed and four wounded,—have missing out of my brigade which sustained the whole fire but 8 or 9 as yet. I hope God will be on our side at last. It is memoriable that I have lost no more and God be praised for it. Our lines are now good and if they dare come on without their shipping I hope we shall give them a drubbing. In the utmost haste

From your faithful husband

WM. DOUGLAS.

I this moment received yours of the 8th inst, but have not got my horse yet. he is left on the road. My love to the children.

WHITE PLAINS 31st Oct^r, 1776.

On Monday the enemy advanced to attack us at this place. I was ordered out with my regiment with three others to meet and endeavor to retard their march. We moved on and at about twelve were attacked by their advanced guard. We drove them back but soon after the main body came on and we stood them until they got on our flank and I ordered a retreat. We had a most severe fire to retreat under, ten men to our one, but we came off in good order and very surely fired on our retreat all the way. I lost three dead and five wounded. They cut my regiment off from our main body and got ahead of me but I took advantage of a wood and got clear of them. My regiment has the honour of behaving most nobly. They·are now near neighbors, our lines are about half a mile.

[Originals in possession of Benj. Douglas, Esq., Middletown, Conn.]

[No. 23.]

GEN. WOODHULL TO THE NEW YORK CONVENTION

HARLEM.

JAMAICA, August 27th, 1776.

GENTLEMEN—I am now at Jamaica with less than 100 men, having brought all the cattle from the westward and southward of the hills, and have sent them off with the troops of horse, with orders to take all the rest eastward of this place, to the eastward of Hempstead Plains, to put them into fields and to set a guard over them.

The enemy, I am informed, are entrenching southward, and from the heights near Howard's.

I have now received yours, with several resolutions, which I wish it was in my power to put in execution; but unless Cols. Smith and Remsen, mentioned in yours, join me with their regiments, or some other assistance immediately, I shall not be able, for the people are all moving east, and I cannot get any assistance from them. I shall continue here as long as I can, in hopes of a reinforcement; but if none comes soon, I shall retreat and drive the stock before me into the woods.

Cols. Smith and Remsen, I think, cannot join me. Unless you can send me some other assistance, I fear I shall soon be obliged to quit this place. I hope soon to hear from you.

I am, gentlemen, your most humble serv't.

NATHANIEL WOODHULL.

WESTWARD OF QUEENS COUNTY, August 27th, 1776.

Inclosed I send you a letter from Col. Potter, who left me yesterday at 11 o'clock, after bringing about 100 men to me at Jamaica. Major Smith, I expect has all the rest that were to come from Suffolk county. There have about 40 of the militia joined me from the regiments in Queens county, and about 50 of the troop belonging to Kings and Queens counties, which is nearly all I expect. I have got all the cattle southward of the hills in Kings county, to the eastward of the cross-road between the two counties, and have placed guards and sentinels from the north road to the south side of the Island, in order to prevent the cattle's going back, and to prevent the communication of the .tories with the enemy. I am within about six miles of the enemy's camp : their light horse have been within about two miles, and unless I have more men, our stay here will answer no purpose. We shall soon want to be supplied with provisions, if we tarry here.

JAMAICA, August 28th, 1776.

I must again let you know my situation. I have about 70 men and about 20 of the troop, which is all the force I have or can expect, and I am daily growing less in number. The people are so alarmed in Suffolk, that they will not any more of them march ; and as to Cols. Smith and Remsen, they cannot join me, for the communication is cut off between us. I have sent about 1100 cattle to the great fields on the plains, yesterday. About 300 more have gone off this morning to the same place, and I have ordered a guard of an officer and seven privates. They can get no water in those fields. My men and horses are worn out with fatigue. The cattle are not all gone off towards Hempstead. I ordered them off yesterday ; but they were not able to take them along. I yesterday brought about 300 from Newtown. I think the cattle are in as much danger on the north side as on the south side ; and have ordered the inhabitants to remove them, if you cannot send me an immediate reinforcement.

[Journals of the New York Provincial Congress.]

[No. 24.]

GEN. WASHINGTON TO ABRAHAM YATES, NEW YORK CON-VENTION

LONG-ISLAND, Aug. 28th, 1776.

SIR—I was just now honored with your favor of this date, with General Woodhull's letter, and should esteem myself happy, were it in my power to afford the assistance required, but the enemy having landed a considerable part of their force, here, and at the same time may have reserved some to attack New-York, it is the opinion, not only of myself, but of all my general officers I have had an opportunity of consulting with, that the men we have are not more than competent to the defence of those lines, and the several posts which must be defended. This reason, and this alone, prevents my complying with your request. I shall beg leave to mention, in confidence, that a few days ago, upon the enemy's first landing here, I wrote to Governor Trumbull, recommending him to throw over a body of 1000 men on the Island to annoy the enemy in their rear, if the state of the colony would admit of it. Whether it will be done I cannot determine. That colony having furnished a large proportion of men, I was, and still am, doubtful whether it could be done. If it could, I am satisfied it will, from the zeal and readiness they have ever shown to give every possible succour. I am hopeful they will be in a condition to do it; and if they are, those troops, I doubt not, will be ready and willing to give General Woodhull any assistance he may want. But cannot the militia effect what he wishes to do? They, I believe, must be depended on in the present instance for relief.

I have the honor to be, in great haste,

Sir, your most obedient servant,

GEORGE WASHINGTON.

[Journals of the New York Provincial Congress.]

[No. 25.]

COLONEL HITCHCOCK TO COLONEL LITTLE

CAMP ON LONG ISLAND.

N. YORK. Aug. 15th, 1776.

DEAR SIR, . . . Great Changes[1] and Alterations have lately been made; it gives me much Uneasiness that your Regiment is not going with mine; can't learn what kind of a Place it is we

[1] Col. Hitchcock had been ordered to Burdett's Ferry, opposite Fort Washington, on the Jersey side, but returned to Long Island on the landing of the enemy.

are ordered to take, but I sat out with a Determination to go anywhere & do anything, that I was ordered to do—were you going up there with your Regiment, with me, I should not wish to be better off. hope however we shall be able to defend Ourselves against Rattle Snakes without you, which I am told are very Plenty there; The General thinks however they [the enemy] will attempt to take & occupy the River on both Sides there & consequently has ordered two more of the established Regiments there ; if they come (& come they certainly will in a few Days) I will defend the Place as long as I can ; they have certainly been embarking for a Day or two ; I am yet fully of the Belief they will Land on Long Island for One of their Places & where else I don't know, but I'm fully persuaded, in more Places than One, I wish you & your Regiment all Happiness. I know you will all play the man—the critical Hour of America is come ; beat 'em once, they are gone—

Compliments Mr. Coleman.

Dear Sir Adieu

DAN HITCHCOCK.

AUG. 29th 1776.

The Wrench I recd in my Back by the Starting of my Horse at my Gun just as I was mounting him, was so great that I scarcely got off from my Bed next Day, but feel much better of it now ; I hear the Regulars have built a Fort on the Hill east of Fort Putnam ; I am astonished that our People are not building two Forts where you & I have always contended for Forts to [be] built For Heaven's Sake apply to the Generals yourself & urge the Necessity of it ; let two Forts be built there, & another just such abbatee as is built between Forts Greene & Putnam, from Water to Water ; it can be done in a Day—cut every apple tree down—if our People are in Spirits ; between us, I think our Salvation depends upon it for their Bombs will drive us out of Fort Putnam, & if they attempt to force & should get thro', we have 'em between two Fires.

[Originals in possession of Chas. J. Little, Esq., Cambridge, Mass.]

[No. 26.]

MAJOR TALLMADGE'S ACCOUNT OF THE BATTLES OF LONG ISLAND AND WHITE PLAINS.

The movements of the enemy indicating an intention to approach New York by the way of Long Island, Gen. Washington ordered about 10.000 men to embark and cross the East River at Brooklyn. The regiment to which I belonged was among the first that crossed over, and, on the 27th of August, the whole British army, consisting of their own native troops, Hessians, Brunswickers, Waldeckers, etc, to the number of at least 25,000 men, with a most formidable train of field artillery, landed near Flatbush, under cover of their shipping, and moved towards Jamaica and Brooklyn. As our troops had advanced to meet the enemy, the action soon commenced, and was continued, at intervals, through most of the day. Before such an overwhelming force of disciplined troops, our small band could not maintain their ground and the main body retired within their lines at Brooklyn, while a body of Long Island Militia, under Gen. Woodhull, took their stand at Jamaica. Here Gen. Woodhull was taken prisoner and inhumanly killed. The main body of our army, under Major-Gen. Sullivan and Lord Stirling, fought in detached bodies, and on the retreat both of those officers were made prisoners. I also lost a brother the same day, who fell into their hands, and was afterwards literally starved to death in one of their prisons ; nor would the enemy suffer relief from his friends to be afforded to him.

This was the first time in my life that I had witnessed the awful scene of a battle, when man was engaged to destroy his fellow man. I well remember my sensations on the occasion, for they were solemn beyond description, and very hardly could I bring my mind to be willing to attempt the life of a fellow-creature. Our army having retired beyond their intrenchment, which extended from Vanbrunt's Mills, on the West, to the East River, flanked occasionally by redoubts, the British army took their position, in full array, directly in front of our position. Our intrenchment was so weak, that it is most wonderful the British General did not attempt to storm it soon after the battle, in which his troops had been victorious. Gen. Washington was so fully aware of the perilous situation of this division of his army, that he immediately convened a council of war, at which the propriety of retiring to New York was decided on. After sustaining incessant fatigue and constant watchfulness for two days and nights, attended by heavy rain, exposed every moment to an attack from a vastly superior force in front, and to be cut off from the possibility of retreat to New York, by the fleet, which might enter the East River, on the night of the 29th of August, Gen. Washington commenced recrossing his troops from Brooklyn to New York. To move so large a body of troops, with all their necessary appendages, across a river full a mile wide, with a rapid current, in face of a victorious, well disciplined army, nearly three times as numerous as his own, and a fleet capable of stopping the navigation, so that not one boat could have passed over, seemed to present most formidable obstacles. But, in the face of these difficulties, the Commander-in-Chief so arranged his business, that on the evening of the 29th, by 10 o'clock, the troops began to retire from the lines in such a manner that no chasm was made in the lines, but as one regiment left their station on guard, the remaining troops moved to the right and left and filled up the vacancies, while Gen. Washington took his station at the ferry, and superintended the embarkation of the troops. It was one of the most anxious, busy nights that I ever recollect, and being the third in which hardly any of us had closed our eyes to sleep, we were all greatly fatigued. As the dawn of the next day approached, those of us who remained in the trenches became very anxious for our own safety, and when the dawn appeared there were several regiments still on duty. At this time a very dense fog began to rise, and it seemed to settle in a peculiar manner over both encampments. I recollect this peculiar providential occurrence perfectly well; and so very dense was the atmosphere that I could scarcely discern a man at six yards' distance.

When the sun rose we had just received orders to leave the lines, but before we reached the ferry, the Commander-in-Chief sent one of his Aids to order the regiment to repair again to their former station on the lines. Col. Chester immediately faced to the right about and returned, where we tarried until the sun had risen, but the fog remained as dense as ever. Finally, the second order arrived for the regiment to retire, and we very joyfully bid those trenches a long adieu. When we reached Brooklyn ferry, the boats had not returned from their last trip, but they very soon appeared and took the whole regiment over to New York; and I think I saw Gen. Washington on the ferry stairs when I stepped into one of the last boats that received the troops. I left my horse tied to a post at the ferry.

The troops having now all safely reached New York, and the fog continuing as thick as ever, I began to think of my favorite horse, and requested leave to return and bring him off. Having obtained permission, I called for a crew of volunteers to go with me, and guiding the boat myself, I obtained my horse and got off some distance into the river before the enemy appeared in Brooklyn.

As soon as they reached the ferry, we were saluted merrily from their musketry, and finally by their field pieces; but we returned in safety. In the history of warfare, I do not recollect a more fortunate retreat. After all, the providential appearance of the fog saved a part of our army from being captured, and certainly myself among others who formed the rear guard. Gen. Washington has never received the credit which was due to him for this wise and most fortunate measure. . . .

As the enemy showed a disposition to cross over into Westchester, Gen. Washington removed the main body of his army up to the White Plains, taking possession of the high ground North and East of the town. Here he seemed determined to take his stand, his lines extending from a mountain on the right, called Chadderton's Hill, to a lake or large pond of water on his left. An intrenchment was thrown up from right to left, behind which our army formed. Long poles with iron pikes upon them, supplied the want of bayonets. Chadderton's Hill was separated from the right of our intrenchment by a valley of some extent, with the river Bronx directly before it; but being within cannon shot of our intrenchment on the right, Gen. Washington thought it best to occupy it, and ordered Gen. McDougall, with 800 or 1000 men, to defend it, and if driven from it, to retire upon the right of the line. The American army were all at their several posts on the last September and beginning of October; and here it looked as if Gen. Washington intended to give battle to the British army. On the 27th October, 1776, it was announced at Head Quarters that the enemy was in motion from Westchester, through Eastchester, directly toward the White Plains. A detachment of

2000, or 3000 men was ordered to proceed on the Old York road to meet the enemy in front. As *our brigade* formed a part of the force, I, of course, was among them. Before the dawn of day, on the 28th of October, we learned that the enemy were in full march directly in front of us. Gen. Spencer, who commanded this body of troops in advance, immediately made the necessary disposition to receive the enemy, having the river Bronx on our right, and between us and the troops on Chadderton's Hill. At the dawn of day, the Hessian column advanced within musket shot of our troops, when a full discharge of musketry warned them of their danger. At first they fell back, but rallied again immediately, and the column of British troops having advanced upon our left, made it necessary to retire. As stone walls were frequent, our troops occasionally formed behind them, and poured a destructive fire into the Hessian ranks.

It, however, became necessary to retreat wholly before such an overwhelming force. To gain Chadderton's Hill, it became necessary to cross the Bronx, which was fordable at that place. The troops immediately entered the river and ascended the Hill, while I being in the rear, and mounted on horseback, endeavored to hasten the last of our troops, the Hessians then being within musket shot. When I reached the bank of the river, and was about to enter it, our chaplain, the Rev. Dr. Trumbull, sprang up behind me on my horse, and came with such force as to carry me with my accoutrements, together with himself, headlong into the river. This so entirely disconcerted me, that by the time I reached the opposite bank of the river, the Hessian troops were about to enter it, and considered me as their prisoner. As we ascended the hill, I filed off to the right, expecting our troops on the hill would soon give them a volley. When they had advanced within a few yards of a stone wall, behind which Gen. McDougall had placed them, our troops poured upon the Hessian column, under Gen. Rahl, such a destructive fire, that they retreated down the hill in disorder, leaving a considerable number of the corps on the field. This relieved me from my perilous situation, and I immediately remounted my horse, and taking my course in the valley, directly between the hostile armies, I rode to Head Quarters, near the Court-house, and informed Gen. Washington of the situation of the troops on Chadderton's Hill. The enemy having rallied, and being reinforced, made a second attempt upon Gen.

McDougall's detachment, who gave them a second warm reception; but, being overpowered, retired upon the right of our line, then in order of battle. A severe cannonade was kept up from both armies through the day, and every moment did we expect the enemy would have attempted to force us from our lines. In the mean time, Gen. Washington had begun to remove his stores and heavy baggage up to Northcastle. After remaining in our lines and on constant military duty for several days and nights, on the 1st of November Gen. Washington retired with his army to the heights in the neighborhood of Northcastle.

[Memoir of Col. Benjamin Tallmadge. Prepared by himself. New York, 1858.]

[No. 27.]

ACCOUNT OF EVENTS ON THE 15TH AND 16TH OF SEPTEMBER, 1776, BY PRIVATE JAMES S. MARTIN, OF COL. WM. DOUGLAS' REGIMENT

. . . . One evening while lying here (Turtle Bay) we heard a heavy cannonade at the city; and before dark saw four of the enemy's ships that had passed the town and were coming up the East River; they anchored just below us. These ships were the Phœnix, of 44 guns; the Roebuck of 44; the Rose of 32; and another the name of which I have forgotten. Half of our regiment was sent off under the command of our Major, to man something that were called "lines," although they were nothing more than a ditch dug along on the bank of the river, with the dirt thrown out towards the water. They staid in these lines during the night, and returned to the camp in the morning unmolested. The other half of the regiment went the next night, under the command of the Lieut.-Colonel, upon the like errand. We arrived at the lines about dark, and were ordered to leave our packs in a copse wood, under a guard, and go into the lines without them; what was the cause of this piece of *wise* policy I never knew; but I knew the effects of it, which was, that I never saw my knapsack from that day to this; nor did any of the rest of our party, unless they came across them by accident in our retreat. We "manned

6

the lines" and lay quite unmolested during the whole night. We had a chain of sentinels quite up the river for four or five miles in length. At an interval of every half hour, they passed the watch-word to each other—"All is well." I heard the British on board their shipping answer, "We will alter your tune before tomorrow night"—and they were as good as their word for once. It was quite a dark night, and at daybreak, the first thing that saluted our eyes, was all the four ships at anchor, with springs upon their cables, and within musket shot of us. The Phœnix, lying a little quartering, and her stern toward me, I could read her name as distinctly as though I had been directly under the stern—. As soon as it was fairly light, we saw their boats coming out of a creek or cove, on the Long Island side of the water, filled with British soldiers. When they came to the edge of the tide, they formed their boats in line. They continued to augment these forces from the Island until they appeared like a large clover field in full bloom. . . . . We lay very quiet in our ditch, waiting their motions, till the sun was an hour or two high. We heard a cannonade at the city, but our attention was drawn to our own guests. But they being a little dilatory in their operations, I stepped into an old warehouse which stood close by me, with the door open, inviting me in, and sat down upon a stool; the floor was strewed with papers which had in some former period been used in the concerns of the house, but were then lying in woful confusion. I was very demurely perusing these papers, when, all of a sudden, there came such a peal of thunder from the British shipping, that I thought my head would go with the sound. I made a frog's leap for the ditch, and lay as still as I possibly could, and began to consider which part of my carcass was to go first. The British played their parts well; indeed, they had nothing to hinder them. We kept the lines till they were almost levelled upon us, when our officers seeing we could make no resistance, and no orders coming from any superior officer, and that we must soon be entirely exposed to the rake of the guns, gave the order to leave the lines. In retreating we had to cross a level clear spot of ground, forty or fifty rods wide, exposed to the whole of the enemy's fire; and they gave it to us in prime order; the grape shot and langrage flew merrily, which served to quicken our motions. . . . We had not gone far (in the highway) before we saw a party of men, apparently hurrying on in the same direction with ourselves; we endeavored hard to overtake them, but on approaching them we found that they were not of our way of thinking; they were Hessians. We immediatel yaltered our course and took the main road leading to King's bridge. We had not long been on this road before we saw another party, just ahead of us, whom we knew to be Americans; just as we overtook these, they were fired upon by a party of British from a cornfield, and all was immediately in confusion again. I believe the enemies' party was small; but our people were all militia, and the demons of fear and disorder seemed to take full possession of all and everything on that day. When I came to the spot where the militia were fired upon the ground was literally covered with arms, knapsacks, staves, coats, hats and old oil flasks, perhaps some of those from the Madeira town cellar in New York. . . . . Several of the regiment were missing among whom was our major; he was a fine man, and his loss was much regretted by the men of the regiment. We lay that night upon the ground which the regiment occupied when I came up with it. The next day in the forenoon, the enemy, as we expected, followed us "hard up" and were advancing through a level field; our rangers and some few other light troops under the command of Col. Knowlton, of Connecticut and Major Leitch of (I, believe) Virginia, were in waiting for them. Seeing them advancing, the rangers, &c, concealed themselves in a deep gully overgrown with bushes; upon the western verge of this defile was a post and rail fence, and over that the forementioned field. Our people let the enemy advance until they arrived at the fence when they arose and poured in a volley upon them. How many of the enemy were killed & wounded could not be known, as the British were always as careful as Indians to conceal their losses. There were, doubtless, some killed, as I myself counted nineteen ball-holes through a single rail of the fence at which the enemy were standing when the action began. The British gave back and our people advanced into the field. The action soon became warm. Col. Knowlton a brave man and commander of the detachment, fell in the early part of the engagement. It was said, by them who saw it, that he lost his valuable life by unadvisedly exposing himself singly to the enemy. In my boyhood I had been acquainted with him; he was a brave man and an excellent citizen. Major Leitch fell soon after, and the troops who were then engaged, were left with no higher commanders than their captains, but they still kept the enemy retreating. Our regiment was now ordered into the field, and we arrived on the ground just as the retreating army were entering a thick wood, a circumstance as disagreeable to them as it was agreeable to us, at that period of the war. We soon came to action with them. The troops engaged being reinforced by our regiment kept them still retreating, until they found shelter under the cannon of some of their shipping, lying in the North River. We remained on the battle ground till nearly sunset, expecting the enemy to attack us again, but they showed no such inclination that day. The men were very much fatigued and faint, having had nothing to eat for forty-eight hours—at least the greater part were in this condition & I among the rest. . . . We had eight or ten of our reg^t killed in the action & a number wounded, but none of them belonging to our company. Our Lt. Col. was hit by a grape-shot, which went through his coat, westcoat and shirt, to the skin on his shoulder, without doing any other damage than cutting up his epaulette.

[*A Narrative of Some of the Adventures, Dangers and Sufferings of a Revolutionary Soldier, etc.* Hallowell, Me. 1830.]

[No. 23.]

CAPT. JOSHUA HUNTINGTON[1] TO ———

CAMP NEAR KING'S BRIDGE, Sept. 20, 1776.

You have most likely heard of our retreat from the city, before this, but I will give you some of the particulars. Sunday morning last, our regiment, with a number of other regiments, were ordered to the lines a little below Turtle Bay, where lay five or six ships within musket shot of our lines. About six o'clock a most furious cannonade began from the ships. At the same time the enemy landed a large body of men a little above where our men were posted, and marched directly for the main road in order to cut off our retreat, which they had like to have effected, as the

[1] Of Col. Samuel Selden's Conn. Regiment.

greatest part of our army were from six to fourteen miles distant from the city. In this skirmish we lost some men though I think not many. I have been unwell about a fortnight, with a slow fever and the camp disorder, which prevented my being in the skirmish. I had not passed the enemy but a little while before the enemy came up ; and if I had been with the regiment at the lines, I was so weak and feeble, I should without doubt have fallen into their hands. I have now left the regiment for a few days, and am with brother Chester, about sixteen miles from the city, getting better. . . .

: [Huntington Family Memoir, p. 164.]

[No. 29.]

LIEUT. TENCH TILGHMAN [1] TO HIS FATHER, PHILA-DELPHIA

HEAD QUARTERS N. YORK 3rd Sepr 1776.

HOND SIR

I have attempted to write to you several times since our Return from Long Island, but have been as often interrupted by the vast hurry of Business in which the General is engaged. He is obliged to see into, and in a Manner fill every Department, which is too much for one Man—Our Retreat [from Long Island] before an Enemy much superior in Numbers, over a wide River, and not very well furnished with Boats certainly does Credit to our Generals. The thing was conducted with so much Secrecy that neither subalterns or privates knew that the whole Army was to cross back again to N. York, they thought only a few Regiments were to go back. General Howe has not yet landed upon this Island, but I imagine something of that kind is in Agitation, as the Fleet drew nearer and nearer, they are now about long Cannon Shot from the Battery, but no firing on either side. We shall be prepared to meet them here or retreat over Kings Bridge as we shall find Occasion, our supernumerary and heavy stores are removed, we must leave our heavy Cannon behind us in Case of

[1] Aide-de-Camp to General Washington.

Retreat, but I dont know that that will be any loss, as we never used them to much advantage. . . .

I am most dutifully & Affect^y Yrs.

Tench Tilghman.

Head Quarters, Harlem Heights, Monday, 16 Sepr. 1776.

Our Army totally evacuated New York yesterday, the Enemy landed a party of about 3000 from Appearance four miles above the City where they encamped last Night. They kept up a very heavy fire from their Ships while their Men were landing, altho' no Body opposed them, I imagine they did it, thinking we might have some men concealed behind some lines on the Water side. We removed everything that was valuable, some heavy cannon excepted, before we left the Town. Our army is posted as advantageously as possible for Security, out of reach of the Fire of the Ships from either River; and upon high Grounds of difficult Access. I dont know whether the New Eng^d Troops will stand there, but I am sure they will not upon open Ground. I had a Specimen of that yesterday. Hear two Brigades ran away from a small advanced party of the Regulars, tho' the General did all in his power to convince them they were in no danger. He laid his Cane over many of the officers who shewed their men the example of running. These were militia, the New England Continental Troops are much better. . . .

Head Quarters Col^o. Morris's 19th Sepr. 1776.

. . . . On Monday last we had a pretty smart skirmish with the British Troops which was brought on in the following Manner. The General rode down to our farthest Lines, and when he came near them heard a firing which he was informed was between our Scouts and the out Guards of the Enemy. When our men came in they informed the General that there were a party of about 300 behind a woody hill, tho' they only showed a very small party to us. Upon this General laid a plan for attacking them in the Rear and cutting off their Retreat which was to be effected in the following Manner. Major Leitch with three companies of Col^o. Weedons Virginia Regiment, and Col^o Knowlton with his Rangers were to steal round while a party were to march towards them and seem as if they intended to attack in front, but not to make any real Attack till they saw our men fairly in their Rear. The Bait took as to one part, as soon as they saw our party in front the Enemy ran down the Hill and took possession of some Fences and Bushes and began to fire at them, but at too great distance to do much execution : Unluckily Col°. Knowlton and Major Leitch began their Attack too soon, it was rather in Flank than in Rear. The Action now grew warm, Major Leitch was wounded early in the Engagement and Col°. Knowlton soon after, the latter mortally, he was one of the bravest and best officers in the Army. Their Men notwithstanding persisted with the greatest Bravery. The Gen¹ finding they wanted support ordered over part of Col°. Griffiths's and part of Col°. Richardson's Maryland Regiments, these Troops tho' young charged with as much Bravery as I can conceive, they gave two fires and then rushed right forward which drove the enemy from the wood into a Buckwheat field, from whence they retreated. The General fearing (as we afterwards found) that a large Body was coming up to support them, sent me over to bring our Men off. They gave a Hurra and left the Field in good Order. We had about 40 wounded and a very few killed. A Serjeant who deserted says their Accounts were 89 wounded and 8 killed, but in the latter he is mistaken for we have buried more than double that Number—We find their force was much more considerable than we imagined when the General ordered the Attack. It consisted of the 2ᵈ Battⁿ. of light Infantry, a Battⁿ. of the Royal Highlanders and 3 Compˢ. of Hessian Rifle Men. The prisoners we took, told us, they expected our Men would have run away as they did the day before, but that they were never more surprised than to see us advancing to attack them. The Virginia and Maryland Troops bear the Palm. They are well officered and behave with as much regularity as possible, while the Eastern people are plundering everything that comes in their way. An Ensign is to be tried for marauding to-day, the Gen¹. will execute him if he can get a Court Martial to convict him—I like our post here exceedingly, I think if we give it up it is our own faults. You must excuse me to my other friends for not writing to them. I can hardly find time to give you a Line.

[Memoir of Lieut. Col. Tench Tilghman. J. Munsell, Albany, 1876.]

[No. 30.]

CAPT. JOHN GOOCH TO THOMAS FAYERWEATHER, BOSTON, MASS.

NEW JERSEY, FORT CONSTITUTION, Sept. 23, 1776.

I know you must be anxious for the certainty of events of which you can have at that distance but a confused account, as I was on the spot will endeavor to give you as Concise & Just account as possible ; on the 15th inst we evacuated New York & took all stores of every kind out of the city, and took possession of the hights of Haerlem eight miles from the City, the Enemy encamp'd about two miles from us ; on the 16th the Enemy advanced and took Possession of a hight on our Right Flank ab^t half a mile Distance with about 3000 men, a Party from our Brigade [Nixon's] of 150 men who turned out as Volunteers under the Command of Lieut. Col^o Crary of the Regm^t I belong to [Varnum's, R.I.] were ordered out if possible to dispossess them, in about 20 minutes the Engagement began with as terrible a fire as ever I heard, when Orders came for the whole Brigade immediately to march to support the first detachment, the Brigade consisted of ab^t 900 men, we immediately formed in front of the Enemy and march'd up in good order through their fire, which was incessant till within 70 yards, when we engaged them in that situation, we engaged them for one hour and eights minits, when the Enemy Broke & Ran we pursued them to the next hights, when we were ordered to Retreat. Our loss does not exceed in killed and wounded twenty five men, the loss of the Enemy was very considerable but cannot be ascertained, as we observed them to carry of their dead and wounded the whole time of the Engagement, they left a Number of killed and wounded on the Field of Battle & a great number of Small Armes, the great Superiority of Numbers and every other advantage the enemy had, when considered makes the Victory Glorious, and tho' but over a part of their Army yet the consequences of it are attended with advantages very great, as they immediately quitted the hights all round us and have not been troublesome since, our people behaved with the greatest Spirit, and the New England men have gained the first Lawrells. I received a slight wound in the Anckle at the first of the Engagement but never quited the field during the Engagement. I'm now Ready to give them the second part whenever they have an appetite, as I'm convinced whenever [they] stir from their ships we shall drubb them.

[N. E. Hist. and Gen. Register, vol. xxx.]

[No. 31.]

ACCOUNT OF THE RETREAT FROM NEW YORK AND AFFAIR OF HARLEM HEIGHTS, BY COLONEL DAVID HUMPHREY

On Sunday, the 15th, the British, after sending three ships o war up the North River, to Bloomingdale, and keeping up, for some hours, a severe cannonade on our lines, from those already in the East river, landed in force at Turtle bay. Our new levies, commanded by a state brigadier-general, fled without making resistance. Two brigades of General Putnam's division, ordered to their support, notwithstanding the exertion of their brigadiers, and of the commander-in-chief himself, who came up at the instant, conducted themselves in the same shameful manner. His excellency then ordered the heights of Harlaem, a strong position, to be occupied. Thither the forces in the vicinity, as well as the fugitives, repaired. In the mean time, General Putnam, with the remainder of his command, and the ordinary outposts, was in the city. After having caused the brigades to begin their retreat by the route of Bloomingdale, in order to avoid the enemy, who were then in possession of the main road leading to Kingsbridge, he galloped to call off the pickets and guards. Having myself been a volunteer in his division, and acting adjutant to the last regiment that left the city, I had frequent opportunities, that day, of beholding him, for the purpose of issuing orders, and encouraging the troops, flying, on his horse, covered with foam, wherever his presence was most necessary. Without his extraordinary exertions, the guards must have been inevitably lost, and it is probable the entire corps would have been cut in pieces. When we were not far from Bloomingdale, an aide-de-camp came from him at full speed, to inform that a column of British infantry was descending upon our right. Our rear was soon fired upon, and the colonel of our regiment, whose order was just communicated for the front to file off to the left, was killed on the spot. With no other loss we joined the army, after dark, on the heights of Harlaem. ——Before our brigades came in, we were given up for lost by all our friends. So critical indeed was our situation, and so narrow the gap by which we escaped, that the instant we had passed, the enemy closed it by extending their line from river to river. Our men, who had been fifteen hours under arms, harassed by marching and counter-marching, in consequence of incessant alarms, exhausted as they were by heat and thirst, (for the day proved insupportably hot, and few or none had canteens, insomuch, that some died at the works where they drank,) if attacked, could have made but feeble resistance. . . .

That night our soldiers, excessively fatigued by the sultry march of the day, their clothes wet by a severe shower of rain that succeeded towards the evening, their blood chilled by the cold wind that produced a sudden change in the temperature of the air, and their hearts sunk within them by the loss of baggage, artillery, and works in which they had been taught to put great confidence, lay upon their arms, covered only by the clouds of an uncomfortable sky. . . . Next morning several parties of the enemy appeared upon the plains in our front. On receiving this intelligence, General Washington rode quickly to the outposts, for the purpose of preparing against an attack, if the enemy should advance with that design. Lieutenant-colonel Knowlton's rangers, a fine selection from the eastern regiments, who had been skirmishing with an advanced party, came in, and informed the general that a body of British were under cover of a small eminence at no considerable distance. His excellency, willing to raise our men from their dejection by the splendor of some little success, ordered Lieutenant-colonel Knowlton, with his rangers, and Major Leitch, with three companies of Weedon's regiment of Virginians, to gain their rear; while appearances should be made of an attack in front. As soon as the enemy saw the party sent to decoy them, they ran precipitately down the hill, took possession of some fences and bushes, and commenced a brisk firing at long shot. Unfortunately, Knowlton and Leitch made their onset rather in flank than in rear. The enemy changed their front, and the skirmish at once became close and warm. Major Leitch having received three balls through his side, was soon borne from the field; and Colonel Knowlton, who had distinguished himself so gallantly at the battle of Bunkerhill, was mortally wounded immediately after. Their men, however, undaunted by these disasters, stimulated with the thirst of revenge for the loss of their leaders, and conscious of acting under the eye of the commander-in-chief, maintained the conflict with uncommon spirit and perseverance. But the general, seeing them in need of support, advanced part of the Maryland regiments of Griffith and Richardson, together with some detachments from such eastern corps as chanced to be most contiguous to the place of action. Our troops this day, without exception, behaved with the greatest intrepidity. So bravely did they repulse the British, that Sir William Howe moved his *reserve*, with two field-pieces, a battalion of Hessian grenadiers, and a company of chasseurs, to succor his retreating troops. General Washington not willing to draw on a general action, declined pressing the pursuit. In this engagement were the second and third battalions of light infantry, the forty-second British regiment, and the German Chasseurs, of whom eight officers, and upward of seventy privates were wounded, and our people buried nearly twenty, who were left dead on the field. We had about forty wounded; our loss in killed, except of two valuable officers, was very inconsiderable. An advantage so trivial in itself produced, in event, a surprising and almost incredible effect upon the whole army. Amongst the troops not engaged, who, during the action, were throwing earth from the new trenches, with an alacrity that indicated a determination to defend them, every visage was seen to brighten, and to assume, instead of the gloom of despair, the glow of animation. This change, no less sudden than happy, left little room to doubt that the men, who ran the day before at the sight of an enemy, would now, to wipe away the stain of that disgrace, and to recover the confidence of their general, have conducted themselves in a very different manner.

[Life of General Putnam, by Colonel Humphrey.]

[No. 32.]

TESTIMONY AT A COURT OF INQUIRY RESPECTING THE RETREAT FROM NEW YORK [1]

. . . . Brigadier General *Parsons*: Says on the 15th, he ordered three regiments of his brigade, viz : *Prescott's, Tyler's,* and *Huntington's,* to march from the lines near Corlear's Hook to assist the troops in the middle division under General *Spencer,* where the enemy were attempting to land ; that he soon rode on after these regiments by General Putnam's order, and found them in the main road ; asked the reason why they were not near the river where the enemy were landing, as he then supposed ; was told by the officers that the enemy's boats were gone farther east- ward, and probably would land at or near *Turtle's Bay,* on which they pursued their march on the road to the barrier across the street ; he, the examinant, being then near the rear of the three regiments, observed the front to advance on the road called *Bloomingdale* road, instead of going in the post-road ; on which he rode forward to the front of the brigade, in order to march them into the other road, when he found Colonel Tyler with his regiment, and was there informed they marched that way by order of Generals *Putnam* and *Spencer,* who were just forward ; this ex- aminant then rode forward on that road some little distance, per- haps sixty or eighty rods, to a road which turned off eastward to the post road, and found General *Fellows'* brigade in that cross road, marching eastward, and also saw Generals *Washington, Putnam,* and others, at the top of the hill eastward, and rode up to them ; General *Washington* directed that the examinant should attend to keep his brigade in order and march on into the cross road ; he accordingly rode back and met the brigade as they came into the cross road ; as he was riding back he saw Colonel Tyler in a lot on the south side the cross road coming from the *Bloomingdale* road to the cross road and asked him why he was

---

[1] Col. Tyler, commanding the 10th Regiment of Continentals (from Con- necticut) was ordered under arrest by General Washington for " cowardice and misbehaviour before the enemy on Sunday, the 15th instant." The testimony at the preliminary trial brought out someof the incidents of that day's confusion and panic.

not with the regiment; he said he was very much fatigued, it being very hot, and was going across the lot to join the regiment, it being nearer than to keep the road; this examinant then rode by the side of the brigade to near the top of the hill, his attention being to keep the brigade in order, and then heard General *Washington* call out, "Take the walls!" and immediately added, "Take the corn-field!" a corn-field being then on the right adjoining east on the main road, and north on the cross road; immediately from front to rear of the brigade the men ran to the walls, and some into the corn-field, in a most confused and disordered manner; this examinant then used his utmost endeavour to form the brigade into some order upon that ground, but the men were so dispersed he found it impossible; he then rode back into the *Bloomingdale* road and there found a considerable part of the brigade but in no order; General *Washington* was then forward in the *Bloomingdale* road, and sent for this examinant, and gave order to form the 'brigade as soon as could be done, and march on to *Harlem Heights ;* as soon as the brigade could be reduced to any form, they marched on to *Harlem Heights;* when they had proceeded about a mile or two, a sudden panick seized the rear of the brigade; they ran into the fields out of the road; the reason he knows not; in the fields he saw Colonel Tyler, which was the first time he recollects to have seen the colonel after the time he saw him crossing the lot to the front of his regiment. . . . . .

Ensign *Wait :* Says that he was in the rear of the first company of Colonel *Tyler's* regiment; that after the brigade had crossed over from the *Bloomingdale* road towards the post road, where they met the enemy, he saw Colonel *Tyler* at the head of the brigade; that when orders were given to man the stone wall, he saw the Colonel at the head of the regiment, who marched up to the fence and presented his piece, and supposes that he fired; that after that he understood that orders were given to go into the corn-field, that after they had got into the corn-field, and a principal part of the brigade were retreating, the examinant heard Colonel *Tyler* say to the men, " Why do you run ? this will never beat them ;" that at that time he supposes the Colonel was nearly in the same place where he was when the fire first began, and that from his behaviour, he has no reason to believe that the Colonel was at all intimidated; that from the situation the Colonel was in at the time of the firing, he has reason to believe that the Colonel was one of the last that retreated from the enemy; that the first time he noticed the Colonel after the retreat from the enemy, was when they had marched about a mile from the cross road up the *Bloomingdale* road, where they got into some order, and that after that the Colonel continued in the front till the brigade reached the Heights of *Harlem.* . . .

Paymaster *Sill :* Says that he had no opportunity of observing Colonel *Tyler's* conduct from the time that they crossed over from the *Bloomingdale* road towards the post road, and had returned back to the *Bloomingdale* road and marched up it one mile ; that when the brigade had marched up that far, there was a cry from the rear that the Light-Horse were advancing, and that a great part of the battalion which Colonel *Tyler* commanded precipitately threw themselves into the lot on the west side of the road ; that the Colonel went into the lot and this examinant with him ; that from the Colonel's conduct at this juncture, it appeared to this examinant that his design in going into the lot was to bring back the men to the brigade, for that in his presence and hearing the Colonel threatened to fire upon them if they did not join the brigade.

Sergeant *Palmer :* Says that when the brigade crossed over from the *Bloomingdale* road towards the post road, he was on the right of the front rank of the brigade which was led by Colonel *Tyler,* and that he had a full opportunity of observing the Colonel's conduct till the time of the retreat ; that on notice that the enemy were approaching and orders given to take the wall, the Colonel advanced to it, still keeping in the front, and was the first man in the brigade who fired ; that this examinant discharged his piece twice at the enemy, and on looking around he saw the whole brigade were retreating, the Colonel still remaining on the ground, with this examinant, and no person within several rods of them ; that upon this the Colonel ordered them to stop, and asked them why they run and commanded the officers to stop them ; that this not being effected, the Colonel and he retreated, the two last men of the brigade, the Colonel along the cross road as far as he remained in sight, and this examinant along the corn-field ; that when this examinant joined the brigade in the *Bloomingdale* road, he saw the Colonel at the head of it ; that when the cry was raised that the Light-Horse were advancing, which occasioned a great part of the battalion in front to betake themselves to the lot on the west side of the road, he heard the Colonel order them back.

Corporals *Brewster* and *Chapman* : Confirm what Sergeant *Palmer* said, that the Colonel was the last man that retreated from the enemy, and that they saw the Colonel, after having marched some distance on the cross road, strike off to the right, with intent, as they conceived, to get to the head of the regiment.

I do hereby certify that the whole Court were of opinion that there is not sufficient evidence to warrant the charge of cowardice and misbehaviour against Colonel Tyler ; and that this report would have been made immediately on taking the examinations, had not the Court apprehended that, the Colonel, having been put under arrest by express order from Head Quarters, some evidence against him might have been pointed out from thence.

CAMP AT WHITE-PLAINS, October 26, 1776.

JOHN MORIN SCOTT, Brigadier-General,
President.

[Force's Archives, Fifth Series, vol. ii. p. 1251.]

[No. 33.]

MAJOR BAURMEISTER'S NARRATIVE OF THE CAPTURE OF
NEW YORK, SEPTEMBER, 1776 [1]

IN CAMP AT HELEGATTE, September 24, 1776.

I had the honor on the 2d inst., of dispatching to Captain von Wangenheim a complete relation, to date, of our doings here with the condition, that he should send an exact copy of it to you, mentioning that the continuation would be forwarded to you, with a similar request to communicate it to Captain von Wangenheim. . . . I announced therefore, that the army camped from New Thown to Blockwels [*Blackwell's*] peninsula, only the brigade of Major-General Grand remained under the orders of General von Heister at Belfort [*Bedford*] opposite New York, with the two Hessian brigades of Major-Generals Stirn and von Mirbach, together with Captain Bitter's English artillery brigade, which were posted behind the hostile works, in order to keep the rebels

[1] Maj. C. L. Baurmeister, of the Hessian Division.

within bounds, in the city as well as in their redoubts thrown up
on the side of the city, for which end 1 Captain and 100 men,
towards noon on the 2nd. of September, were obliged to occupy
Gouverneurs Island, upon which were found 10 iron cannons
spiked, 4 18- and 6 32-pounders, many unfilled bombs, some thousand bullets, flour and salt meat in barrels. Every 24 hours this
post was relieved by the pickets of the English and Hessian regiments; the shore was occupied from Helgatte to Reed-Hurck.
Before Helgatte 2 frigates lay at anchor: la Brüne and Niger,
both of 32 guns, with a bombarding vessel, and on terra firma, just
to the left side of these vessels, a battery was erected of 2 24-
pounders, 4 12-pounders and 2 howitzers. Blockwell Island was
occupied by 1 Captain and 100 men of the English infantry, and
in the night of the 3d. of September the frigate Rose of 32 guns
sailed out of the fleet up the East River, with 30 boats, leaving
New York on the left, and without the slightest difficulty anchored
in Whall Bay [Wallabout] and Buschwickfeste. All the enemy's
cannon were put into a serviceable condition and conveyed to the
batteries, which were found in part and also erected on the rising
ground to the left of the village ferry as far as to Gouverneurs
Island. . . . Often in the night rebels came over to the English
camp in small boats, asked to serve, and enlisted in the newly
raised brigade, 2000 men strong, of a Colonel de Lancy, whose
ancestors settled on York Island, and who had much to suffer from
the present rebels. Some 100 men, from the prisoners of the
attack of August 27th., are also enrolled in this brigade. On the
4th. of September, the English left their post on Blockwells Island,
the rebels occupied it in force, and so strong, that the outposts on
the main shore were exposed to a continuous fire, which even the
great battery could not silence. The 5th. of September, 5 wagons
and the requisite draught horses were furnished to every regiment,
in New Thown also a forage magazine was erected, and the inhabitants of Long Island recognized the royal authority, excepting
the county of Suffolck, in which several thousand rebels still remain, not collected together but scattered, ready to fight against
us everywhere on the first opportunity; why now Brigadier General
Erkskine with his strong detachment advanced no farther than 9
English miles beyond Jamaika and the 6th of September was
obliged to return is not to be divined; it was then, that this best
part of Long Island should have been kept for the winter-quarters,

for till now wherever the army has been the country is stripped of
provisions, cattle and horses, as everything is declared rebel property; there is no longer an English regiment to be found incomplete in horses, and this want will soon no longer appear in the
Hessian regiments, as many officers obtain the horses they need
for little money and even for nothing. I myself have 3 in this
way.

The happiness of the inhabitants, whose ancestors were all
Dutch, must have been great; genuine kindness and real abundance
is everywhere, anything worthless or going to ruin is nowhere to
be perceived. The inhabited regions resemble the Westphalian
peasant districts, upon separate farms the finest houses are built,
which are planned and completed in the most elegant fashion.
The furniture in them is in the best taste, nothing like which is to
be seen with us, and besides so clean and neat, that altogether it
surpasses every description.

The female sex is universally beautiful and delicately reared,
and is finely dressed in the latest European fashion, particularly
in India laces, white cotton and silk gauzes; not one of these
women but would consider driving a double team the easiest of
work. They drive and ride out alone, having only a negro riding
behind to accompany them. Near every dwelling-house negroes
(their slaves) are settled, who cultivate the most fertile land, pasture the cattle, and do all the menial work. They are Christians
and are brought on the coasts of Guinea, being sold again here
among the inhabitants for 50 to 120 York pounds a head; 20
York shillings are such a pound and 37 York shillings make the
value of a guinea.

On the 7th the fleet was stationed between Reed Huck and
Governeurs Island nearer to New York, and the baggage of the
Hessian corps, remaining for the chief part on board was loaded
upon one transport for the greater convenience of each regiment,
whereby there was a great relief from the repeated sending, frequently in vain for want of boats. The Brocklands-Leinen was
to be demolished, but on the representation of General von Heister, that this could not be done by soldiers without compensation,
especially as it would be the work of four weeks, General Howe
recalled this order. . . . . .

Many subjects are returning to the legitimate authority, and on
Long Island the villages of Grevesand, New Utrecht, Flattbusch,

Brockland and Ferry are filled with the fugitive settlers, most of
whom however find their dwellings empty, furniture smashed, not
a window left whole and their cattle gone forever. . . . .

I am to present the compliments of General von Heister.
Colonel George Orboune, our Muster-Commissioner has already
reviewed us.   Major-Gen. Mirbach has had an attack of apoplexy,
but he expects to recover; but Major-General Stirn and Col. von
Hering are more sick.   *

With the greatest respect

(Signed)   BAURMEISTER.

IN THE DETACHED CAMP, AT HELGATTE, Sept. 24, 1776.

Magazine of American History, N. Y., January, 1877. Original in the possession of Hon. George Bancroft.]

[NO. 34.]

COLONEL JOHN CHESTER TO JOSEPH WEBB

WEATHERSFIELD, CONN.

FROM THE OLD HOUSE AT Yᴱ MANOR OF FORDHAM,

Oct. 3ᵈ, 76.

 . . . . The Enemy have not altered their situations much
since you left us.   Not long since Genˡ Putnam with a party of
16 or 1800 men as covering party went on to Harlem plains &
with a number of waggons brought off a large quantity of Grain,
but not the whole, for just at Day break the Enemy had manned
their lines & were seen in collumn advancing : as our party were
not more than half theirs it was thought best to retreat which was
done in good order & without a skirmish.   We are daily fetching
off large quantities of Hay & Grain from Morrisania as we are
daily in expectation of Landing & an attack there, though we are
determined not to leave the Ground without disputing it Inch by
Inch.   Whilst you was here there was a frigate opposite the Widᵒ
Morris's House.   Since that there has another come through &
anchored just above Hell Gate opposite Harlem Church almost.

Another has moved up East of Morrisania a mile or two near Frogs point where if they land they will probably march up through West Chester & come upon us by Williams's Tavern.

[Original in possession of Rev. Dr. John Chester, Washington.]

[No. 35.]

COL. JOHN GLOVER TO HIS MOTHER

MARBLEHEAD, MASS.

FORT CONSTITUTION, }
Oct. 7 : 1776. }

DEAR MOTHER :

. . . . On the 23^d (Sept.) a detachment from several Corps commanded by Lieut. Col. Jackson, consisting of 240 men were sent off to dislodge the enemy from Montressor's (Ward's) Island, for which purpose six boats were provided to carry 40 men each. Col. Jackson led, Major Hendly, of Charlestown with him. They were met by the enemy at the water's edge before they landed, who gave them a heavy fire. Notwithstanding this the Col. landed with the party in his boat, gave them battle and compelled them to retreat, called to the other boats to push and land, but the scoundrels, coward-like, retreated back and left him and his party to fall a sacrifice. The enemy seeing this, 150 of them rushed out of the woods and attacked them again at 30 yards distance. Jackson with his little party nobly defended the ground until every man but eight was killed on the spot, and himself wounded, before he ordered a retreat. Major Hendly carrying off Col. Jackson was shot dead as he was putting him into a boat, and not a single man of the 8 but what was wounded. One of them died at the oar before they landed on the Main. The officers who commanded the other boats are all under arrest and will be tried for their lives. In short if some example is not made of such rascally conduct, there will be no encouragement for men of spirit to exert themselves. As the case now is they will always fall a sacrifice, while such low-lived scoundrels, that have neither Honour nor the Good of their Country at heart, will skulk behind and get off clear. Yours &c JOHN GLOVER.

[Collections of the Essex, Mass., Institute, vol. v. No. 2.]

[No. 36.]

GENERAL GREENE TO COLONEL KNOX

WHITE PLAINS.

FORT LEE, Nov. [17], 1776.

Your favor of the 14th reached me in a melancholy temper. The misfortune of losing Fort Washington, with between two and three thousand men, will reach you before this, if it has not already. His Excellency General Washington has been with me for several days. The evacuation or reinforcement of Fort Washington was under consideration, but finally nothing concluded on. Day before yesterday, about one o'clock, Howe's adjutant-general made a demand of the surrender of the garrison in the general's name, but was answered by the commanding officer that he should defend it to the last extremity. Yesterday morning, General Washington, General Putnam, General Mercer, and myself, went to the island to determine what was best to be done; but just at the instant we stepped on board the boat the enemy made their appearance on the hill where the Monday action was, and began a severe cannonade with several field-pieces. Our guards soon fled, the enemy advanced up to the second line. This was done while we were crossing the river and getting upon the hill. The enemy made several marches to the right and to the left,—I suppose to reconnoitre the fortifications and the lines. There we all stood in a very awkward situation. As the disposition was made, and the enemy advancing, we durst not attempt to make any new disposition; indeed, we saw nothing amiss. We all urged his Excellency to come off. I offered to stay. General Putnam did the same, and so did General Mercer; but his Excellency thought it best for us all to come off together, which we did, about half an hour before the enemy surrounded the fort. The enemy came up Harlem River, and landed a party at head-quarters, which was upon the back of our people in the lines. A disorderly retreat soon took place; without much firing the people retreated into the fort. On the north side of the fort there was a very heavy fire for a long while; and as they had the advantage of the ground, I apprehend the enemy's loss must be great. After the troops retreated in the fort, very few guns were fired. The enemy approached within small-arm fire of the lines, and sent in a flag, and the garrison capitulated in an hour. I was afraid of the fort; the redoubt you and I advised, too, was not done, or little or nothing done to it. Had that been complete, I think the garrison might have defended themselves a long while, or been brought off. I feel mad, vexed, sick, and sorry. Never did I need the consoling voice of a friend more than now. Happy should I be to see you. This is a most terrible event: its consequences are justly to be dreaded. Pray, what is said upon the occasion? A line from you will be very acceptable.

I am, dear sir, your obedient servant,

N. GREENE.

No particulars of the action as yet has come to my knowledge. [Mem. on the back.] I have not time to give you a description of the battle.

[Life and Correspondence of Henry Knox, Maj. Gen., &c. By Francis S. Drake, Boston, 1873.]

[No. 37.]

DIARY OF REV. MR. SHEWKIRK, PASTOR OF THE MORA-
VIAN CHURCH, NEW YORK [1]

1775.

Sunday April 23rd.—In Town were many Commotions tho' it was Sunday, on account of various Reports, especially from Boston, that Hostilities had been begun between the King's Troops and the Provincials.

---

[1] A part of this diary was published in the *Moravian*, Bethlehem, Penn., in 1876, with notes prepared by Rev. A. A. Reinke, present pastor of the Moravian congregation in New York. The extracts for 1775 appear in print now for the first time, and, of the whole, only those which bear upon public affairs are given here. In 1776, the Moravian Church stood in Fair street (now Fulton), opposite the old North Dutch Church on the corner of William street.

Thursday 27th. Late in the evening, Br. & Sr. Van Vleck arrived from Bethlehem; but finding the Town in such Commotions, he did not think it proper to stay for the present, apprehending that he might be called upon to be a Member of the Committee, &c.; and therefore went the following Evening to Jacobsen's at Staten Island.

Saturday 29th.—This whole week, ever since last Sunday all was alarmed in the City; there was nothing but Comotion & Confusion. Trade & publick business was at a stand;—soldiers were enlisted; the Port was stopt, and the Inhabitants seized the Keys of the Custom House; took the Arms & Powder into their Custody, not trusting the Corporation, &c. A Panic & Fear seized the People; many were for moving into the Country, & several did. The case was the same with some of our People, & especially the Sisters;—we comforted & encouraged them as well as we could. To-day matters as to the Town took a Turn; the Divisions & Animosities among one another ceased; from whence [the most was to be feared at present;—they all in general agreed to stand by one another, & use moderate measures; & since then it is grown more quiet; & not so many fearful reports are spread.

Sunday 30th. This afternoon some of the new England Provincials came to Town.

Friday May 26th.—Being informed this Ev'ning that the Provincial Congress which has begun in this City, had made out that all those Ministers that preach in English are by Turns to open each day the Congress's Consultations with Prayers, some further Inquiry was made into this Matter, & we understood,

Saturday 27th that the Matter is not so general as it is thought, & that if it should be offer'd one may excuse one's self.

Tuesday June 6th.—There was again a Hurry in the Town on account of the King's Soldiers being taken on Board of the Man of War. But we remained in Peace.

Sunday 25th.—In the Town it was very noisy; for our Governor, W^m. Tryon was expected to come in on his return from England; and at the same time General Washington of the Provincials, who has been appointed Chief Comander of all the Troops by the Continental Congress. They would show some regard to the Governor too, but the chief attention was paid to Gen. Washington. At one Church the Minister was obliged to give over; for the People went out, when the General came, who was received with much ado. The Governor came on shore late in the Ev'ning.

Thursday August 24th.—Last night was a great Disturbance in the City. About Mid-night some of the Town Soldiers began to take away the Cañons from the Battery. The Asia Man of War watched their motion; the Captain Vandeput who is an humain Man & has no Intention to hurt the Town, but must protect the King's Property, fired a couple of guns about 12 o'clock;—his Barge & the Town People fired upon one another; on both sides some were wounded, & one of the Barge Men killed. The whole city got up; all was in alarm; the Drums beating, & the soldiers gathering together. They got away 21 Cañons; the Man of War fired a Broadside with balls, &c. Several houses were damaged. Many people flew from their houses, & among them Sr. Kilburn, who was but yesterday with her Effects, and many of Abr. V. Vlecks & his 2 little children, &c. come back to her own house. Thus things went on till Morning, & now the whole day thro' there is nothing but moving out of the Town; & fearful Reports. Several of our People moved likewise Abm. V. Vleck's family & Kilburn moved to Jas. Cargyll's, & on fresh alarming news the next day, with Eliz. Vandeursen & Hil. Waldron to Second River [New Jersey].

Friday 25th.—Things were the same in the Town as yesterday, & rather worse. A correspondence was carried on between the Capt. of the Asia, & the Mayor of the City, & thro' the latter with the Committee or Congress, to adjust matters. Gov. Tryon acted as Mediator. Some hot-headed Men seemed to insist on pursuing their rash measures, while others, & rather the Majority, did not approve of it.

Monday 28th.—The Moving out of the Town continues, & the City looks in some Streets as if the Plague had been in it, so many Houses being shut up. Br. & Sr. Seuneffs, with their 7 children, moved to-day to Philadelphia, for good & all.

Another measure in the Town, which takes place this Week, namely to divide all Men between 16 & 50 years into Ward companies, caused Troubles, & was one reason why Seuneff made Haste to get away, tho' he will doubtless meet with the same in Philad.

Monday Sept. 11*th.*—Last week & to-day several of the Inhabitants came back again to Town ; also some of our People.

Monday 18*th.*—The Town-Soldiers, or the Minute Men made a great Parade to-day ; marching with their Baggage & Provision, &c. It was thought they went on an Expedition, but it was only a Trial. They went but 5 miles, & came back in the Ev'ning ; they made not only for themselves, but for the greatest Part of the Inhabitants an idle, noisy, & exceedingly ill-spent Day ; & they got, most of them, drunk ; fought together where they had stopt ; & when they came back to Town ; so that many are now under the Doctor's & Surgeon's Hands. May the Lord have Mercy on this poor City.

Tuesday Oct. 10*th.*—On account of an attempt which had been made to take Blankets, Sheets, &c. out of the King's Store, the city was again in danger of being fired upon, & it caused new fear & alarm. However upon Consultations of the Comittee or Congress & the Corporation, the goods were carried back again, & this Storm blew over, tho' some ill designed Persons were not pleased with it.

Other accounts & Reports this Week made that several families move again out of the Town ; & it is observed that some of the Head-Men begin to hang down their Heads, & many believe they will be ruin'd men.

Monday 16*th.*—The Report that the Crown Officers, & also our Governor here, will be taken up, & on which account Gov. Tryon had wrote a Letter to the Mayor, which appeared in print, caused new Alarm this week.

Thursday 19*th.*—In the Afternoon a Captain [1] of the Rifle Men

---

[1] Capt. Michael Cresap, of Maryland.

who some time ago marched with his Company thro' Bethlehem, & now coming from Cambridge near Boston died here, was interred in Trinity Church-yard, with great Pomp, & military Honours. All the Companies, many of the Clergy Men, & a great Concourse of the People attended.

Saturday 21st.—In the afternoon Br. & Sr. Henry Van Vleck all on sudden resolved to leave N. York & to return to Bethlehem, or at least for the present to go to Brunswig. The Reason was because a Report was spread that a Transport with Troops had been cast away on the Jersey Coast; from whence it was concluded, & they thought to have sure Intelligence, that some Troops, with the Fleet from England, would be here soon. They went this Ev'ning to Powl's Hook.

1776.

Thursday 18th January.—Last night and to-day Troops came in from the Jerseys; the troubles begin again.

Monday 29th.—The troubles in the town increased. Tenbroeks' moved to Second River on Wednesday. They would have gone on Tuesday, but the weather was too bad.

Sunday 4th February.—This afternoon Mr. Lee, a General of the New English (New England) troops came to town; as also the " Mercury," a man of war, with General Clinton. The men of war *here* took a merchant ship coming in, &c.; all which made many commotions in the town.

Monday 5th.—Soldiers came to town both from Connecticut and the Jerseys, and the whole aspect of things grew frightful, and increased so from day to day. The inhabitants began now to move away in a surprising manner. The weather was very cold, and the rivers full of ice, which proved a great obstruction to the People's moving. However, in the middle of the week it thawed fast, which seemed also to answer the prevention of designs against the men of war, the execution of which might have proved very fatal to the city. One could not pass the streets without feeling a great deal; and at last we were obliged to encourage it that our sisters and young People might retreat. At the end of the week about 40 of our People were Moved.

Sunday 11th.—This was a gloomy day. The carts went all the day with the goods of the people that are moving; moreover, in the forenoon the Soldiers began to take away all the guns from the Battery and the Fort, and continued till late. This caused an hourly expectation, especially in the afternoon, that the men of war would fire; however they did not. It did not at all look like a Sunday. In some churches they had no service; in others hardly any People. In the forenoon we had a discourse from behind the table, from the yesterday's watch-word; "I the Lord do keep it; I will water it every moment, lest any hurt it," &c. In the afternoon was preaching on Lamentations III. 39–41: "Wherefore doth a living man complain, &c. Let us search and try our ways," &c. Both times we had more hearers than we expected.

Monday 12th.—His Majesty's ship, the "Mercury," with Genl. Clinton, and the "Transport" with the soldiers left the harbour yesterday, to proceed on their voyage southward. The moving out of the town continues.

Saturday 17th.—The whole week those of our people who are yet in town were visited. This morning the "Phœnix" went out of the harbor, down to the watering place and the hook. In the afternoon the "Asia," the ship with the Governor and the two Prices, moved also out of the east river, and when she was opposite the White Hall she was fast upon a rock. All was in agitation in town; and it seemed there was a thought of attacking her, &c.; but they dropt it; and with the high water the "Asia" got afloat and lies now in the bay below the Island.

Wednesday 21st.—In the afternoon Sister Esther Pell came to town from Middle Town Point. The boat she came in, laden with wood, was stopped by the men of war, and was sent back; but the passengers were allowed to come to town.

Sunday 25th.—In the forenoon only a discourse was kept on the watch-word of to-morrow. In the afternoon a sermon was preached on the day's gospel. Several of the New England people were present. In the town the work at the entrenchments continued, and some branches of trade were likewise working. At night Sister Shewkirk came back from Second River.

Wednesday 13th March.—A packet from England arrived once again, and brought an uncommon number of letters; but they came not on shore. The postmaster would not take them, for fear that they might be seized without the postage being paid. The people were not suffered to go on board to fetch them; unless they took an oath to tell nothing that is done in the city. A packet for Bethlehem, directed to Bro. Shewkirk, had been sent from England along with the government despatches post-free, and was brought by Mr. Ross in the King's Service, who had been on board privately.

Sunday 7th April.—Easter. To-day and last night the commotions in the city begin to be greater; attacks have been made on the little islands, and at the watering place.

Monday 8th.—Sister Kilburn who had got the officers, &c., out of her house, got it cleaned and in order again. Tho' these lodgers had been better than common soldiers, yet she found her house and premises much injured. Sister Hilah Waldron on the following days got likewise the soldiers out of one of her houses, but she has suffered a great deal more. Indeed it is beyond description, how these uncivilized, rude, and wild People, abuse the finest houses in the city.

Tuesday 30th.—Sisters Kilburn and Hilah Waldron, and Sister Boelens have got the soldiers out of their houses.

Friday 17th May.—This day had been appointed a day of fasting and prayer throughout the country; therefore we had preaching in the fore and afternoon. The Text, a. m., was from Joel ii. 12, 13, 14. "Therefore also now, saith the Lord, turn ye even to me with all your heart, and with fasting and with weeping, and with mourning; and rend your hearts and not your garments, and turn unto the Lord your God; for He is gracious and merciful, slow to anger and of great kindness, and repenteth Him of the evil. Who knoweth if He will return and repent, and leave a blessing behind Him?" The text, p. m., was from Hosea xiv. 1–3: "O Israel, return unto the Lord thy God, for thou hast fallen by thine iniquity," &c. Our Saviour gave grace, in this critical juncture of affairs, to keep in the speaking to the subject of the text, and to avoid in the application what might be exceptionable. We had a pretty numerous auditory in the afternoon; also some of the officers. All behaved with attention. To-day the news came that the Provincials have raised the Siege of Quebec, with the loss of their artillery, baggage, and some hundreds of sick.

Thursday 13th June.—Here in town very unhappy and shocking scenes were exhibited. On Munday night some men called Tories were carried and hauled about through the streets, with candles forced to be held by them, or pushed in their faces, and their heads burned; but on Wednesday, in the open day, the scene was by far worse; several, and among them gentlemen, were carried on rails; some stripped naked and dreadfully abused. Some of the generals, and especially Pudnam and their forces, had enough to do to quell the riot, and make the mob disperse.

Friday 14th.—A printed letter from the Continental Congress was distributed, which gave intelligence that for certain, within ten days, the fleet from Halifax would be here, and it was strongly recommended to make all possible defence. In consequence of this, many more troops came to town, and all was in alarm.

Tuesday 18th.—To-day men were drafted out of the different Ward Companies. This matter gave us some anxiousness. Our brethren could not stand out, as times and circumstances are, and had none to apply to. One Alleviation is, that a man drafted may hire another man, if he can get one. Of our people were only drafted Robt. Thomas and Abraham Van Vleck. The town is now pretty full again of the soldiers that are come from Pennsylvania and other parts; and the moving of the inhabitants out of town continues.

Saturday 22d.—Yesterday and to-day the news came that the fleet was arrived at the Hook, and the troops from Halifax; which caused new alarm.

Sunday 30th.—Some of the inhabitants moved to-day out of town ; the Provincial Soldiers were busy, and had no service ; and in general there is little attention paid to the Sunday. Our preachings were yet tolerably well attended. The to-day's Word was, " The work of Righteousness shall be Peace, &c." At 5 was the Congregational Meeting, in which we called to mind that to-day we conclude the first half of this year ; and how graciously our dear Lord has helped us through in the troubles of the country, that begun to increase much with the beginning of the year, and have lasted more or less ever since ; and now, as they approach yet more seriously, the watch-word with which we begin the next half year, is very comfortable, and was spoke upon : " Thou shalt know that I am the Lord, for they shall not be ashamed that wait for me." Our brethren and sisters parted as if there might again be a scattering, and it proved so ; for, the following week several more left again the town.

Monday 1st July.—The watch-word of the first day of this month was very comfortable, and suitable to the time we are in. In the evening the news came that the fleet, or part of it, had left the Hook, and was coming nearer.

Tuesday 2d.—This, and more so when towards noon the first ships appeared in sight this side the narrows,—put the whole town into commotion. On the one hand every one that could was for packing up and getting away ; and on the other hand the country soldiers from the neighboring places came in from all sides ; and *here* the Ward companies were likewise warned out. Theodore Sypher's wife and child came to our house, and staid with us this night ; but the next day went to a house a couple of miles out of town. In the evening we had our usual meeting.

Wednesday 3d.—Bro. Sleur who had brought his wife and daughter into the country put several of his things into Bro. Henry Van Vleck's vault ; we put also in some goods belonging to the house, &c. To-day we heard that the shop goods and clothes belonging to Sr. Hilah Waldron and sons, Henry Ten Broeck, Eliz. Van Deursen, Sr. Reed, Sr. Kilburn, Abr. Van Vleck, &c., to the amount of above £700, which went in a boat yesterday with several other people's goods were taken, with the boat,

by a Man of War. Our people would not have sent their goods
with this boat, if they had not been encouraged by the people be
longing to the boat, whom they knew ; and who repeatedly told
that they could not nor would they go *down* the river, but go *up*
the North river, or put the goods down at or about Powl's Hook ;
and yet they went straight down towards the fleet. There were
also some passengers on board. From all circumstances it
appeared plain that it was done designedly.

Thursday 4th.—The fear that the fleet would come up to the
town began to subside. It was heard that they had taken possession of Staten Island ; and that they would hardly advance
farther before the fleet from England arrives. The country
soldiers of the neighboring places were sent back again ; on the
other hand more of the New England troops came in.

Wednesday 10th.—Sr. Hilah Waldron, who had applied to
Washington to get a pass to Staten Island, but got none, went
again to Second river, in order to go with Sr. Kilburn to Elizabethtown, to try whether they could get one there ; for the captain of the Man of War had told them that he wished they would
come for their goods.

Friday 12th.—A few more ships came in through the Narrows,
and it was reported that the great fleet from England began to
arrive. In the afternoon about 3 o'clock there was unexpectedly
a smart firing. Two Men of War, with some Tenders came up.
They fired from all the batteries, but did little execution. The
wind and tide being in their favor, the ships sailed fast up the
North river, and soon were out of sight. When they came this
side of Trinity Church, they began to fire smartly. The balls and
bullets went through several houses between here and Greenwich.
Six men were killed ; either some or all by ill-managing the cannons ; though it is said that a couple were killed by the ship's
firing ; one man's leg was broke, &c. The six were put this evening into one grave on the Bowling Green. The smoke of the
firing drew over our street like a cloud ; and the air was filled
with the smell of the powder. This affair caused a great fright in
the city. Women, and children, and some with their bundles
came from the lower parts, and walked to the Bowery, which was
lined with people. Mother Bosler had been brought down into

their cellar. Phil. Sypher's, with their child, which was sick, came again to our house. Not long after this affair was over, the fleet below fired a Salute, Admiral Howe coming in from England. The Srs. Van Deursen and Reed would fain have gone out of town this evening, but they could not bring it to bear.

Sunday 14th.—It was a wettish day, and it looked as if all was dead in the town. The English (Church of England) churches were shut up, and there was services in none, or few of the others ; we had not many hearers either.

Tuesday 16th.—Bro. Wilson who came to town last Friday,—for he could be in peace no more at Second River, as the country people will have the Yorkers to be in town,—asked for a pass to go over on business ; but they would give him none. This week they have begun to let no man go out of the city. Last Sunday, a flag of truce brought a letter to Washington ; but having not the title which they give him here, it was not received. Yesterday a message was sent down from here ; to-day an answer came, (Geo. Washington, Eqr., &c., &c.,) but was again returned on account of the direction.

Thursday 18th, was the day appointed when Independence was to be declared in the City Hall here ; which was done about noon ; and the Coat of Arms of the King was burnt. An unpleasant and heavy feeling prevailed.

Saturday 20th.—About noon a General Adjutant from Lord Howe came, and had a short conversation with General Washington, in Kennedy's house. When he went away he said, it is reported, to Washington and the others with him : " Sir and gentlemen, let it be remembered that the King has made the first overture for peace ; if it be rejected, you must stand by the consequences ;" and thus—which seems to have been the main errand —he departed. Much politeness passed on both sides.

Monday 22nd.—Our Bro. Wilson looking at the ferry, whither his negro was come with some goods from Second River, was put under arrest by one Johnson, and treated very basely by him, on account of a charge laid against him by one Gordon, at the Falls, about 12 miles from Second River ; that he and his son had spoken against the American cause; were dangerous persons; and had done much mischief to their neighborhood, &c. Bro. Wilson appeared before the Committee, the chairman knew nothing of the charge. Wilmot, one of the Committee did, but they could prove nothing; and Wilson could easily clear himself. The result was,—if he resided at Second River, they thought he should stay there. Many persons were ordered to-day to quit the town, because they were suspected.

Tuesday 23*d.*—Bro. Wilson got a pass, and went to Second River to-day.

Monday 29*th.*—Bro. Wilson came from Second River; he had got a certificate of the Committee there, which cleared him sufficiently of the late charge; and the Committee here gave him a pass to go to Pennsylvania. He brought letters from Bethlehem, where he intends to go this week; and returned to Second River this afternoon. He also brought word that our people have got their goods that were taken with the boat.

Wednesday 14*th August.*—There was much alarm in the town, as it was expected that the next morning an attack would be made on the city by the King's troops; which however, did not prove so.

Saturday 17*th.*—Towards night a proclamation was published, in which all women, children, and infirm people were advised to leave the city, with all possible speed; as a bombardment was expected; those that were indigent should be assisted and provided for. This caused a new fright. Some of the sisters yet in town came to Br. Shewkirk to advise with him about it.

Sunday 18*th.*—Early in the morning the two men of war and their tender, that had been up the North River, came back; which caused again a sharp cannonading till they were passed. Yesterday, a fortnight ago, they had been attacked by the Row-gallies and a Privateer, which were obliged to desist from their attempt; having been gradually worsted by the men-of-war, and lost several of their men. Last week they attacked them with fire-ships, but could not obtain their end, and lost one of their captains; they then sunk vessels, and thought to be sure of having stopped their passage; however, they came back. It was a rainy morning, with a north east wind. The fright seemed to be not as great as it was when they went up; and yet the balls hurt more houses; some men were likewise hurt.

Phil. Sypher's experienced a kind preservation. A nine pounder came through the old German church on the Broad Way, into the house they lived in, opposite the Lutheran church, and into the room where they slept; but they were up and out of the room. The ball come through the window, which it mashed to pieces, with part of the framework; went through the opposite wall near the head of the bedstead; crossed the staircase to another room; but meeting with a beam in the wall, came back and went a part through the side wall, and then dropt down on the stairs. A thirty-two pounder, supposed coming from the Powlis Hook battery, fell into Sr. Barnard's garden, just before her door. If there was service kept, it was but in one church. Our preaching in the forenoon was on Jer. 45 : 19; "I said not unto the seed of Jacob, seek ye me in vain," &c., and in the evening from Matt. 6, 19 20; "Lay not up for yourselves treasures on earth" &c.

Wednesday 21st.—In the evening . . . a very heavy thunder storm came on. It lasted for several hours, till after 10 o'clock; an uncommon lightning; one hard clap after the other; heavy rain mixed at times with a storm like a hurricane. The inhabitants can hardly remember such a tempest, even when it struck into Trinity church twenty years ago; they say it was but one very hard clap, and together did not last so long by far. Upon the whole it was an awful scene. Three officers, viz., one Captain, and two Lieuts., were killed in one of the Camps; they were all Yorkers; and one soldier of the New English People was likewise killed in a house in the square; several others were hurt, and the mast of one of the row gallies mash'd to pieces.

Thursday 22d and *Friday 23d.*—The king's troops landed on Long Island. The troops from here went over, one Battalion after the other, and many kept on coming in; yet, upon the whole their number certainly was not so great as it commonly was made. In the evening we had the congregational meeting with the little company that was present. We resolved to drop

8

the Wednesday meeting for the present, and to begin that on
Tuesday and Friday at 6 o'clock.

Monday 26th.—A good deal of firing was heard on Long
Island, and several skirmishes happened between the scouting parties, wherein the Provincials sustained loss.

Tuesday 27th was a Fast and Prayer-day in this Province;
which had been appointed by the Convention; but here in the
city it was not and could' not be observed. On the one hand,
there are but few inhabitants in the town, and the soldiers were
busily employed; on the other hand there was much alarm in the
city. Soon, in the morning, an alarm gun was fired in expectation,
that the ships were coming up; which however proved not so;
but on Long Island there was a smart engagement, in which the
Americans suffered greatly. Two generals, Sullivan and Sterling,
and many other officers and soldiers were taken prisoners. All
the troops now went over; those from King's Bridge came likewise, and went over the next morning. As very few of our
people came, we kept only a little meeting in the forenoon, in
which a short discourse was kept on Jer. 48, 17 and 18.; and
concluded with a moving prayer, kneeling. This (the result of
the battle) was an agreeable disappointment for all honest men;
for what could such a fast signify, when men want to pursue
measures against the Word and Will of God, &c.

Wednesday 28th.—The different parties on Long Island kept on
to be engaged with one another; the firing was plainly heard.
Bro. Shewkirk met with a young man, who waited on Ensign Good-
man, and who was come back from Long Island. He told him
that he, and a small number of his regiment—Huntington's,—had
escaped with their lives. It had been a sight he should never forget; such as he never wished to see again. This young man is
of a serious turn, and religious more than common, and promises
to be the Lords'. In the afternoon we had extraordinary heavy
rains and thunder. From one of the Forts of the Continental
army on Long Island, two alarm guns were fired in the midst of
the heavy rain; supposing that the regulars would attack their
line somewhere between Flatbush and Brockland; all the men
were ordered out though it rained prodigiously; it was found,

after some time, that it was a false alarm. The sound of these alarm guns had just ceased, when, immediately after, a flash of lightning came, followed by a clap of thunder. It was awful. The very heavy rain, with intermixed thunder, continued for some hours till towards evening. In the night the battling on Long Island continued, and likewise,

Thursday 29th; and in the afternoon such heavy rain fell again as can hardly be remembered; nevertheless the operations on Long Island went on more or less; and behold, in the night, the Americans thought it advisable to retreat, and leave Long Island to the King's troops. They found that they could not stand their ground, and feared to be surrounded, and their retreat cut off. The great loss they had sustained, the want of provision and shelter, in the extraordinary Wet; the unfitness of many of their troops for war, &c.; undoubtedly contributed to this resolution.

Friday 30th.—In the morning, unexpectedly and to the surprize of the city, it was found that all that could come back was come back; and that they had abandoned Long Island; when many had thought to surround the king's troops, and make them prisoners with little trouble. The language was now otherwise; it was a surprising change, the merry tones on drums and fifes had ceased, and they were hardly heard for a couple of days. It seemed a general damp had spread; and the sight of the scattered people up and down the streets was indeed moving. Many looked sickly, emaciated, cast down, &c.; the wet clothes, tents, —as many as they had brought away,—and other things, were lying about before the houses and in the streets to-day; in general everything seemed to be in confusion. Many, as it is reported for certain, went away to their respective homes. The loss in killed and wounded and taken has been great, and more so than it ever will be known. Several were drowned and lost their lives in passing a creek to save themselves. The Philadelphia, Pennsylvania, and Maryland people lost the most; the New England people, &c., it seems are but poor soldiers, they soon took to their heels. At night, the few that came or would come, had a meeting on the texts; and the next day we ended this troublesome month with the watch-word, " He that believeth shall not make haste." " Grant me to lean unshaken, &c."

Sunday 1st September.—We had our preaching in the forenoon, and in the evening as usual; and in the afternoon the Congregation meeting. At the preachings we had goodly companies of strangers.

Tuesday 3d.—The evening meeting was on the Watchword and Text. The rebel army begun to re-collect themselves; and the greatest part marched towards Harlem, and along the East River, some miles from here; the king's army advanced eastward on Long Island, opposite the Hell Gate, and thereabouts.

Monday 9th.—Whereas the troubles of War were now near Watts' House, Phil. Sypher fetched his wife, child, and goods back from thence to town, as also the things out of the Chapel House that had been there; and it was just high time, else they might have been lost; for this house soon after was plundered by the king's troops. Several other people came back from those parts. By the measures and proceedings of the Rebel army, it appeared evident, that they intended to leave the city; for as they had begun last week, so all this week, they removed their sick, their stoves, and ammunition, and gradually the soldiers marched away. They likewise took the bells out of all the Churches and conveyed them away.

Wednesday 11th and *Thursday 12th.*—Night and day they were busy to bring their things away; and it appeared plain, that there would be a change soon; the reports were various. Almost daily there was firing from Long Island to Horn's Hook, and the ship yards here.

Friday 13th.—In the afternoon, some. Men of War went up the East river; the few cannons left, fired on the ships, which caused that they fired back from Long Island and Governor's Island and very smartly. Isaac Van Vleck, who is too much bewildered in the matter, made haste to get out of town.

Saturday 14th.—In the afternoon more ships went up the East River, which being fired on again, brought on another smart cannonading; some Houses were damaged and it was very unsafe to walk in the streets. The remainder of the Rebel army hasted away, and so did the members of the Committee, and others of the deluded people.

Sunday 15th.—Soon in the morning when the tide served, more ships passed up both the North and East river; and though what was yet in town of the Rebel troops got away as fast as they could, yet they fired again on the ships, as they did likewise from Powles Hook; which caused a cannonading which made the houses shake, and the sound of it was terrible. One large ball, supposed to come from Powles Hook flew against the North Church, just opposite the chapel broke, and a part of it went back into a neighboring cellar kitchen, where a negro woman was, who came running over to the kitchen of the chapel-house; where also Syphers' family was, who had been there all night, as they lived near the fort, where the houses were most exposed to the firing. After some time the firing ceased, and at the usual time we had the forenoon's preaching, in all stillness; the only service kept in the city. About this time the king's troops had landed on York Island, about three miles from the city; there was some slaughter, and the rebels were made to retreat towards Harlem. In the afternoon at three was the congregation meeting; but the evening preaching we thought proper to drop. There was a good deal of commotion in the town; the Continental stores were broke open, and people carried off the provisions; the boats crossed to Powles' Hook backward and forward yet till toward evening; some people going away and others coming in; but then the ferry boats withdrew, and the passage was stopped. Some of the king's officers from the ships came on shore, and were joyfully received by some of the inhabitants. The king's flag was put up again in the fort, and the Rebels' taken down. And thus the city was now delivered from those Usurpers who had oppressed it so long.

Monday Sept. 16th.—In the forenoon the first of the English troops came to town. They were drawn up in two lines in the Broad Way; Governor Tryon and others of the officers were present, and a great concourse of people. Joy and gladness seemed to appear in all countenances, and persons who had been strangers one to the other formerly, were now very sociable together, and friendly. Bro. Shewkirk, who accidentally came to it, met with several instances of that kind.—The first that was done was, that all the houses of those who have had a part and a share in the Rebellion were marked as forfeited. Many indeed were marked by persons who had no order to do so, and did it perhaps to one or the other from some personal resentment. Bro. Shewkirk, walking through the streets, saw to his grief, that several houses belonging to our people were likewise marked; as Sr. Kilburn's, Hilah Waldron's, and Sr. Bouquet's, King's, Isaac Van Vleck's, &c. He wrote afterwards to Governor Tryon, congratulating him on the late happy event, and at the same time interceded in behalf of the 2 Ww's houses. The word of this day was remarkable : " Israel shall be saved in the Lord, with an everlasting salvation ; ye shall not be confounded world without end." The following day everything was pretty quiet, though almost daily they brought in prisoners, who were lodged in the Dutch and Presbyterian churches. The fear one had of the city's being destroyed by fire subsided, and the inhabitants thought themselves now pretty secure ; little thinking that destruction was so near.

Friday 20th.—Bro. Jacobsen came from Staten Island, and it was a true mutual joy to see one another; as, for a couple of months we could have no communication with Staten Island. By him we heard that our people there were all well.

Saturday 21st.—In the first hour of the day, soon after midnight, the whole city was alarmed by a dreadful fire. Bro. Shewkirk, who was alone in the chapel-house, was not a little struck, when he saw the whole air red, and thought it to be very near ; but going into the street, he found that it was in the low west end of the town ; and went thither. When he came down the Broad Way, he met with Sr. Sykes and her children. She was almost spent carrying the child, and a large bundle besides. He took the bundle, and went back with them, and let them in to our house ; when he left them, and returned with their prentice to the fire, taking some buckets along. The fire was then in the lower part of Broad street, Stone street, &c. It spread so violently that all what was done was but of little effect ; if one was in one street and looked about, it broke out already again in another street above ; and thus it raged all the night, and till about noon. The wind was pretty high from southeast, and drove the flames to the northwest. It broke out about White Hall ; destroyed a part of Broad street,

Stone street, Beaver street, the Broadway, and then the streets going to the North River, and all along the North river as far as the King's College. Great pain was taken to save Trinity church, the oldest and largest of the English churches, but in vain ; it was destroyed, as also the old Lutheran church ; and St. Paul's, at the upper end of the Broadway, escaped very narrowly. Some of our families brought of their goods to our house. Bro. Shewkirk had the pleasure to be a comfort to our neighbors, who were much frightened the fire might come this way ; and indeed, if the wind had shifted to the west as it had the appearance a couple of times, the whole city might have been destroyed. The corner house of our street, going to the Broadway, catched already ; Bro. Shewkirk ordered our long ladder, and the others to be fetched out of our burying ground ; which were of service in carrying the water up to the roof of said house in buckets ; and by the industry of all the people the fire was put out. Several of our people have sustained considerable loss : Sr. Kilburn has lost two houses ; Pell's three houses ; Jacobson one, and Widow Zoeller her's ; and others have lost a part of their goods ; as Lepper, Eastman, &c.

There are great reasons to suspect that some wicked incendiaries had a hand in this dreadful fire, which has consumed the fourth part of the city ; several persons have been apprehended ; moreover there were few hands of the inhabitants to assist ; the bells being carried off, no timely alarm was given ; the engines were out of order ; the fire company broke ; and also no proper order and directions, &c. ; all which contributed to the spreading of the flames.

Monday 23d.—The fire has thrown a great damp on the former joyful sensation ; numbers of people were carried to Jail, on suspicion to have had a hand in the fire, and to have been on the Rebel's side ; it is said about 200 ; however, on examination, the most men were as fast discharged.

Bro. Conrad, also, was taken to Jail, but after a couple of days he came out again. Daniel Van Vleck expected the same, which made his wife and family much distressed ; for he had often talked too inconsiderate, and in a wrong spirit ; however it blew over. After all, it is observable, that those of our people who had kept themselves free from the Infatuation, were acknowledged as such, and met with nothing disagreeable of that kind.

November.—In November new troubles began on account of the quartering of the soldiers, of whom more and more come in ; as also many of their women and children. Many of the public buildings were already filled with Prisoners, or sick, &c ; especially all the Dutch and Presbyterian churches, as also the French church, the Baptists, and new Quaker meeting ; and we were not without apprehension, that something of that nature might come upon us ; and this the more, as the Chapel-House has the appearance of a spacious building ; and just opposite the same they were fitting up the fine north church of the English Dutch for Barracks.

Saturday 16th.—From early in the morning till towards noon, a heavy cannonading was heard, tho' at a considerable distance ; one heard afterwards that the king's troops had attacked the lines and the famous Fort Washington, and carried it ; several thousands of the rebels were taken prisoners, &c. The king's army has been about 2 months thereabouts ; and there have been, from time to time, sharp engagements, at the White Plains, &c ; till at last they have driven them away from the York Island ; and it was a matter of moment, as now one may hope that the communication with the Jerseys will be open'd, as also with the places up the East River ; so that the Inhabitants may come to the city and provisions be brought in ; especially wood, which is not to be had, and is extremely dear ; a cord of oak wood, bought formerly for 20s. now 4£s. Fort Constitution, or Lee, opposite Fort Washington, now Fort Kniphausen, on the Jersey side surrender'd, or was left by the rebels ; and the king's troops got soon master of this part of the Jerseys, and advanced swiftly towards Philadelphia.

Monday, 18th.—In the forenoon, about 11 o'clock, 2 officers, with 2 other gentlemen came to see the chapel and house ; Bro. Shewkirk showed them about ; one of the officers asked whether service was kept in the chapel ; and hearing it was, said, it would be a pity to take it ; the other ran about very swiftly, and saw every part of the premises. Bro. Shewkirk, who easily could guess what the meaning was, as soon as they were gone, made application to the present commanding General Robertson, and to Governor Tryon. The former was not at home ; the latter received him kindly, but said he could do nothing in the matter, as now all the power was lodged with the army; yet he would recommend the matter to the General; and this he did in a few lines he wrote under the petition, referring it to the favorable consideration of the General. Bro. Shewkirk carried it to him, but he was not come home yet, and so he left it there. He did not know that the 2000 and more prisoners taken in Fort Washington, had come already to town. In the afternoon about 4 o'clock he saw at once the street before the window full of people. The serjeant of the guard came to the door, and asked whether this was the Moravian meeting? He was order'd to bring these 400 prisoners here by command of the Generals Smith and Robertson. If the latter had order'd it, it may be it was done before he came home to his quarters. Bro. Shewkirk, who was alone in the house, did not know what to do; he could not go away. By and by the Major who had command of the prisoners and another man came in; they looked at the Chapel, and said it was too small; the latter said he had told that before, he had been in the place before now, and knew it. He spoke to Bro. Shewkirk, and condoled with him that the place should be taken; they began to doubt of the certainty, and thought there was a mistake in the matter; another young man of the city who knwos Bro. Shewkirk, and has now the care of the provisions for the rebel prisoners, was likewise inclined in our favour. These 3 persons went backward and forward to make another inquiry; at last one of them came back and told he had met with the Deputy Barrack Master, a Jew; who had told him they must be here. Well—the gate on the men's side was open'd.

The serjeant of the guard, quite a civil man, advised to take all loose things out of the chapel before the prisoners came in. This was done accordingly. Phil. Sykes, who was come before this time, and extremely welcome, while Bro. Shewkirk was alone in the house, assisted herein; as also young Wiley; and it took up some time, during which the Major came again, and order'd the serjeant to wait awhile longer; he would go to Genl. Robertson. After some time he came back, and addressed Bro. Shewkirk in a friendly manner; saying, he had believed they would have been a disagreeable company; and took the prisoners to the North Church. Bro. Shewkirk thanked the Major for his kindness; may the Lord reward him as also the other two men. The pris-

oners, with the guard, stood above half an hour in the street before our door, and many spectators, of whom none, so far as one
could see, showed a wish for their coming in, but several signified
the reverse, and were glad when it did not take place. An old
gentleman, several weeks after, accosted Bro. Shewkirk in the
street, and told him how sorry he had been when he saw these
people standing before our door; he had heard Bro. Rice, &c.
After this affair was over, Bro. Shewkirk retreated to this room,
and thanked our Saviour, with tears, for his visible help; He has
the hearts of all men in His hands. If these prisoners had come
in, how much would our place have been ruined, as one may see
by the North Church; not to mention the painful thought of
seeing a place dedicated to our Savior's praise, made a habitation
of darkness and uncleanness. Praise be to Him and the Father!

As the winter quarters of the soldiers in this city were not
settled yet, the apprehension was not over, that some would be
put to us; and so one of our neighbors thought, who in time of
peace was one of the Common Council men; but at the same
time he assured Bro. Shewkirk that as far as he knew, none of
the creditable and sensible men of the town, wished it out of
spite, &c. Bro. Shewkirk's character was well-known, but the
house was large, and there was want of room.

Sunday, December 1st.—In the afternoon about two o'clock, a
company of officers came into the House, looking for some quarter for themselves. It was assured by some that they would not
disturb our church and service; some talked but of some rooms;
others said they must have the whole house, and the chapel too.
One, a Cornet of the Light Horse marked one room for himself;
desired to clear it this afternoon, and let him have a table and a
couple of chairs, and he would willingly pay for it. After they
were gone, Bro. Shewkirk, and Wilson who was just with him,
went to Genl. Robertson. The Genl. was kind; he said he had
given them no orders; he intended to have no place disturbed
where service was kept. He took down Bro. Shewkirk's name
and the matter; which chiefly was, not to disturb our chapel, nor
to desire the whole house, Bro. Shewkirk offer'd a couple of rooms
if necessary; and at last said he would go to Alderman Waddel.
He was along with the officers in the street, before they came in,
but told Wilson he had nothing to do with it; he only upon their

desire had gone along with them, and hear what he knew of the matter, and they should come along with him. When they were on the way, they met one of those officers, (the Genl's clerk) and indeed him, who spoke the most imperiously, and that he would have the chapel; upon which the Genl. and they returned to the Genl's house. The officer spoke here quite in another tone and said he had already told the other to look out for another place, etc. The Genl. said he would see about the matter, and give an answer the next morning. The brethren went home, and Bro. Shewkirk held the congregation meeting for which the brethren and sisters were gathered together. Upon this occasion we found again that our neighbors were not against us. One said, it cannot be that they would take your place, the only place where public service was held when there was none in the whole city. In the evening the room which the Cornet had marked was cleared, in case he should come; but none of them came again. Some time after, Dr. Edmunds, belonging to the hospital came one day, and with much civility and modesty inquired after a room. Bro. Shewkirk, thinking perhaps it might be a means to be free from a further endeavor of somebody's being quartered here,—and moreover wishing to have a man in the house in these days,—offered him the room the Cornet had marked; and after some weeks he came, and proves a very civil and quiet gentleman, who causes little or no troubles.

Monday 2nd.—The commissioner's extraordinary gracious proclamation in the name of the King, was published in the public papers; by virtue of which all rebels within 60 days may return without suffering any forfeiture or punishment; and it has had a great effect; numbers are come in, have signed the prescribed declaration, availed themselves of the benefit of the proclamation, and returned to the peaceable enjoyment of their property; though afterwards some of them have shown their insincerity and bad principles, going back again to the rebels. The officers yesterday doubtless thought in a hurry to secure lodgings to themselves before the proclamation was published, as now they can't take houses as they please. This was also the answer Genl. Robertson gave to Bro. Wilson this morning, when he carried in his name, and mentioned again our house and chapel. The Genl. said the proclamation would settle these matters.

Tuesday 31st.—Whereas it is at present very unsafe in the evenings to be out, on account of several late robberies, and persons having been knocked down besides, we were obliged to submit to the 'times and circumstances; and therefore the congregation members met at 4 o'clock in the afternoon, and had a love feast; to praise together our dear and gracious Lord for all his goodness bestowed on us during this year full of troubles. Indeed these times have been a time of shaking, and what had no root is dropped off.

1777.

Tuesday 7th January.—Since the attack and defeat which the Hessians sustained near Trenton some time ago, the rebels are again in high spirits; and whereas the King's troops have been ordered down towards Philadelphia from Newark, and about Hackensack, the rebels are come again to these places, and distress the inhabitants greatly. Several are come to town, having fled from thence.

Tuesday 14th.—Upon the request of General Howe to lend our benches for the entertainment on the Queen's birthday, several wagons full were fetched.

Saturday 18th.—Several reports prevailed that a part of the rebel army was approaching this city, and early this morning they had made an attack upon a fort above King's Bridge; but they were repulsed. Some of the soldiers here were ordered up that way to-day, and all the night soldiers kept a look-out.

Monday 20th.—It appears from the public papers, that intelligence has been had of a further intention to destroy this city by fire. For this reason the city watch has been regulated anew, according to which about 80 men watched every night in the different wards. Besides this, some of the Light Horse patrol the streets in the night. Some other regulations were likewise published, which give again an aspect of matters coming again into some order. The effect has also shown itself, the breaking down of fences, &c., does not go on as it did for a while; the bread is larger &c.

To-day a beginning was made with the inhabitants to take the oath of allegiance to his Majesty. Every day 2 wards are taken ; it is done before the governor, mayor, &c.

Thursday 6th February.—Our burying ground at Fresh Water, (corner of Mott and Pell streets) lies entirely open ; not the least of a board or post is left.

Sunday 16th.—The evening preaching at 6, was on a part of the to-day's Epistle : 2 Cor. vi : 1, 2 ; the subject,—" not to receive the grace of God in vain." When near the conclusion, another cry of fire was heard in the street, so that the last verses could not be sung. It happened to be in the Broadway, but was put out soon.

Monday 17th.—Towards evening there was another alarm of fire, but it proved to be a false one, and the engines were ordered back.

Thursday 4th March.—In the afternoon was the burial of Dr. Autchmuty, Rector of Trinity Church here, who departed this life last Tuesday. Bro. Shewkirk was invited, and was one of the ministers that were pall-bearers. There was a large company of ministers present ; the most of them were strangers, partly belonging to the army. He was buried in St. Paul's. The weather was bad, raining and snowing, yet there was a great concourse of people. Mr. Inglis kept the funeral service.

Sunday 16th.—Some wild officers who came into the evening meeting disturbed the devotion somewhat; however they went away soon ; the auditory was pretty large and attentive.

Tuesday 18th.—We have had fine weather of late. On Sunday night about 100 of the rebels being in a house somewhere above King's Bridge, some of the King's troops went to take them prisoners ; and as soon as they saw and heard nothing of an opposition, they surrounded the house, and the Captain and some men went in ; but some of the rebels took up their guns, and killed the captain, and 4 or 5 men ; upon which the others rushed in with their fixed bayonets, killed about 40, and took the rest prisoners. In the Jerseys some fightings have likewise been within these days.

Wednesday 29th May.—The King's troops are preparing for the campaign, and to leave the town and winter quarters. The day before yesterday some of the fleet with fresh troops from home arrived, and yesterday a large number of troops came in from King's Bridge to embark.

Saturday 31st.—As many troops are come in, some were lodged in the North Church opposite us, who made a great wild noise. They were of the recruits that are come from England. Others were lodged in the Methodist meeting, and in the old Dutch church, &c.

Tuesday 3rd June.—The packet came in, as also more troops; but we got no letter.

Wednesday 4th.—At noon a salute was given from all the ships in the river, this being His Majesty's birthday. In the evening meeting we blessed our dear king; afterwards the front of our house was illuminated with 48 candles, and made a fine sight to the satisfaction of the beholders. To-day our Sister Len. Venema came back out of the country to our joy.

Thursday 5th.—In these days the troops were moving, and everything was in an emotion; and on

Friday 6th.—Many went away into the Jerseys; more of the German troops were arrived.

Wednesday 25th.—An account had come to town within these days, that the intended expedition of the army had not succeeded:—finding the rebel army too much entrenched and fortified; and therefore they had returned to Amboy; would leave the Jerseys, embark, and go upon another expedition. A good many of the army came to town, especially also women and children, so as to make the place and streets pretty full again. Several of the Jersey inhabitants flocked likewise to the city. In the evening the xii. chapter of the Hebrews was read, and spoken on.

Saturday 28th.—Since Thursday, a report prevailed that there had been a smart battle in the Jerseys. After the King's troops had embarked, and the day was appointed to sail on an expedition, the general got intelligence that part of the rebel army was come within three miles from Amboy; upon which the troops were ordered back on shore, and march'd in the night to surround the rebels, with whom Washington was, it is said. The reports vary much, and were exaggerated exceedingly : 1,100 killed of the King's troops; 5 or 6,000 of the rebels; as many taken prisoners, and their artillery; they were surrounded with Washington; that they could not escape; nay, Washington was among the slain; Stirling dead of his wounds; Genl. Livingston likewise, &c.; 400 Pennsylvanians had grounded their arms, and come over to the regulars, &c., &c. To-day, the account fell very much, and came down to a few hundreds lost on the rebel side; how many on our side, is not said at all. Seventy were taken prisoners, who were, together with a couple of field-pieces, brought to town early in the morning. Matters go but slow, and cause concern to all disinterested well-wishers.

Thursday 3rd July.—The King's army has left the Jerseys, and is come back to Staten Island. Many came to town daily; so that it grows quite full again for the present. The rebels have now the whole Jerseys again except Powless's Hook; and we are just where we were last year, after the being in possession of N. Y. Island. 'Tis very discouraging, may the Lord pity this poor country.

[Original in the Archives of the Moravian Church.]

[No. 38.]

MAJOR NICHOLAS FISH TO RICHARD VARICK

NEW YORK, April 9, 1776.

I have since my last been on Several Excursions in military Capacity—That to West Chester County to Guard the Cannon & find out the Authors of Spiking them, has probably ere this time reached you; I shall not therefore trouble you with a detail.

You wish to hear what we are about in New York [   ]

To be informed, picture to yourself the once flourishing City evacuated of most of its Members (especially the fair). Buisiness of every kind stagnated—all its streets that lead from the North and East Rivers blockaded, and nothing but military opperations our Current Employment.

I have been engaged for near three Weeks with the first independent Battalion on fatigue duty, in erecting a Redoubt round the Hospital, which we compleated on the 2^d instant. This, tho' you will suppose it did not agree well with the tender Hands & delicate Textures of many, was notwithstanding with amazing agility and neatness, and laying vanity aside, is generally judged to be the best work of the kind in the city; the Hospital round which our Works are, is made an Arsenal for Provisions. On Bayards Mount now called Montgomerie Mount, as a Monument to that great Heroe, who honorably fell supporting freedom's cause, there will be a Fortification superior in Strength to any my Imagination could ever have conceived. Several hundred Men have been daily employed there for upwards of four Weeks. The Parapet of the old Battery is raised to a proper Height, with a sufficient number of Ambersures—As also the Parapet on the Fort Wall. There are two fortifications on Long Island opposite this City to command the shipping, one on Gou^{rs} Island, one at red Hook, and the City itself and Suburbs filled with them. Sundays we have none of, all Days come alike when [   ] is in question. We have $Genl^s$ Putnam, Sullivan, Heath, Thompson, & Ld Sterling among us, with I believe about 14 Thousand Troops; fresh arrivals from Cambridge Daily. And Washington hourly expected with many more—On Sunday the 7th instant there was an Exchange of many shot between our Rifle Men on Staten Island, and the Man of War, who sent Barges there for Water, of which the Riflemen prevented their supplying themselves—We know of four of their Men being killed, nine wounded, and have 12 Prisoners. Our Com^y now Guards the Records of the Province which are removed to Mr. N. Bayards Farm. . . . .

[Hist. Mag., Second Series, vol. v. p. 203. Communicated by Hon. Hamilton Fish.]

[No. 39.]

SURGEON WILLIAM EUSTIS TO DR. TOWNSEND

BOSTON, MASS.

NEW YORK, 28th June, 1776.

MY DEAR FRIEND,

. . . . You will be in Boston long before this can reach you, and will doubtless have heard of the Discovery of the greatest and vilest attempt ever made against our country: I mean the *plot*, the infernal *plot* which has been contrived by our worst enemies, and which was on the verge of execution: you will, I say, undoubtedly have *heard* of it, but perhaps I may give you a better idea of it than as yet you have obtained. The Mayor of York with a number of villains who were possessed of fortunes, and who formerly ranked with Gentlemen, had impiously dared an undertaking, big with fatal consequences to the *virtuous* army in York, and which in all probability would have given the enemy possession of the city with little loss. Their design was, upon the first engagement which took place, to have murdered (with trembling I say it) the best man on earth: Genl Washington was to have been the first subject of their unheard of SACRICIDE: our magazines which, as you know, are very capacious, were to have been blown up: every General Officer and every other who was active in serving his country in the field was to have been assassinated: our cannon were to be spiked up: and in short every the most accursed scheme was laid to give us into the hands of the enemy, and to ruin us. They had plenty of money, and gave large bounties and larger promises to those who were engaged to serve their hellish purposes. In order to execute their Design upon our General, they had enlisted into their service one or two from his Excellency's *life-Guard*, who were to have assassinated *him:* knowing that no person could be admitted into the magazines or among the cannon but those who were of the Artillery they have found several in our Regiment vile enough to be concerned in their diabolical Designs—these were to have blown up the Magazines and spiked the cannon. (Tell Homans, one Rotch, a fellow he bled for me in Morton's company at N° 1 is taken up

9

with his brother for being concerned.)   Their Design was deep, long concerted, and wicked to a *great Degree*.   But happily for us, it has pleased God to discover it to us in season, and I think we are making a right improvement of it (as the good folks say). We are hanging them as fast as we find them out.   I have just now returned from the Execution of one[1] of the General's Guard: he was the first that has been tried: yesterday at 11 o'clock he received sentence, to-day at 11 he was hung in presence of the whole army.   He is a Regular-Deserter . . . . he appeared unaffected and obstinate to the last, except that when the Chaplains took him by the hand under the Gallows and bad him adieu, a torrent of tears flowed over his face; but with an indignant scornful air he wiped 'em with his hand from his face, and assumed the *confident look*.   You remember General Greene commands at Long Island; with his last breath the fellow told the spectators, that unless Gen[l] Greene was very cautious, the Design would *as yet* be executed on him.

The trial will go on, and I imagine they will be hung, gentle and simple, as fast as the fact is proved upon them.

That any set of men could be so lost to every virtuous principle, and so dead to the feelings of humanity as to conspire against the person of so great and good a man as Gen[l] Washington is surprising; few of our countrymen (as you may well imagine) are concerned; they are in general foreigners: upwards of 30 were concerned, and 'tis said Gov[r] Tryon is at the bottom. . . . . .

Our Expedition against the Light house did not succeed; they command it so well with y[e] shipping that 'tis thought wise to let it stand. . . . .   W. EUSTIS.

Monday Morning July 1st.—Since writing the above upwards of 100 sail have arrived: we conclude that the whole fleet is there: for we have counted 140 topsail vessels; some say there are 160: people are moving out of York; and I think we must very soon come to action; the flower of our Reg. is picked for a field fight, which we imagine will take place on long island.   Wherever I am, whatever I am doing, my best wishes will be for the felicity of my friend.   Adieu.   Heaven preserve us to meet again.

[New England Hist. and Gen. Register, vol. xxiii. p. 205.]

[1] Thomas Hickey.

[No. 40.]

CAPTAIN NATHAN HALE TO HIS BROTHER

New York, Aug. 20th, 1776.

Dear Brother,

I have only time for a hasty letter. Our situation has been such this fortnight or more as scarce to admit of writing. We have daily expected an action—by which means, if any one was going, and we had letters written, orders were so strict for our tarrying in camp that we could rarely get leave to go and deliver them.— For about 6 or 8 days the enemy have been expected hourly, whenever the wind and tide in the least favored. We keep a particular look out for them this morning. The place and manner of attack time must determine. The event we leave to Heaven. Thanks to God! we have had time for compleating our works and receiving reenforcements. The militia of Connecticut ordered this way are mostly arrived. Col. [Andrew] Ward's Reg^t has got in. Troops from the Southward are daily coming. We hope, under God, to give a good account of the Enemy whenever they choose to make the last appeal.

Last Friday night, two of our five vessels (a Sloop and a Schooner) made an attempt upon the shipping up the River. The night was too dark, the wind too slack for the attempt. The Schooner which was intended for one of the Ships had got by before she discovered them; but as Providence would have it, she run athwart a bomb-catch which she quickly burned. The Sloop by the light of the fire discovered the Phœnix—but rather too late —however, she made shift to grapple her, but the wind not proving sufficient to bring her close along side or drive the flames immediately on board, the Phœnix after much difficulty got her clear by cutting her own rigging. Serg^t Fosdick who commanded the above Sloop, and four of his hands, were of my Company, the remaining two were of this Reg^t.

The Genl has been pleased to reward their bravery with forty dollars each, except the last man who quitted the fire Sloop, who had fifty. Those on board the schooner received the same.

I must write to some of my brothers lest you should not be at home. Remain

Your friend and Brother

N. HALE.

MR. ENOCH HALE.

[*Life of Captain Nathan Hale, the Martyr-Spy of the American Revolution.* By I. W. Stuart, Hartford, 1756.]

[No. 41.]

EXTRACT FROM A LETTER FROM NEW YORK

NEW YORK, April 12 1776.

" If you have any idea of our situation, you must be solicitous to hear from us. When you are informed that New York is deserted by its old inhabitants, and filled with soldiers from New England, Philadelphia, and Jersey—you will naturally conclude, the *Environs* of it are not very safe from so undisciplined a multitude, as our Provincials are represented to be; but I do believe, there are few instances of so great a number of men together, with so little mischief done by them; they have all the simplicity of ploughmen in their manners, and seem quite strangers to the vices of older soldiers. They have been employed in erecting fortifications in every part of the town; and it would make you sorry to see the place so changed: the old fort walls, are demolished in part, although that is an advantage to the Broadway. There is a Battery carried across the street, erected partly at Lord Abingdon's expense, for the Fascines, were cut out of the *wood* that belonged to the Warren estate: it was beautiful *wood*—Oliver De Lancey, had been nursing it these forty years; it looks in a piteous state now: Mr. D. hoped to have it somewhat spared by telling the New England men, who were cutting it, that a third part belonged to one of the *Protesting Lords.* One of them answered, ' Well, and if he be such a great liberty boy, and so great a friend to our country, he will be quite happy that his wood, was so *happy* for our use.' You remember Bayard's Mount covered with cedars? It commanded a prospect exceedingly extensive! The top of it is so cut away, that there is room enough for a house and garden; a fortification is there erected as well as round the *Hospital:*—in short, every place that can be employed in that way, is or will be, so used. You may recollect a sweet situation at Horn's Hook, that Jacob Walton purchased, built an elegant house, and greatly and beautifully improved the place; he was obliged to quit the place; the troops took possession, and fortified there. Oh, the houses in New York, if you could but see the insides of them! Kennedy's house, Mallet's, and the next to it, had six hundred men in them. If the owners ever get possession, they must be years in cleaning them. The merchants have raised their goods to an enormous price; many articles are scarce indeed; and there is quite a hue and cry about *pins.* Common rum, 6 to 7 shillings per gallon; poor sugar, 4l a hundred; molasses none; cotton 4s per pound."

[From the Historical Magazine.]

[No. 42.]

EXTRACTS FROM THE LONDON CHRONICLE

SEPT.—OCT. 1776.

FROM A BRITISH OFFICER AT NEW YORK, SEPT. 6, 1776.

"General Howe finding himself at the head of 21,000 men, in high health and fit for action, was determined to begin upon it as soon as possible; accordingly a great number of regiments were reimbarked on board the transports, and everything prepared for an Expedition, so secret, that neither the second in Command at land or sea could guess where the blow was to fall.

Everything being prepared, and the Cannon embarked in the night of the 21st of September [August], the Rainbow of 50 guns, commanded by Sir George Collier, got under weigh, and anchored near a strong post of the enemy's, called Denysys, upon Long Island, who fled from thence instantly, expecting the man of war would level the place to the ground.

A little after nine, the transports all anchored in Gravesend-bay on the southern part of Long Island; the flat-bottom boats immediately landed the troops, and the gallant Lord Howe was present to direct the operation.

The army, when landed, consisted of 18000 men, the rest being left upon Staten Island. Lord Cornwallis Commanded one of the advance-posts, Gen. Grant another, and Earl Percy had a post of difficulty and danger, to which he on all occasions shewed himself equal. The King's forces lay still, getting ashore Cannon &c. for 3 or 4 days, and then encamped at Flatbush; after this they moved on in three bodies, and surprised many of the enemy's outposts, and killed and took a number of men."

LETTER FROM NEW YORK.

OCT. 20, 1776.

" No doubt but before you receive this you'll be informed of the King's troops being in possession of New York, to the great satisfaction of the loyal part of its inhabitants, who have for a long time suffered every hardship from a set of tyrants that is possible to be conceived; however, they are now rewarded who have withstood the traitors, and remained firm to their King. The Howes do all that is possible to alleviate the sufferings of a persecuted people, who rather than turn rebels have despised death and ruin; and if it had not pleased God to send us death and relief, dreadful would have been the consequence to every person that dared to be honest; however, we are now protected in our lives and properties; and some thousands have joined the King's troops; and every time they attack the rebels they rout them with great loss; they fly before our victorious army on every onset; and I don't doubt but in a very little time this daring rebellion will be crushed. It would before now have been the case, had not the Americans been fed with hopes from the Court of France. But now let France or any other Power dare to assist them, we are prepared, and don't at all fear but we shall be able to give them a proper reception. It is resolved to attack Washington directly. Proper dispositions are making for that purpose; and I hope by the next letter to give you an account of an end being put to a government that have dared to call themselves the Independent States of America. Almost all the New Yorkers have returned to their allegiance, and there is not a doubt but the other Colonies will do the same when they dare declare themselves, and be properly supported by government.

There is a broad R put upon every door in New York that is disaffected to government, and examples will be made of its inhabitants; on the other hand, every person that is well affected to government finds protection."

LETTER FROM WHITE PLAINS.

"The following Letter is from an officer of eminence, who was present at the engagement at White Plains, to his friend in Edinburgh:

Camp at White Plains, 31 Miles from New York, N.E. within six Miles of Hudson's River, Nov. 2, 1776.

" Our whole army, except about 2000 men, left New York Island, and on the 12th of Oct. passed Hell-gates in our flat boats, and landed on a part called Frogs-neck, in Westchester county ; here we halted a few days, until provisions were brought to us; and on the 18th we again took to our boats, and passed a creek, in order to move this way, and to cut the rebels off from King's-Bridge. On our march the 18th, we had two pretty smart skirmishes, but made the provincials give way as fast as we advanced. After marching about three miles, we halted to get cannon, provisions, &c. brought forward. On the 26th we marched again by New Rochelle, about four miles without opposition, where we halted till the 28th ; and finding that the rebels had moved to this place from King's-bridge, we followed them, and drove them from hill to hill, until we came within three quarters of a mile of their entrenched camp, where they made a shew of disputing a commanding ground. A brisk Cannonade ensued, and we attacked them on the top of a rugged hill, where, though covered behind stone walls and fences, we drove them off. We had about 200 killed and wounded. The rebels left about 50 killed, besides what they carried off. We then encamped on the ground, with an intent to drive them from their entrenchments; but yesterday at day-break they went off of themselves and took post on another hill, about three-quarters of a mile further on where they are now. They have left a post behind them in New York Island, near King's-bridge of about 1500 men, [Fort Washington] which, I think, we shall give a very good account of. We have taken in their abandoned works 74 pieces of cannon. Their whole force is now opposed to us. They burn all the country as they retreat; they are a set of base fellows. I do not imagine we shall go much further this campaign, but just force them to go towards New England. I heard from Col. Campbell the other day. He is well and anxious to be relieved. I write on my knee very cramped, and have lain in a waggon for three nights past, one of which was very wet."

[No. 43.]

EXTRACT FROM THE MEMOIRS OF COLONEL RUFUS PUTNAM [1]

WRITTEN BY HIMSELF

The 31st of March 1776, I received General Washington's orders " to march to New York by the way of Providence, to afford Governor Cooke my best advice and assistance in the construction of the work there." In this tour I went to visit Newport again, where I laid out some additional works; on my return from Newport to Providence I met with General Washington there, I believe the 6th of April, and obtained leave to go by Brookfield to New York. I believe I tarried with my family part of two days and then pushed for New York where I arrived about the 20th. On my arrival at New York I was charged as chief engineer with laying out and overseeing the works which were erected during the campaign at New York, Long Island and their dependencies with Fort Washington, Fort Lee, King's Bridge, etc., most of which, but not all, appear in a plan of New York island etc., and obstructions in the river, which accompanies Marshall's Life of Washington. This was a service of much fatigue, for my whole time was taken up from daylight in the morning until night in the business, besides sometimes going in the night by water from New York to Fort Washington.

September 8th 1776, a council of general officers had determined on holding the City of New York. See General Washington's letter of that date. On the 12th of September having been out with General Miflin, by order of General Washington, to reconnoiter the

[1] Washington's Chief Engineer in 1776.

country between Kingsbridge and Morrisania and eastward, on our return we met with General Washington near Harlem Heights, where we made our report to him, in consequence of which a council of general officers was convened, whose advice was the withdrawing the army from the city,—see the General's letter of the 14th of September,—and this measure was the salvation of the army, and which probably would not have been but for the discoveries made by Mifflin and myself.

My being appointed engineer by Congress was wholly unexpected. I had begun to act in that capacity through pure necessity, and had continued to conduct the business more from necessity and respect for the General than from any opinion I had of my own abilities, or knowledge of that art; true it is that after my arrival at New York I had read some books on fortification, and I knew much more than when I began at Roxbury, but I had not the vanity to suppose that my knowledge was such as to give me a claim to the first rank in a corps of engineers, yet my experience convinced me that such a corps was necessary to be established, therefore near the last of September, I drew up a plan for such an establishment and presented it to General Washington, and which he transmitted to Congress—see his letter to that body of the 5th of November 1776. In my letter to General Washington on the subject I disclaimed all pretension of being placed at the head of the proposed corps, and signified it would be my choice to serve in the line of the army.

October 19th 1776, the British landed on Pell's point and some skirmishing took place in the afternoon between part of Glover's brigade and some advance parties of the enemy near East Chester, the next morning by order of the General I set out from Kingsbridge to reconnoiter their position etc. I set out in company with Col° Reed, the adjutant-general and a foot guard of about twenty men, when we arrived on the heights of East Chester we saw a small body of British near the church, but we could obtain no intelligence; the houses were deserted. Col° Reed now told me he must return to attend to issuing general orders. I observed that we had made no discovery yet of any consequence, that if he went back I wished him to take the guard back for I chose to go alone. I then disguised my appearance as an officer as far as I could, and set out on the road to White-plains; however, I did not then know where White-plains was, nor where the road I had taken would carry me. I had gone about two and a half miles when a road turned 'off to the right, I followed it perhaps half a mile and came to a house where I learned from the woman that this road led to New Rochelle, that the British were there and that they had a guard at a house in sight; On this information I turned and pursued my route toward White-plains (the houses on the way all deserted) until I came within three or four miles of the place; here I discovered a house a little ahead with men about it. By my glass I found they were not British soldiers; however I approached them with caution. I called for some oats for my horse, sat down and heard them chat some little time, when I found they were friends to the cause of America, and then I began to make the necessary enquiries, and on the whole I found that the main body of the British lay near New Rochelle, from thence to White-plains about nine miles, good roads and in general level open country, that at Whiteplains was a large quantity of stores, with only about three hundred militia to guard them, that the British had a detachment at Mamaraneck only six] miles from White-plains, and from Whiteplains only five miles to the North river, where lay five or six of the enemies ships and sloops, tenders, etc. Having made these discoveries I set out on my return. The road from Ward's across the Brunx was my intended route unless I found the British there, which haply they were not, but I saw Americans on the heights west of the Brunx who had arrived there after I passed up. I found them to be Lord Sterling's division; it was now after sunset. I gave my Lord a short account of my discoveries, took some refreshment, and set off for headquarters by the way of Philip's at the mouth of Sawmill river, a road I had never travelled, among tory inhabitants and in the night. I dare not enquire the way, but Providence conducted me. I arrived at headquarters near Kingsbridge (a distance of about ten miles) about nine o'clock at night. I found the General alone. I reported to him the discoveries I had made, with a sketch of the country; he complained very feelingly of the gentlemen from New York from whom he had never been able to obtain a plan of the country, that from their information he had ordered the stores to Whiteplains as a place of security. The General sent for General Greene and Gen¹ George Clinton, since Vice-President of the United States. As soon as General Clinton came in my sketch and statement was shown to him and he was asked if the situation of those places was as I had reported. Gen¹ Clinton said it was.

I had but a short time to refresh myself and horse when I received a letter from the General with orders to proceed immediately to Lord Sterling's, and I arrived at his quarters about two o'clock in the morning October 21st 1776. Lord Sterling's division marched before daylight and we arrived at Whiteplains about 9 o'clock A.M. and thus was the American army saved (by an interposing providence from a probable total destruction.). I may be asked wherein this particular interposition of providence appears, I answer, first, in the stupidity of the British general, in that he did not early on the morning of the 20th send a detachment and take possession of the post and stores at Whiteplains, for had he done this we must then have fought him on his own terms, and such disadvantageous terms on our part, as humanly speaking must have proved our overthrow; again when I parted with Col⁰ Reed on the 20th as before mentioned, I have always thought that I was moved to so hazardous an undertaking by foreign influence. On my route I was liable to meet with some British or tory parties, who probably would have made me a prisoner (as I had no knowledge of any way of escape across the Brunx but the one I came out). Hence I was induced to disguise myself by taking out my cockade, loping my hat and secreting my sword and pistols under my loose coat, and then had I been taken under this disguise, the probability is that I should have been hanged for a spy.

October 29th, the British advanced in front of our lines at Whiteplains about 10 o'clock A.M., I had just arrived on Chatterton hill in order to throw up some works when they hove in sight, as soon as they discovered us they commenced a severe cannonade but without any effect of consequence. General McDougal about this time arriving with his brigade from Burtis's and observing the British to be crossing the Brunx below in large bodies in order to attack us, our troops were posted to receive them in a very advantageous position. The British in their advance were twice repulsed; at length however their numbers were increased so that they were able to turn our right flank. We lost many men but from information afterwards received there was reason to believe they lost many more than we. The rail and stone fence behind which our troops were posted proved as fatal to the British as the rail fence and grass hung on it did at Charlestown the 17th of June 1775.

After the affair of the 29th of October my time was employed in examining the nature of the country in a military point of view in our rear towards North Castle, Croton river, etc., until about the 5th of November when I received the following order from the General which I shall take the liberty to transcribe.

HEADQUARTERS WHITEPLAINS, November 5th 1776.

SIR :—You are directed to repair to Wright's mills and lay out any work there you conceive to be necessary, in case it is not already done, from thence you are to proceed towards Croton bridge, and post the two regiments of militia in the most advantageous manner, so as to obstruct the enemies passage to that quarter, you are also to give what directions you think are proper to those regiments, respecting the breaking up the roads leading from the North river eastward, after this you are to go up to Peekskill and direct Lasher's detachment to break up the roads there. You are likewise to lay out what works will be advisable there and order them to be set about

Given under my hand—

G°. WASHINGTON.

To Col° Putnam, Engineer.

November 11th 1776, Gen¹ Washington came to Peekskill and I went with him to visit Fort Montgomery, on the same day or the next he crossed the North river, leaving instructions with me to ascertain the geography of the country with the roads and passes through and about the highlands, a report of which I afterwards made with a sketch of a plan.

December 8th 1776, I wrote to Gen¹ Washington informing him that I had accepted of a regiment in the Massachusetts line of the Continental army, with my reasons for so doing, assuring him at the same time of my attachment to him and readiness to execute any service.

[Original in the archives of Marietta College, Marietta, Ohio.]

[No. 44.]

SCATTERING ORDERS BY GENERALS LEE, SPENCER, GREENE
AND NIXON

[*Colonel Little's Order Book*]

GENERAL SPENCER'S ORDERS.

NEW YORK, Sept. 8th.

All the guards in the posts are to be continued as large as at any time, & be very vigilant & alert. All the Reg[ts] are to lie on their arms this night & be ready to turn out at the shortest notice, as it is not improbable we may be speedily attacked. Gen. Wadsworth to send an adjutant to Head Quarters tomorrow for orders.

Sept. 9th.

Guard same as this day & fatigues. The several Brigades in this Division are to lodge on their arms this night & be ready to turn out on the shortest notice. Cols. &c are to take particular care of the arms & ammunition. Col. Chester to send an adjutant to Head Quarters for orders.

GENERAL NIXON'S ORDERS.

NEW YORK Sept 9th.

A serjeant, Corporal & 12 men daily to mount as a guard at Gen. Nixon's quarters. Officers of guard in the night are to send visiting rounds between every relief. Complaints are made that orders are not made known to soldiers. The General expressly enjoins that the adjutant see that the orders are daily read to the several regiments, that the soldiers may not plead ignorance thereof.

Sept. 10th.

The Gen. desires officers not to suffer their men to straggle as we may expect a sudden attack, when one is made. The Gen[l] desires all the officers to lodge in camp, as in the critical situation of affairs, much depends on their vigilance.

GENERAL GREENE'S ORDERS.

FORT CONSTITUTION Sept. 30th.

Major Box is appointed & requested in conjunction with the Engineers of this Department & Col. Bull to oversee & forward the fortifications at Fort Constitution. Lt. Col. Cornell is appointed Dep. Assistant Adj. Gen¹. for this Division. The Q^r. M^r. Gen¹ is directed to provide tools of all kinds necessary for a Blacksmith's & Armorer's shop, large enough to do the business of this part of the army. Many trangressions of gen¹ orders happen for want of their being read & explained to the men. The Gen¹ directs that all orders issued be read to the men in Reg^ts or Companies, & that every Captain provide himself with an orderly book that the men may be fully informed of their duty. The adj^ts of regiments are to report any neglect.

Oct. 2^d.

The Brig^rs. or officers commanding Brigades are requested to send the Brig^de Majors˷or some other proper officers to fetch the new regulations of the army, & distribute them among the Reg^ts of their Brigades & the C. officers of each reg^t or corps are directed to have them read—to have the rules & regulations read first to the whole regiment drawn up for that purpose & then order the Captains to read them again to each of their companies the day after they have been read to the reg^ts—to be continued the first Monday in every month. Lt. Mills of Col. Hitchcock's Reg^t is requested to collect a party of carpenters from either of the Brigades, reg^ts or corps in this Division of the army, that are willing to enter the work for the same pay, that was allowed last campaign. Officers for the day. Major Bailey—for fatigue Major Bartholomew.

Oct 4th.

A guard to mount to-morrow at 8 A.M. to relieve the guard over Hackensack River—to take 3 days provision with them. Officers for the Day Lt Col. Crary—for fatigue Lt Col. Culbertson.

Oct. 6th.

The Post to be carried out at any time when he arrives, night or day. No person under guard in the main guard to be released without permission from the guard. A fatigue party of 400 to complete the fortifications at Fort Constitution—Cols. Durkee's, Bradley's, Rolling's & William's Reg^ts. to form a brigade under Gen¹ Roberdeau, until his Excellency's pleasure be further known. The D. Adj^t. Gen¹ is directed to appoint a grand parade, where all guards for different posts are to parade.

Oct. 7th.

A guard of 50 men to relieve the guard at Hoebuck's Ferry

immediately, to take 4 days provisions. The commanding officers of Regts—in the English neighborhood are to take care that none of the rails are burnt in their Reg^{ts} for fire wood. Reg^{ts} are to be furnished with firewood daily, apply to Q M. Genl for teams. A sub. & 30 men to go immediately for the stock brought from Bergen.

Oct. 8th.

Application for leave of absence from camp for a short time on the occasional business of the regt. is to be made to the Brig^r Genl or the commanding officers of Brigade—Brig^{rs} are desired not to grant liberty of absence unless on real business. The houses upon the waterside, near the ferry are to be cleared of the present inhabitants for the use of the guards & ferrymen. A cap. & 40 men well acquainted with rowing to be drawn for the management of the ferryboats. This party to be excused from other duty & to be continued in that employ. All the Axes in the different reg^{ts} are to be delivered to the Q. M. Genl Col. Biddle, & he is to deliver an equal proportion to the Reg^{ts} retaining enough for the Public works. Cap. Olney of Col. Hitchcock's Reg^t & Cap. Warner of Col. Little's are appointed to assist in overseeing the fortifications & are to be excused from all other duty. Commanding officers of Reg^{ts} are requested to fix upon proper places for Barracks, none to be nearer the fort than 50 rods. The Genl desires com^g officers to divide the reg^{ts} into messes of 8 men. The men must build timber huts, as boards are not to be had. Boards are to be had only for the roof. The huts are to be 12 feet long by 9 wide, to have stone chimneys & to be ranged in proper streets. The guard at the Bridge to be relieved immediately. The Cap. of the Artillery is directed to examine the state of the amunition in the magazine & report to the D. A^t. Q^r. The Genl directs that none of the troops go out of drum call, without liberty from the Com^g officer of the reg^t. The rolls of companies are to be called 4 times a day. Men not to be found when the reg^{ts} are called to parade may expect to be severely punished & the officers if negligent of their duty are to be arrested—Adjutant Colman is appointed to do the duty of Brigade Major for Genl Nixon's Brigade while Major Box is employed on the Fortifications.

Oct. 13th.

Gen. Nixon's & Gen. Roberdeau's Brigade are to draw & cook themselves 3 days provisions immediately. The guard to be relieved from Col. Ewing's Brigade, the guards at Bergen to be excepted. The other two Brigades to hold themselves in readiness to march at a moment's warning. Cap. Spurr from Col. Hitchcock's reg^t is to oversee fatigue parties employed on Fortifications. The Com^y is desired to kill all the fat cattle brought from Bergen, that the inhabitants don't claim—take an account of all the marks & numbers & have their value estimated by 2 or 3 good men. The sheep that are fit are to be killed for the use of the Army. An exact account of their number & marks and value is to be kept. The Q^r. M. Gen. is directed to take all horses brought from Bergen & not claimed & to employ such as are fit in the service ; the rest to be disposed of at Public Vendue. Lest any should be injured that cannot claim his property, a record is to be kept describing the natural & artificial marks & the value of each.

GENERAL NIXON'S ORDERS.

FORT CONSTITUTION Oct. 13th.
It is Gen. Greene's orders that my Brigade move over the Ferry immediately. The regiments to leave a careful officer & 12 men each to bring forward their baggage to King's Bridge, who is to take care that none of it be left behind or lost. When the Reg^{ts} are over the ferry, they will march to Mt Washington & remain there till further orders—You will hurry the march as fast as possible, as they must cross the ferry this night—

J^{xo} NIXON B. G.
To Dudley Colman, A.B.M.

EAST CHESTER Oct. 16th.
The several reg^{ts} in this Brigade are to draw 4 days provision & have it cooked immediately. The Q. M. will apply to the assistant Q. M. Genl for carriages to transport their provisions. Col. Varnum's Reg^t to relieve Col. Nixon's at Froggs Point this P.M.

Oct. 16th.
Sir—You are to order Col. Varnum's reg^t to march immediately to Froggs Neck to relieve Col. Ritzema's or Col. Malcolm's reg^t (which of the two you find there not relieved). You will get a pilot from Col. Nixon's reg^t to direct them thither.

J^{xo}. NIXON, B. G.
To Dudly Colman, Brigade Major.

MILES SQUARE, EAST CHESTER Oct. 18th.

Sir—You will have a working party of 300 men & officers ready to go to work as soon as the tools arrive, which I have sent for & you will see that suitable guards are mounted by each regiment.

J^{no}. NIXON, B. Gen.

To D. Colman, B. Major.

GENERAL LEE'S ORDERS.

MILES SQUARE, Oct. 19th.

Gen. Lee returns his warmest thanks to Col. Glover, and the Brigade under his command, not only for his gallant behavior yesterday, but for their prudent, cool, orderly & soldier like conduct in all respects. He assures these brave men that he shall omit no opportunity of showing his gratitude. The wounded are to be immediately sent to Valentines Hill at the second Liberty pole where surgeons should at once repair to dress their wounds. They are afterwards to be forwarded to Fort Washington.

[No. 45.]

GENERAL LEE TO COLONEL CHESTER

CAMP [MORRISTOWN ?] Dec^r: 7th 1776.

SIR—

You are to proceed from hence to a certain mill about 8 miles distant where you are to take Post in the most advantageous manner possible, with half your Party, and remain yourself: The other half you are to detach under the most understanding, cool officer you can select. He is to proceed to Harrington Township, where they are to collect, all the serviceable horses, all the spare Blankets (that is to leave a sufficient number to cover the People) they are to collect any spare shoes, great Coats, to serve as Watch Coats—The People from whom they are taken are not to be insulted; either by actions or language; but told that the urgent necessity of the Troop, obliges us to the Measure—That unless we adopt it, their liberties must Perish—That they must make an Estimate, of what is taken and the Publick shall pay them—The officer who commands the

10

Party detach'd, above all, must take care to advance a Party, to look out, on the Road of Hackinsack in the Front of the Party who are collecting, that they may not be surprised, whilst they are thus occupied—A Canadian and Monsr: Vernajou will conduct you; when the whole is finished, you are to march by another Road to Morristown : By a Road which will be indicated : you are not to suffer any Country People to pass by you, who might inform the Enemy of your motions—if the Collecting Party should be attacked, they will naturally return (but in good order to your Post—the horses and necessaries collected are to be brought up to Morris Town and then be disposed of by the General—

CHARLES LEE, Major-General.

COLONEL CHESTER.

[Original in possession of Rev. Dr. John Chester, Washington, D. C.]

[No. 46.]

CAPTAIN BRADFORD'S ACCOUNT OF THE CAPTURE OF GENERAL LEE[1]

" Gen. Lee had advanced with his Division to Baskenridge, about twenty-two miles from the Enemy's advanced Guards, where they lodged the night of Dec. 12th, Gen. Sullivan being with the body of the Division, & Gen. Lee in the Rear, or on the flank of the rear about 2 Miles from the body, having with him only his aid-de-camp, Mr. Bradford, a Major with an express from Gen. Gates, a French Colonel, a French Captain, the latter in our service, the former just from Paris by the way of Dartmouth in Mass. with dispatches for Congress, & perhaps a dozen guards. The house was surrounded on one side with a wood, on the other an orchard. The Gen. had just sent forward Gen. Sullivan, who marched with the Division about 8 o'clock in the morning, tarrying himself to finish dispatches to Gen. Gates, which having just done, dressed & sent for his horses, was ready to mount, & would have been gone in 5 or

---

[1] Capt. Bradford, of Rhode Island, was Aide-de-Camp to General Lee at the time of the latter's capture, and gave this account of the affair to the Rev. Dr. Stiles, then at Dighton, R. I.

10 minutes, when about 10 o'clock they were surprised with about 50 horse, which came on the house from the wood & orchard at once & surrounding fired upon it. The French Col. escaped & was pursued & overtaken. Gen. Lee looked out of the window to see how 'the ' guards behaved, & saw the enemy twice with his hanger cut off the arm of one of the Guards crying for quarter—the guard behaved well, fired at first, but were rushed upon & subdued. The Gen. sees then that they must submit, & after walking the chamber perhaps 10 or 15 minutes, told his aid-de-camp to go down & tell them Gen. Lee submitted. Mr. Bradford went to the door & on opening it a whole volley of shot came in the door—he spoke loud & opened again & delivered his orders. Gen. Lee came forward & surrendered himself a prisoner of war, saying he trusted they would use him like a gentleman. Of this one of them gave assurance & ordered him instantly to mount. He requested His Hat & Cloke and Mr. Bradford went in to fetch it, but changing his clothes on his return they did not know him from a servant & laying down the General's Hat and Cloke he escaped back into the house. They immediately rode back in triumph with the Genl."

[From the Stiles MS. Diary, Yale College Library.]

[No. 47.]

GENERAL OLIVER WOLCOTT TO HIS WIFE

LITCHFIELD, CONN.

PHILADELPHIA[1] December 13 1776

MY DEAR SPOUSE

The 11th in the Evening a Detachment of the Enemy took possession of Burlington, about 20 miles from this City on the Jersey shore. The Rest of their Army are at Trenton, and upon the Banks of the River above it; their numbers are uncertain, but are computed about twelve thousand, and as their Designs, are undoubtedly to gain Possession of this City, the Congress, upon the advice of Genls Putnam and Mifflin (who are now here to provide for the Protection

[1] Gen. Wolcott, at this date, was a delegate in Congress from Connecticut.

of the Place,) as well as the Result of their own Opinion, have adjourned themselves to Baltimore in Maryland, about 110 miles from this City, as it was judged, that the Council of America, ought not to sit in a Place liable to be interrupted by the rude Disorder of Arms, so that I am at this moment, going forward for that place. Whether the Army will succeed in their cruel Designs against this City, must be left to time to discover. Congress have ordered the General to defend it to the last extremity, and God grant that he may be successful in his Exertions.

Whatever Event may take place, the American Cause will be supported to the last, and I trust in God that it will succeed. The Grecian, Roman and Dutch States were in their Infancy reduced to the greatest Distress, infinitely beyond what we have yet experienced. The God who governs the Universe and who holds Empires in His Hand, can with the least Effort of His Will, grant us all that Security Opulence and Power which they have enjoyed.

The present scene it is true appears somewhat gloomy, but the natural or more obvious cause seems to be owing to the term of enlistment of the Army having expired. I hope we may have a most respectable one before long established. The business of war is the result of Experience.

It is probable that France before long will involve Great Britain in a war who by unhappy Experience may learn the Folly of attempting to enslave a People who by the ties of Consanguinity and Affection ever were desirous of promoting her truest Happiness.

Gen. Howe has lately published a Proclamation abusing the Congress as having sinister Designs upon the People and has offered to such as will accept of Pardon upon an unlimited Submission, " Royal Forgiveness." But who is base enough to wish to have a precarious Care dependent upon the caprice of Power, unrestrained by any Law and governed by the dangerous thirst of Avarice and Ambition ?

My best love to my children and friends. May the Almighty ever have you and them in his protection

yours with the most
Inviolable affection
OLIVER WOLCOTT.

To MRS. LAURA WOLCOTT
   Litchfield
     Connecticut.

[Original in possession of Frederick H. Wolcott, Esq., Astoria, L. I.]

BATTLES

OF

TRENTON AND PRINCETON.

TRENTON AND PRINCETON.

[No. 48.]

CAPTAIN WILLIAM HULL TO ANDREW ADAMS

LITCHFIELD, CONN.

TRENTON, Jany 1ˢᵗ, 1777.

DEAR SIR:

Have but a moment which shall embrace with Pleasure to inform you of the present State of our Army and our late Success. After we had recruited a few days of a fatiguing March of more than 250 Miles (thro' all our Windings) Genl. Washington gave orders for us to be every way equiped for Action. On the Evening of the 25th Ult. we were ordered to March to a ferry [McConkey's] about twelve Miles from Trenton, where was stationed near two Thousand Hessians. As violent a Storm ensued of Hail & Snow as I ever felt. The Artillery and Infantry all were across the Ferry about twelve O'clock, consisting of only twenty one hundred principally New England Troops. In this Violent Storm we marched on for Trenton. Before Light in the Morning we gained all the Roads leading from Trenton. The Genl. gave orders that every Officer's Watch should be set by his, and the Moment of Attack was fixed. Just after Light, we came to their out Guard, which fired upon us and retreated. The first Sound of the Musquetry and Retreat of the Guards animated the Men and they pushed on with Resolution and Firmness. Happily the fire begun on every Side at the same instant, their Main body had just Time to form when there ensued a heavy Cannonade from our Field Pieces and a fine brisk and lively fire from our Infantry. This continued but a Short Time before the Enemy finding themselves flanked on every Side laid down their Arms. The Resolution and Bravery of our Men, their Order and Regulariety gave me the highest Sensation of Pleasure. Genl. Washington highly congratulated the Men on next day in Genl. Orders, and with Pleasure observed, that he had been in Many Actions before, but always perceived some Misbehaviour in some individuals, but in that Action he saw none. Pennsylvania itself is obliged to acknowledge the Bravery of New Eng'd Troops. I have a List from Head Quarters of the Killed and taken, which was taken the day after the Action, since which many more have been brought in: 1 Col. wounded since dead, 2 Lieut. Col^s. taken, 3 Majors, 4 Capts. 8 Lieuts., 12 Ens'ns, 92 Serj'ts, 9 Musicians, 12 Drums, 25 Servants, 842 Privates, 2 Capt's Killed, 2 Lieuts. killed 50 privates Six Brass Field Pieces, One Mortar, and about 1500 Stand of Arms. A large Number of Horses and a vast Quantity of Plunder of every kind. And this, Sir, I will assure you with only the Loss of six or seven on our side, this is no Exaggeration but simple fact, 'tis impossible to describe the scene to you as it appeared. We immediately retreated across the River and did not get to our Tents till next Morning—two Nights and one day in as violent a Storm as I ever felt. What can't Men do when engaged in so noble a Cause. Our Men's Time Expired Yesterday, they have generally engaged to tarry six weeks longer. My company almost to a man. Orders have now come for us to march for Princetown. We have a Rumor that it was burned last night by the Enemy, who we suppose are about retreating. Compliments to Miss Adams & Children. Adieu and believe me to be sincerely yours,

WM. HULL.

[*Legacy of Historical Gleanings.* By Mrs. C. V. R. Bonney. Vol. I., p. 57. Munsell, Albany. 1875.]

[No. 49.]

COLONEL KNOX TO HIS WIFE

DELAWARE RIVER, NEAR TRENTON,
Dec. 28, 1776, near 12 o'clock.

. . . . . Trenton is an open town, situated nearly on the banks of the Delaware, accessible on all sides. Our army was scattered along the river for nearly twenty-five miles. Our intelligence agreed that the force of the enemy in Trenton was from two to three thousand, with about six field cannon, and that they were pretty secure in their situation, and that they were Hessians—no British troops. A hardy design was formed of attacking the town by storm. Accordingly a part of the army, consisting of about 2,500 or 3,000, passed the river on Christmas night, with almost infinite difficulty, with eighteen field-pieces. The floating ice in the river made the labor almost incredible. However, perseverance accomplished what at first seemed impossible. About two o'clock the troops were all on the Jersey side; we then were about nine miles from the object. The night was cold and stormy; it hailed with great violence; the troops marched with the most profound silence and good order. They arrived by two routes at the same time, about half an hour after daylight, within one mile of the town. The storm continued with great violence, but was in our backs, and consequently in the faces of our enemy. About half a mile from the town was an advanced guard on each road, consisting of a captains guard. These we forced, and entered the town with them pell-mell; and here succeeded a scene of war of which I had often conceived, but never saw before. The hurry, fright, and confusion of the enemy was [not] unlike that which will be when the last trump shall sound. They endeavored to form in streets, the heads of which we had previously the possession of with cannon and howitzers; these, in the twinkling of an eye, cleared the streets. The backs of the houses were resorted to for shelter. These proved ineffectual; the musketry soon dislodged them. Finally they were driven through the town into an open plain beyond. Here they formed in an instant. During the contest in the streets measures were taken for putting an entire stop to their retreat by posting troops and cannon in such passes and roads as it was possible for them to get away by. The poor fellows after they were formed on the plain saw themselves completely surrounded, the only resource left was to force their way through numbers unknown to them. The Hessians lost part of their cannon in the town; they did not relish the project of forcing, and were obliged to surrender upon the spot, with all their artillery, six brass pieces, army colors, &c. A Colonel Rawle commanded, who was wounded. The number of prisoners was above 1,200, including officers,—all Hessians. There were few killed or wounded on either side. After having marched off the prisoners and secured the cannon, stores, &c, we returned to the place, nine miles distant, where we had embarked. Providence seemed to have smiled upon every part of this enterprise. Great advantages may be gained from it if we take the proper steps. At another post we have pushed over the river 2,000 men, to-day another body, and to-morrow the whole army will follow. It must give a sensible pleasure to every friend of the rights of man to think with how much intrepidity our people pushed the enemy, and prevented their forming in the town.

His Excellency the General has done me the unmerited great honor of thanking me in public orders in terms strong and polite. This I should blush to mention to any other than to you, my dear Lucy; and I am fearful that even my Lucy may think her Harry possesses a species of little vanity in doing [it] at all.

MORRISTOWN Jan. 7 1777.

I wrote to you from Trenton by a Mr. Furness which I hope you have received. I then informed you that we soon expected another tussle. I was not out in my conjecture. About three o'clock on the second of January, a column of the enemy attacked a party of ours which was stationed one mile above Trenton. Our party was small and did not make much resistance. The enemy, who were Hessians, entered the town pell-mell pretty much in the same manner that we had driven them a few days before.

Nearly on the other side of Trenton, partly in the town, runs a brook [the Assanpink], which in most places is not fordable, and over which through Trenton is a bridge. The ground on the other side is much higher than on this, and may be said to command Trenton completely. Here it was our army drew up with thirty or forty pieces in front. The enemy pushed our small party through the town with vigor, though not with much loss. Their retreat over the bridge was thoroughly secured by the artillery. After they had retired over the bridge, the enemy advanced within reach of our cannon, who saluted them with great vociferation and some execution. This continued till dark when of course it ceased, except a few shells which we now and then chucked into town to prevent their enjoying their new quarters securely. As I before mentioned, the creek was in our front, our left on the Delaware, our right in a wood parallel to the creek. The situation was strong, to be sure; but hazardous on this account, that had our right wing been defeated, the defeat of the left would almost have been an inevitable consequence, and the whole thrown into confusion or pushed into the Delaware, as it was impassable by boats.

From these circumstances the general thought best to attack

Princeton, twelve miles in the rear of the enemy's grand army, and where they had the 17th, 40th, and 55th regiments, with a number of draughts, altogether perhaps twelve hundred men. Accordingly about one o'clock at night we began to march and make this most extra manœvre. Our troops marched with great silence and order, and arrived near Princeton a little after daybreak. We did not surprise them as at Trenton; for they were on their march down to Trenton, on a road about a quarter of a mile distant from that in which we were. You may judge of their surprise when they saw such large columns marching up. They could not possibly suppose it was our army, for that they took for granted was cooped up near Trenton. They could not possibly suppose it was their own army returning by a back road; in short, I believe they were as much astonished as if an army had dropped perpendicularly upon them. However they had not much time for consideration. We pushed a party to attack them. This they repulsed with great spirit, and advanced upon another column just then coming out of a wood, which they likewise put in some disorder; but fresh troops coming up, and the artillery beginning to play, they were after a smart resistance put totally to the rout. The 18th regiment used their bayonets with too much severity upon a party they put to flight; but they were paid for it in proportion, very few escaping. Near sixty were killed on the spot besides the wounded. We have taken between three and four hundred prisoners, all British troops. They must have lost in this affair nearly five hundred killed, wounded, and prisoners. We lost some gallant officers. Brigadier-General Mercer was wounded: he had three separate stabs with a bayonet. A Lieutenant-Colonel Fleming was killed, and Captain Neil of the artillery an excellent officer. Mercer will get better. The enemy took his parole after we left Princeton. We took all their cannon, which consisted of two brass six-pounders, a considerable amount of military stores,,blankets, guns, &c. They lost, among a number of other officers, a Captain Leslie, a son of the Earl of Leven and nephew to General Leslie: him we brought off and buried with honors of war.

After we had been about two hours at Princeton, word was brought that the enemy was advancing from Trenton. This they did, as we have since been informed, in a most infernal sweat,—running, puffing, and blowing, and swearing at being so outwitted. As we had other objects in view, to wit, breaking up their quarters, we pursued our march to Somerset Court House, where there were about thirteen hundred quartered, as we had been informed. They, however, had marched off, and joined the army at Trenton. We at first intended to have made a forced march to Brunswick; but our men having been without rest, rum, or provisions for two nights and days were unequal to the task of marching seventeen miles further. If we could have secured one thousand fresh men at Princeton to have pushed for Brunswick, we should have struck one of the most brilliant strokes in all history. However the advantages are very great: already they have collected their whole force, and drawn themselves to one point, to wit, Brunswick.

The enemy were within nineteen miles of Philadelphia, they are now sixty miles. We have driven them from almost the whole of West Jersey. The panic is still kept up. We had a battle two days ago with a party of ours and sixty Waldeckers, who were all killed or taken, in Monmouth County in the lower part of the Jerseys. It is not our interest to fight a general battle, nor can I think, under all circumstances, it is the enemy's. They have sent their baggage to Staten Island from the Jerseys, and we are very well informed they are doing the same from New York. Heath will have orders to march there and endeavor to storm it from that side. 'There is a tide in the affairs of men, which taken at the flood leads on to victory.'

[*Life, etc. of General Knox.* By Francis S. Drake. Boston, 1873.]

[No. 50.]

COL. HASLET TO CÆSAR RODNEY

ALLENTOWN January 2nd 1777.

This morning we were called up at 2 o'clock under a pretended alarm that we were to be attacked by the enemy but by daylight we were ordered to march for Trenton, and when we reached Crosswicks found that the brigade had gone. We reached Trenton about 11 o'clock and found all the troops from our different posts in Jersey, collected and collecting there under General Washington himself; and the regular troops were already properly disposed to receive the enemy, whose main body was then within a few miles and determined to dispossess us.

Trenton stands upon the River Delaware, with a creek called the Assanpink passing through the town across which there is a bridge.

The enemy came down on the upper side of this creek, through the town, and a number of our troops were posted with Riflemen and artillery to oppose their approach.

The main body of our army was drawn up on a plain below, or on the lower side of the Assanpink, near the bridge, and the main force of our Artillery was posted on the banks and high ground along the creek in front of them.

Gen. Mercer's brigade was posted about 2 miles up the creek, and the troops under Gen. Cadwallader were stationed in a field on the right about a mile from the town, on the main road, to prevent the enemy from flanking. We had five pieces of Artillery with our division and about 20 more in the field, near, and at the town. Our numbers were about five thousand, and the enemy's about seven thousand. The attack began about 2 o'clock and a heavy fire upon both sides, chiefly from the artillery continued untill dark.

At this time the enemy were left in possession of the upper part of the town, but we kept possession of the bridge, altho' the enemy attempted several times to carry it but were repulsed each time with great slaughter. After sunset this afternoon the enemy came down in a very heavy column to force the bridge. The fire was very heavy and the Light troops were ordered to fly to the support of that important post, and as we drew near, I stepped out of the front to order my men to close up ; at this time Martinas Sipple was about 10 sets behind the man next in front of him ; I at once drew my sword and threatened to cut his head off if he did not keep close, he then sprang forward and I returned to the front. The enemy were soon defeated and retired and the American army also retired to the woods, where they encamped and built up fires. I then had the roll called to see if any of our men were missing and Martinas was not to be found, but Leut. Mark McCall informed me that immediately upon my returning to the head of the column, after making him close up, he fled out of the field.[1] We lost but few men ; the enemy considerably more. It is thought Gen. Washington did not intend to hold the upper part of the town.

[Original in possession of Cæsar A. Rodney, Esq.]

[1] Sipple afterwards joined the Delaware Regiment under Col. David Hall, and is said to have proved a brave and faithful soldier.

[No. 51.]

JOURNAL OF CAPTAIN THOMAS RODNEY [1]

January 3rd 1777.

. . . . At two o'clock this morning, the ground having been frozen firm by a keen N. West wind, secret orders were issued to each department and the whole army was at once put in motion, but no one knew what the Gen. meant to do. Some thought that we were going to attack the enemy in the rear; some that we were going to Princeton; the latter proved to be right. We went by a bye road on the right hand which made it about 16 miles. During this nocturnal march I with the Dover Company and the Red Feather Company of Philadelphia Light Infantry led the van of the army and Capt. Henry with the other three companies of Philadelphia Light Infantry brought up the rear. The van moved on all night in the most cool and determined order, but on the march great confusion happened in the rear. There was a cry that they were surrounded by the Hessians, and several corps of Militia broke and fled towards Bordentown, but the rest of the column remained firm and pursued their march without disorder, but those who were frightened and fled did not recover from their panic until they reached Burlington.

When we had proceeded to within a mile and a half of Princeton and the van had crossed Stony Brook, Gen. Washington ordered our Infantry to file off to one side of the road and halt. Gen. Sullivan was ordered to wheel to the right and flank the town on that side, and two Brigades were ordered to wheel to the left, to make a circuit and surround the town on that side and as they went to break

---

[1] Captain Rodney marched with a Delaware company to the relief of Washington in the dark days of the campaign. Four other companies from Philadelphia, joined with his, formed a battalion under Captain Henry—Rodney being second in command. He was with Cadwallader's force during the battle of Trenton ; and his vivid description of the storm that night, and the condition of the river [*Force*, fifth series, vol. iii.], has frequently been quoted by historical writers. His interesting account of subsequent events, as given above, is now published for the first time. It has been made the subject of a highly interesting paper prepared and read by Cæsar A. Rodney, Esq., of Wilmington, before the Historical Societies of Delaware and Pennsylvania.

down the Bridge and post a party at the mill on the main road, to oppose the enemy's main army if they should pursue us from Trenton.

The third Division was composed of Gen. Mercer's Brigade of Continental troops, about 300 men, and Cadwalader's brigade of Philadelphia Militia to which brigade the whole of our light Infantry Regiment was again annexed.

Mercer's brigade marched in front and another corp of infantry brought up the rear. My company flanked the whole brigade on the right in an Indian file so that my men were very much extended and distant from each other; I marched in front and was followed by Sargeant McKnatt and next to him was Nehemiah Tilton. Mercer's brigade which was headed by Col. Haslet of Delaware on foot and Gen. Mercer on horseback was to march straight on to Princeton without turning to the right or left.

It so happened that two Regiments of British troops that were on their march to Trenton to reinforce their army there, received intelligence of the movements of the American Army (for the sun rose as we passed over Stony Brook) and about a mile from Princeton they turned off from the main road and posted themselves behind a long string of buildings and an orchard on the straight road to Princeton.

The two first Divisions of our army therefore passed wide to the right and left, and leaving them undiscovered went into Princeton. Gen. Mercer's Brigade, owing to some delay in arranging Cadwallader's men had advanced several hundred yards ahead and never discovered the enemy until he was turning the buildings they were posted behind, and then they were not more than fifty yards off.

He immediately formed his men, with great courage, and poured a heavy fire in upon the enemy. But they being greatly superior in number returned the fire and charged bayonets, and their onset was so fierce that Gen. Mercer fell mortally wounded and many of his officers were killed, and the brigade being effectually broken up, began a disorderly flight. Col. Haslet retired some small distance behind the buildings and endeavored to rally them, but receiving a bullet through his head, dropt dead on the spot and the whole brigade fled in confusion. At this instant Gen. Cadwallader's Philadelphia Brigade came up and the enemy checked by their appearance took post behind a fence and a ditch in front of the buildings before mentioned, and so extended themselves that every man could load and fire incessantly; the fence stood on low ground between two hills; on the hill behind the British line they had eight pieces of artillery which played in cessantly with round and grape shot on our brigade, and the fire was extremely hot. Yet Gen. Cadwalader led up the head of the column with the greatest bravery to within 50 yards of the enemy, but this was rashly done, for he was obliged to recoil; and leaving one piece of his artillery, he fell back about 40 yards and endeavored to form the brigade, and some companies did form and gave a few vollies, but the fire of the enemy was so hot, that, at the sight of the Regular troops running to the rear, the militia gave way and the whole brigade broke and most of them retired to a woods about 150 yards in the rear; but two pieces of artillery stood their ground and were served with great skill and bravery.

At this time a field officer was sent to order me to take post on the left of the artillery, until the brigade should form again, and, with the Philadelphia Infantry keep up a fire from some stacks and buildings, and to assist the artillery in preventing the enemy from advancing. We now crossed the enemy's fire from right to Left and took position behind some stacks just on the left of the artillery; and about 30 of the Philadelphia Infantry were under cover of a house on our left and a little in the rear.

About 150 of my men came to this post, but I could not keep them all there, for the enemies fire was dreadful and three balls, for they were very thick, had grazed me; one passed within my elbow nicking my great coat and carried away the breech of Sargeant McKnatts gun, he being close behind me, another carried away the inside edge of one of my shoe soles, another had nicked my hat and indeed they seemed as thick as hail. From these stacks and buildings we, with the two pieces of Artillery kept up a continuous fire on the enemy, and in all probability it was this circumstance that prevented the enemy from advancing, for they could not tell the number we had posted behind these covers and were afraid to attempt passing them; but if they had known how few they were they might easily have advanced while the two brigades were in confusion and routed the whole body, for it was a long time before they could be reorganized again and indeed many, that were panic struck, ran quite off. Gen. Washington having rallied both Gen. Mercer's and Gen. Cadwallader's brigade, they moved forward and when they came to where the Artillery stood began a very heavy platoon fire on the march. This the enemy bore but a few minutes and then threw down their arms and ran. We then pushed forwards towards the town spreading over the fields and through the woods to enclose the enemy and take prisoners. The fields were covered with baggage which the Gen. ordered to be taken care of. Our whole force met at the Court House and took there about 200 prisoners and about 200 others pushed off and were pursued by advanced parties who took about 50 more. In this engagement we lost about 20 killed, the enemy about 100 men killed and lost the field. This is a very pretty little town on the York road 12 miles from Trenton; the houses are built of brick and are very elegant especially the College which has 52 rooms in it; but the whole town has been ravaged and ruined by the enemy.

As soon as the enemy's main army heard our cannon at Princeton (and not 'til then) they discovered our manouvre and pushed after us with all speed and we had not been above an hour in possession of the town before the enemy's light horse and advanced parties attacked our party at the bridge, but our people by a very heavy fire kept the pass until our whole army left the town. Just as our army began our march through Princetown with all their prisoners and spoils the van of the British army we had left at Trenton came in sight, and entered the town about an hour after we left it, but made no stay and pushed on towards Brunswick for fear we should get there before him, which was indeed the course our General intended to pursue had he not been detained too long in collecting the Baggage and Artillery which the enemy had left behind him. Our army marched on to Kingston then wheeled to the left and went down the Millstone, keeping that River on our left; the main body of the British army followed, but kept on through Kingston to Brunswick; but one division or a strong party of horse took the road to the left of the Millstone and arrived on the hill, at the bridge on that road just as the van of the American Army arrived on the opposite side. I was again commanding the van of our army, and General Washington seeing the enemy, rode forward and ordered me to halt and take down a number of carpenters which he had ordered forward and break up the bridge, which was done and the enemy were obliged to return. We then marched on to a little village called Stone brook or Summerset Court House about 15 miles from Princeton where we arrived just at dusk. About an hour before we arrived here 150 of the enemy from Princeton and 50 which were stationed in this town went off with 20 wagons laden with Clothing and Linen, and 400 of the Jersey militia who surrounded them were afraid to fire on them and let them go off unmol-

11

ested and there were no troops in our army fresh enough to pursue them, or the whole might have been taken in a few hours. Our army now was extremely fatigued not having had any refreshment since yesterday morning, and our baggage had all been sent away the morning of the action at Trenton; yet they are in good health and in high spirits. . . . .

MORRISTOWN January 6ᵗʰ 1777.

We left Pluckemin this morning and arrived at Morristown just before sunset. The order of march, was first a small advance guard, next the officers who were prisoners, next my Light Infantry Regiment, in columns of four deep; next the [prisoners flanked by the riflemen, next the head of the main column, with the artillery in front. Our whole Light Infantry are quartered in a very large house belonging to Col. Ford having 4 Rooms on a floor and Two stories high. This town is situated among the mountains of Morris County, about 18 miles from Elizabethtown, 28 from Brunswick and 20 from Carroll's Ferry.

[Originals in possession of Cæsar A. Rodney, Esq.]

[No. 52.]

POSITION OF THE BRITISH AT THE CLOSE OF THE CAMPAIGN

" The following were the exact stations of Gen. Howe's army on the 6th of January, 1777, from an authentic account.

At New York.—The first brigade of British consisting of the 4th, 15th, 27th, and 45th regiments; a squadron of light dragoons of the 17th; and three Hessian regiments, viz. Hereditary Prince, Cassel and Donop.

At Harlem.—The sixth brigade, British, consisting of the 23d, 44th, and 6th regiments, and a brigade of Hessians.

At Amboy.—33d and 71st regiments, and remains of 7th and 16th [?] regiments; a detachment of dragoons, and the Waldeck regiment.

At Brunswick.—The guards, grenadiers, and light infantry.

Second brigade, British, consisting of the 5th, 28th, 35th, and 49th regiments. Fourth brigade, British, consisting of the 17th, 40th, 46th, and 55th regiments, and the 42 regiment, which is not brigaded. Also Donop's corps, Hessian grenadiers, and chasseurs.

At Bergen.—The 57th regiment, ordered to Amboy, and preparing to embark.

At Rhode Island.—Third and fifth brigades of British, consisting of the 10th, 37th, 38th, and 52d; of the 22d, 43d, 54th, and 63d regiments; a battalion of grenadiers, and one of light infantry; a troop of light dragoons; a detachment of artillery, and two brigades of Hessians.

This account shews clearly what places Gen. Howe is in possession of, and what he is not; that in Jersey he has only Brunswick and Amboy, and in New York only York city and Harlem. All other places are in possession of the Americans, who seem by the last accounts to be endeavoring to cut off the troops at Brunswick."

[*London Chronicle*, March 1-4, 1777.]

RETURNS AND STATEMENTS

OF

PRISONERS.

———•••———

1776.

Returns and Statements of Prisoners

[No. 53.]

NARRATIVE OF LIEUT. JABEZ FITCH

TAKEN PRISONER ON LONG ISLAND.

. . . "I myself was so happy as to fall at first into ye hands . . of ye 57th Reg^t who used me with some degree of Civility, altho, some perticular Offrs were very liberal of their favourite Term (Rebels) & now & then did not forget to Remind me of a halter, &c; they did not Rob or Strip me of any of my Clothing, only took my Arms & Amunition, & after keeping me in ye Field sometime, in Confinment with several others under a Strong Guard, was sent off to Gen^{l1} Grants Quarters, at Gowaynes. In this March we passd through ye Front of several Brigades of Hessians who were peraded on several Emininences in order of Battle; they Indeed made a very Warlike appearance, & as no power appear'd at yt [that] time to oppose them, their whole attention seemed to be fixed on us, nor were they by any means, sparing of their Insults; But their Offrs Esspacially, Represented to ye life (as far as their Capacitys would admit) ye conduct of Infernal Spirits, under Certain Restrictions; Having pas'd through those Savage Insults, we at length came to a hill nigh to the place where we at first engaged ye Enimy ye morning; we were here met by a number of Insolent Soldiers among whom was one Woman who appeared remarkably Malicious and attempted several times, to throw Stones at us, when one of our Guard Informed me yt her husband had been killed in this Day's Action; we were then conducted down to a barn near ye water side, where we were drove into a Yard among a great number of Offrs & men who had been taken before us; soon after we came here, Capt. Jewett with a number of others were brought in, & Confin'd with us; Capt

---

[1] Of Colonel Huntington's regiment.

Jewett had Recd two Wounds with a Bayonet after he was taken &
Strip'd of his Arms, & part of his Cloths, one in ye Brest & y^e
other in ye Belly, of wich he Languished with great pain untill y^e
Thirdsday following when he Died; Sarg^t Graves was also Stab'd
in ye Thigh with a Bayonet, after he was taken with Capt Jewett, of
wich wound he recovered altho' he afterward perrish'd in Prison
with many hundred others at N. York. . . . . After being
some time confined in this Yard, Capt Jewett & some others who
were wounded were ordered to some other place in order to have
their Wounds dress'd, & I see no more of them this Night. . . .
Early next morning Capt Jewett came to us in excessive pain with
his wounds already dress'd, but yet notwithstanding ye applications of
several of ye Enimy's Cirgions, Especially one Doc^r Howe (a young
Scotch Gen^t) who treated him with great civility & tenderness, he
Languished untill ye Thirdsday following (viz: ye 29th of Augt at about
5 oClock in ye Morning) when he Expired, & was Buried in an
Orchard nigh s^d House, at about 8 ye same morning, with as
much Deacence as our present Situation would Admit; I myself
[was] Indulg'd by Gn^ll Grant, at ye application of Maj^r Brown,
who Attended us in this place, to Attend ye Captains Funeral; The
aforesaid Maj^r Brown treated us with ye greatest Civility & Comples-
ance, during our confinment in this place, & Endeavour'd to make
our Accomodations, as agreable as possable; Gen^ll Grant also was
so good as to send us (with his Compliments,) two Quarters of Mut-
ton well Cook'd, & several Loves of Bread, which were Acceptable
to us, as most of us had eat nothing since ye Monday before."

[From copy of original in possession of Mr. Chas. I. Bushnell, New York.]

[No. 54.]

EXTRACT FROM THE JOURNAL OF LIEUT. WILLIAM
McPHERSON [1]

TAKEN PRISONER ON LONG ISLAND.

W^m McPherson, Lieut. was taken Prisoner the 27th Day of
August by the Hathians [Hessians] and was taken to Flatbush, that
evening and staid there five days and then they marched us down to

---

[1] Of Colonel Miles' regiment. The journal, McPherson says, was "wrote
at John Lott's, Flatbush, L. I."

the river and sent us aboard of one of their transports. Sept. the
15th. I am as hearty as the time will admit. The Generals who
were taken on Long Island are Gen¹ Sullivan, Lord Sterling. They
were taken the 27th of Augt. 1776. That day there were twenty-
three thousand of the King's troops on Long Island and about
twenty-six hundred of the Continental troops against them which was
suffered very much. Sept. 22ᵈ. We sailed from below the Narrows
up near New York and there we —— the 23ᵈ day. There was some
firing from the Rowbuck & another small vessel against our work
on Paulus Hook which continued about half an hour. Col. Miles
got leave to go to Philadelphia this 26th of November 1776, from
New York where he was prisoner. The 7th of October we all left
the Snow Mentor and were taken into New York and was put into a
close house there. All the officers signed their parole this day
& got a small bound to walk round to stretch their legs, which
we found grateful. Nov. 20, 1776, all the officers got leave to
walk in the bounds of the City of New York."

[Original in the possession of Hon. Edward McPherson, Gettysburg,
Penn.]

[No. 55.]

DEPOSITION OF PRIVATE FOSTER

TAKEN PRISONER ON LONG ISLAND.

Thomas Foster of full age being duly sworn, deposeth and saith
that he was a soldier in the first battalion of the Pennsylvania Riflemen, commanded by Colo. Miles; that he was made a prisoner on
Long Island; that immediately after he was made prisoner he was
stripped by the Hessians of all his clothes, except his frock and a pair
of drawers; that after they had stripped him, they put a cord about
his neck and hanged him up to the limb of a tree, where they suffered him to remain until he was almost strangled; that they
then cut him down and gave him a little rum to recover his spirits;
that they repeated this cruel sport three times successively; that
he has frequently heard it said among the British troops that the

Hessians hanged several of our prisoners, and further this deponent says not.

his

THOMAS **X** FOSTER,

mark

examined and sworn in the presence of

GENᴸ MCDOUGALL
JOHN SLOSS HOBART
NATHL. SACKET
WILLIAM DUER

[Journal of the New York Provincial Congress, Vol. II.]

[No. 56.]

LETTERS FROM CAPT. NATHANIEL FITZ RANDOLPH, OF NEW JERSEY

WRITTEN WHILE PRISONER.[1]

MY DEAR SPOUSE—these with my Love to you and Children may informe you of my present situation, which is that I am wounded in the head and arm but not dangerous. Should be glad that you will send me some necessary Clothing as I now remain in close confinement. I would not have you make yourself uneasy about me as I have been

[1] Captain Randolph was a very brave officer from Woodbridge, N. J., who, during the war, undertook several hazardous scouting expeditions. He belonged to the Continental army, was five times wounded, twice made a prisoner, and finally killed, in July, 1780, in a skirmish near Springfield, New Jersey. He was the officer who captured the famous Colonel Billop. He appears to have been with Colonel Heard, when the latter was sent to seize tories on Long Island, in January, 1776; in which connection the following letter to his wife will be of interest:

. . . When we Shall Return Home is unceartain we have Been Busy a Hunting up and Disarming the Tories ever Since we Have Been Here. Have collected upwards of two Hundred Muskits with ammunition &c. We was two nights at Jamaica where I had to take Jonathan Rowland an own uncle to Roberts wife. Likewise Samˡ Doughty an acquaintance of Roberts. Charles Jackson is well and Desires to Be Remembered to his fammily and I Request of you to Show his wife this Letter. I Remain yours &c.,   NATHL. FITZ RANDOLPH.
HEMPSTEAD, Jan. 24th, 1776.
P. S. We proceed from Here to Oyster Bay.

treated with the greatest kindness by Col. Prescott who commanded the party of King's Troops whose hands it was my misfortune to fall into. Likewise by most of the officers of the 28th and 35th Ridgements. I have been before Lord Cornwallace, who I believe looks upon my conduct nothing more than becoming a soldier—and Major Generl. Grant has for my conduct in taking his steward and stores kindly sent me word that I may send to him for any necessarys which I may want and shall be wellcome to. I would request to procure some person to bring what necessarys you may send to me and believe they will not be molested or detained if received protection. I now conclude wishing you every happyness these times can afford and remain your ever affectionate Husband,

NATHL. FITZ RANDOLPH.

ON BOARD GAURD HOUSE AT NEW BRUNSWICK Jan. 26th, 1777.

P. S. Joseph Combes is well and hearty, and desires that his brother Stephen may send him some clothes, but in particular to send a pair of Buckskin Breeches.

To Mrs. EXPERIENCE FITZ RANDOLPH—
to the care of
John Hampton
at
Woodbridge.

_____

I make no doubt but every intelligence you have had concerning me has been favorable and wish it was in my power to send you such intelligence now—But must informe you in as few words as possible that the wound in my head is verry painfull and dangerous and am now close confined in the Provost Goal, By a positive order from Generl. Howe. I would not have you make yourself uneasy about me as it will be of But Little Service to either of us—But wish you every Happyness the world can afford and remain your ever affectionate Husband,

NATH'L. FITZ RANDOLPH.

NEW YORK Feb. 25th 1777.

P. S. Our men who are prisoners here is verry sickly and are Dying Dayly—John Parker an Indian Israel dyed here a few days ago—Please to send enclosed by some safe hand.

To Mrs. EXPERIENCE FITZ RANDOLPH
in
East Jersey.

These with my love to you and Children may informe you that I remain close Confined in the Provost Goal but in vain might attempt to discribe in a particular manner the misserys that attend the Poor Prisoners Confined in this Horrid place, they are dying dayly with (what is called here) the Goal fever but may more properly be called the Hungry fever which rages among the prisoners here confined in goals they being deprived of allmost every necessary of Life. As to the treatment I have received since a prisoner has been varrious Sometimes like a Gentleman other times like a Ruffin, have been for a week without a Surgeon to attend me. At other times have been attended by eight or ten different Surgeons in one day, But have for three weeks past had verry regular attendance. My wounds is in a fair way of doing well and am in prety good Health. Being in great haste must conclude, desireing you to make your self as happy as possible in your present Situation and wait with patience until time brings a change. I remain with sincere affection, ever your affectionate Husband,   NATHL. FITZ RANDOLPH.

NEW YORK, March 10, 1777.

P. S.   David Tappin is confined in a Room where the Small Pox is and Reuben Potter has been unwell for some days past.

[Originals in possession of Captain John Coddington Kinney, Hartford, Conn.]

[No. 57.]

EXTRACT FROM THE JOURNAL OF CAPT. JAMES MORRIS, PRISONER AT FLATBUSH, L. I.[1]

" I was put on board with the other prisoners of war [at Philadelphia] and sailed down the river Delaware, and went to New York. We were 12 days on our passage. I was then put on my parole of honour and boarded with a plain Dutch family in Kings County, at

[1] Captain James Morris was a Connecticut officer. He first entered the service as ensign in Colonel Gay's Regiment, and was engaged in the battle of Long Island. In the following year, as lieutenant, he fought at the battle of Germantown, where he was taken prisoner, and closely confined in Philadelphia until removed to Long Island. When released, in 1781, he was

the west end of Long Island. We were confined within the limits of said County.

At Flat Bush I became acquainted with a Mr Clarkson a man of science and of a large property, he owned the most extensive private Library that I had ever known in the United States, his wife had a capacious mind and she was remarkably distinguished for her piety. Mr. Clarkson made me a welcome visitor at his house and gave me access to his library. He allowed me to take as many books as I chose and carry them to my lodgings. I there lived two years and six months devoting my time to reading. I read through a course of ancient and modern history. My exercise was hand labour and walking. I tended a garden one summer upon shares and my net profits were about twelve dollars. The next summer I obtained the use of a small piece of Land and planted it with potatoes from which my net profits were 30 dollars. I was treated with great kindness by the family with which I lived. I endeavored to be always on the pleasant side with them and to be sure, not to be wanting in my attentions to my landlady. Here I learned that the little nameless civilities and attentions were worth a great deal more than they cost me. Here I was peculiarily situated to learn the human character: for the inhabitants in this county were all attached to the British Government and said the officers paroled there were all rebels, and that they would finally be hung for their rebellion, so that if any of us received any injury or met with any abuse from the inhabitants we could have no redress we must patiently bear it. The Dutch inhabitants were uncultivated yet many of them possessed strength of mind and were intelligent. They were mostly strangers to the sympathies and tender sensibilities which so much rejoiced the heart of friends with friends and promote the happiness of society. But not-

detailed to Scammell's Light Infantry Corps, and took part in the capture of Yorktown, Virginia. One of his letters, written from Flatbush while prisoner, is as follows:

FLATBUSH, LONG ISLAND, June 30, 1778.

Wednesday, the 17th inst., the American Prisoners of war left Philadelphia. I embarked on board the Sloop Nancy, Capt. Hill. Sailed as far as Billings Port ; then went on board the Brig Minerva, Capt. Smith, in order to sail for New York. After a passage of 12 days arrived at New York, being the 28th inst. The 29th I was paroled upon Long Island, and went to live at the House of Mr. John Lott. Our treatment, both officers and soldiers, while on board the shipping, was much better than I expected ; our situation was as agreeable as circumstances would admit. We had the liberty of any part of the ship, and both officers and soldiers had a supply of provisions and a gill of Rum per man per day.

withstanding I was thus secluded from my particular friends and acquaintances yet I enjoyed my share of comfort and worldly felicity. I felt no disposition to murmer and repine in my then condition. Every day afforded me its enjoyments excepting a time when I had a pretty severe attack with the ague and fever which reduced me low. The whole term of my Captivity was three years and three months lacking one day. I was exchanged on the 3rd day of Jany 1781. I was taken from Flat Bush to New York and from thence conveyed to Elizabethtown in New Jersey and set at liberty."

[Original in possession of Hon. Dwight Morris, Bridgeport, Conn.]

[No. 58.]

BRITISH PRISONERS TAKEN BY THE AMERICANS ON LONG ISLAND

KINGS BRIDGE, August 29, 1776.

GENTLEMEN: I send to your care and safe keeping the following prisoners of war, taken on *Long Island*, on the 27th instant viz: Lieutenant *John Ragg*, of the Marines, Sergeant *David Wallace*, Corporal *Thomas Pike* and *Edward Gibbon*, *William Smith*, *Isaac Hughs*, *Thomas Haraman*, *John Woodard*, *Edward Cavil*, *William Williams*, *William Coortney*, *Stephen Weber*, *John Smith*, *Samuel Morral*, *Thomas Sarral*, *Joseph Distant*, *Benjamin Jones*, *William Jones*, *William Pearce*, *John Hopkins*, *Henry Weston*, *Evan Evans*, and *John Morten*, Privates.

You will please to secure them in such manner as to prevent their escape, observing the order of Congress in this respect.

I am, gentlemen, with Esteem,

Your humble Servant

W. HEATH, Major General.

To the Committee of the Town of Fairfield [Conn.]

[*Force*, 5th Series, vol. i, p. 1215.]

A RETURN OF THE PRISONERS TAKEN IN YORK DURING THE CAMPAIGN 1776

When taken	Where	Generals	Colonels	Lt. Colonels	Majors	Captains	Lieutenants	Ensigns	Chaplains	Q. Masters	Adjutants	Surgeons	Commissaries	Engineers	Wagon Masters	Volunteers	Privates	Wounded
Aug.t 27th	Long Island	2	3	4	2	18	43	11	3		1	3				3	1006	9 Officers, 56 Privates
Sep.t 15 & 16th	York Island		1	2	3	4	7										354	
Oct.r 12th	White Plains					1	2			1							35	
Nov. 16th	Fort Washington		4	4	5	56	107	31	1,1	2	2	5	2	1	1		2637	6 Officers, 53 Privates
Nov. 18th	Fort Lee						1	1		1		3					99	
	Total	2	8	10	10	79	160	43	4	4	3	11	2	1	1	3	4131	

Copy

CHATHAM Jan.y 30th 1777   A true copy taken from the Commissary General's, &
P. S. The original taken in New Jersey sent to Gov.r Brooks. | brought from York by Major Wells.

[Original among Lieut.-Col. Henshaw's papers.]

[No. 60.]

LIST OF AMERICAN OFFICERS TAKEN PRISONERS AT THE BATTLE OF LONG ISLAND[1]

THREE GENERALS.

Major General John Sullivan,
Brigadier General Lord Stirling,
Brigadier General Nathaniel Woodhull.[2]

THREE COLONELS.

Penn. Rifle Reg't........	1	............Col. Samuel Miles,
Penn. Musketeers........	1	............Col. Sam. John Atlee,
New Jersey Militia.......	1	............Col. Phillip Johnston.[2]

FOUR LIEUT.-COLONELS.

Penn. Rifle Reg't.... 1 [Miles'].......Lt. Col. James Piper,

Penn. Militia......... 2 .... { Lt. Col. Nicholas Lutz,
{ Lt. Col. Peter Kachlein,

17th Continental Regt. 1 [Huntington's] Lt. Col. Joel Clark.

THREE MAJORS.

Penn. Militia........	1 [Lutz's]	..........Maj. Edward Burd,
17th Continental Reg't	1	.................Maj. Browne,[3]
22d Continental Reg't	1 [Wyllys's]	.........Maj. Levi Wells.

EIGHTEEN CAPTAINS.

Penn. Rifle Reg't.... 2 ...... { Capt. Richard Brown, 1st Batt.,
{ " Wm. Peebles, 2d Batt.

Penn. Musketeers.... 4 [Atlee's]. { Capt. Thomas Herbert,
{ " Joseph Howell,*
{ " Francis Murray,*
{ " John Nice.*

[1] The left-hand column, naming the regiments, with the rank and number of officers captured, is taken from the report of Joseph Loring, the British Commissary of Prisoners.—*Force*, 5th Series, vol i., p. 1258. The names added opposite have been collated from official rolls, published and in manuscript, unless otherwise stated in notes.

[2] Reference has already been made to Gen. Woodhull and Col. Johnston in the chapter on "The Battle of Long Island."

[3] Huntington's regiment appears to have had no major at this date; certainly none was taken prisoner. In the return of prisoners exchanged Dec. 9, 1776, there is this memorandum in regard to Maj. Browne: "Taken on Long Island, not in arms. It is preposed that he be exchanged for Major Wells, of Connecticut."

Penn. Militia........ 5 .....
{
Lutz' Battalion.

Capt. Jacob Crowle,
" Joseph Heister,*
" Jacob Mauser.*

Kachlein's Battalion.

Capt. Garret Graff,*
" Henry Hogenbach,*
" Timothy Jayne.*
}

The officers designated by the asterisk were exchanged Dec. 9, 1776.
See list in *Penn. Archives*, Second Series, vol. i., p. 426.

17th Continental..... 4 .....
{
Capt. Joseph Jewett,[1]
" Ozias Bissell,
" Jonathan Brewster,
" Caleb Trowbridge,
" Timothy Percival,
" Eben. F. Bissell.
}

Train of Artillery.... 1 ....Capt.-Lieut. John Johnston.[2]

Maryland Provincials. 2 [Smallwood's] Capt. Daniel Bowie.[3]

FORTY-THREE LIEUTENANTS.

Provincial Rifle Reg'ts 11 ....
{
1st Battalion.

1st Lieut. William Gray,*
" John Spear,
" John Davis,
" George Wert,
2d Lieut. Joseph Triesbach,
" Wm. McPherson,
" Luke Broadhead.*

2d Battalion.

1st Lieut. Matthew Scott,*
" Daniel Topham,
Lieut. Brownlee.

Cunningham's Regiment.

Lieut. Patterson.
}

[1] There is a discrepancy here. The English give four Captains, while Huntington's return gives six. So also in Lieutenants and Ensigns.

[2] This name does not appear on any roll, but no doubt Johnston was the Captain intended, no other having been taken prisoner.

[3] Bowie was the only Maryland Captain taken, the rest being accounted for. Possibly one of the Lieutenants—six having been taken instead of five, as the English report—was rated by mistake as a Captain.

12

Penn. Musketeers.... 1 ....Lieut. Walter Finney.

Penn. Militia........ 6 .....{

Lutz' Battalion.
Lieut. Stephen Baldy.[1]
Kachlein's Battalion.
Lieut. Lewis,
" 　　Medow [Middagh]
" 　　Shoemaker.

17th Continental Reg't 6 .... {

Lieut. Solomon Orcutt,
" 　　Jabez Fitch, Jr.,
" 　　Thomas Fanning,
" 　　Solomon Makepeace,
" 　　Nathaniel Gove,
" 　　Jonathan Gillet.

Delaware Battalion........ 2 {

Lieut. Jonathan Harney,
" 　　Alex. Stewart.

1st Battalion N. Y. }
Continental... 5 } [Lasher's] {

Lieut. Edward Dunscomb,
" 　　Robert Troup,*
Adj. Jeronimus Hoogland,
Lieut. Gerrit Van Wagenen,[2]
" 　　Wm. Gilliland.

11th Battalion Continental... 1 [Hitchcock's] Lieut. John Blunt.

New Jersey Militia......... 1 [Johnston's] 1st Lieut. John Toms.

1st Batt. Maryland }
Independents... } [Veazey's 2 {
Co.]

Lieut. Samuel Wright,
" 　　Edward De Courcy.

Long Island Militia........ 2 {

Lieut. Coe,[3]
" 　　———.

Train of Artillery.......... 1 ..Cadet John Callender.[4]

[1] There was but one Lieutenant taken in Lutz's Battalion. See Rolls in *Force*, Returns of Col. Haller's regiment.

[2] Lieuts. Van Wagenen and Gilliland did not belong to Lasher's battalion, but were taken with Dunscomb, Troup, and Hoogland, and probably rated with them.

[3] In Onderdonk's Revolutionary Incidents it is stated that Coe was a Lieutenant of the troopers, and was taken the day after the battle. The other Lieutenant was taken at the time of Gen. Woodhull's capture, but his name does not appear.

[4] Callender is doubtless meant. He was rated as a Lieutenant afterwards, and was confined in officers' quarters.

Maryland Provincials........ 5
{
1st Lieut. Wm. Sterret,
" Joseph Butler,
Lieut. Hatch Dent,
" Walter Ridgely,
" Walter Muse,
" Edward Praul.
}

ELEVEN ENSIGNS.

Penn. Musketeers........... 4
{
Ensign W. Henderson,
" Alexander Huston,*
" Michael App*,
" Septimus Davis.*
}

17th Continental Reg't...... 5
{
Ensign Anthony Bradford,
" Joseph Chapman,
" Cornelius Higgins,
" John Kinsman,
" Elihu Lyman,
" Joel Gillet.
}

Maryland Provincials........ 2
{
Ensign Wm. Courts,
" James Fernandez.
}

STAFF.

Adjutant............. ...... 1 [Huntington's] Adj. Elisha Hopkins.

Surgeons 3
{
Miles' Battalion.
Dr. John Davis,
Dr. Joseph Davis.*
Huntington's Regt.
Dr. Silas Holmes.
}

Volunteers................ 2
{
Lieut. David Duncan,
" —— Young.[1]
}

[1] These were two Pennsylvania officers, and it is supposed that they were serving as volunteers at the battle. Their names appear in *Force*.

[No. 61.]

LIST OF AMERICAN NON-COMMISSIONED OFFICERS AND SOLDIERS TAKEN PRISONERS, KILLED, OR MISSING, AT THE BATTLE OF LONG ISLAND

COL. TYLER'S REG'T.—TENTH CONTINENTAL [CONN.]

KILLED.—Antony Wolf.

MISSING.—Samuel Everett, Amasa Pebody.

COL. HITCHCOCK'S REG'T.—ELEVENTH CONTINENTAL [R. I.]

Captain Kimball's Company.

MISSING.—Richard Wallen.

Captain Symond's Company.

KILLED.—John Elliott.

MISSING.—Nath. Ramson, John Patten.

Captain C. Olney's Company.

MISSING.—Caleb Herenden, Benjamin Foster, Daniel Williams, London Citizen [a negro].

Captain Bowen's Company.

MISSING.—William Deputrin.

COL. LITTLE'S REG'T.—TWELFTH CONTINENTAL [MASS.]

Captain Parker's Company.

KILLED.—Peter Barthrick.

Captain Wade's Company.

MISSING.—Archelaus Puleifer.

Captain Dodge's Company.

MISSING.—Elijah Lewis.

COL. HUNTINGTON'S REG'T.—SEVENTEENTH CONTINENTAL [CONN.]

Captain Tyler's Company.

MISSING.—Bartlet Lewis, Elisha Benton, Sergeants; Reuben Bates, Olive Jennings, Joseph White, Jesse Swaddle, Corporals; Joseph Arnold, Joel Ballard, Azariah Benton, Lemuel Lewis, Seth Rider, John Smith, Jeremiah Sparks, Jonathan Witherd, Josiah Benton, Luke Kimball, Jonathan Barnard, James Lindsey, Privates.

Captain *Jewell's* Company.

MISSING.—Stephen Otis, Rufus Tracy, Roswel Graves, Sergeants; Nathan Raymond, Peleg Edwards, Corporals; Joshua Blake, Billa Dyer, Theophilus Emerson, Jaspar Griffin, Elisha Miller, Adam Mitchel, Charles Phelps, Silas Phelps, Oliver Rude, Ebenezer Smith, Jacob Sterling, Timothy Tiffany, Peter Way, Lebbeus Wheeler, Nathan Wood, David Yarrington, Duron Whittlesey, William Eluther, Zadock Pratt, Eliphalet Reynolds, Rufus Cone, Privates.

Captain *Trowbridge's* Company.

MISSING.—Daniel Ingalls, Daniel Farnham, Moses Smith, Sergeants; George Gordon, Levi Farnham, Corporals; Silas Bottom, Drum-Major; William Bedlock, Alexander Brine, Joseph Clarke, John Colegrove, Luke Durfee, George Forster, Caleb Green, John Gardner, Ebenezer Keyes, John Kingsbury; Robert Lithgow, Benjamin Lounsbury, Ishmael Moffit, Joseph Munsur, Daniel Malone, Solomon Mears, John Pollard, Stephen Potter, Joseph Russell, Allen Richards, Monday Smith, David Saunders, John Talmage, William Turner, John Thomas, Samuel White, John Winter, Privates.

Captain *Ozias Bissell's* Company.

MISSING.—Ebenezer Wright, Howard Moulton, Sergeants; Freegrace Billings, Nathan Barney, Abner Belding, Seth Belding, Daniel Church, Lemuel Deming, George Edwards, Thomas Green, Jesse Judson, David Lindsey, Michael Mitchel, Samuel Moulton, Joseph A. Minot, Giles Nott, James Price, Jonathan Price, Benjamin Ripnor, Timothy Risley, Joel Skinner, Daniel Thomas, Robert Wallas, Privates.

Captain *Brewster's* Company.

MISSING.—Theophilus Huntington, Sergeant; Jabez Avery, William Button, Corporals; Simon Armstrong, Jesse Barnet, Joseph Ellis, Asa Fox, Samuel Fuller, Elijah Hammond, Solomon Huntley, Sanford Herrick, Luther Japhet, John Lewis, Thomas Matterson, Rufus Parke, Amasa Pride, Jehiel Pettis, Roger Packard, Samuel Tallman, John Vandeusen, Calvin Waterman, John Williams, Privates.

Captain *Percival's* Company.

MISSING.—Roger Coit, Uriah Hungerford, Rous Bly, [killed,] Sergeants. Samuel Agard, Daniel Bartholomew, Silas Bates, John Bray, David Brown, Solomon Carrington, John Curtis, John Dutton,

Daniel Freeman, Gad Fuller, Abel Hart, Jason Hart, Timothy Isham, Azariah Lothrop, John Moody, Timothy Percival, Isaac Potter, Elijah Rose, Elijah Stanton, Benjamin Tubbs, Abraham Yarrington, Jesse Roberts, Privates.

Captain Fitch Bissell's Company.

MISSING.—Cornelius Russell, Eleazer House, Hezekiah Haydon, Sergeants; Samuel Bordman, Aaron Porter, Elisha Boardman, Corporals; Robert Newcomb, Drummer; John Atwood, Orias Atwood, William Craddock, Ira Clark, Roderick Clark, Lemuel Fuller, Abner Fuller, Roger Tyler, Carmi Higley, Erastus Humphy, Jonathan Halladay, John Willson, John White, John Fletcher, Privates.

Captain Hubbard's Company.

MISSING.—William Talmage, Samuel Skinner, William Parsons, Ebenezer Coe, Sergeants; Eleazer Brooks, Samuel Buck, Jr., Cornelius Coverling, Aaron Drake, Benjamin Hills, Alexander Ingham, Elias Leet, Levi Loveland, Elijah Roberts, Reuben Shipman, Samuel Strictland, Seth Turner, Nathan Whiting, Job Wetmore, Privates.

COL. JONATHAN WARD'S REG'T.—TWENTY-FIRST CONTINENTAL [MASS.].

Captain King's Company.

MISSING.—Moses Whitney, James Barker, Privates.

Captain Bartlet's Company.

MISSING.—Cornelius Warren, Private.

COL. WYLLYS' REG'T.—TWENTY-SECOND CONTINENTAL [CONN.].

Captain Pettibone's Company.

MISSING.—William Gaylord, Private.

Captain Scott's Company.

MISSING.—Eliezur Loveland, Private.

Captain Wright's Company.

MISSING.—Joel Taylor, Private.

Major Holdridge's Company.

MISSING.—Abner Rider, Sherman Shadduck, Elijah Smith, Joseph Watrous, Privates.

Captain Mills' Company.

MISSING.—Robert Lusk, Jonathan Ingham, Privates.

COL. MILES' REG'T.—[PENN.] [1]

(Two Battalions.)

First Battalion.—Captain Farmer's Company.

MISSING.—Robert Garrett, Drummer; Alexander Anderson, John Barger, Henry Cordier, Creewas Bastian, Cornelius Dauel, George Dillman, 'George Edwards, Jacob Engelhart, Chushan Foy, Philip Feese, George Garling, Benjamin Hackett, Lawrence Homan, Nicholas Hause, Martin Haynes, Jonathan Hager, Jacob Koppinger, Adam Kydle, Conrad Meserly, George Miller, Jr., Adam Swager, Jacob Shifle [wounded], Francis Shitz, Jacob Shutt, Jacob Slottner, Goodlip Voolever, Henry Wise, John Young, Privates.

Captain Brown's Company.

MISSING.—James Anderson, Sergeant; William Lever, Drummer; Hugh Barkley, Hezekiah, Biddle, William Bradley, Peter Carmichael, Samuel Crosson, Peter Develin, Timothy Driskil, Adam Growss, Alexander Holmes, Robert Huston, John McGriggor, Christy Mc-Michael, William Moore, Jonathan Nesbit, Richard Roberts, Nathanael Scott, Degory Sparks, Robert Stokes, Privates.

Captain Long's Company.

MISSING.—Thomas Higginbottom, Sergeant; Henry Donely, Drummer; James Nelson, Fifer; John Beatty, Thomas Christopher, Abraham Dunlap, John Elliot, Jr., John Elliot, Sen., Benjamin Harverd, Patrick Kelly, Daniel McLean, Hugh Mulhalon [wounded], John Williams, Privates.

Captain Albright's Company.

MISSING.—Thomas Wilson, Robert Tate, James Geddes, Sergeants; Andrew Boned, Alexander Boyd, Edward Carleton, James Cuxel, Thomas Fosler, Hugh Gobin, Jacob Helsley, John Henary, Philip Kennedy, William Kilpatrick, Thomas Knee (or Karee), Conrad Lead, Henry McBroom, Hugh McClughan, John McElnay, James McFarland, Bartholomew McGuire, Jacob Newman, John Rinehart, Henry Shadon, Charles Spangler, Charles Stump

---

[1] The returns of the losses in the Pennsylvania regiments, as here given, are copied from the original manuscript rolls in the public archives of that State. I am indebted to the Hon. John A. Linn, Assistant Secretary of the Commonwealth, Harrisburg, not only for the authenticated copies, but for several of the documents in Part II., and for much other information respecting the troops from Pennsylvania.—ED.

[wounded], John Swartz, George Wampler, Edward Wells, Thomas Williams, Privates.

Captain Shade's Company.

MISSING.—Isaac Gruber, Sergeant; Henry Baker, Henry Bolla-baker, John Bower, Henry Goodshalk, Jacob Isenhart, Adam Kerchner, George Keibler, John Lee, John McAry, Lorentz Miller, Christopher Neighhast, John Simmins, Elias Schwartz, Frederick Tickard, Henry Weaver, Privates.

Captain Weitzell's Company.

MISSING.—John Gordon, Sergeant-Major; Thomas Price, Sergeant; William Allison, Peter Brady, Andrew Carter, Robert Caruthers, Henry Gass, John Hardy, Dennis Huggins, Martin Kershller, Joseph Madden, William McCormick, Patrick McVey, Robert Morehead, Andrew Ralston, John Rice, Jacob Speiss, James Watt, Privates.

Second Battalion.—Captain Murray's Company.

MISSING.—Thomas Dudgeon, John Galloway, Daniel McCoy, Thomas Plunkett, Privates.

Captain Peebles' Company.

MISSING.—P. Heylands, Sergeant; James Carson, Drummer; Edmund Lee, Fifer; James Atcheson, Samuel Dixon, Samuel Montgomery, David Moore, James Moore, James Mortimore, John Neil, Robert Nugent, Patrick Quigley, Thomas Rogers, William Witherspoon, Privates.

Captain Marshall's Company.

MISSING.—Robert Andrews, Robert Slemen, Privates.

Captain Erwin's Company.

MISSING.—James Dugan, John Justice, William Lindsay, Samuel Roddy, Sergeants;[1] Daniel Brownspeld, Jeremiah Gunnon, John Guthry, William Guthry, John Henry, Philip Kelly, Andy McKenzie [a volunteer], William Moore, William Mull, James Nelson, William Nelson, Stephen Singlewood, Charles Stamper, John Stoops, William Twifold, Angus Wilkinson, Privates.

---

[1] One of these sergeants escaped, but the rolls do not show which one.

Captain Grubb's Company.

MISSING.—George Brown, John Hehm, Robert Henderson, Joseph McFarland, Privates.

Captain Christ's Company.

MISSING.—Matthew Whitlow, Jeremiah Geiss, Sergeants; Paul Frederick, Yost Fuchs, Privates.

COL. ATLEE'S REG'T.—[PENN.]

Captain Anderson's Company.

MISSING.—Francis Ferguson, William Harper, John Madden, William McCormick, Hector McGowan, John Moore, Benjamin Nain, Hosea Rigg, Edward Wood, Privates.

Captain Lloyd's Company.

MISSING.—William Nemrich, Sergeant [wounded]; Jesse Moore, Fifer; Michael Clary, Michael Derry, Folk Matthias, Archibald Graham, James Hidden, Robert Kinen, Adam Kingfield, Patrick McCullough, James Moore, Edward Murphy, William Powel, James Tyrer, Richard Wallace, William Watson, Privates.

Captain Murray's Company.

MISSING.—Joseph Atkinson, James Davis, William Gillespie, John Guthrie, Thomas Logan, Thomas McConnell, John McEnrae, John Moody, Patrick Mullan, David Robinson, Privates.

Captain McClellan's Company.

MISSING.—James Mitchell, Sergeant [wounded]'; Joseph Moor, Corporal [killed]; John Calhoon, James Elder, Michael Kenaday, Robert Love, Justin McCarty, James McClure, Daniel McElroy, James McElvay, William McIlvain, Thomas Mitchel, Thomas Moore [wounded], William Murray [wounded], O'Trail Morris, Privates.

Captain Herbert's Company.

MISSING.—Eleazer Crain, John Everhart, John Ingram, George Ridge, Boston Wagoner, Michael Weaver, Privates.

Captain De Huff's Company.

MISSING.—Michael Loy, Jacob Marks, Christian Mentzer, Patrick Mulrang, Peter Wile, Godlip Wiseman, Privates.

Captain Nice's Company.

MISSING.—Edward Barnhouse, Edward Baxter, Michael Domiller, John Gee, John Huston, Robert Jones, Edward Justice, Richard Robeson, Michael Stucke, Privates.

Captain Howell's Company.

MISSING.—Michael Carmodey, John Ervine [killed], John Gilkey, James Gallagher, William Jones, William McMaunagel, William Tweedy, Privates.

LIEUT.-COL. KACHLEIN'S REG'T.—[PENN.]

Captain John Arndt's Company.

MISSING.—Andrew Hessher, Andrew Reefer, Sergeants; Thomas Sybert, Martin Derr, George Fry, Lawrence Gob, Anthony Frutches, Peter Froes, John Harpel, Jacob Dufford, Joseph Stout, Mathias Stidinger, Peter Beyer, Peter Lohr, Bernhard Miller, Richard Overfeld, Jacob Weid Knecht, Henry Bush, Sr., Peter Kern, Philip Bush, Abraham Peter.

COL. GAY'S REG'T.—[CONN.]

Captain Goodwin's Company.

MISSING.—Clement Maxfield, Martin Nash, Privates.

Captain Wells' Company.

MISSING.—Joseph Bidwell, Private.

Captain Wilson's Company.

MISSING.—Benjamin Frisby, Private.

COL. CHESTER'S REG'T.—[CONN.]

MISSING.—Maygot, Cheney, Marret, Upham, Fling, Alderman, Humphry, Gillet, Martin, Shawn, Sasanan, Tassett, Privates.

BIOGRAPHICAL SKETCHES.

In the few following sketches the writer has simply incorporated such facts of personal interest as have come to his knowledge while preparing the work.

As for the generals who took part in this campaign, Washington, Stephen, and Mercer were from Virginia ; General Beall, of Maryland, commanded part of the Flying Camp from that State ; Generals Mifflin and St. Clair were from Pennsylvania—also Generals Cadwallader, Roberdeau, and Ewing, who commanded Pennsylvania " Associators" for a short time (Roberdeau also having a brigade under Greene at Fort Lee) ; Generals Stirling and Heard, from New Jersey ; Generals James and George Clinton, McDougall, Scott, and Woodhull, from New York ; Generals Putnam, Spencer, Wadsworth, Wolcott, and Parsons, from Connecticut ; General Greene, from Rhode Island ; Generals Heath, Nixon, Fellows, and Lincoln, from Massachusetts ; and General Sullivan, from New Hampshire. General Lee was born in Wales, had served in the British army, and settled in Virginia. General De Fermoy was a Frenchman.

CALLENDER, CAPTAIN JOHN.—This officer, who behaved so well on Long Island, was the son of Eliezer Callender, of Boston. At the close of the war he became a merchant in Virginia, and died at Alexandria, in October, 1797.

CLARK, LIEUTENANT-COLONEL JOEL.—Lieutenant Fitch states that Clark, who commanded Huntington's regiment at the battle of Long Island, and was taken prisoner, died about one o'clock on the morning of December 19th, after a long sickness, and was buried in the New Brick Churchyard [now Park Row], in New York. Officers followed his remains to the grave.

DOUGLAS, COLONEL WILLIAM.—Born in Plainfield, Conn., January 17th, 1742. Afterwards lived in Northford. Served as Putnam's orderly-sergeant in the French and Indian War. In 1775 joined Montgomery, who put him in charge of the flotilla on Lake Champlain, in view of his nautical experience. In 1776 he raised a regiment for the army at New York, where, as appears in the narrative, he proved himself a thorough soldier. In 1777 he raised a Continental regiment, but his health broke down, and he died May 28th of that year. His death was a loss to the service, as he was a man of faith, character, and personal courage. The regiment he raised was given to the famous Colonel Return Jonathan Meigs.

13

DUNSCOMB, LIEUTENANT EDWARD.—Born May 23d, 1754, in New York. Died November 12th, 1814. Graduate of Columbia College in 1774. He was son of Daniel Dunscomb, a firm friend of the colonial cause. After his capture at the Jamaica Pass, August 27th, he was confined on a prison ship and fell sick, but recovered, and on his exchange rejoined the army, where, in 1780, he appears as Captain of the Fourth New York Line. After the war he became clerk of the United States Courts. He was also a vestryman of Trinity Church, and a trustee of Columbia College. The tradition in his family is that he was asked to be Hamilton's second in the duel with Burr, but declined in disapproval of the practice.

FISH, MAJOR NICHOLAS.—Born in New York, August 28th, 1758; died June 20th, 1833. He was at Princeton a short time, but leaving college, studied law with John Morin Scott, whose brigade-major he became in 1776. Fish afterwards served with the New York Line through the war, and as major of light infantry under Hamilton at Yorktown. In 1786 he became adjutant-general of New York, was afterwards an alderman of the city and president of the Cincinnati. He was the father of the Hon. Hamilton Fish, ex-Secretary of State.

GAY, COLONEL FISHER.—Of Wadsworth's brigade. He came from Farmington, Conn., having served also at the siege of Boston. His regiment was for some time on Long Island, but the colonel had been sick, and either died or was buried on the day of the battle, August 27th.

HALE, CAPTAIN NATHAN.—The most authoritative account of his capture and death is given by Hull, who was captain with him in Webb's regiment. Lossing states that he was hanged from an apple-tree in Rutgers' orchard. Hale was a young graduate of Yale ; came from Ashford, Conn. The sketch of his life by I. W. Stuart, Hartford, 1856, contains the particulars of his career. See page 262, Part I.

HAMILTON, CAPTAIN ALEXANDER.—See chapter on " The Two Armies." Hamilton was stationed in New York at the Grand Battery and Fort George, and doubtless participated in the firing on the ships whenever they passed up either river. At White Plains his guns did good execution, also in the subsequent actions in New Jersey. In March, 1777, he became aid to Washington with rank of lieutenant-colonel, and particularly distinguished himself at Monmouth, and afterwards as commander of a light infantry battalion at Yorktown. He had few if any superiors among the younger officers of the Revolutionary army.

HENSHAW, LIEUTENANT-COLONEL WILLIAM.—Born at Boston February 20th, 1735, and removed to Leicester in 1745. He served in the French war under Amherst. The Lexington alarm he answered promptly, and marched to Boston at the head of his militia regiment. The Massachusetts Provincial Congress appointed him adjutant-general of the army mustered around Boston, and he held that position until relieved by General Gates in July. He was actively engaged through the entire campaign in 1776, being in the midst of the fighting on Long Island, at Harlem Heights, and at Princeton. At the close of the campaign he retired from the service. A full and interesting sketch of him, together with his Order Book of 1775, has lately been published by the Massachusetts Historical Society. Colonel Henshaw died February 20th, 1820.

HUGHES, COLONEL HUGH.—Of Welsh extraction. Taught a select grammar school, in 1765, in the French Church Consistory Rooms in Nassau Street, New York. He served most efficiently in the quartermaster's department during much of the war, and died in 1802, seventy-five years of age.

JOHNSTON, CAPTAIN JOHN.—After partially recovering from his severe wounds received at the battle of Long Island, Captain Johnston took up the artist's profession, and painted several historical portraits, among them that of Samuel Adams and his wife. He also painted his own, which is in possession of his grandson, Mr. J. J. Soren, of Boston.

KNOWLTON, LIEUTENANT-COLONEL.—Born in West Boxford, Mass., November, 1740, and removed to Ashford, Conn. He served in the French war as private in Captain Durkee's company. A full and accurate sketch of him may be found in the *New England Historical and Gen. Register* for January, 1861, by Ashbel Woodward, M.D., of Franklin, Conn.

LASHER, COLONEL JOHN.—Born March 3d, 1724, probably in New York. A merchant of some wealth. He lost four houses in the fire of September 21st, 1776. On the expiration of the term of service of his battalion, he was elected a lieutenant-colonel of one of the New York Continental regiments, but declined. He died in New York at an advanced age. See references to him in the chapter on "The Two Armies."

LITTLE, COLONEL MOSES.—Frequently mentioned in the account of the campaign. He was one of the "Descendants of George Little, who came to Newbury, Mass., in 1640"—the title of a handsome little work compiled by Mr. George T. Little, and printed in 1877. During the retreat through New Jersey, Colonel Little was sick at Peekskill, and could not participate with his men at Trenton and Princeton. He rendered further service at various times during the war.

McDOUGALL, GENERAL ALEXANDER.—Born in Scotland in 1731 ; died in New York, June 8th, 1786. It is understood that a biography of this officer is in the course of preparation. As he was so closely identified with the Revolutionary struggle, it could be made a valuable work, if his papers are all preserved. He was a leader of New York's "Liberty" party before 1776, and served continuously through the war.

MILES, COLONEL SAMUEL.—Born March 22d, 1739, probably in Philadelphia. Served in the French war. After the Revolution, held positions as

Judge of the High Court of Errors, member of the Governor's Council, and Mayor of Philadelphia. He died at Cheltenham, Montgomery County, Pa., December 29th, 1805.

PARRY, LIEUTENANT-COLONEL CALEB.—Killed on Long Island. See notice of him on page 196, Part I. A genealogy recently prepared by Richard Randolph Parry, Esq., of Philadelphia, contains much interesting personal history of the family.

PIPER, LIEUTENANT-COLONEL JAMES.—He was lieutenant-colonel of Miles' First Battalion, and "a very worthy gentleman." Taken on Long Island, and died in New York not long after the battle. Captain Peebles, of Miles', Captain Bowie and Lieutenant Butler, of Smallwood's, and Lieutenant Makepeace, of Huntington's, who were all wounded and taken prisoners, died afterwards in New York, says Fitch.

RUTGERS, LIEUTENANT-COLONEL HENRY.—Of New York City. Brother of Harmanus Rutgers, killed on Long Island. He was connected with the army much of the time in the Commissary of Musters Department. Rutgers College takes its name from him. He left many Revolutionary papers, which have been unfortunately lost.

SCOTT, GENERAL JOHN M.—Born in New York in 1730 ; died September 14th, 1784. He was the only child of John and Marian Morin Scott, and fourth in the line of descent from Sir John Scott, Baronet of Ancram, County Roxburgh, Scotland, who died in 1712. At the age of sixteen he graduated at Yale College in the class of 1746, and took up the profession of law in New York, where he rose steadily in practice and reputation. With Wm. Smith, the historian of New York, and Wm. Livingston, he became identified with the Whig element in the colony, and at an early date advocated principles which paved the way for the final opposition to ministerial measures. These three—Smith, Livingston, and Scott—became leaders at the bar, and the two latter also in politics. Scott's residence stood at about the corner of Thirty-third Street and Ninth Avenue, as appears from Ratzer's official map of the city and island in 1766–67, and contained 123 acres. At that date it was some three miles out of town. From papers still preserved it appears that, very soon after the Revolution, this fine estate, which had become embarrassed, was sold for $8250, and that as early as 1813 it was worth $100,000. Scott associated himself with enterprises that contributed to the progress and social advancement of the city, becoming in 1754 one of the founders of the Society for the Promotion of the Arts, and also of a City Library. From 1757 to 1762 he was alderman of the Out-ward of New York. He contributed to the *Watch Tower* and *Reflector*, and was the author of several official and literary papers and reports during his lifetime. When the Revolutionary troubles opened, he was made one of the committee of one hundred citizens in 1775, took a foremost part against England's designs, and, as a powerful public speaker in favor of the colonial cause, might be called the Samuel Adams or James Otis of New York. As stated in the text, he became a member of the provincial committee and Congress in 1775–76, and brigadier-general of State troops in March, 1776, taking active part in the campaign around, his native city. At the close of the year he offered his last month's salary to those of his troops who would remain in the service a few weeks longer, and served himself a month without pay. In 1777 he was appointed secretary of the State, and continued in the public service in that capacity and as State senator and member of Congress until his death. His remains lie buried .in Trinity Church-yard, near the line of Broadway, north of the church.

SELDEN, COLONEL SAMUEL.—Of Hadlyme, Conn. Son of Samuel and Deborah Dudley Selden. Born January 11th, 1723. His grandfather was Thomas Selden, one of the original founders of Hartford. A genealogy of the family is in the course of preparation by Mr. Henry M. Selden, of Haddam Neck. Colonel Selden was taken prisoner in the Kip's Bay retreat, being prostrated by the exertions of the day. He was confined in the present Register's building, in the City Hall Park, where he died of fever, " on Friday P.M., October 11th, about three o'clock." In the latter part of his sickness he was attended by Dr. Thacher, a British surgeon, who paid him every attention. He was buried in the Brick Church-yard. See chapter on " The Two Armies" for further reference. Among this officer's great-grandsons are Chief-Justice Waite, Hon. Lyman Trumbull, General McDowell, Judge Selden of Rochester, Colonel Joseph Selden of Norwich, and many others, the descendants being numerous.

SMITH, CAPTAIN ROBERT.—Born in New York in 1752 ; of Scotch ancestry. Entered the counting-house of his brother, Alex. Robertson Smith, a wealthy merchant. In 1776 he raised a company of Scotsmen and sons of Scotsmen, and joined Malcom's New York Regiment. He was on Long Island with Scott's brigade, and at White Plains received a severe contusion from a spent shot. Obliged by ill-health to retire from the service for a time, he appeared again as a volunteer at Monmouth, and fought on foot, having given up his horse to a general officer. After the war he settled in Philadelphia, where he was a bank director for forty-eight years, holding also other offices of trust. He was a man of liberal disposition, a Presbyterian elder, and gave freely for all charitable purposes.

STIRLING, GENERAL LORD.—This officer's name was properly William Alexander. His father claimed the title of the Earl of Stirling, and he himself continued it. There is this description of the general in Surgeon Waldo's diary, kept at Valley Forge (*Historical Magazine*, vol. v.) :

" Major-General Lord Stirling is a man of a very noble presence, and the most martial Appearance of any General in the Service ; he much resembles the Marquis of Granby—by his bald head—the make of his face, and figure of his Body. He is mild in his private conversation, and vociferous in the Field."

TILGHMAN, CAPTAIN TENCH.—Aid to Washington.   Born near Easton, Talbot County, Md., December 25, 1744 ; died April 18th, 1786.   From Maryland, Tilghman went to Philadelphia, became captain of a city military organization, and joined Washington as volunteer secretary and aid in August, 1776.   He served with his chief through the war, participating in many battles, and having Washington's closest confidence.   His rank as lieutenant-colonel was dated from April, 1777, by his own desire, that he might not outrank Hamilton and Meade, who had been appointed aids earlier in the year.   His descendants preserve many relics of his Revolutionary service.

TROUP, LIEUTENANT ROBERT.—His father was an officer in the British Navy, and died before the Revolution.   Troup graduated from Columbia (old King's) College in 1774, and after his capture on Long Island as one of the patrol at the Jamaica Pass was exchanged in December following, with a few others.   In March, 1777, he accepted a captain-lieutenancy in the artillery, offered by Knox, but soon after joined General Gates' staff.   In May, 1778, Gates wrote to Laurens, President of Congress :

" Having neglected when I left York to recommend a proper person for D. A. General [deputy adjutant-general] to the army under my command, I beg to mention Lieut Col: Robert Troup, and desire the Favor you will propose him to Congress for that office ; my knowledge of his Honor, Merit, Integrity induces me apart from any personal regard, thus earnestly to wish his promotion."—*MS. Letter.*

After the war, Troup studied law in New York, became intimate with Hamilton and Burr, and was one of the very few who retained his friendship for the latter after the duel.   Colonel Troup was appointed the first United States District Judge for New York.

VAN WAGENEN, LIEUTENANT GERRIT H.—Son of Huybert Van Wagenen and Angenietje Vredenburg, was born in New York at No. 5 Beekman Slip (now Fulton Street), 1753, January 21st.   He went to Canada in August, 1775, as second lieutenant in the Eighth Company of the First Regiment of New York State troops under Colonel McDougall.   Was at the storming of Quebec, in the columns of General Montgomery.   In May, 1776, he was sent to New York, and then to Philadelphia, in charge of some prisoners.   On returning to New York and finding that the British were landing on Long Island, he offered his services to General Sullivan, and was sent by him with four other officers to the Jamaica Pass, as described in the chapter on the battle.   The party were all taken prisoners, and he continued a prisoner twenty-two months, when he was exchanged.   He then received an appointment in the Commissary of Prisoners Department, and continued in that office about three years.   (For a full account of his services, see the " Gen. and Biog. Record," vol. viii., page 44).   In 1783, March 11th, he married Sarah, daughter of Derrick Brinckerhoff and Rachel Van Ranst.   He now engaged in the hardware business with his father at No. 5 Beekman Slip, where the business had been carried on by his father since about 1760.   The volume entitled " New York during the Revolution" says, under date of 1767, " In Beekman Slip, near Queen Street, was the extensive hardware store of Huybert Van Wagenen, whose sign of the golden broad axe was so often referred to in the annals of the period." He lived at Beekman Slip till 1811, when he removed to 69 Gold Street, near Beekman, and in 1821 removed with his family to Oxford, Chenango County, where he died, 1835, November 20th.

WEBB, LIEUTENANT-COLONEL S. B.—Born in Wethersfield, Conn., December, 1753. He went to Boston on the Lexington alarm, and was at Bunker Hill as Captain Chester's lieutenant. He became aid to General Putnam and then to Washington in 1776. In 1777 he raised a Continental regiment in Connecticut, and served as its colonel to the end of the war, though for two years he was a prisoner on parole. His lieutenant-colonel was Ebenezer Huntington, and major, John P. Wyllys, both young officers in this campaign. Colonel Webb resided in New York until 1789, and then removed to Claverack, where he died December 3d, 1807.

WOODHULL, GENERAL.—There is a good sketch of General Woodhull in " Thompson's History of Long Island," vol. ii. In regard to his capture, Lieutenant Jabez Fitch, of Huntington's regiment, says in his narrative · " On ye 6th [of Sept.] Genll Woodhull, of ye Long Island malitia, was sent from ye Mentor to ye Hospital at Newatrect [New Utrecht] ; he was an aged Gentleman, & was taken by a party of ye Enemy's light Horse at Jameca, & altho he was not taken in arms, yet those Bloodthirsty Savages cut & wounded him in ye head & other parts of ye body, with their Swords, in a most Inhuman manner of which wounds he Died at ye Hospital; and altho ye Director of their affairs took but little care to preserve his Life yet they were so generous to his Lady, as to endulge her with liberty to carry home ye General's corpse and bury it with Deacence."

THE MAPS.

PLAN OF THE BATTLE OF LONG ISLAND AND THE BROOKLYN DEFENCES.

THE outlines and topography of this " Plan" have been compiled from Ratzer's and United States Coast Survey maps. Bernard Ratzer was a British Engineer, ranking as lieutenant in the Sixtieth Royal American Regiment of Foot in 1756. In 1767–8, he made an official survey of New York and part of Long Island with many details, the accuracy of which is beyond question.

There is an advertisement in the *Connecticut Gazette* for October 25th, 1776, in which Samuel Loudon (late printer and bookseller in New York, but now in Norwich) offers for sale " Ratzer's elegant map of New York and its Invirons from Actual Surveys, showing the present unhappy seat of War." This survey on Long Island extends nearly to the line of the hills. All beyond is reproduced from maps of the coast survey, farm lines, and Brooklyn maps. The whole represents the ground almost exactly as it lay in 1776. One correction should be made at the Jamaica Pass. The name belongs to the dotted roundabout line which represents the original pass, the straight road having been cut afterwards.

THE STILES SKETCH OF THE BROOKLYN WORKS.

Now published for the first time, and quite important as confirming the Hessian map in vol. ii. of the Society's " Memoirs." The fortifications at Red Hook are undoubtedly exactly reproduced. Taken in connection with General Greene's orders, the sketch is valuable, enabling us to locate the works! The drawing, of course, is not precise, but the names and relative positions are enough as long as we have Ratzer to follow in the matter of outline and topography. The writer is indebted to the librarians of Yale College, Profs. Van Name and Dexter, for the favor of tracing the sketch from the original.

EWING'S DRAUGHT.

This is a one-half reduction from the original in the possession of Mr. Stauffler, of Lancaster, Pennsylvania, who has kindly furnished the writer with a tracing. It was drawn by John Ewing, Colonel Hand's brother-in-law, but in topography is far out the way. It contains, however, several important items in the references, which are noticed in the text.

MAP OF NEW YORK CITY AND OF MANHATTAN ISLAND, WITH THE AMERICAN DEFENCES IN 1776.

So far as known, no contemporary map exists showing the whole of Manhattan Island, except the very small and inaccurate sketches in Stedman, Sparks, and some other works. The one presented in this volume is believed to be the first to give the entire island, with its roads, settlements, and topographical features, as it lay in 1776. In the compilation, Ratzer and Montressor have been followed as far as they go—namely, from the Battery to about Fiftieth Street. From this point to King's Bridge the map of the commissioners who first laid out the island into streets in 1814 has been adopted. This is official, and gives the old roads as they existed during the Revolution. The Bloomingdale and King's Bridge roads are laid down in the present map as the commissioners have them, the surveys being made by Randall. The fortifications at Harlem Heights are from Sauthier's English map as given in New York Hist. MS. and Stedman.

FIELD OF THE HARLEM HEIGHTS AFFAIR.

Reference has been made to the topography of this battle-field in a note in Chapter VI. The outlines are taken from Randall's city map, and the ground has been frequently visited by the writer. Point of Rocks has been partly cut away, but the main features in the vicinity remain.

NEW YORK AND BROOKLYN WITH THEIR ENVIRONS IN 1776.

In this outline map, a bird's-eye view is presented of the entire position in this vicinity. Details will be found in the larger maps. Care has been taken to give the outlines, roads, and relative distances with accuracy. The plan is a photographic reduction of Ratzer's, Randall's, and Coast Survey charts.

THE PORTRAITS.

[The portraits are those of representative officers—men who rendered good service, not only during the campaign, but, in the case of three of them, during the war. Lasher's and Hand's have never been published ; and the other two are not found in any general work. They are given here (two of them, at least) as contributions to the list of Revolutionary portraits. All have been specially photographed and transferred to steel by Mr. Egloffstein's process, for the present volume.]

COLONEL LASHER'S portrait is enlarged from a finely-painted and well-preserved miniature in the possession of Mrs. Kernochan, of New York.

COLONEL HAND'S portrait is in the possession of his granddaughter, Mrs. S. B. Rogers, of Lancaster, Pennsylvania.

COLONEL GLOVER'S portrait appeared first in the publications of the Essex Institute at Salem, Massachusetts.

COLONEL HUNTINGTON'S portrait appears in the Huntington family *Memoir*. The original is a miniature by Trumbull, in possession of General Huntington's descendants at Norwich.

INDEX.

S.

W.

Y.

ERRATA.

———

Page 37, line 26—The old City Hall stood at the corner of Nassau and Wall streets, site of present Sub-Treasury Building.

Page 119, line 1—Lieutenant-Colonel Cornell became member of the Board of War, not Commissary-General.

Page 243, line 10—But one of the regiments suffered as much as any other.

Page 280, line 21—Rall's column reached Fort Washington first.

Page 289, line 31—Read December 25th.

Page 291, line 5—Read December 25th.

Page 295, line 23—Read Cadwallader's *and* Mercer's men.

Part II., page 99, third line in Glover's letter—Read [Randall's] for (Ward's).

E   Johnston, Henry
232   Phelps, 1842-1923.
J73
1971   The campaign of 1776
         around New York and
         Brooklyn

DATE			